Three Great Escape Stories

Three
Great Escape Stories
from the Second World War

The Wooden Horse

Escape Alone

Return Ticket

Collins
St James's Place
London

The Wooden Horse was first published in 1949
Revised edition 1955
Reprinted 1967
© this edition Eric Williams 1965
Escape Alone was first published under the title
We Die Alone in 1955
Revised Edition 1960
© this edition David Howarth 1965
Return Ticket was first published in 1953
© this edition Anthony Deane-Drummond 1965

First Impression 1965
Second Impression 1967
Third Impression 1969
Fourth Impression 1971
Fifth Impression 1972
Sixth Impression 1973

ISBN 0 00 192324 2

Printed in Great Britain
Collins Clear-Type Press
London and Glasgow

THREE GREAT ESCAPE STORIES

Contents

The Wooden Horse

by

ERIC WILLIAMS

Contents

CONTENTS

Introduction

THIS IS an adventure story of the Second World War. It is my own story, but to make it more vivid I have told it as fiction and used the names " John " and " Phil " for my friends, Captain Michael Codner, M.C., R.A., and Flight-Lieutenant Oliver Philpot, M.C., D.F.C., R.A.F. I have called myself " Peter."

It is some years now since I wrote THE WOODEN HORSE, and even longer since the events described in it took place. In re-reading it to make this special edition, it seems to me scarcely believable that a mere plywood box could have fooled the Germans for so long. Nor does it seem possible that I, or my younger self, could have crossed wartime Germany as I did, knowing so little of that country or its language.

How the escape was contrived and how much of it I owe to the resourcefulness and courage of my companions you will discover in the book, but before I begin my story I would like to describe the prison camp.

The barbed-wire compound, because of its very simplicity, was an extraordinarily difficult nut to crack. In the stone castle or other fortress, the prisoner could always cherish the possibility of secret rooms, underground passages or even sewers. In the simple rectangular barbed-wire cage, there were no such possibilities.

Stalag-Luft III was typical of hundreds of these compounds which the Germans had made all over Europe to keep the prisoners of their early rapid advance. Later, when the Allies had prepared themselves and were fighting back, the Germans took fewer captives, and these, mostly aircrew shot down over enemy territory, were collected in this one enormous camp.

The camp was set in a clearing of the pine forest. The flat grey surface of the compound was broken only by the squat wooden huts raised on piles above the ground to discourage tunnelling. Round the huts the double twelve-foot fence of bristling barbed wire, strong and heavily interlaced, was guarded by high wooden sentry towers which the prisoners called goon-boxes. There were two guards, or goons, in each box, connected by telephone to the main guardroom at the prison gates. They were armed with machine-guns and searchlights which swept the camp continually during the hours of darkness. Between the sentry towers were arc lamps suspended from poles above the wire, while below it, sunk deep under the ground, were seismographs which recorded in the guardroom the vibrations caused by tunnelling.

Outside the wire fence, sentries armed with rifles patrolled between each pair of watch-towers. At night, when the prisoners were locked in their huts, these guards were doubled, and savage police dogs, occasionally visible in the searchlight beams, roamed the deserted compound.

Fifteen feet inside the main fence was a single strand of barbed wire twelve inches above the ground. This was the trip-wire, and anyone stepping over it was shot at by the guards. A narrow pathway trodden by the feet of the prisoners ran round the camp just inside the trip-wire. The camp was so crowded that it had become a convention to walk only in an anti-clockwise direction round the circuit.

The surface of the compound was a mixture of sand, powdered leaf-mould and dirt, which in the summer formed a thick layer of soft dust. In the winter this dust was churned by the prisoners' feet into a grey sea of clinging mud.

Under this top layer the subsoil was clean hard yellow sand; yellow when damp, but drying to a startling whiteness in the sun. The Germans knew that every tunnel carried its embarrassment of excavated sand and viewed each disturbance of the grey upper layer with suspicion. Every excavation made for a drain, rubbish pit or garden was carefully watched by the ferrets, or security guards. It was only by elaborate camouflage that the tell-tale yellow sand could be hidden in these places.

The skin of grey dust formed one of the most effective defences of the camp.

ERIC WILLIAMS

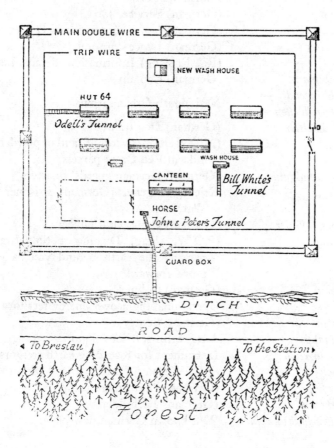

Glossary

Abort	(German) Latrine
Appel	(German) Roll Call
Arbeitskarte	(German) Workman's identity card
Ausweis	(German) Identity card
Chocker	(slang) Unhappy, discontented
Cobber	(slang) Mate, friend
Cooler	Punishment cell
Dienst	(German) Service, Job
Feldwebel	(German) Non-Commissioned Officer
Gefreiter	(German) Lance-corporal
Gen	(R.A.F. slang) Information, details, news
Hauptmann	(German) Captain
Hitlerjugend — *Hitlermädchen*—	Nazi Youth Organisations
Hundmeister	(German) Dog trainer
Klim	(Milk spelt backwards) Brand of powdered milk in Red Cross parcels
Kommandantur	(German) German guards' quarters
Kriegie	Kriegsgefangener (German) Prisoner of War
Lager Offizier	(German) Compound Officer
Moling	(P.O.W. slang) Digging a tunnel and packing the earth behind you as you move forward
Oberst	(German) Colonel
Op	Operational flight over enemy territory
Posten	(German) Sentry
Schnapps	A powerful spiritous liquor
Seismograph	Instrument for recording earth tremors
Stooge	(P.O.W. slang) Person on a " Dienst "
Straflager	(German) Punishment camp
Verboten	(German) Forbidden
Völkischerbeobachter	Well-known German newspaper

PHASE ONE

CHAPTER ONE

The Daily Round

IT WAS early morning. Inside the room everything was hushed; the eerie, impermanent lifelessness of a room where everyone is sleeping. On the four two-tier bunks ranged round the walls the prisoners slept rolled like cocoons in their blankets. Beside each bunk, sentinel-like, stood a narrow wooden locker. On the table in the centre of the room, softly illuminated by the light that crept in under the closed blackout shutters, lay in disordered heaps the clothes of the sleeping prisoners. Thinly, from the direction of the Kommandantur, came the sound of a distant bugle call.

In one of the upper bunks a figure stirred, grunted and turned over on its back. It lay still for a while; then with a convulsive jerk that shook the whole room it sat up, rubbed its eyes and yawned. Peter Howard, lying in the bunk below, opened his eyes. A few scraps of wood shavings dislodged from the mattress above fell slowly down and rested on his face. He brushed them off, turned over and pulled the thin grey blanket tightly round his ears. It was too early to wake yet. He closed his eyes. He knew it all so well. A pair of legs covered with long sandy hair would appear over the side of the bunk above. Legs that would wriggle their toes disgustingly as their owner prepared to land like an avalanche beside his head. He had seen it all too often before. He tensed himself expectantly. Crash! Bang! Ger . . . doyng! The whole hut shook. One of the shrouded figures moved impatiently and swore in an undertone. A stool slid noisily across the floor. The man who had cursed pulled the blanket up over his head. Heavy footsteps stamped across the room. A short silence, then clang! as the lid of the tea-jug was banged down. Another short silence and then the sound of a spoon being stirred violently inside a pottery mug. Presently the whole room shook again as the door was slammed.

Peter relaxed and slowly opened his eyes. He knew exactly what had happened since the first convulsive thrashing of limbs had jerked him from his sleep. First Bennett had pulled on his socks, then his wooden clogs which had spent the night resting beside his head. Next he had leaped for the wooden stool, missed it and sent it slithering across the floor. He had looked surprised and stamped over to the tea-jug to see if the next-door stooge had fetched the water. Finding the jug contained only a handful of dried tea he had again forced an expression of exaggerated surprise and had filled a mug with cold water from a large pottery jug which stood near the stove. He had added a spoonful of lemonade powder and stirred violently. After drinking the mixture in three great gulps he had gone out, slamming the door after him, to walk round the circuit until breakfast-time.

Every morning since they had arrived at Stalag-Luft III Peter had awakened to the same abrupt reveille. At first he had opened his eyes at the preliminary crash. Now he kept them closed until after Bennett had left the room.

All was silent again. Not a sound from the other six occupants of the two-tier bunks. Either they were asleep or grimly hanging on to the last shreds of slumber until the storm had passed. Bennett had gone now. He would be walking round the compound—just inside the wire—leaving the others to gather together the ragged edges of their slumber. Peter often wondered what Bennett found in prison life attractive enough to get him out of bed so early. Most of them lay in bed as long as possible, reluctant to begin another day. Bennett was a queer chap. Starting the day half an hour before everyone else and then sleeping on his bunk all afternoon. Perhaps he was right. The camp would be deserted at this hour of the morning. Bennett needed plenty of space all round him. He was too bull-like, too virile to live cooped up with seven other people. He needed wide open spaces and a job of work to do. Peter wriggled himself more comfortably into his mattress of wood shavings and tried to sleep again.

From the corner on his right hand came the mumbled ends of Robbie's morning hymn of hate . . . " Blast, what a noisy devil that fellow Bennett is." There was bitterness in it, and finality. They would quarrel soon. Peter could see it coming. Starting over some small detail it would flare up into a violent feud. One of them would move into another room and life would go on. It was like that in the prison camp. A man would stand the boredom for so long and then, slightly at first, the personal habits of one of his seven companions would begin to wear him down. Little things such as the way the man ate, or possibly his accent. Life with him would become unbearable.

Poor old Robbie, he had been a prisoner for nearly three years ; and a flimsy wooden hut was not Bennett's ideal background. He couldn't have been silent in a padded cell with a thick cork floor. Peter sighed. The thought of a cork floor made him think of bathrooms. He hadn't had a bath for two years—unless a length of hosepiping and a punctured cocoa-tin could be called a bath—and he lay thinking of porcelain baths in all the colours of the rainbow. Green, yellow, pink, black. . . . No, he didn't like black. He liked a bath that lent its colour to the water. Green was the best. A green bath, darker green tiles on the wall and a cork floor. Or perhaps a sunken bath. Yes, a sunken bath. . . .

He forced his mind away. What about this tunnel ? There must be a place to start one if you could only think of it. David had nearly got away with it. David with his blue seaman's eyes and halo of rosy-red beard. David the farmer. Good old dependable David. David who ran a farm on paper. Over his bunk there was a rough bookshelf made from bed-boards, the narrow cross planks of the two-tier bunks. All the books were about farming. At the right time of the year David would sow his crops and in due course he would harvest them. He kept a profit and loss account. Funny how seriously he took it. If it rained on the day when he had decided to reap he would walk about with a

face like thunder. If during a heatwave one of the others remarked
on the fine weather he would mutter something about the crops
needing rain. Good old farmer David, he was compensating for
his imprisonment. But he still tried to escape. He was the room's
representative on the Escape Committee. And yet his farm was
very real to him.

The only man who knew more about farming than did David
was Bennett. But Bennett knew more about everything than
anyone else. Bennett the authority. Bennett the bull. Full of
" bull." You couldn't discuss anything with Bennett in the room.
No matter what the discussion Bennett would finally deliver
himself of a categorical authoritative pronouncement which
would kill the topic dead. Abortive attempts would be made to
revive it but under the weight of authority behind the pronouncement the opposition would languish and finally relapse into a
baffled and disgruntled silence.

They were always arguing. Paul caused a lot of the trouble.
Tall and thin, so tall that you wondered how he had managed
to fit into the Hurricane in which he had been shot down early in
the war, he had gone straight from school into the R.A.F. His
whole world was flying and the wide freedom of the sky. Paul
found prison life more irksome than did most of his fellow
prisoners. It tried his patience beyond endurance and it was in
these times that he turned to Robbie for consolation.

Robbie was the peacemaker.

Peter forced himself into wakefulness. It was his turn to be
cook. Of all the chores of prison life cooking was the one he
hated most. It had been harder for the early prisoners. They
had had to cook on wood fires in the open air. He had a stove.
At least, he had a hundred-and-twelfth share in a stove. There
were fourteen rooms in the hut. Each room had eight prisoners
and for every eight men there was one cook. At the end of the
hut stood a cast-iron stove with one cooking ring and a small
oven. Fourteen dinners for eight had to be cooked on that stove
every evening. He began to think about the evening meal. If

he peeled the potatoes and put them on about ten o'clock ... His
thoughts were interrupted by Robbie.

" What about a spot of tea, Pete ? "

" O.K., Robbie. Just going. Bags of time yet." He stretched
and rolled out of his bunk. " 'Morning, Nig ! "

" 'Morning, Pete." Nigel Wilde and John Clinton slept in
the bunks nearest the stove. Like most advantages in prison life,
this had its compensating disadvantages. Although warmer in
winter it meant that the bunks were used as seats during the
daytime. Peter preferred the colder privacy of the wall farthest
from the stove.

Nigel lay on his back in the upper bunk, his right arm curled
round the top of his head. His right hand was gently stroking the
left-hand side of his moustache. His expression was blissful.

Peter stood watching him. Nigel winked.

" Why do you keep doing that ? " Peter asked.

" I like it, old boy. Feels as though someone else is doing it."

" You're crazy."

" I know, it's nice."

In the bunk below, John Clinton lay dreaming, his dark head
resting on a folded pair of trousers, a seraphic expression on his
face.

" What's the weather like ? " Nigel asked.

Peter padded over to the window. It was late spring and across
the wire he could see the pale fronds of a silver birch graceful
against the dark olive background of the pine forest. Peter was
fond of that silver birch. He had tried to paint it in all its moods.
As a sharp but twisting and fragile silhouette against a winter sky.
And as he saw it now, a cascade of delicate green, almost yellow
in the morning sun. He had painted it often but had never been
able to capture its isolated beauty, its aloofness against the darkness
of the pines. Overhead the sky was clear and still, the hushed
expectancy that foretells a burning day. Under the window the
sand was moist with dew, and dew sparkled on the barbed wire.
The rows of long green-painted barrack huts looked washed and
cool.

"It's a lovely morning, Nig."

"*Gut zeigen*. What about a cup of tea?" Nigel specialised in translating air force slang literally into German. "*Gut zeigen*" was his way of saying "good show." In the same way "bad show" became "*schlecht zeigen*," and "fair enough" "*blond genug*." When he was particularly morose he considered himself to be "*gebraünt weg*," or "browned-off." He sometimes used this queer German on the guards and was genuinely surprised when they didn't understand.

Peter, still looking out of the window, saw Bennett come striding furiously round the circuit. Wearing heavy army issue boots, a woollen skull-cap and R.A.F. battledress, he came past the window at full speed.

"Come on, Pete," Nigel called. "What about that tea?"

Peter crossed to a wooden shelf over the stove and took down seven mugs. The tea-jug had been left just inside the door the night before with a handful of tea-leaves in the bottom. It was the turn of the cook in the next mess to take both jugs across to the kitchen and have them filled with boiling water. It would be Peter's turn to-morrow. He poured three mugs, one for Nigel, one for Robbie and one for himself. He would not waken the others yet. There was still plenty of time.

Crossing again to the shelf, he took from a cardboard box a heavy German loaf; ninety per cent potato meal and a liberal sprinkling of sawdust. A loaf that, if allowed to dry, would split into great fissures and become as hard as stone. The cardboard box had once contained a Red Cross parcel from England. There were dozens of similar boxes littered round the room, holding all the personal possessions of the eight prisoners. Boxes piled on top of the cupboards. Boxes under the beds. Boxes round the stove, filled with brown coal, old potatoes and waste paper. Eight such boxes were delivered to the room each week and yet they never seemed to have enough of them.

He cut twenty-four thin slices. A seventh of a loaf a day was each man's ration. By cutting very thin slices he could make three for breakfast, one for lunch and three for tea. He spread them thinly with margarine from a Red Cross parcel, opened a tin of jam, and breakfast was prepared.

He was still in pyjamas.

"What about a cold shower before breakfast, Nig?"

"*Blond genug*, old boy." Nigel unwound himself from his blankets.

"O.K. Let's wake John."

"What? Wake the child? Have a heart, old boy!" Nigel treated John with a teasing respect. Respecting him for his fine intelligence and ready courage; teasing him because of his youth and absent-mindedness. John's mind was always on his books or schemes of escape. So far removed from his environment that Nigel often had to go and find him and bring him to his meals. Nigel loved John and masked his affection under a veil of chaffing and elaborate practical jokes. He called him "the child" and respected him above everyone.

"Yes, go on! Wake him up, it'll do him good."

"Shall I?"

"Yes, go on!" Peter waited for the joke that had amused him every morning for days.

Nigel reached for his latest invention, his latest method of teasing John. This time it was an elaborate waking device. A cocoa-tin suspended by a harness of string hung just above John's head. Through a hole in the top of the tin ran another string suspended on the end of which was a bunch of bent and rusty nails. By pulling rapidly on the centre string Nigel could conjure forth a most satisfactory noise. He pulled the string.

John did not wake.

"I think the loose bed-boards were a better idea," Peter said.

"Yes, but a bit dangerous." Nigel grinned as he remembered the last waking device he had invented. A device which had effectively removed the one remaining board which had held John's shaking bed together and had deposited him, complete with mattress, on the floor.

"Come on," Peter said. "Once round the compound and then a shower."

Leaving John asleep they clambered out of the window. It was quicker than the door and quieter.

Once more the room was silent. Robbie lay lazily flapping at the flies that were doing circuits and bumps inside his bed space. There was the whole room for them to fly in and they had to come and buzz round him. He gave it up and pulled the blanket over his head. Presently a figure in one of the upper bunks began to curse.

" What's the matter, Pomfret ? " Robbie lowered his blanket.

" Oh, it's those two noisy blighters. They're much too hearty. What do they want to take a cold shower at this hour for ? And that tin can thing. It's too silly."

" Keeps them happy, I suppose."

" Well, it shouldn't. They shouldn't be happy in a prison camp. Nobody should be happy in a prison camp. It's not decent. And talking of decency, I suppose they're going to sunbathe in the nude again. The S.B.O. ought to stop it. It shouldn't be allowed."

" Why in heaven not ? " Robbie asked.

" It's not decent," Pomfret said.

" Oh, don't be so lily-livered. I shall sunbathe myself when the weather gets a bit warmer." Robbie pulled the blanket over his head and lay thinking of the play he was producing. The feminine lead was the trouble. Young Matthews had played it in the last four shows and the audience were getting used to him. He might ask Black. It was the very devil, this feminine lead. So many chaps were shy of taking it on. He'd go round and see young Black later on and try to persuade him to do it.

" Come on, show a leg ! " It was Peter and Nigel returned from their cold shower. " Breakfast up, *appel* up ! *Appel* in ten minutes. Who wants breakfast in bed ? "

Pomfret rolled out of his bunk, rubbing his eyes and growling under his breath. Putting on a Polish army greatcoat over his pyjamas he took a cardboard Red Cross box containing his washing materials from a shelf above his head, and shuffled off to the washroom.

" What's the matter with her this morning ? " Nigel asked.

" Oh, she's a bit touchy this morning," Robbie told him. " You woke her with your infernal machine."

" That's more than I did to the child. Hey, John, wake up ! On appel bitty, mein Herr ! "

" He's all right," Robbie said. " He'll have breakfast after appel."

In the far corner David Bruce lay thinking. He was planning his day. He was going to drench his new calf. It was not doing so well. To lose a calf now would be a serious thing. Make a hole in the little reserve of capital that he had accumulated.

The door was flung open and a German guard entered the room. " *Raus ! Raus ! Ausgehen ! Alle rausgehen !* "

" Goon in the block ! " Paul stood by his bunk, trousers in his hands, hair on end, still in the lower school. " *Deutschland kaput !* "

The guard shouted at him in German.

" Buzz off ! " Paul said. " We don't understand German here."

The guard shouted again in German ; a long sentence that ended with the English word " cooler."

" You're for it," Robbie said. " It's the cooler for you."

The guard shouted again. He was nearly screaming now.

" Buzz off ! " Paul made his stock retort.

The guard began to unsling his rifle. The bayonet was fixed.

" Better be careful," Robbie said.

A Feldwebel came walking down the centre corridor of the barrack hut. The guard sprang to attention and made a long, involved complaint in German. The Feldwebel turned to Paul.

" You have been impertinent again, eh ? " He spoke in English.

" I object to being shouted at."

" Come ! " The Feldwebel was used to this sort of thing.

Paul finished pulling on his trousers. He was no stranger to the cooler. He was almost happy there. He felt that he was carrying on the fight. He gathered up his blankets and his toilet things and accompanied the Feldwebel down the corridor.

" *Ausgehen, alle rausgehen !* " the guard shouted, unmoved by his victory.

" *Gut zeigen*, Joe. Just coming." Nigel said it quietly. " Hi, John ! On appel bitty ! Come on, you'll be late for appel."

John opened his eyes. He looked blank. Suddenly he realised what it was all about. " Give me a cup of tea, somebody ! "

Peter handed him a cup of tea. John swallowed once and handed it back. He rolled out of his bunk and stood putting on his clogs, a lean brown figure with a mop of black hair like an Abyssinian warrior. His pyjama trousers which had been cut short above the knee were of a different pattern from the jacket, which had no sleeves. The jacket had blue stripes and the trousers had once been pink. He took another gulp of tea, hurled a blanket round his shoulders, snatched up a book and shuffled off to roll-call, a slice of bread-and-jam in one hand and his book in the other. Once on appel he stood reading his book, taking occasional bites at the slice of bread-and-jam.

Outside the barrack the prisoners stood in fives. Peter stood next to David who, pipe jutting from the depths of his red beard, puffed clouds of smoke into the cool morning air.

" Why do we always stand in fives ? " Peter complained. " It used to be threes in the last camp."

" These are air force goons," David said. " The others were army goons. Army goons can only count in threes."

The guards walked down the rows counting them ; the guards in uniform, the prisoners huddled under blankets or defying the morning air in pyjamas or shorts. Slowly the guards walked down the ragged lines, counting as they walked. *Drei-und-fünfzig . . . vier-und-fünfzig . . . fünf-und-fünfzig . . . sechs-und-fünfzig . . . sieben-und-fünfzig. . . .*

The British adjutant called them to attention. The Lager Offizier, tall and immaculately uniformed, was mincing across the square to where the Senior British Officer was standing. After saluting the S.B.O. he turned to the assembled prisoners, and bowing from the waist saluted and shouted " *Guten Morgen, meine Herren !* " The Kriegies replied with an incoherent roar.

" Guten Morgen, meine Herren ! "

While the more prudent replied " *Guten Morgen, mein Herr*,"
the wilder spirits chanted their single-syllabled reply of derision ;
the two replies combating one another and resulting in an enthusiastic greeting which made the Lager Offizier beam with
pleasure. He was popular with these wild-looking British, was
he not ?

After appel Nigel returned to his bunk. He was plotting his
post-war career. He had already decided to be a doctor, a game
warden, a gold prospector, a holiday camp proprietor, a farmer
(he dropped this almost immediately under the scorn of David
Bruce), a big game hunter and a bookmaker. He took one course
of study after another, dropping each one as another more
attractive career caught his fancy. He lived in a frenzy of enthusiasm—but nothing lasted for long with him.

Peter lay on his bunk waiting for John to finish his breakfast.
" Parcels to-morrow," he said.

"Good show!" John spoke through a mouthful of bread and butter. "We'll have the last tin of salmon for dinner to-night."

"Don't burn it this time," Bennett said. "If you'd only do it the way I told you. You want to cover the top with greased paper."

John said nothing. It was too early in the day to start an argument.

"If we get any raisins we'll swop them for biscuits," Peter said. "Then we can make a cake."

"We'll bake it in the afternoon," John said, "and then if it turns out to be a pudding we can have it for dinner."

"And if it turns out to be porridge we'll have it for breakfast," Robbie added.

"I wouldn't mind running a restaurant after the war," Nigel said. "Run it for a bit, and then leave a manager to look after it. Then I could start a small farm and supply the restaurant from the farm. The waste food from the restaurant would do to feed the pigs and . . ."

"Sort of perpetual motion," John said.

"And then when I'd got the farm running I could put a bailiff in that and start on something else."

"You have to know something about cooking to run a restaurant," Bennett said. "Judging by your last effort you wouldn't last long."

"Farming's a job for the expert," David said from out of his misery. "You can lose a lot of money. I've got a calf now that's doing very badly. It's a Friesian. The book says they're difficult to rear. I wish I'd decided on Herefords."

"Friesians look nicer," Peter said.

David snorted.

When the others had finished their breakfast Peter collected the eight knives and mugs—they had no plates—and took them over to the washhouse to clean them.

Outside the washhouse was a long queue of prisoners waiting for their morning shower. The camp, which housed nearly a thousand men, possessed six cold water taps. Two of them had been converted by the prisoners into rough shower baths. The remaining four supplied all the water for washing clothes and crockery and for cooking. The Germans had agreed to build shower baths. They had been building them for nearly a year. The unfinished structure stood inside the camp surrounded by its own wire barrier to prevent the prisoners from stealing nails and odd pieces of timber. They had long since given up any hope of using the showers.

Squeezing his way past the crowd of bathers, Peter entered the washhouse. It was full of men washing dirty clothes on long wooden benches; dipping them in water, laying them on the benches, soaping them, and scrubbing them with nail brushes. In one corner several men were trying to wet themselves under the meagre trickle of water falling from the cocoa-tin shower. In the opposite corner a prisoner stood on the wash-bench, his face pressed to the window. All over the camp there were similar figures, watching through holes cut in the walls of the huts, hiding under the huts, peering through half-open doors; spying on the German guards. Every subversive activity in the camp had its nimbus of stooges. Every ferret who came into the camp was shadowed by a stooge, his every movement was reported to the duty pilot who sat at the main gates of the camp.

In the middle of the floor was a dark, gaping hole about two feet square, cut through the six inches of solid concrete on which the brick floor was laid. Next to the hole lay the trap. Built of solid brick on a wooden frame, it could be lowered into position by means of hooks fitting into slots in the sides of the frame. Once the trap was in position and the joints made good with soap mixed with cement dust, it was impossible to tell that the floor had been disturbed. Head and shoulders out of the trap stood a man named White.

" Hallo, Bill," Peter said.

" 'Morning, Pete."

" How's it going ? "

" Piece of cake ! " White lifted his hand, palm open, forefinger touching the tip of his thumb, and made a clicking noise with his tongue. " She's doing fine."

" How far have you got ? "

" About forty feet."

" Ferret approaching ! " It was the stooge calling urgently from the window.

White was down the hole in a flash and the trap was lowered on top of him. A crowd of bathers and washers of dirty linen surged over the trap, swamping the floor, camouflaging the trap. Peter set to and washed his crockery, while a running commentary on the guard's progress came from the watcher at the window. The German passed without entering the washhouse and work on the tunnel was resumed.

When Peter returned to the hut he found Bennett " tin-bashing." The prisoners were forced to cook in utensils of their own making. Nothing at all was provided by the Germans. The usual thing was a flat dish about twelve inches long by eight inches wide and two and a half inches deep. It was made by taking both ends off a Klim tin and rolling the cylinder into a flat sheet. When a number of these sheets had been collected they were joined together by folding the edges one over the other and filling the joints with silver paper salvaged from cigarette packets. A blunt nail was used as a punch and a narrow groove punched along the double thickness of metal. The edges of the flat sheet thus formed were turned up and the four corners folded to form a dish.

Bennett, surrounded by pieces of rolled-out tin, was bashing furiously, bashing the tin with a personal vindictiveness that made the hut shake and the tins rattle on the shelves.

" It's a lovely day," Peter offered.

Bennett grunted.

" Wouldn't you rather do that outside in the sun, old boy ? Besides, the hut wouldn't shake so much if you bashed on the sand."

Bennett grunted again.

Peter sighed. He put the crockery and breakfast cutlery on

the shelves and went out to walk round the circuit until lunchtime.

Outside the hut he met Robbie mooching round clad in an old pullover and army slacks cut down to make shorts. The ragged ends of his shorts flapped round his lean brown legs. He was wearing home-made sandals.

" Hallo, Pete. Mail come in yet ? "

" Not yet, Robbie—it's late this morning."

" Is Bennett still bashing ? "

" Yes."

" God ! I wish that chap would move into another mess. Y'know, he's not like an ordinary man. If he wants to open a door he doesn't just turn the handle. He throws himself at it with all his strength and then when he finds the lock won't break he turns the handle."

They walked several circuits in silence.

" This is an awful life, y'know, Pete."

" Yes. Pretty foul. Makes you appreciate life at home though. What wouldn't I give to walk on grass again ! " He savagely kicked the sand at his feet. " There's a place in Warwickshire I'd like to be now, on the Avon. There's a place where I used to bathe, a steep bank where you can dive into a deep pool." He thought of the sun dappling through the trees on to the river bank and the earthy smell of the brown river, the warm grass under his naked feet. " I'm going there as soon as I get back to England."

" I shall go back to my wife and kids," Robbie said.

Peter kicked a stone that lay on the path in front of him. His feet were bare but hardened. His life before the war seemed long ago, a different life. Softer and less real than the life he was living now. " I often wonder whether it's better or worse for you married men—imprisonment, I mean. At least you've got something waiting for you and the old shekels piling up in the bank. You've got your life fixed. This is just an interlude for you. I sometimes feel that life is running past me and when I get back it will be too late."

" Too late for what ? " Robbie asked, smiling.

Peter kicked another stone. " Oh, too late to begin life again.
. . . It's this awful feeling of time passing. I'm not getting anywhere—not even fighting. . . . It's such a waste of time."

" I'm wasting time too, you know," Robbie said gently. " My
youngest will be two and a half next week and I haven't seen
her yet."

" That's just what I mean, you've got something concrete
ahead of you. Something behind you too, to look back on."

" Well, you can build for the future. Lots of chaps are taking
degrees in all sorts of subjects."

" Yes, I know," said Peter moodily. " But I can't settle
down to that sort of thing. I'm browned off this morning.
Gebräunt weg, as Nig would say. I want to escape and get back
to England."

" Bah, escape ! How many people have got back from this
camp so far ? None ! "

" But there's no harm in trying," Peter said. " It gives you
something to do. You're not just sitting down waiting for the end
of the war."

" How long has Bill White's crowd been on the washhouse
dienst ? "

" Just over two months."

" And how far have they got ? "

" About forty feet."

" There you are. They've another three or four months'
work yet before they're even under the wire. They haven't an
earthly, Pete. Not an earthly. The goons are bound to tumble
to it before then."

" Oh, I don't know. People have got out before now."

" Yes, but what percentage ? Out of every thirty tunnels
started I suppose one gets through. Once you're outside the camp
your difficulties have only just begun. It's no good, Pete. They'll
never make it. It's just a waste of time." Robbie walked on, hands
in pockets, head lowered, kicking up the sand of the circuit as he
walked. A sharp wind ruffled his soft grey hair and carried the
dust from the circuit across the trip-wire. It brought with it the

sound of gramophone music from one of the wooden barracks and the smell of burning brown coal blocks.

"What's the time?" Peter asked.

Robbie looked at his watch. "Just after twelve."

"Good gracious. It's time I went for the tea water."

"You've time for another circuit," Robbie said. "You can get hot water until twelve-thirty."

"O.K. I'll avoid the queue then."

They walked on in the warm sunshine.

"I'd like to get out," Peter said. "I'd like to get out even if it's only for a few days. You feel so cut off here. I often wonder if the world's going on just the same outside. I'd like to see a cinema show and use a telephone—how I'd like to use a telephone! And I'd like to go up and down in a lift—and walk on carpets—and climb stairs. I'd like to spend money and have to make a decision."

"You can make a decision now," Robbie said. "What to have for dinner."

Peter laughed. "Not even that. Parcels come to-morrow. We've only got a tin of salmon left."

"Well, you can decide what book to take out of the library—or what socks to wear to-morrow."

"I can't—I haven't any clean."

"I wonder you don't cut your feet to blazes." He looked down at Peter's bare feet.

"Oh, I haven't worn shoes since the winter." He lifted one of his feet. Its sole was brown and hard as leather. "Have to get this hard skin off before next winter—I don't think I could wear shoes for long now."

"There you are," Robbie said. "That's a decision."

"Yes—and here's another. I'm going for the tea water."

"See if there's a letter for me as you go by, will you?" Robbie said. "I'll wait here and you can chuck it out of the window."

"Right."

He found that Bennett had finished his tin-bashing. The

room was empty. Lying on the table were several Kriegsgefangener letter forms. He sorted them out. One for John, two for Nigel, three for Pomfret, one for himself. He crossed over to the window and called out to Robbie. He held out his fist with thumb extended downwards. Robbie shrugged his shoulders and mooched on, hands in pockets.

While Peter and Robbie walk round the circuit Paul is in the cooler. It is a narrow cell high up in the German barrack. It has one small window at the level of the ceiling. The window is covered from the outside by a metal plate which stands a foot away from the wall. A certain amount of air finds its way round the edges of the plate but the prisoner cannot see the sky.

He has had no breakfast. His shoes have been taken from him and even if he had a book he could not read in the dim light of the cell. He knows the cell. He has been here before. He knows that shortly after two o'clock, if the sun is shining, a stray beam of light will enter the cell, creeping in through a small space between the metal plate and the window-frame. He will watch this beam of light. In it specks of dust will be floating, beautiful faerie specks that will dance and swirl in the sunlight as he fans the air with his hand. He will sit looking at them until, with the movement of the sun, the beam of light is there no more.

Presently he hears footsteps in the corridor and the sound of a key in the lock. The door opens and a guard is there with his midday meal. He knows this too. He will have the same meal every day he is in the cooler. A small bowl of cabbage water and two potatoes cooked in their jackets. He sits on the bed while the guard places the food on the table. He likes to treat the guard as a waiter. Physically, he suffers the hardships of solitary confinement; mentally he wins a battle in the constant war against the enemy.

He spends the long afternoon lying on his bunk and thinking of home. He thinks, too, of the barrack room he has just left. In a way, it is good to be in the cooler again, away from the insistent company of his fellow prisoners. He is an individualist, a natural fighter pilot. Not for him the dependence of the bomber crew. He is the lone wolf, alone in the cockpit of his Hurricane, far above the clouds in the blue sky, with the sun above him gilding his wings and turning the fleecy clouds below him into a carpet of snow. His is the lone encounter above the clouds, his prey the full-bellied bombers escorted by the waspish vicious fighters. Two three-hundred-miles-an-hour fighters twisting and turning in the sky. The rattle of machine-guns, and the loser plunging burning into the clouds that wait below.

He imagines himself in the cockpit of his Hurricane (the kick of the controls as you go into a flick roll, the matchless rhythm of a perfectly timed roll off the top, and the way the patchwork quilt of the earth slides over you and the sudden smell of petrol as you pull out of a loop). He remembers the smell of glycol and the way the parachute bumps against the back of your legs as you run out to the waiting aircraft, the bounding over the rough turf, the smoothness as you become airborne, the quick climb through the clouds and the thrill of sighting the enemy below you, silhouetted against the clouds. He remembers the attacking dive when you clench your teeth and press the firing button and the aircraft judders with the firing of the eight Browning guns, the sudden blackout as you pull out of a dive and the quick look round for the enemy as you recover. The slow roll over the airfield before you come in to land, the peace and quiet as you switch off the engine, the smell of the grass as you climb down from the aircraft and the small friendly sounds of the countryside as you stand there smoking a cigarette, waiting for the truck to take you back to the dispersal hut.

He lies thinking of this as the cell grows dark. He falls asleep lying on his bunk, the shoddy blanket across his chest, his face young in sleep, untroubled, free.

CHAPTER TWO

John Has An Idea

A FEW WEEKS later the ferrets pounced and Bill White's tunnel was discovered. These ferrets were ubiquitous in the camp. Clad in blue boiler suits and three-quarter boots, they would be found lying underneath the huts or hidden in the roofs listening for incriminating evidence. They came in and out hidden in the rubbish carts and even climbed in over the wire during the night so that the duty pilot who sat patiently at the main gates could not book them into the camp. Some of the ferrets with a sense of humour would report to the duty pilot as they came and went. There was politeness between them, and mutual respect. It was a constant game of counter-espionage.

The compound was deserted. It was afternoon. Most of the prisoners were sleeping on their beds. Outside the barbed-wire fence the posten paced their beat, their rifles slung high across their backs. Beyond the wire the forest, remote and unreal from inside the camp where no trees grew and the ground was arid and beaten hard by the feet of the prisoners, lay dark and cool beneath a cloud of pale green leaves.

Peter and John walked slowly, hands in pockets, round the circuit of the wire, idly watched by the sentries in the boxes. As they walked they were speaking in low tones.

" Pity about Bill's scheme," Peter said. " I thought they stood a chance with that."

" It was too far from the wire," John told him. " Think of all the sand you've got to hide to dig a tunnel three hundred feet long. The only way to get out is to make the tunnel as short as possible—start somewhere out here, near the trip-wire."

"You couldn't do it. There's nowhere near the wire to start a tunnel from. They chose the nearest building to the wire."

"Why start from a building at all? Why not start out in the open here—camouflage the trap. We could come out to it every day and take it slowly."

"But that's impossible. It's like the top of a billiard table. Every spot of ground near the trip-wire is in full view of at least three goon boxes and two outside posten. You couldn't possibly sink a shaft out here. Besides—how would you get the sand away?"

"It was done once. Ages ago by some chaps in another camp. A crowd of them went out with a chap who played an accordion. While he played they all sat round in a big circle and sang. And while they were singing they dug a hole in the middle, passed the sand round and filled their pockets with it. They got the hole as deep as a man's arm, put some boards across it and replaced the surface sand. Then they all went back to their huts with their pockets full of sand."

"What happened?"

"Oh, a sentry came into the compound that night, walked over the trap and fell down the hole. The whole thing was too slapdash and hurried."

They walked on in silence. To Peter the idea was new and worth considering. "There must be a way," he said. "All we need is something to cover it with, some sort of innocent activity like the accordion. But we can't do that again—must be a classic by now."

"Might do something like it," John said.

"I don't know—it's all so bare. If only there were some trees."

"Goons hate trees."

"The trouble is you've always got to have such a good reason for anything you do. If we start mucking around with the landscape we've got to show it's for some definite purpose, something quite different."

"I sometimes get tired of working out goon reactions," John said. "All this 'we think that they think that we think' stuff. You're so frightfully in the dark." He shivered and looked up. "Hallo, look at the trees. There's another of those whirlwind things on the way."

Peter stopped. Over to the south the tops of the trees were bending and waving while the air in the camp was cold and still. Then sudden gusts of wind came across the camp, catching at windows left loosely open, blowing up spouts of sand, snatching at the washing hung on lines outside the huts. The swastika over the Kommandantur flared out suddenly, then drooped again.

"I'm going in to shut the windows," Peter said. "Left the food on the table. Coming?"

"I'll stay and watch," John said.

He shivered again as Peter hurried off. The whole camp had come to life. Prisoners dashing out of the huts and snatching washing from the lines, windows slamming. By now the nearest trees were bowing to the wind and John moved into shelter behind a hut as the fine sand whipped across and stung his legs.

Here she comes, he thought, and quickened his pace, reaching the side of the hut as the whirling column of dust and sand left the trees and swept towards the wire. Leaves and bits of paper were caught up and flung into the air and as he watched a large sheet of newspaper whirled upwards, mounting the spiral, up and up, fifty or sixty feet, floating and staggering; crowning the whirlwind as it hit the camp. The nearest goon box was enveloped in a cloud of sand and John had a sudden impulse to rush the wire while the sentry was blinded.

In a moment it was all over. The fine dust still hung in the air but the sand was gone and the rushing in the trees had fallen to a sigh.

Far away from the camp the piece of newspaper was floating downwards and, as he watched, it drifted on to the tops of the pines, hung absurdly for a moment and then slipped out of sight.

Wish that was me, he thought. I could do with a miracle like that. Like old Elijah. Or the Greek tragedies. *Deus ex machina*.

When the plot got stuck you lowered him down in a box and he sorted everything out. He pictured a genial old man with an olive wreath drifting down into the camp and offering him a lift. " Any more for the *Skylark* ? Penny a ride on Pegasus. . . ."

And then he found himself running across the camp, an idea racing through his mind. The god in the box—the Trojan horse. Peter—he must find Peter.

He found Peter lying on his bunk, listening to Robbie's latest complaint about Bennett. His eyes were closed.

John tried to appear calm. " Pete, the wind's dropped. What about finishing that walk ? "

" O.K." Peter was grateful for the interruption. " Just a minute while I light my pipe." He took the cigarette from Robbie's hand and held it to the bowl of his pipe. " I should let it drop, Robbie—you can't do anything about it."

" I'm getting moved to another mess," Robbie said. " If that noisy blighter doesn't . . ."

" Come on, Pete," John said.

" I'm with you." Peter handed the cigarette back to Robbie. " Come for a walk. It'll do you good."

" The circuit gives me the willies," Robbie said.

They walked on the firm sandy soil in the circuit. The wind-storm had passed leaving the camp clean, scoured. The air was still now and the prisoners were hanging their washing on the lines.

John was trying to appear calm. He was still tense with the excitement of the idea, but he spoke calmly.

" Pete—you know the idea of camouflaging the outside trap ? "

" Yes ? "

" I was thinking after you'd gone in. You said the last one was a classic by now."

" Well, it is, in a way."

" So is this. What about the wooden horse of Troy ? "

Peter laughed. " The wooden horse of Troy ? "

" Yes, but a vaulting-horse, a box horse like we had at school. You know, one of those square things with a padded top and sides that go right down to the ground. We could carry it out every day and vault over it. One of us would be inside digging while the others vaulted. We'd have a good strong trap and sink it at least a foot below the surface. It's foolproof."

" What about the sand ? "

" We'll have to take it back with us in the horse. Use a kitbag or something. We'll have to keep the horse in one of the huts and get the chaps to carry it out with one of us inside it. We'll take the sand back with us when we go in."

" It'll have to be a strong horse."

" Oh, we'll manage it all right. There's bags of timber in the theatre. You'll be able to knock one up all right." John could see it already. See it clearly and finished. As a complete thing. The wooden vaulting-horse, the vertical shaft under it and the long straight tunnel. He could see them working day after day until they got the tunnel dug. And he saw them going out through the tunnel.

" Let's go and see the Escape Committee now," he said.

" There's no hurry. Let's get the whole thing worked out first."

" We'll go now," John said. " Someone else might think of it while we're still talking about it."

An hour later they were back on the circuit. They had put the scheme before the Committee, who were at first incredulous, then mocking, finally intrigued. They had registered the idea as their own and had been told that if they could produce the vaulting-horse the scheme would have the full backing of the Committee.

" We'll have to get some strong pieces of wood for the frame-work," Peter said. " Four pieces about three inches square and five feet long would do for the legs. Then we've got to have pieces to go round the bottom to tie the legs together—the same round the top. . . . And then we've got to cover the sides. I don't see how we can possibly do it."

" I was thinking of that. Why not cover the sides with canvas ? "

Peter considered the idea. " I don't think that would do, because the sides will have to be solid, otherwise there's no point in covering them at all. And if we do anything pointless the goons will get suspicious and wonder why we've done it. No, this will have to be an absolutely pukka vaulting-horse without anything phony at all."

" Why not cover the whole of the four sides with bed-boards ? "

" No, that won't do ! " Peter said it emphatically.

" Why not ? We've plenty of bed-boards. All the chaps will give up one or two each."

" That's not the point. Do you realise what the thing would weigh if we made the sides of solid wood ? It would be as much as we could do to lift it, let alone carry someone inside it. No, we'll have to think of something else."

They walked on in silence, pacing slowly round the wire.

" I've got it, John ! " Peter said suddenly. " There's our supply "—pointing to the unfinished washhouse—" we'll pinch some of the rafters out of the roof of the new shower baths. Get some nails too while we're about it."

" We'll have to do it after dark," John said. " There's no moon now, let's do it to-night."

" What about the dogs ? "

" We'll have to risk them. The searchlights worry me more than the dogs. I'll dig a sunbathing pit outside the window and we can crawl from under the hut into that. Then if we leave a few benches or chairs lying outside the other windows we can crawl from one to the other."

" I'm more worried about the dogs."

" We'll get Tony Winyard to look after the dogs. He'll make a row and attract them down to that end of the camp. What's worrying me is where to hide the wood we get out."

" Oh—bury it in the sand under the hut or somewhere. When we get it sawn up we can hide it in our beds."

" O.K.—that fixes the framework all right. But what about

the sides? There's not much point in getting the stuff for the framework until we know what we're going to use on the sides."

"It'll come," Peter said. "It'll come. Don't look too far ahead. Let's get organised for to-night. We'll think about the sides to-morrow."

At dusk each evening the guards came into the compound and herded the prisoners into the huts. From dusk until dawn the prisoners were locked in the huts while outside in the compound the darkness was stabbed and dissected by the searchlight beams which swept the camp continually throughout the night.

There was no system in the sweeping of the searchlights. Peter had spent hours sitting at the abort window watching them. At times it would appear that the men on the lights were following a strict routine—one light following the other in its restless movement across the camp. There seemed just time to dash quickly from one hut to another in the interval between the beams. Then, with startling abruptness, the beam would stab out in a totally unexpected quarter, utterly confounding the system.

It was quite dark in the centre of the compound. Round the wire, covering an area of some sixty feet in width, the ground was brilliantly lit by the arc lamps hanging above the wire, a ring of white light surrounding an area of darkness in which stood the blacked-out wooden huts. In each hut, cold and dead from the outside, a hundred prisoners, each with his own private problem, crowded into family intimacy. Each darkened hut seething inside with living cells, loving, hating, chaffing, wrangling.

It was eight twenty-five in the evening. Five minutes before zero hour. In Peter's room the men sat round the table talking nervously. It was like the crew room before take-off. An air of tension and an eagerness to get it started. To get it over with.

During the afternoon Peter had loosened several boards in the floor. The huts stood on wooden piles raised a few feet above the level of the sand. Often during the night Peter had heard the dogs sniffing and prowling about under the floor. He was thinking of this now as he sat, dressed in Australian dark blue battledress, his face blackened with wood-ash, waiting to slip out through the trap he had made.

He was frightened of the dogs. There was something terrifying to him in the thought of the dogs prowling about in the darkness of the compound. Animals trained by men to hunt men. Men themselves were all right. They knew when to stop. But where would the dogs stop if they caught you ? He had seen them being trained outside the wire. He had seen them set on the masked and padded " quarry " by the *Hundmeister*. Seen them bring him to earth and stand over him growling softly. He rubbed his right hand slowly up and down his left forearm and glanced impatiently at his watch.

John sat, a mirror in front of him, smearing wood-ash on his face. " What time is it, Pete ? "

" Twenty twenty-five. Better wait until twenty-thirty before we go. I hope they don't bungle things at the other end."

" Who's doing it ? " Robbie asked.

" Tony Winyard."

" What's he going to do ? "

John was still rubbing wood-ash on his face. " He's going to crawl out of the bottom hut to attract the dogs up to that end of the camp."

" Sooner him than me," Pomfret said.

" And me," Peter said. " He's done it several times. He carries a bag of pepper and reckons he can throw it in the dog's face. Sounds rather like putting salt on a sparrow's tail to me. Still, it'll be useful to us if he can keep the dogs up at that end for about ten minutes. They stage it rather like a bull fight. Tony's the matador. The cape-handlers each have a hole in the floor of their room and call to distract the dog's attention. Must be rather funny. The brute doesn't know which way to go." He looked again at his watch. " O.K., John. Off we go."

He crossed to the trapdoor and lowered himself into the darkness under the hut. The sand felt cool to his hands and the air was musty and full of the odour of pinewood. He crawled towards the edge of the hut and lay waiting until John joined him. " After the next beam has passed," he said, " we'll make a dash for the sand pit."

They reached the sand pit and lay there in its friendly darkness, waiting for the right moment to start the long crawl to the washhouse. It was over a year since Peter had been out of the hut after dark, and he lay on his back looking up at the sky. There were no clouds, and the heavens were trembling with a myriad of stars. He lay there feeling the night air on his face, the cool sand under his hands.

It took them some time to crawl through the wire surrounding the new shower house, but once inside, with the wire replaced, they were free from the dogs and searchlights and could work in peace. They worked fast. There were some long wooden rafters lying against one of the walls and these Peter sawed into suitable lengths with a small hacksaw blade. John searched for nails and any odd tools lying around. He found a bricklayer's trowel and about a dozen good long nails.

When Peter had collected sufficient timber he passed it to John who had crawled back through the wire, and between them they dragged it to the hut.

Several times on the way back they had to lie flat while a searchlight enveloped them in its blinding light. It's just like being over Berlin, Peter thought. Just the same feeling of naked vulnerability.

Once they heard a dog bark; a short sharp yelp of rage that made them grin nervously in the darkness as they squirmed towards the hut.

There was more than the usual noise coming from the hut that night. A carefully orchestrated background to drown the sound of their working. Peter knew that every blackout shutter in the hut was unfastened, that men were waiting in every room to drag them inside should they have to bolt for it.

They gained the hut without being discovered and buried the timber and the trowel in the sand under it.

The next morning Peter went along to the camp theatre to

borrow some tools, while John canvassed the compound for prisoners who were willing to vault.

The camp theatre was a large room formed by removing two of the partition walls in one of the centre huts. A low stage had been built at one end of the room. Behind the stage was a small dark recess used as a dressing-room, property room and carpenter's shop.

For some weeks past he had been helping to construct and paint the scenery for the next dramatic show. It was made up of narrow " flats "—wooden frames covered with thin brown paper. If the covering of the frames was done on a damp day the paper contracted when the weather changed, and split. If the covering was done on a dry day the paper expanded and sagged. It was the usual thing to paint an entire " flat " one evening and return the following morning to find it split from top to bottom.

He found McIntyre, the stage carpenter, making easy-chairs from the plywood chests in which the Red Cross parcels arrived from England.

" 'Morning, Mac," he said.

McIntyre was a typical stage carpenter, taciturn, pessimistic, and a genius at improvisation. He grunted.

" How's it going, Mac ? "

" O.K."

" I've come to see if I can borrow a hammer."

" Aye."

Peter sat back in one of the finished arm-chairs and looked round the small cluttered room. Mac's retreat. The bulwark that Mac had built himself against the boredom of prison life. Pieces of furniture, machines for " noises off," properties. All Mac's. He leaned comfortably back in the chair and sighed.

" This is a comfortable chair, Mac."

" Aye." (Hammering at one of the chairs.)

" We could do with one of these in our room."

" Aye," Mac said. " I dare say."

Peter sat up. " Mac, could you spare me any of this plywood ? "

" What for ? "

" I want to make a vaulting-horse."

" A what ? "

" A vaulting-horse. You know—one of those box horses. I want to cover the sides with plywood."

McIntyre straightened up. " Aye, you'll need quite a number of boxes for that. I'm having a load sent in from the Kommandantur. I'll have some extra ones put in for you."

" Thanks a lot, Mac. Could you spare me any three-inch nails ? I'll get on with making the framework this morning and then I'll be ready for the plywood when it arrives."

" Aye," McIntyre said. " Why the sudden interest in gymnastics ? "

Peter dropped his voice to a whisper. " Camouflage for a hole."

" Sorry, Pete." McIntyre's attitude became at once cold and antagonistic. " I can't let you use these tools for escape purposes. You know that as well as I do. They're on parole. Even if they weren't, you'd mess 'em up. Why on earth don't you give it a rest ? "

" O.K., Mac." He understood McIntyre's jealousy for his tools. His not being able to escape himself and not wanting other people to try either. " O.K., Mac," he said. " I shouldn't have asked you really," and he started to move towards the door.

" Why not go along and see ' Wings ' Cameron ? " McIntyre said. " He's got a few illicit tools and he'll lend a hand in making it."

" I'll go along now," Peter said. " Thanks all the same, Mac." As he walked towards the wing-commander's room he wondered why McIntyre had suggested that. Just to get rid of him, or with a genuine desire to help ? How little I know of him, he thought. How little I know of any of them. Old Mac, completely absorbed in his carpentry. Proud of his resourcefulness in making something out of nothing. Making a vocation out of imprisonment.

" Wings " Cameron lived in a small room at the end of Block 64. As a wing-commander he enjoyed the privilege of a room to himself. He needed it. Because he was another enthusiast. And enthusiasts are not easy to live with in a prison camp. He, too, loved making things. Give him a piece of string, some bent nails, a few empty Klim tins, leave him alone for a while and he would produce a lamp, a cooking stove, a patent device for digging tunnels—whatever you had asked him for.

As Peter walked down the corridor of Block 64 he could hear the sounds of hammering coming from the room at the end of the hut. Good show, he thought, he's in the mood for heavy work.

He stopped at the wing-commander's door. Stuck to the centre panel was a cartoon cut from an American magazine. It showed a convict digging a hole in the floor of his cell. He was using a pickaxe. Outside the barred door, over which the convict had draped a blanket, stood two wardens talking. " I don't know what he's making," one of them was saying, " but it's keeping him very quiet."

Peter grinned and knocked on the door.

" Come in," called a friendly voice, and Peter entered the cell-like room.

" Wings " Cameron was a small man with a large moustache. A plumber's moustache. He was wearing a pair of Egyptian sandals, rose-coloured socks, a pair of faded grey flannel trousers and a bright yellow shirt with a large red handkerchief of Paisley design knotted loosely round his neck. He had been shot down wearing these strange clothes. " Thought I'd dress like a foreigner," he explained later, " then I shouldn't be noticed if I had to bale out. But I must have dressed as the wrong sort of foreigner, because I was arrested quite soon."

The room was twelve feet by six feet. Across the narrowness of it, at the end farthest from the door, stood a two-tier bunk. The bottom bunk was made up for sleeping. The top bunk was a confusion of old Klim tins, bits of wire, bed-boards, the pieces of a broken-down cast-iron stove, and the remains of a wooden bicycle that " Wings " had started to make and never finished. Klim tins stood in rows on wooden shelves fixed to the walls. Klim tins stood on the table and on the chairs. Klim tins overflowed all these and stood in serried rows under the bunks. The tins were filled with nails, pieces of string, screws, nuts and bolts, small pieces of glass, odds and ends of paint from the theatre. Everything that " Wings " had acquired from years of diligent scrounging.

Along one wall, under the window, were fixed a drawing-board and a work-bench. On the drawing-board was pinned a scale drawing of a sailing yacht. On the work-bench lay another confusion of odds and ends, a vice made by " Wings " out of the parts of an old bed, and a model steam engine constructed from Klim tins and a German water bottle.

As Peter entered the room, the wing-commander was nailing a wooden batten to the floor. The batten formed a frame round a large square hole he had cut in the floor.

" What's that for ? " Peter asked.

" To stop me falling down the hole." The wing-commander replied without looking up from his work.

" No, I don't mean the piece of wood. I mean the hole itself."

" Oh, that ! " He straightened himself. " That's part of an air-conditioning plant I'm fitting."

" How will it work ? "

" I'm fitting a fan under the floor. I've got the parts of it here." He pointed to a wheel with propeller-like blades cut from plywood. " The fan is driven by a belt and pulley from a large wheel under the floor. A shaft runs from the wheel up through the floor to the top of the work-bench. I shall have this old gramophone turntable mounted on the top of the shaft. The winding-handle of the gramophone will be fixed to the turntable as a crank. When the room gets too hot I merely turn the handle and cold air is driven up through the hole in the floor. The hot air leaves through another hole I'm going to cut near the ceiling."

" Why don't you use the gramophone motor to drive the fan ? " Peter asked.

" Oh, the motor's broken. I used the parts to make a clock."

" Wait till the goons see it. They'll be after you for damage to Reich property."

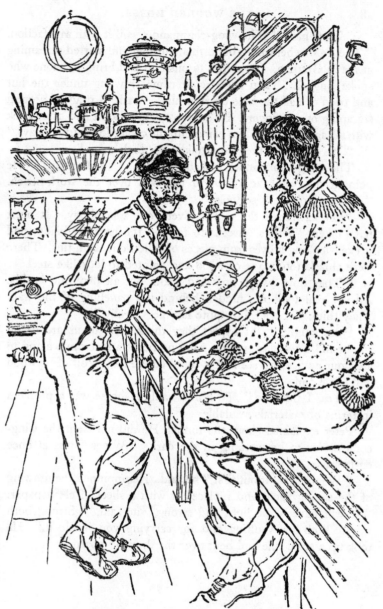

"*It will have to be light and strong,*" he said

" They have." The wing-commander said it with satisfaction. " The Feldwebel came round this morning and started screaming at me in German. I told him to push off and bring someone who spoke English. Then a Gefreiter came crawling under the hut and tried to nail the hole up from underneath. I pranced around stamping on his fingers. He went away after a bit and came back with a Lager Offizier. I'm going into the cooler for fourteen days."

" It's a wonder they don't take your tools away."

The wing-commander looked cunning. " Look at this." He pointed to a tool-rack fixed to the wall over the work-bench. " Have a look at these tools."

Peter examined the tools. Every one was phony. It must have taken " Wings " weeks to fashion the hacksaw blades and wicked-looking knives from pieces of rolled-out Klim tins. There were chisels too, made of wood and painted to look like steel.

" They do a swoop now and again, but all they find is this. All my real tools are hidden behind the panelling of the wall. They think I'm mad, but quite harmless, really."

Peter laughed. " I expect they think most of us are round the bend. I want to make a vaulting-horse and I came along to ask your advice and see if you could let me have a bit of plywood and some nails."

" Yes, I think so." To him a vaulting-horse was a problem in terms of materials available.

Peter explained about the tunnel. He did not want the wing-commander to be working in the dark. " Wings " was at once enthusiastic.

" We must set it out first," he said. He unpinned the drawing of the sailing yacht and replaced it with a sheet of clean paper. " It will have to be light and strong," he said. " Strong both ways. Both for vaulting and for carrying you inside it." He took up a scale rule and bent over the drawing-board.

CHAPTER THREE

The Tunnel Is Started

BETWEEN THEM they had built the vaulting-horse. It stood four feet six inches high, the base covering an area of five feet by three feet. The sides were covered with two-feet square plywood sheets from Red Cross packing-cases stolen from the German store. The sides tapered up to the top which was of solid wood boards padded with their bedding and covered with white linen material taken from the bales in which the cigarettes arrived from England. There were four slots, four inches long by three inches wide, cut in the plywood sides. When pieces of rafter six feet long and three inches by two inches thick had been pushed through these holes the horse could be carried by four men in the manner of a sedan chair.

The horse was kept in the canteen. A canteen in name only— a long, low extension to the camp kitchen, containing the barber's shop and a large empty room used as a band practice room. Like all the other buildings in the compound, it was raised above the surface of the ground ; but it was built on a brick foundation and more solidly than the living quarters. The entrance was by double doors reached by a short flight of wide wooden steps.

While the horse was being built John had been recruiting prisoners for the vaulting. He had posters made which he stuck up round the camp, advertising gym classes which would be held every afternoon. Special prisoners were detailed to talk to the German guards, remarking on this typical English craze for exercise and telling them, casually, about the vaulting-horse.

Some days later the few afternoon walkers on the circuit were surprised to see the double doors of the canteen open and a team of prisoners dressed only in shorts march down the wooden steps and form up in a line near the trip-wire. They were followed by the four strongest members of the team carrying a box-like object slung on wooden poles. The box was carried to a spot about thirty feet inside the trip-wire where it was carefully placed on the ground and the poles withdrawn.

The team formed up and under the direction of one of the prisoners began to vault over the box. The guards, bored with watching the prisoners walking the endless circuit of the wire, turned towards the unusual spectacle. They did not give their whole attention to the vaulting. A boxing match or a faked spontaneous fight was a well-known Kriegie method of distracting the attention of the guards while an attempt was being made on the wire. So the guards watched the vaulting but cast an occasional glance along the strip of wire for which they were responsible.

The standard of vaulting was high. The captain of the team led his men in a complicated series of jumps. Only one of the men was not so good. His approach was clumsy and his vaulting not up to the standard of the others. The guards soon singled him out as the butt of the party and grinned whenever he failed to clear the horse. The vaulting had drawn a crowd of amused prisoners, who jeered and cat-called whenever he made his run up to the box. Every time he failed to clear the horse he drew a guffaw of laughter from the surrounding prisoners.

Soon the guards in the boxes were leaning on their elbows waiting for him to make his run. It was not often they had the chance to laugh at the British prisoners. The boot was usually on the other foot. The more the spectators laughed the more determined this man appeared to be to clear the obstacle. He took a final, desperate leap and in missing his footing he lurched into the horse and knocked it over. He knocked it over on to its side so that the interior was in full view of the guards.

The horse was empty. The vaulters righted the box and went on with their sport. Soon they carried the horse back into the canteen, where they left it until the following afternoon.

Before they left the canteen they tied pieces of black cotton across the doorway and from the edge of the horse to the skirting-board. The following morning the cotton was broken. The ferrets were taking no chances. During the night the vaulting-horse had been examined.

It was after breakfast, a week after the vaulting had first started. Peter and John were walking round the circuit. The subject of their conversation—it had been nothing else for a week—was the vaulting-horse.

" I think we might start digging to-morrow," John said. " The

Vaulting-horse showing one lifting bar in position

goons have got used to the vaulting now. We've knocked the horse over often enough for them to see that there's nothing going on inside. Besides, the chaps who are vaulting want to get some return for their labour. They won't just go on vaulting if nothing happens."

" Yes, I know, I'm rather worried about the vaulters. It's tough going on the little food we get. How long do you think it'll take us to dig the tunnel ? "

" Let's see." John hitched his shorts with his elbows. " We've got about forty-five feet to go to the trip-wire, thirty feet across the danger strip. That's seventy-five feet. The wire itself is about eight feet thick so that makes eighty-three feet. We should break at least thirty feet away from the wire because of the outside sentries. That gives us one hundred and thirteen feet altogether. That's if we go straight. Allow a bit for going round rock or tree roots and make it a round figure of one hundred and twenty feet. . . . A hundred and twenty feet. If we do five feet a day it will take us twenty-four days."

" We shan't do five feet a day," Peter said.

" Oh, I don't know. I could dig five feet in a day. Make it three feet if you like, that will make it about six weeks."

" It's not a matter of how much we can dig in a day—it's a matter of how much we can carry away in the horse. Do you realise how much sand weighs ? "

" You should know that—you're the construction boss."

" As far as I can remember a yard of sand weighs about ten hundredweight, but I don't know whether that's wet or dry. Ours will be wet, of course. But knowing that wouldn't help us much. What we want to know is how big a pound of sand looks, so that we can figure out how much we can dig in one session. How much do you think they can carry in the horse—with one of us inside as well ? "

" What do you weigh ? "

" I don't know. I was eleven-three when I was shot down. I expect I'm about ten-seven or ten-ten now."

" Then I'm about ten. Supposing we say we can carry ten stone of sand."

" That's a hundred and forty pounds—let's go and weigh a pound of sand and see how much it looks. I think a foot a day seems more reasonable than three feet."

" What shall we use as a pound weight ? I think a gallon of water weighs about ten pounds."

" We'll use an unopened tin of Klim—that weighs exactly a pound nett. We'll make some scales, put an empty Klim tin on the other end and fill it with damp sand until the scales are even. Then we'll know what a pound of sand looks like."

"Right," John said. "We can't go in yet. They're holding a Latin class in our room."

"I suppose I ought to be going to German classes really."

"Oh, I shouldn't bother. After all, we shan't travel as Germans. A little knowledge is dangerous. If you start learning German now and start talking outside you'll get us both in the cart. Your best role is dignified silence. We'd better travel as Frenchmen and I'll do the talking. As long as you can say ' *Ich bin Ausländer—night verstehen*,' that should get you through."

"O.K.," Peter said. "*Ich bin Ausländer—night verstehen*. Sounds impressive. What does it mean ? "

"It means ' I'm a foreigner—I don't understand.' "

"That seems a good line. I suppose I just keep on saying that until you come along."

"You can pretend to be deaf and dumb if you like."

"I know! I'll have a pronounced stutter. Then if they ask me anything I'll just stutter and you interrupt and tell them what they want to know."

"Yes, I'll do that if they talk French, but if they don't you just stick to the *nicht verstehen* business."

"Right," Peter said. "*Ich bin Ausländer—night verstehen*." He walked on round the circuit thinking of the escape. *Ich bin Ausländer—nicht verstehen.* What a vocabulary to try to cross Germany with. But even if I spoke fluent German, how much better off would I be ? It's all a matter of luck, this escaping business. Chaps have got through to England without any German at all. And fluent German speakers have been brought back. And that's looking too far ahead too. We've got to get out of the camp first. Let the morrow look after itself. It would be nice to be back in England though. Feeling as though you were doing something instead of stewing here waiting for the end of the war. Back on the squadron with the flying and the fear, and the relief, and the parties in the mess, and the feeling that it could happen to anyone else but not to you. And the feeling of thankfulness the next morning that it hadn't happened to you and that you could go out that night and you wouldn't have to worry again until the night after. . . .

That evening Peter made the top section of the shoring for the vertical shaft. He made it with four sides of a plywood packing case reinforced and slotted so that they could be assembled into a rigid four-sided box without top or bottom. The box would stand a considerable inwards pressure.

John spent the evening in making twelve bags from the bottoms of trouser legs. Several of the prisoners had made themselves shorts by cutting their trousers off above the knee. When John had sewn the bottoms together, roughly hemmed the tops and inserted string, the trouser legs had become bags about twelve inches long. He fashioned hooks from strong wire with which he intended to suspend the bags inside the horse.

During the week they had made two sand pits, one at the side and one at the head of where the horse was standing. They had made these ostensibly to soften the shock of landing on their bare feet. Actually they served as a datum mark to ensure that they always replaced the horse on the exact spot.

The next afternoon they took the horse out with John inside it. He took with him a cardboard Red Cross box to hold the surface sand, the trouser-leg bags and hooks, one side of the vertical shoring and the bricklayer's trowel they had stolen from the unfinished shower baths.

This is worse than going on your first " op," Peter thought. He was holding one end of the front transverse pole and walking slowly towards the spot where they would place the horse.

John crouched inside the horse. His feet were on the bottom framework, one on each side of the horse. In his arms he held the equipment. The horse creaked and lurched as the bearers staggered under the unaccustomed weight. They got the horse into position and began to vault.

Inside the horse John worked quickly. Scraping up the dark-grey surface sand, he put it into the cardboard box and started to

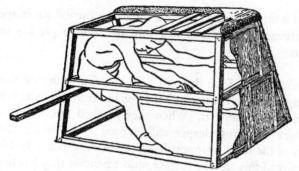

Showing the framework construction of the vaulting-horse with one man in position for being carried

dig a deep trench for one side of the shoring. He put the bright yellow excavated sand into the trouser-leg bags.

As the trench grew deeper he had difficulty in reaching the bottom. He made it wider and had to bank the extra sand against one end of the horse. It was hot inside the horse and he began to sweat.

He finished the trench and put the plywood sheet in position. He replaced the surface sand, ramming it down with the handle of the trowel, packing the shoring tight. The top of the shoring was six inches below the ground.

Standing on the framework of the horse, he carefully spread the sand over the plywood sheet, packing it down hard, finally sprinkling the grey sand over the whole area covered by the horse —obliterating his foot and finger marks.

Calling softly to Peter, he gave the word that he had finished.

The vaulters inserted the carrying poles and staggered back into the canteen with John and the bags of sand.

Once inside the canteen they transferred the sand from the trouser-leg bags into long, sausage-like sacks made from the arms and legs of woollen underwear. These they carried away slung round their necks and down inside their trouser legs.

The sand was dispersed in various places around the compound, some of it finding its way by devious routes to the latrines, some of it buried under the huts, some of it carried out in specially made trouser pockets and dug into the tomato patches outside the huts.

It took them four days to sink the four sides of the box. Working alternately, they sank the box in the ground and removed the sand from inside it. When they reached the bottom of the woodwork they dug deeper still, putting bricks under the four corners of the box to support it. They made a trap of bed-boards and replaced this and the surface sand whenever they left the hole.

Finally they had made a hole five feet deep and two feet six inches square. They had dropped the wooden box twelve inches as they worked. The top of the box was now eighteen inches below the surface of the ground. This eighteen inches of sand above the wooden trap gave them security from the probing-rods of the ferrets and was also deep enough to deaden any hollow sound when the trap was walked on. But it was too much sand to remove each time before reaching the trap. To make this easier they filled bags, made from woollen undervests. These they placed on top of the trap, covering them with merely six to eight inches of surface sand. The bags were thin enough not to impede the progress of the ferret's probe, and enabled them to uncover and recover the trap more quickly.

The wooden box stood on four brick piles two feet high. On three sides the shaft below the wooden box was shored with pieces of bed-board. The fourth side was left open for the tunnel.

It was possible to stand in the shaft, but it was not possible to kneel. To get into the tunnel they were forced to make a short burrow in the opposite direction. Into this they thrust their feet while kneeling to enter the tunnel.

The first seven feet of the tunnel was shored solid with bed-boards. The shoring was made by Peter, in the evenings, in the security of their room, and taken down to the tunnel in sections and reassembled there. The whole of the work was done with a table-knife and a red-hot poker. To assemble the shoring Peter lay on his back in the darkness of the narrow tunnel, scraping away sufficient sand to slide the main bearers into position before inserting the bed-boards. He had to work slowly and carefully, fearful all the time that a sudden fall of sand would bury him. He was alone down there and even a small fall of sand would be enough to pin him, helpless, on his back in the narrowness of the tunnel.

When the ceiling of the tunnel was in position they had to fill the space between the top of the tunnel and the wooden ceiling with sand. If this were not done the sand would fall and the

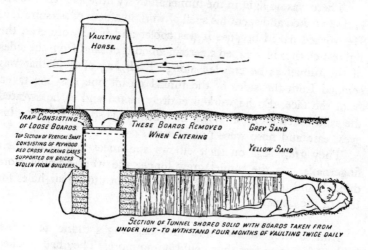

Section of Tunnel shored solid with boards taken from under hut—to withstand four months of vaulting twice daily

ceiling become higher and higher until a tell-tale subsidence of the surface would reveal the path of the tunnel.

After the first seven feet of shoring, which they built to take the force of the impact of the vaulters on the surface, the tunnel ran on without any shoring whatever.

The tunnel was very small. They had quickly seen that the progress of the work would be determined by the speed with which they could get the excavated sand away. The smaller they made the tunnel the less sand they would have to dispose of and the faster would go the work.

While one of them supervised the vaulting the other dug in

the tunnel. He worked alone down there. Once he got into the tunnel with his hands in front of his head he had to stay like that. He could not get his arms behind him again. Nor could he crawl with them doubled up. It was fingers and toes all the way until he got to the end of the tunnel. Once he got there he scraped some sand from the face with the trowel and crawled backwards down the tunnel, dragging the sand with him. When he got back to the vertical shaft he had brought enough sand to fill half a bag. And there were twelve bags to fill.

There was no light in the tunnel and very little air. He worked entirely naked and spent his spell of work in a bath of perspiration. He worked naked because it was cooler and if he wore even the lightest clothes he scraped a certain amount of sand from the sides of the tunnel as he crawled along. Each bag of sand that was scraped from the sides of the tunnel meant one less bag taken from the face. So he worked entirely naked and as he sweated the sand caked on him. When he finished his spell of digging his eyes, ears and nose were full of sand.

They grew segs on their elbows and knees and broke their fingernails. As the tunnel grew longer the work became more difficult and the air more foul. They did not put up air-holes for fear of the dogs.

And so they worked until they had dug a tunnel forty feet long. After forty feet they could do no more. They had reached the limit of their endurance. The farther they pushed the tunnel the more difficult the work became. The air was bad ; and they were taking two hours to fill the twelve bags.

Not only were the tunnellers exhausted by the twenty-four times repeated crawl up the tunnel, but the vaulters—who had been vaulting every afternoon of the two months that it had taken to dig the forty feet—were exhausted too. The tunnellers were given extra food, but the vaulters were not, and they had little energy to spare.

Peter and John had devised games and variations on the theme of vaulting. A dozen men could not vault for two hours without looking unnatural about it. The whole time one of the tunnellers was below ground the other would be in the vaulting team trying to make the two hours that the horse stood there appear as natural as possible. It was not easy, especially when the ferret was standing within earshot of the horse, watching the vaulting.

They organised a medicine-ball and a deck-tennis quoit and stood in a circle round the horse throwing them to one another. They even organised a run round the circuit—leaving the horse vulnerable and alone with the trap open below it.

It was a considerable physical strain working in the tunnel; yet both of them preferred it to organising the vaulting.

The end came one afternoon while John was in the tunnel. Peter had gone to the main gate to find out how many Germans were in the compound. It was ten minutes before they were due to take the horse in.

As he was walking back towards the horse he was met by one of the vaulters, pale-faced and running.

" What's wrong ? " Peter asked.

" There's been a fall."

" Where ? "

" Near the horse."

" Is John all right ? "

" We shouted to him, but we can't get a reply."

Peter ran towards the horse. A fall probably meant that John was trapped. There were no air-holes. He would be caught in the end of the tunnel, suffocating, trapped by the fall of sand.

The vaulters were grouped round a man who was lying on the ground. Peter glanced quickly towards the sentry boxes above the wire. The guards were watching.

" Where's the fall ? " he asked.

" Wilde's lying on it. A hole suddenly appeared, so Wilde lay on it to stop the guards seeing it. He's pretending he's hurt his leg."

" How's John ? "

" We can't get a reply."

Peter wanted to overturn the horse at once and go down, but

the thought of the discovery of the tunnel stopped him. Old John would be furious if he panicked for nothing.

"Send someone for a stretcher," he said. "We must make this look as natural as possible."

Two of the vaulters went for a stretcher. Peter crouched by Nigel's feet, his head near the horse. "John," he called. "John!"

No answer.

"Roll over, Nig," he said.

Nigel rolled over. There was a hole, about as thick as his arm, going down into the darkness of the tunnel.

"John," he called. "John!"

"Hallo, Pete." The answer was weak.

"What happened?"

"There's been a fall, but I can clear it. I've taken some of the shoring from the shaft. I'll have it fixed in a jiffy. Can you fill it from the top?"

"O.K. Let me know when you've got it fixed." He pretended to attend to Nigel's leg.

"The goons seem interested," Nigel said.

"The chaps with the stretcher will be here in a minute," Peter told him. "They'll carry you to your hut. That'll explain what we've been doing."

Presently he heard John's voice, thinly, from inside the tunnel. "I'm just putting the shoring in. You can fill-in in about five minutes."

What a man, Peter thought. What a man. Good old John. He poked solicitously at Nigel's leg. The two vaulters returned with the stretcher and a first-aid kit. Peter made a great business of bandaging Nigel's leg while the others, shuffling round, kicked the sand towards the hole.

"It'll sink a bit," Peter said. "We'll kick some more over it later on. What's the time?"

"Three-thirty."

"It's roll-call at four! We must get John up before then." He banged on the side of the horse. There was no reply.

Ten minutes passed. Still there was no sign from John.

There was a hole, about as thick as his arm

We've had it, Peter thought. If we can't get him up before roll-call we've had it. "Come on, chaps, let's get vaulting," he said. "We can't just stand around here."

They began to vault again. Then he heard John's voice, urgently, from inside the horse. "Hey, Pete, what's the time?"

"You've got five minutes."

"It's an awful mess."

At the end of the five minutes they carried him into the canteen. He could hardly stand. "It's an awful mess," he said. "There's a bit of tree root there and the vaulting must have shaken it loose. I've jammed it up temporarily but it needs proper shoring."

"I'll take some down with me to-morrow," Peter said.

The next afternoon he went down with some wooden shoring. He found the tunnel choked with sand. Soft shifting sand that continued to fall as he worked. He worked in the dark, entirely by feel, and the air was bad so that he panted as he worked. Sand fell into his eyes and his mouth. He worked furiously, clearing the sand away and fitting the shoring into position.

When the shoring was fitted he managed to pack some of the sand away between the shoring and the sides of the tunnel. The rest of it he spread about the floor, lying flat on his belly and pressing it down with his hands.

When he finally got back into the horse he could hardly find the strength to replace the trap. He put it back, and the sand above it, and gave John the signal that he was ready to be taken in. When he reached the canteen he crawled out from under the horse and fainted.

That evening he was taken to the camp hospital. It was a total collapse. He had taken too much out of himself with the digging, the vaulting and the worry. The British doctor prescribed a week in bed. The matter was out of Peter's hands and he lay in bed wondering what John was doing.

During the week he was in the hospital no digging was done ; but the horse was taken out every afternoon to avoid the suspicion of the guards.

CHAPTER FOUR

Peter Bribes A Guard

PETER HAD been given a sedative and put to bed. He woke during the night, sweating. Outside it was raining. Outside the window the rain poured down, beating on a corrugated-iron roof somewhere close at hand, drumming and beating and sluicing away into the gutter. Occasionally there was a flash of lightning and a low rumble of thunder in the distance.

He lay in bed and listened to the rain. It sounded cool and soft—summer rain. He imagined it falling on the leaves of a tree outside the window, pattering on the leaves and then falling in large slow drops on to the dark earth below. He imagined it, earth-brown, swirling and gurgling as it made a way for itself down the gravel path ; eddying but imperative, with small twigs and leaves like rudderless boats twisting and turning on its surface. Twisting and turning but always following the flow of the stream, underneath the wire, into the ditch outside the wire ; the freedom of the outside world.

He lay for a long time listening to the rain and finally fell asleep, cool now, soothed by the patter of the rain.

When he awoke again it was morning. The blackout shutters had been taken from the windows and the sunlight streamed into the room. It seemed more friendly than in the night, and more untidy. The other patients were sitting up in bed, washing themselves. Through the open door he could hear the clanging of buckets and the swish of water as the orderlies washed the floor of the corridor.

He lay still for a while listening to the friendly banter of the other patients. They were ragging the man in the bed next to his own. By his lack of repartee and the sounds coming from his bed it was obvious that he was gargling.

When the gargling was finished he was able to reply. He spoke with a marked Australian accent. " It was bad luck, that's all. If it hadn't been for that darned sentry we'd have got away."

Peter raised his head and looked towards the next bed. His neighbour had a bandage round his head and his arm was in a sling.

" 'Morning, cobber. Feeling better ? "

" I've got a lousy head," Peter said. " What's wrong with you ? "

" I got a bullet through the shoulder. We were just getting a boat at Danzig and a sentry saw us. Took a pot at me and got me through the shoulder. I cut my head open when I fell down."

" He's got a sore throat," one of the other men said. " There's nothing wrong with him except the sore throat. He got that talking about his escape. He's done nothing but talk about it since he's been here."

" He's chocker," the Australian said. " Broke his arm jumping off a train. Hadn't been out more than a few hours and he breaks his arm falling off a train. He needs to get some hours in."

" Where are you from ? " Peter asked.

" The North Compound. Four of us got out under the wire. I'd have made it if it hadn't been for that sentry."

" How long were you out ? "

" Three days. I caught this cold sleeping in a ditch."

" What happened to the other two ? "

" In the cooler. Put their hands up as soon as he started shooting. Wish I'd had the sense to do the same."

" How did you get to Danzig ? " Peter asked.

" Jumped a goods train. Riding on the rods, cobber. That's the way for a man to get around."

" What's Danzig like ? "

" Rotten. Wouldn't go there again. No future for a joker there. Too many sentries in the docks."

" Are the docks fenced in ? "

" No, but they're stiff with troops. No future there, cobber."

That week Peter lay in bed dreaming of escape. He listened carefully to the experiences of the others, comparing them with his own ; trying to trace a common weakness in their plans. He thought back over his last attempt, an abortive escape made from Dulag-Luft when he was first captured. That had been over a year ago. A year since then spent in escape, and he had never got within fifty feet of the wire. People said it was impossible to escape, and here were two men who had just been brought back.

He questioned them about their attempt and tried to analyse the causes of its failure. He ran over in his mind all the stories he had heard from prisoners who had been outside the wire. He went over each escape step by step until he came to the moment of capture. In every case they had been caught on foot and usually within a few days of leaving the camp. Most of them had walked, covering sometimes only a very few miles before they were recaptured. Of those who had jumped trains only these two had reached their destination, and they had been caught in the docks in Danzig. They had boarded the train in the goods yard outside the camp and had travelled all the way without a stop.

" That seems to be the answer," he said one night after lying for some time, pondering, on his bed. " Buy tickets and travel as passengers. There must be hundreds of foreign workers travelling about Germany on the railway."

" It's not safe," the Australian said. " Bound to get caught first time they ask you for your papers. The things we make aren't good enough to stand a train check."

" But you are getting somewhere," Peter persisted. " If you do get past the booking office you travel quickly and safely to where you want to go."

" They have train checks," the Australian said. " I had a cobber who did that. He got past the booking clerk all right but got picked up on the train. Joker came round looking at the tickets and asking for their papers. When he showed his papers they ran him in straight away. Those jokers are used to looking for forged papers and they spot 'em right away."

" It must have been a fast train," Peter said. " You don't want a corridor train. You want to get on a slow local train, one without a corridor. Once you're in, you're in. Nothing can happen until you get to the other end."

" Unless you get into conversation with anyone."

" You can pretend to sleep. Besides, you'd obviously be a foreigner and the Germans wouldn't talk to you anyway."

" How do you know that they allow foreign workers on the trains ? Probably transport 'em in cattle trucks."

" We'll have to find that out."

" I'd rather walk," the Australian said. " Or jump goods trains. Too nerve-racking to sit in the same carriage with a lot of goons for several hours. Might fall asleep and start talking in English. Besides, they smell. Give me the open air every time."

" I'm not so sure," Peter said. " I think there's something in this train travel."

After the tension of the last few days it was a relief to lie back and do nothing. It was a queer place, this inner sanctum of captivity. A place remote from barbed wire and goon boxes. The patients were no more prisoners than were the patients in any military hospital. Even the guards were more friendly and, not being supervised, were able to come into the wards and talk to the patients.

Peter used this period of enforced idleness to complete his pictorial record of Kriegie life. He wanted to make a record of the untidiness of boxes and old tin cans in which they lived, the bearded figures wrapped in a multitude of sweaters, scarves and greatcoats, hobbling in their wooden clogs out of the barrack huts to attend the morning appel. The appel itself, rows and rows of ragged figures in balaclava helmets, clad in every type and colour of uniform from French horizon blue through air force blue and

English and Polish khaki to the dark blue of the Fleet Air Arm. Every colour of beard from bright red to black, every form of footwear from clogs to flying-boots.

He wanted to paint the hospital, its bare wooden walls and rows of untidy beds. The rough home-made bedside tables, chairs made from packing-cases, and the pale angular patients.

Above all he wanted to capture the spirit of undefeated humour that was so typical of the camp—the humour that inspired the cartoon that hung on the wall of one of the messes in his block. The drawing showed two Kriegies wrapped up like parcels in scarves and sweaters, trying to heat a tin of food over a fire made from a broken packing-case, the remains of which still lay beside them on the floor. Around them was an indescribable chaos of old tins, bits of wire and sticks or wood, and over all hung the pall of smoke and steam which gathered as soon as the prisoners were locked in for the night. The caption ran, " Not the Berkeley, old boy—wouldn't be seen dead in the place ! "

The first Sunday evening that Peter was in the hospital the camp padre brought a portable gramophone and played a selection of classical records. He played Beethoven's Second Piano Concerto and as Peter lay listening his thoughts travelled back to the night that he had been shot down. The quiet stooging along miles from the target, the moon and the stars, the flickering searchlights far away on the horizon. The lighthearted conversation of his crew. Then suddenly the hammer and din of machine-gun bullets and the heavier tearing impact of cannon shells as a night fighter closed in from behind them. The wild jinking to avoid the attack, the dry-mouthed sick fear of the smashing, tearing impact of the shells. The smell of cordite, the sudden red mushrooming fire in the cockpit, the fumbling with the parachute and the sickening swaying of the flapping parachute as he descended into Germany.

He lived again his feeling of relief to be safely, unhurt, on the ground. The three days hunted across the German countryside, the capture, interrogation, solitary confinement, the prison camp. Improvisation, making the best of things, attempting to escape.

He thought of his first camp, Oflag XXIB in Poland. It had been snowing when the new batch of prisoners had arrived and the night had been clear, smelling of snow and pinewoods. They had been marched into the barrack block where a hundred prisoners had been locked since dusk. After the freshness of the night outside, the strench had been appalling. A long low room lit by dozens of home-made goon lamps, lamps made from tobacco tins filled with rancid animal fat. Lamps which gave off a feeble red glow and clouds of black evil-smelling smoke. They threw weird, distorted shadows on the walls which had once been white-washed but now were grey and smeared by smoke and steam. There were windows in each of the side walls but these were covered from the outside by wooden blackout shutters. The air was thick with tobacco smoke and steam from the row on row of damp washing which hung down almost to head level from lines strung across the room. Smoke from the goon lamps mixed with the steam and tobacco smoke to form a thick fog which eddied and billowed just below the ceiling.

He remembered his horror at the uncouth appearance of the bearded, haggard-looking men who sat huddled round the flickering goon lamps. Life had been pretty grim in those early days. The days before the Red Cross parcels had begun to arrive and the prisoners had lived on turnip soup and rotten potatoes. It seemed almost impossible now, in the heat of the summer, that he had been so cold. He remembered waking in that long damp room, waking fully dressed, even to his issue greatcoat. He wore a woollen skullcap on his head and mittens on his hands. A film of water lay on the grey blanket which covered his head and the woodwork of the bunk on which he lay was damp.

He grinned as he remembered the reveille, the door crashing open and the hoarse baying cry of " *Raus ! Raus !* " as the guards came into the room. The equally hoarse shout of " Push off ! " with which the prisoners replied. It had been an abrupt intro-duction to imprisonment, but he had learned a lot at Oflag XXIB.

It had been there that he had met John, the lone army officer among so many airmen. At first he had seemed aloof, but later, when you got to know him, you discovered his eagerness, his consuming desire to escape, to wipe out the disgrace of being captured. It was a disgrace not shared by the airmen because it involved a surrender of arms.

His thoughts were suddenly broken by the clatter of footsteps and the yelping commands of a German officer. The door crashed open and a German major with an escort of soldiers clanked into the ward. They had come to conduct a " blitz appel." The major paused, stood looking at the gramophone and its operator, softly illuminated by the flickering yellow glow of a goon lamp. The padre was playing the last movement of the Second Piano Concerto.

" Ach, Beethoven," the major said. " He is a good German."

" Yes," said the Australian's voice from out of the darkness. " He's dead ! "

The Australian had " tamed " one of the guards. He called him " Dopey " and treated him with affectionate contempt. Dopey was a simple man, a man of small loyalties. For a bar of chocolate he would forget his obligation to the Third Reich. For a cigarette he would agree that the Allies would probably win the war.

One day when Dopey came in for his cup of cocoa Peter talked to him about the state of the railways. He began by asking for news of the latest air raids.

" *Hamburg kaput*," the guard said. " *Duisburg kaput. Haben Sie Zigaretten ?* "

Peter gave him a cigarette.

" *Danke*." He took off his cap. " *Hitler kaput. Deutschland kaput*."

" Good show, Dopey," the Australian said. " How long will the war last ? "

" One month, two month."

" How're the Ruskies doing ? " the Australian asked. This

stock question always brought the same reply. Dopey was terrified of the Russians.

"Russland no good! Stalingrad no good!" He lifted the leg of his trousers to show where he had been wounded. He had been wounded in the battle of Stalingrad and left lying in the snow. He had been returned to Germany badly frost-bitten, for Home Defence duties. His greatest fear was of being sent back to the Russian front.

"Ruskies good fighters," the Australian said. "Ruskies better fighters than Germans."

"Ruskies no good," Dopey repeated. "Ruskies mad devils. Stalingrad no good. Mud. Snow. Ice. Ruski women fight like devils. Not good to fight against women."

"Not when they're armed," the Australian said. "You're not bad at it when they're not."

"Russland no good," the guard repeated.

But Peter wanted to get the conversation back to the railways. "*Hamburg Bahnnof kaput?*" he asked.

"*Hamburg kaput.*" The guard knew this by heart. He had been paid a cigarette to say it. He might, with luck, get another. "*Duisburg kaput, Berlin kaput.*"

Peter laughed and tried again. After much questioning he discovered that the railways were overcrowded, trains were running late and, above all, that foreign workers were allowed to travel on the trains. But they had to have special passes. Further indirect questions brought the information that a foreign worker needed permission from the firm by whom he was employed and a special permit from the police before he could leave the town where he was registered.

From that time onward until he left the hospital Peter cultivated Dopey in every way. He gave him cigarettes and cocoa and bribed him with his small ration of chocolate to bring eggs into the hospital. When the time was ripe he asked Dopey to borrow one of the foreign workers' passes and bring it into the camp for him to see.

Dopey refused. He was terrified. Nothing would make him

budge. He was willing to trade for small, innocent commodities, but stuck at the passes. It was not patriotism. He was afraid of the consequences.

Peter played his trump card. " You have been trading with the prisoners. I have three witnesses. If you do not bring me the passes I shall report you to the Camp Kommandant. We shall go to the cooler. But you—you will be shot."

Dopey whined and pleaded, but he was caught and he knew it. The next morning he brought the passes. Peter made a careful copy of them and returned them to Dopey the same evening. The passes would have to be forged properly when he got back to the camp ; but he knew what they were like. He was equipped now and he bided his time. During the long hours of idleness in the hospital he had completed his plans for the journey to neutral territory. He waited impatiently to get back to the tunnel.

CHAPTER FIVE

The Third Man

WHEN PETER came out of hospital he and John discussed the tunnel. As usual they discussed it while walking round the circuit, the only place in the compound safe from the ears of the ferrets.

" It's quite obvious," Peter was saying, " that we can't go on as we are. We've done forty feet out of the hundred and ten and already we're taking two hours to dig out twelve bags. The farther we get the longer it will take. It looks as though we've come to a full stop."

" I suppose we couldn't take the horse out twice a day ? Once in the morning and once in the afternoon ? "

" We could do that but then we could only take six, or at most eight, bags out at a time. And that would grow less and less the farther we got. No, I can't see how we can finish the job under the present system. We've got to think of something altogether new. It's not the digging, it's getting the blasted sand back from the face to the shaft. It's bad enough at forty feet. It's going to be impossible to drag it back the whole length of the tunnel. Why, it'll take about half an hour to crawl up to the face once we get to a hundred feet. It's not like wriggling on the surface. It looks as though we've bitten off more than we can chew."

" There's always a way," John said. " Let's study the problem. It's how to get the sand from the face to the shaft. Why not use a toboggan like they did at Schubin ? "

" That was a big tunnel and they could have as many down there as they liked. Here we've got no air and no light. Besides, if you took two men out in the horse you couldn't bring any sand back. It would be as much as the vaulters could do to carry the two men, let alone twelve bags of sand as well. And I don't see how a toboggan would help you if you were down there alone."

" Then we'll *have* to take two down at once, that's all."

Peter grunted and they walked on in silence. He was still feeling the strangeness of walking on the circuit after the closer confinement of the hospital. We must do it, he thought. It's too good a thing to drop. There must be *some* way of getting the sand out of the place. . . .

Then he saw it. " I've got an idea," he said. " It'll be slow going but I think we'll cope with the whole length of the tunnel."

" How ? "

" We'll go down together, as you suggested. We'll have to stand head to head, one at each end of the horse. The chaps should be able to carry us. Then we'll have to make thirty-six bags instead of the original twelve. And we'll have to make a small chamber at the end of the tunnel to give us room to work. We'll run a toboggan between us with a rope at each end. One will work in the chamber and the other in the vertical shaft. We can dig enough in one session to fill the thirty-six bags—it's not the digging that takes the time. When we've filled the thirty-six bags we'll stack them all in the shaft and go back in the horse without any sand."

" You mean, leave all the thirty-six bags in the tunnel ? "

" I'm coming to that. We do that in the afternoon. The same evening one of us goes out alone in the horse and brings back twelve of the bags. The next afternoon the other brings back twelve more, and the last twelve that evening. The next afternoon we both go out and dig another thirty-six."

" We shan't average more than six inches a day," John said.

" We'll have to revise our ideas, that's all ; and we'll have to bring someone else in to organise the vaulting. We can't both be underground without having someone up there who's in the scheme."

" I thought just we two were going to be in it. I thought we were going to keep it small."

" Yes, but we've got to adapt our plans as we go along. It's too much to ask a chap to organise all the vaulting and not give him a chance to go out with us."

" O.K. Whom do you suggest ? "

" Let's ask Tony Winyard. He's done a moling dienst himself and he might help with the digging."

" O.K. You go and find him and I'll organise some more trouser bottoms and get on with the extra bags."

Peter found Winyard in the library, looking for a book on old glass. " Hallo, Tony," he said. " Care for a turn round the circuit ? There's something I'd like to ask you."

" Sure—I'm getting bored with glass anyway." And they walked out into the sunshine of the compound.

" How the dienst going ? " Tony spoke casually.

" That's what I wanted to see you about. We need a third man and we wondered if you'd care to join us."

Winyard did not answer immediately. He seemed slightly embarrassed. " Well, as a matter of fact, I'm just preparing for a dienst myself. It's a one-man show—under the wire in the Vorlager—but it won't come off until the autumn. I've got to wait for the dark evenings."

" Oh, we shall be out before the autumn," Peter said. " We're just starting a new system. We hope to get cracking again at once."

Winyard appeared to be thinking it over. " I'd like to," he said finally, " but I'll have to turn it down, I'm afraid. You see I've been caught so often that they've told me that next time I'm caught I'm for the Straflager and once you get there you're finished. My next attempt has got to be pretty nearly a dead certainty. Not that yours isn't a good show," he added quickly, " but frankly I don't think you stand much chance of getting out."

" O.K.," Peter said. " I can see your point."

" Don't think I'm knocking your show in any way," he repeated. " There's nothing wrong with the idea except that it's going to take so long. I'm afraid the goons are bound to tumble to it before you're finished."

" Oh, I don't think so. We've got over the worst part. The

horse has been accepted as a camp institution now. The goons are used to it and think no more about it."

" How much have you done now ? "

" About forty feet."

" How much have you got to do in all ? "

" A hundred and ten."

" And you've been at it how long—two months ? "

" Yes."

" It's the end of August now—that puts you well into November."

" No, I reckon October. We'll mole the last ten or fifteen feet and do it in one go."

" Oh, well, I wish you luck. I've had moling, but if you want any tips I'll be glad to tell you all I can."

" Thanks a lot," Peter said. " I shall be glad of that. We've never tried a moling dienst before."

He found John at the far end of the camp canvassing for trouser-leg bottoms. " How's it going, John ? "

" Oh, I've exhausted all the people who've cut their trousers down. I'm now persuading people that shorts are a good thing and getting 'em to cut 'em down while I wait."

" Winyard doesn't want to come in with us," Peter said. " He doesn't think we've an earthly chance of getting out."

" That's his funeral. I've got enough bottoms for another ten bags."

" Who do we ask now ? " Peter said. " I'd like to ask old Nig, but his leg's so dicky I don't think he'd make it."

" We shouldn't have let him do so much vaulting. With a wounded leg like his it was asking for trouble. He can hardly walk now and yet he comes out every day and hops round the horse—just to make it look a crowd. He ought to go into hospital."

" What's wrong with his leg exactly ? "

" Oh, it was badly patched up by a goon doctor. They shot at him while he was coming down in a parachute."

" How do you know they shot *at* him ? I expect they were just popping off wildly at everything in general."

" Why do you always stand up for the Hun, Pete ? You must have lost more than most people in the war."

" Oh, I don't know. It wasn't anyone's fault. You can't go blaming the whole nation. Nig doesn't blame them for his leg."

" Old Phil blames them—makes goon hatred a sort of religion. He gets up every morning cursing the goons and keeps it up all day."

" I suppose some chaps work up a hate to keep them going—a useful way of expending surplus energy."

" He's helped us a lot," John said. " He's organised practically all the dispersal, as well as vaulting with the best of them."

" He's not much good at vaulting."

John smiled. " I love to see him when he gets really angry. He grits his teeth and charges at the horse with his arms going like piston-rods."

" But the nearer he gets to the horse the slower he runs."

" Yes, but he does keep at it. He's improved enormously since he started."

" Let's ask him to come in," Peter said. " We'll do the digging and he can organise the vaulting and the dispersal. I'd rather no one else went down the hole because we know exactly how small we want it, and Phil would have grand ideas about enlarging it and putting in an air pump. If he'd look after the vaulting—you know how methodical he is, he'd draw up lists and organise it so that everyone had a certain time on a certain day to vault. Now that we're going to go out twice a day the problem of the vaulters is going to be more difficult than ever."

" O.K.," John said, " let's go and find him."

They ran Philip Rowe to earth near the gate leading to the Vorlager. He had a list of names in his hand and was looking worried.

" What's the gen, Phil ? " asked Peter. " Come for a turn round the circuit."

"I can't at the moment. I'm supposed to be organising the hot showers. But no one seems to want one."

"Then leave it," Peter said. "Come for a walk instead."

"I can't. It's all right for you—you've no sense of responsibility. I've got a job to do. Someone's got to help run the camp."

"Come on, Phil," John said. They fell in one each side of him and began to walk him firmly round the circuit.

"All right," he said, accepting the inevitable. "But only once round. I've got to find these people for their showers."

"We've more important things than showers," Peter said. "We're going to get you out of the camp and send you home to your wife."

"You're mad," Philip said. "You're both mad. Let me go —find someone else to pester. I've got a job to do."

"We mean it, Phil," John said. "We want you to join us in the dienst."

Philip looked suspicious. "Why ask me?"

"Well," Peter began, "knowing your organising ability . . ."

"And your almost touching faith in our efficiency . . ." John continued.

"We thought you'd jump at the idea," Peter concluded.

"What do you want me to do?"

"We're going to work on a new system now. We're both going down together—with a toboggan and rope—and we'll dig thirty-six bags in one session and then spend the next three sessions taking twelve out at a time. We'd like you to organise the vaulting and the dispersal of the sand."

"I'm practically doing that already."

"That's why we want you to come in. We can get three out as easily as two."

"O.K.," Philip said. "I'll come in. But I don't think we've a hope in hell of ever getting out."

"You stick by us," John assured him. "You'll get out."

In Peter's mess there was a growing air of tension. They had been at Sagan now for five months, and five months' intimate knowledge of one another was becoming unbearable.

It was lunchtime. The biscuits had not been buttered. No one had gone for the tea water. Five morose figures sat round a bare table. Presently Pomfret spoke. " It's a matter of principle. I've done it every day this week and now it's Friday. It's not that I mind doing it, but I've done more than my share. Clinton must do it to-day as a matter of principle." He advanced his chin obstinately. He was dressed in the full uniform of a flight-lieutenant. His collar, ironed with a tin of hot water, was frayed round the edges.

" That's all very well," Bennett pointed out, " but it's lunch-time and we're hungry. You and Clinton share the duty of cook and it's up to you to see that the meal is prepared." Apart from his odd assortment of clothing Bennett might have been addressing a board meeting. He delivered his opinion as an ultimatum and glanced round the table for approval. His red, hairy arms were crossed upon the table. Having delivered his speech, he sucked his teeth with an air of finality.

" Well, I'm not doing it," Pomfret said. He appeared about to cry. " It's not fair ! Just because he's digging a tunnel it doesn't mean he can neglect all his duties in the mess. I'm fed up with doing two people's work. All they think about is their wretched tunnel. I'm sick to death of seeing them sitting in the corner whispering all evening. It was bad enough before they started the tunnel. Clinton was always missing at meal times. But for the last two months I've done all the work. It's not right, you know."

" That's for you and Clinton to settle between yourselves," said Bennett judicially. " What about our lunch ? It's only a matter of buttering eight biscuits and walking over to the canteen for some hot water."

" That's not the point ! It's a matter of principle."

" So the whole mess must suffer for the sake of your principles," put in Robbie, who was sitting at the head of the table disgustedly studying his fingernails.

"It's not my principles at fault, it's Clinton's laziness."

"I don't call it laziness to dig in a tunnel and vault over a horse for several hours a day," Robbie said. "Surely you and he can come to some arrangement so that you both do an equal amount of work, but his share doesn't interfere with his tunnelling."

"You can't come to any arrangement with Clinton," Pomfret said. "He always forgets. He hasn't grown up yet. He's got no sense of responsibility."

"He's not the only one who hasn't grown up," Robbie said.

"This is all very well," Bennett interrupted, "but do we get our lunch?"

"I'm not doing it!" said Pomfret obstinately.

The five men looked at one another angrily. The food cupboard was sacred. No one but the cook was allowed to open it. It was a custom of the mess. In a life where hunger was ubiquitous, food had strict taboos.

"Supposing we split the mess in two," Pomfret said. "Let them mess together and we five will mess together. They can do what they like then."

"They always do." Bennett sucked his teeth.

"Well, what do you say?" Pomfret asked. "I think it would serve them right."

"Very likely buck them no end," Robbie said.

"I think we ought to," Pomfret said. "Howard and Clinton can't cook anyway."

They hesitated. It was a decision. Some of them had not made a decision for years. Some were reluctant to cast the three into the outer darkness of their dissociation.

"I think we should," Pomfret said.

"Let's take a vote." Bennett was once more addressing the board of directors.

"I say yes," Pomfret said.

Bennett looked at Robbie, who thought of coping with the eccentricities of the other three. He decided not to risk it. Anyway, their tunnel would be finished soon.

"I think it's childish," he said, "and it'll be damned inconvenient having two messes in one room."

"Would you rather go with them? Then you can do all the cooking for them," said Pomfret spitefully.

"No, I'll go with you. But I don't like the idea of splitting up."

When the others came in they found the biscuits ready buttered and the tea water in the can. John had been working at the face and Peter at the tunnel entrance. Nigel had been hiding the excavated sand under the floor of the canteen. John, yellow from head to foot with caked sweat and sand, threw himself on his bunk and closed his eyes.

"Lunch, John?" Peter asked.

"Not for the moment, thanks, old boy."

"Feeling rotten?"

"I'm O.K. I'll be O.K. in a minute. I'll wash before I eat." He lay back with his eyes closed. His body was brown but his face was colourless. His hair, matted with sand and sweat, was damp on his forehead. There were long streaks down his chest and arms where the sweat had washed away the sand. The sand was under his broken fingernails and in his eyes. As he lay there, Peter could see that his nostrils too were filled with sand.

Pomfret cleared his throat. "I prepared the lunch to-day."

"Thanks, old boy," John said. "Was it my turn?"

"It was your turn," Pomfret replied. "It has been your turn for the last three days. As a matter of principle I, at first, refused to do it to-day."

"Thanks for doing it all the same," John said. "I'll do the dinner."

"That will not be necessary," Pomfret said. "We five have decided to mess separately."

"After due consideration," said Bennett, addressing an audience of at least five hundred, "we have decided that we five shall mess on our own."

Pomfret looked at him angrily. After all, he was in the chair.

"We are tired of Clinton's impossible attitude," Bennett

continued, " and we presumed that you three would want to be together. We have separated the food, and starting with dinner to-night we shall cater for ourselves."

" O.K.," Peter said. " That suits us." In a way he was glad as very soon they would begin to save their food for the escape. " What do you say, Nig ? "

" *Blond genug*, old boy," Nigel replied.

So the mess was split into two and settled down to a new way of living. There was still friction among the five, particularly between Robbie and Bennett, but the three drifted into an ideal way of living where no one was stooge and yet at the right time, for them, the meals appeared. Most of their time was spent in vaulting and digging, making civilian clothes and tracing maps. When they had nothing to do they lay in the sun. They had dug a sand pit outside the window of the mess and, despite spirited opposition from the " purity league " led by Pomfret, used to lie for hours soaking in the sun that beat back in a shimmering haze from the burning sand. They bathed in a brick fire-water tank and made fantastic sun-hats from Red Cross boxes. But Pomfret hated the sun. He would lie on his bunk cursing the heat, flapping at the flies that buzzed and whined around his head.

The place was thick with flies. Sometimes Peter, John and Nigel would organise a " daylight sweep." They closed the doors and windows and attacked the flies with tightly rolled copies of the *Völkischer Beobachter*, slashing and cutting at the enemy as he settled on table, stools and bunks. It was glorious while it lasted. A slaughter that relieved the tension of their nerves. Finally, flushed and elated with their victory, they would all descend on the sole remaining insect, upsetting stools and tables in their mad rush to claim the last of the intruders. Having cleared the room, they would go and swim in the fire-water tank, returning to find the room as thick with flies as ever.

Peter made a refrigerator consisting of an open-sided wooden cupboard standing on two bricks in a shallow metal tray of water. A loose cover made from a blanket was fitted over the cupboard, its ends falling into the water in the tray. Another metal tray of water was placed on top of the cupboard and "feeders"—narrow strips of blanket—were led from the upper tray on to the loose cover. By keeping both tins full of water the absorbent loose cover was always moist and the constant evaporation of this moisture considerably lowered the temperature inside the cupboard. So effective was the refrigerator that tins of food placed inside it soon became coated with beads of moisture.

They filled a canvas kitbag with water and hung it from the ceiling of the room. Water oozing through the canvas and evaporating cooled the atmosphere that otherwise would have been unbearable. The sun blazed down on the wooden huts and turned them into ovens. At intervals German soldiers came round with hoses and sprayed water both on the roofs and under the huts.

In the evenings after dinner the prisoners would sit on the steps of their huts or stand in groups against the wooden walls engaged in desultory conversation. It reminded Peter of the slums in Liverpool where he had lived before the war. He had often pitied the people in those slums, sitting in rows on their doorsteps and on chairs on the pavement outside their houses, too hot to go inside their overcrowded tenements. Now he, too, sat in shirt sleeves, smoking his pipe on the doorstep, the dust of the circuit between his toes and the friendly gossip of his neighbours all around him. And sitting there he would feel a quiet contentment, a lazy acceptance of conditions. An acceptance that he knew was dangerous and which he banished with redoubled efforts to escape.

CHAPTER SIX

They Plan Their Journey

IT WAS evening and they had been locked in for the night. Peter and John sat on one of the bunks sewing the trouser-leg bags. It was unbearably hot in the small room. While the lights were on the prisoners were not allowed to remove the wooden blackout shutters, and the air was stale and thick with tobacco smoke. Outside in the corridor the duty stooge sat reading a book.

In other rooms along the corridor other prisoners were making parts of a secret wireless set, forging passports or making civilian clothing from odd bits of uniform. Through the thin partition wall on one side could be heard the strains of a well-worn jazz record. From the other side came the raised voices of two of the prisoners who were quarrelling.

Robbie, Bennett, David and Paul were playing bridge. Pomfret, an angry expression on his face, was trying to read a book.

Nigel was making a golf ball. He had searched for several days in the compound before he had found the right stone. Smooth, round and not too heavy, it was an ideal stone for the core. Next he had unravelled the top of a pair of woollen socks, carefully winding the wool on to a piece of stick. It was good, resilient wool, resilient enough to give the ball sufficient " life " to enable him to drive it fifty or sixty yards. He had cut down a pair of issue boots to make shoes and saved the soft leather of the uppers to make the cover of the ball. He had borrowed a paper template and cut two pieces of leather shaped like a solid figure eight. After winding the wool on to the stone until the ball had reached the regulation size, he had soaked the leather in water and was now sewing it together with thread waterproofed with candle grease. Sitting on his bunk, tongue between his teeth, he was gently stretching the damp leather round the ball.

Through the thin partition came the sound of next door's worn-out gramophone.

"That's the end," Pomfret said. "That's the end of reading for to-night."

"Bet you what you like the next tune's 'Boynk Boynk,'" Nigel said.

"Right," said Peter, "I'll take you on. Twenty Player's it's 'Ah, Sweet Mystery of Life.'"

"I'm in this," John said. "Bet it's 'Intermezzo.'"

Patiently they waited for the record to begin.

"There you are," Nigel said. "It's 'Boynk Boynk.'"

"It isn't 'Boynk Boynk' anyway," Pomfret said, "it's 'Oynk Oynk.'"

"It's not," Nigel said, "it's 'Boynk Boynk.'"

"It's 'Oynk Oynk' I tell you! " Pomfret said. "Listen! "

"Oh dear! Are you two arguing again?" John said.

Reedily the stupid tune ground its way into the chorus. "Oynk Oynk, Boogie Boogie Woogie."

"It's 'Boynk'! " Nigel said.

"It's 'Oynk'! " Pomfret said.

There was a knock on the door and Stafford, the hut representative on the Escape Committee, brought in a Red Cross box filled with invalid food—the special diet sent from England for the hospital. A certain amount of this food usually found its way into the hands of the Committee and was rationed out to prisoners who were working in tunnels.

Peter made a place for him among the trouser-leg bags on the bed.

"I've got the extra rations," Stafford said.

"Thanks," Peter said. "Any news of the torch?"

"Yes—we'll have it to-morrow. We've only two batteries so you'll have to use it as sparingly as you can."

" How did you manage it ? " John asked.

" Oh, we've got one of the goons taped. Why are you making so many bags ? "

They told him of the new system.

" We thought you'd have to do that in the end," Stafford said. " Far too much for one man to do. Have you decided on your route and what you're going as ? "

" We thought we'd go up to the Baltic and try to stow away on a Swedish boat," Peter said.

" How are you travelling ? As Poles ? "

" No," John said. " Good-class French workers. Not ex-P.O.W.s, but French craftsmen who've been brought over from France. My French is fairly good. Lived in France some time before the war. And we're both dark enough to pass as Frenchmen."

" Can you let us have any money ? " Peter asked.

" We've got a bit in the kitty—what about two hundred marks apiece ? "

" Like a bit more than that if you can manage it. Y'see, we thought we'd travel first class and stay at decent hotels if necessary."

Stafford looked surprised. " I say—that's going it a bit, isn't it ? Don't you think that's rather sticking your necks out ? "

" No," John said. " We've thought it over pretty carefully. Most chaps who've tried to escape have gone out looking like tramps. They may have been out some time but they haven't got very far. If you travel by passenger train it's all or nothing. You're either where you want to be in a few days—or you're caught. We don't think anyone has stayed in a hotel yet, so we thought we'd try it."

" Perhaps you're right—anyway, it's your show. We'll let you have the money and fix you up with papers and everything you want. If you make it you'll be the first out for over a year."

" Thanks a lot, Stafford," Peter said. " What about a spot of vaulting to-morrow ? "

Stafford grinned. " Opportunist, aren't you ? O.K., I'll come and vault. Call in at my room as you go out."

"Right," Peter said.

"Oh, by the way," Stafford added, "they're starting a tunnel from Block 64. Shouldn't interfere with yours in any way. It's an old one that was sealed up some time ago and Odell is getting it going again. It'll be a blitz job—they'll work continually, in shifts, and stuff all the sand in the roof of their hut."

"But that's silly," Peter said. "The goons search the roof once a week."

"That's just the idea. They'll wait until the next search and start immediately afterwards. They won't hide the sand at all—just bung it up in the roof—and by working in shifts all day and all night they hope to get out by the next time the roof is searched."

"How far have they got to go?" Peter asked.

"About a hundred and fifty feet."

"They won't get all that in the roof. The whole hut'll collapse with all that weight."

"They'll just put all they can in the roof and then the last few days they'll put it in their beds and in Red Cross boxes under the beds."

"How many are going out?"

"The whole hut."

"They won't have a chance." Peter was getting angry now. The quick, prison camp anger that fades as quickly as it comes. "That's about a hundred men. If a hundred men get out now they'll have a country-wide search and then where will *we* be? They won't have all the papers—or the proper clothing. And there'll be such a flap that it'll completely spoil our show."

"Oh, it's not as bad as that," Stafford said. "The whole thing will be over inside a fortnight and it will be at least two months before yours breaks. The flap'll be over by then. Personally, I don't think they'll last more than a few days. But it's an attempt and they're so few and far between these days that we back anything that's put forward." He grinned. "Otherwise, you wouldn't have stood much chance."

"They'll be picked up by the seismographs," John said.

"Yes, particularly if they work at that speed," Peter agreed. He was feeling better now.

"It's a wonder you haven't been picked up," Stafford said.

Peter laughed. "Ours isn't such a dim scheme as you imagine. Anything picked up by the seismographs is blanketed by the vibration of the vaulters landing on the surface."

"I hadn't thought of that!" Stafford said.

"No, nor did we until the tunnel had been going for some time," John admitted. "Must have been that. The seismographs would have recorded it otherwise."

"Oh, well," Stafford yawned. "I've got to relieve the stooge." He stood up and stretched. "Don't forget to call for me to-morrow."

"We won't forget," John said.

When he had gone Peter turned to John. "It's a good thing about Odell, really. I think the goons are getting a bit suspicious and if they find any of our sand they'll blame it on Odell. Now, what about that sketch?" He crossed to his locker and came back with a half-finished sketch of John.

Pomfret sat at the head of the table deeply immersed in his book. Pomfret hated women novelists. In his opinion, everything written by a woman was bad. Pomfret had very fixed ideas about a woman's duties and writing books was not one of them. One of his favourite forms of self-torture was to take a book by one of the more popular women novelists and read it slowly word by word, suffering as much as he could in the process. This evening he was enjoying himself. Sitting, head in hands, he tried to deafen himself to the bridge post-mortem that was raging at the end of the table. He looked up.

"Pete," he said, "what's a solid bar of misery?"

"What, old boy?"

"A solid bar of misery."

Peter was busy with an india rubber.

"What's that, old boy?"

"That's what I want to know. It says here 'a solid bar of misery seized her by the throat.' Now, what's a solid bar of misery ? Just imagine "—he made a gesture with his hands indicating a bar—" a solid bar "—he illustrated it on the table— " seized her by the throat." He seized his throat with both hands and nearly throttled himself. " I don't get it, do you ? "

" No," Peter said, " I don't. Hey, Nig, what's a solid bar of misery ? "

Nigel thought for a moment. " A crowded pub that's run out of beer, I should think."

" What about a brew ? " John asked.

" Good show," said Bennett. " Our jug's on the fire now. It was pretty hot when I went down there ten minutes ago."

Although the mess had split in two they still shared the tea, coffee and cocoa. It was more economical.

" I'll do it," Robbie offered. " I've finished my book." He took down the eight mugs and put them on the table.

" Which shall it be," he asked, " cocoa, or Nescafé ? "

" There's not much Nescafé left," said Paul, who was cook.

" O.K.," Robbie said, " cocoa." He put the cocoa in the mugs and went down the corridor, returning with the jug of hot water. " Someone's got a lovely cake in the oven," he said.

" It's mess three," Paul told him. " It's Smith's birthday."

" Well, that's that ! " Peter said, laying down the drawing. " It's not much like you, I'm afraid, John. But that's about all I can do to it." He leaned the drawing against the table and stood back. It was a full-length study in pencil and charcoal. It lacked finish but it had caught something of the character of the sitter. It showed a young man in a creased, collarless, woollen shirt, sitting with a book in his lap, his back propped against one of the wooden uprights of the bunk. His right leg was crossed over his left knee. A wooden-soled sandal hung from his right foot, secured by strips cut from an R.A.F. greatcoat. The face was in repose. Dark-skinned, with large brown eyes and heavily marked eyebrows, it was at once sensitive and mischievous. There was something faun-like in the setting of the ears and the long black hair. The subject looked as though he were about to speak. He looked as though what he was to say would be of interest.

"It's not good," Peter said, "but it's the best I've done. Sorry I kept you sitting so long."

"That's O.K. What about a game of chess?"

"Right." He knocked out his pipe on the stove and filled it from a tin on the table. He lit it with a cigarette end and a piece of paper. "If you ever see anyone do this after the war," he said, "you'll know he's been a Kriegie."

"You won't see anyone do it," John said. "There'll be plenty of matches."

"'The listening horizon,'" Pomfret quoted. "How can a horizon listen?"

"That's poetic licence," Bennett told him. "She means it was quiet."

"Then why doesn't she say 'it was quiet'?" Pomfret asked plaintively. "'She raised her eyes to the listening horizon'— it's nonsense."

"It gives you a lot of pleasure anyway," Robbie said.

"If I start anything I like to finish it," Pomfret said. "I started the book and I'm going to finish it." He scowled and returned to his torture. Pomfret was enjoying his evening.

John fetched the chess set from a shelf over his bed and put it on a corner of the table. He set out the men. "I'll give you a knight, if you like, Pete."

"It would make a better game," Peter agreed. He sat cross-legged on the bench, puffing at his pipe. He was not a good chess player but he enjoyed the game. He had never beaten John.

The bridge four had broken up and the players were preparing for bed. Bennett was washing his feet in a bowl of water near the stove.

"Have you heard about the new chap in room ten?" Bennett asked.

"What chap?" Nigel said.

"The chap they call 'Harry the Horse'?"

"Oh, you mean 'Gilbert the Gelding'—the type who's just had his head shaved."

"Yes, he's an incredible type. Too good-natured to be true.

The chaps in room ten have been pulling his leg left, right and centre."

"I heard about it," Robbie said. "It's a darn' shame."

"What did they do?" Nigel asked.

"They were all sitting in their room one night," said Bennett, "when a chap came in and said, 'Have you heard the new order from the S.B.O.?' 'No,' they said, 'what's that?' 'Oh,' says the first type, 'the S.B.O. says we've all got to have our heads shaved as a demonstration against the Hun.' Well, they argued who was to be done first and then someone said, 'Harry's the newest arrival, let's do him first.' So they sat him in a chair and got a razor and soap and shaved his hair off. He had a terrific mop too. Just as they'd finished another type came in and said, 'You know about the order to shave our heads—well, it's been cancelled!'"

When the laughter died down Bennett continued, "The next day they told him they were digging a tunnel from underneath the room and explained that they wanted a lot of water to wash the sand. They collected some buckets and kept Harry staggering between the washhouse and room ten with buckets of water all afternoon. As fast as he brought a full bucket they handed him an empty one and tipped the full one out of the opposite window. Kept it up for about two hours."

"I think it's a shame," Robbie said.

"Oh, he doesn't mind—he likes it. You know that skeleton old Mac got from Berlin for his medical studies? They dressed that up one night and sat it up in a chair. When Harry came in he got the fright of his life. 'What's that?' he asked. 'That's old Joe,' they said. 'He was one of the earliest Kriegies—died years ago and we're still drawing his rations.'"

"It's quite true," Nigel said, "and he doesn't turn a hair. I was in room ten the other night. We were all sitting talking and Harry was reading a book. Presently the door opened and a chap dressed in full uniform came in on all fours. No one except Harry took any notice. This type crawled solemnly round the room four times, then stopped in front of Harry and barked, 'Stand up when I talk to you! Don't you know I'm your C.O.?' Then he crawled out. One of the chaps closed the door after him and said to Harry, 'Don't mind him—he's round the bend.'"

The lights flickered twice. "Lights out in five minutes," Bennett said. "You types had better get to bed."

"O.K.," Peter said. "I can't win anyway. Your game, John."

"Yes, I think so," John said.

They undressed and Peter put out the light. He crossed to the window and opened the blackout shutters. The night air was clean and cool after the atmosphere of the room. The compound was flooded with moonlight. The sand was silver and the posts of the wire fence stood out straight and dark and edged with light. The top of the sentry box was silver too. Even the yellow searchlights seemed powerless against the silver of the moon.

"The goon's in his box and all's well with the world," he said.

"I hope he falls out of it," said Robbie.

CHAPTER SEVEN

The Tunnel is in Danger

THE CAMP BARBER was clipping the hair of a newly-arrived prisoner. On chairs arranged along the wall sat other clients looking at German magazines and waiting their turn to be clipped. Near the window stood a tall, gangling prisoner with a shaven head and long sensitive face. He held a violin under his chin and played a low, sad melody, rising and falling and endlessly repeating the same few notes. He gazed out of the window seemingly unconscious of the other people in the room. Except for the low notes of the violin, the sound of a blue-bottle buzzing against the window-pane and the snip-snap of the barber's scissors, the room was silent.

It was nearly tea time. Outside in the compound a football match was noisily coming to an end ; the vaulters were packing up and before long the circuit would be deserted while the prisoners ate their tea.

The newly-arrived prisoner—this was his first visit to the barber's shop—was presently astounded to see the door open and a naked, brown tousle-headed, sand- and sweat-stained figure crawl in on all fours carrying with him a khaki-coloured bag tied at the neck with string.

Without saying a word, ignored by the barber and his waiting clients, the strange figure crawled to the window, opened a trap in the floor and disappeared from view, dragging after him the bag tied with string. Then another fully-dressed figure appeared with another bag, followed by others who formed a human chain, passing the bags from hand to hand down to the naked one under the floor.

Suddenly the vacant-eyed violinist stopped playing. The trap was at once closed on the man under the floor and the human chain became an orchestra earnestly playing the various instruments which had been lying close to hand.

A few minutes later one of the ferrets sauntered past the window. He did not look in. He would have seen only a prisoner having his hair cut, the waiting clients and the camp orchestra practising in one corner of the room. The orchestra continued to play. There was a loud knock on the door. They laid down their instruments and opened the trap. The violinist resumed his melancholy tune. Twelve empty bags were handed up from the hole in the floor and the naked one emerged, carefully dusting the moist sand from his body on to the floor near the trap. He was handed his clothes in silence and in silence he put them on. The sand was brushed into the hole in the floor and the trap carefully replaced. The empty bags were collected while one of the vaulters carefully swept the floor with his handkerchief to remove the last traces of the sand.

After some months of work in the tunnel the space below the floor of the barber's shop was filled. The bags of sand were then carried out by the camp glee-singers, who rehearsed in the next room. The full bags were passed up through a trap door in the ceiling to Nigel, who spread the sand evenly between the joists in the beaverboard ceiling. They could not put much sand in the roof as the weight threatened to bring down the ceiling ; so after a time another trap door was made over the kitchen. The bags were now handed up to Nigel, who carried them, bag by bag, across the rafters to the new trap door, where he hid them until the late evening.

Next door to the kitchen was the office of the " kitchen goon " —the German soldier who supervised the issue of the prisoners' rations. After the kitchen goon had left for the night the bags were handed down into the kitchen, where David was waiting to receive them. When the bags had all been passed down into the kitchen they were carried through to the kitchen goon's office where they were taken down through another trap door and the sand hidden under the floor.

During the daytime the kitchen goon sat in his office completely unaware of the results of the previous evening's work lying directly beneath his feet.

The week that Odell's tunnel was started the Germans pounced again. Peter and John had been digging in the tunnel that afternoon and Peter had been out in the early evening to bring in twelve of the bags. After helping to pass the bags up to Nigel in the roof he had washed himself in the kitchen and was walking back to the hut when he saw the compound gates open and a German army lorry drive at full speed towards the canteen.

He knew at once what was about to happen and he could do nothing to stop it. The lorry would be outside the canteen before the stooges were aware that anything was wrong. The dispersal team was in the roof and under the floor. It was finished. All those months of work would be wasted. All their carefully laid shoring, the brick piles and the cunningly made trap would be exposed, lying on the surface, a pitiful heap of boards and sheets of rotted plywood. He felt sick and walked blindly on round the circuit, his hands in his pockets, walking hard to fight down the sickness and the choking obstruction in his throat. Someone passed him on the circuit and said something about " Bad luck." But he did not reply. They had been digging for three months and now the tunnel would be discovered. Three months of pinning your faith to a hole in the ground. Three months of waking up in the morning just a little happier because you were doing something to get out of the place. Three months of jealous anxiety that the hole would be discovered; subterfuge and improvisation, hilarity and panic. Every inch of the narrow hole that had been scraped with their bare hands and a bricklayer's trowel. And now it was all going for nothing.

He would recover. In half an hour he would be grinning and saying, " It was a lousy tunnel anyway "; but for the moment he was very near to tears and he wanted to be alone.

One of the ferrets sauntered past the window

Soon he was joined by John and they walked on in silence. Peter spoke first. " Have they caught Nig and the others ? " He was deliberately casual.

" No. If you remember we started an hour earlier to-day. David was just climbing out of the kitchen window as the goons rushed in at the door. He was the last one out."

" Where did Nig go ? "

" He climbed down into the canteen and joined the glee-singers. When the goons rushed in they were singing ' He shall set His angels guard over thee.' The Feldwebel stood under the trap while they sent a ferret up from the kitchen side. All they got out was the ferret."

" They'll find the sand in the roof," Peter said.

" I'm afraid they will. They turned the singers out but Nig stayed behind as long as he could collecting the sheets of music. When he left they were tearing up the floor of the barber's shop."

" I'm afraid we've had it."

" There's still a chance. They may not connect the horse with it. They may think we were dispersing the sand from somewhere else. Or if they do think of the horse they may think it was part of the stooging system."

" Were there any bags left in the kitchen ? "

" Yes—they'd all finished except Nig and David who were stowing the stuff away under the office floor. When the alarm went they still had three full bags, so they stuffed the three full ones and all the empty ones down the trap, closed it up, and David went out of the window and Nig went up through the trap, over the roof and down into the canteen."

" That was jolly good work."

John laughed. " It was Nig and David. They'd rather go to the cooler than leave a trap open. If the ferrets don't discover the trap under the office all they'll find will be a lot of sand and nothing to tell them where it came from."

" If they do find the bags we're finished," Peter said. " They're much too big for the goons to think we carried them under our coats. If they do find them they'll know the tunnel's somewhere in the canteen and when they can't find it they'll either watch the place so closely that we can't work or they'll connect them with the horse. If only we could lay a false trail away from the canteen we might stand a chance."

" Let's walk round there," John suggested, " and have a look."

There was an armed guard posted outside the canteen. From inside came the sounds of hammering and the hoarse commands of the German N.C.O.

" They're enjoying themselves," John said gloomily. "They're tearing the place to pieces."

Peter did not speak.

" This puts paid to Odell's scheme," John said. " The ferrets will ransack the camp looking for the tunnel and more dispersal. They're bound to examine all the roofs—especially after they found our sand in the canteen roof."

" Have you got the rest of the bags ? " Peter asked quickly.

" There are twenty-four full ones in the tunnel and a few odds and ends in my bed."

" Let's go and get them," Peter said, " and bung them in with Odell's sand. If it's not discovered it will be O.K.; and if it *is* discovered it won't do Odell any harm. But it'll make the goons think our dispersal was part of Odell's tunnel. I don't think trouser-leg bags have been used before and they're bound to put two and two together and think Odell's men got them across in some way or other from their hut to the canteen. If we can persuade them that the canteen sand came from Odell's tunnel we can lie low for about a week and then go on using the canteen for dispersal. They won't search there again for a bit once they think they know where the sand came from."

" Right," John said. " You go and tell Odell and I'll get the bags and meet you in his room."

The next morning when the prisoners went out to appel they took with them enough food to last them all day. They knew the camp would be searched and during the evening they had hidden most of their *verboten* possessions behind the panelling of the walls and in the sand under the huts. Some of them, risking the possibility of a personal search, carried their most cherished possessions with them.

During the day Odell's tunnel was discovered. It was discovered by the ceiling of Hut 64 collapsing and burying the searchers in a shower of sand. They soon found the tunnel and with it the bags that Peter had hidden there the night before. Apparently satisfied that this was the only tunnel in existence, they called off the search and took the senior officer of the hut to serve his sentence in the cooler.

That night, after they had been locked in the huts, Stafford came in to cheer them up. He brought with him the weekly ration of milk food.

" They've found the trap in the floor of the kitchen goon's office," he said. " Marcus was over there getting water just before lock-up time."

" That means they've found the bags," Peter said.

" What are you going to do ? "

" Nothing," Peter said. " Nothing for a week—or perhaps more. We shall take the horse out every day and vault as usual. But no digging. No digging until we're sure they're not suspicious of the horse. Then we shall start again and carry on as we were before. We're just about under the trip-wire now and it would be silly to rush things. We'll rest for a week and then work all-out until we're through."

" The horse needs re-upholstering," John said. " We'll do that during the next week and get our clothing fixed up."

" What are you wearing ? "

" I've got my own brown shoes," John said, " and a pair of Australian navy-blue battledress trousers that I swapped for a pair of khaki ones. Jim Strong's lent me his air force mackintosh and I've got a beret that I swapped with a Pole in the last camp. All I need really is a jacket of some sort and a civilian shirt and tie."

" We've managed to get two shirts for you," Stafford said.

" And I've got a Fleet Air Arm jacket that ought to fit you. Used to belong to my pilot. I'm afraid one sleeve's torn and a bit bloodstained, but if you wash it and take the gold braid off it should pass as a civilian jacket. You can either cover the buttons or replace them."

" We've got some buttons," Peter said. " We've been collecting them for some time."

" How are you fixed up for clothes ? " Stafford turned to Peter.

" Old Tettenborne's got a black B.O.A.C. trench coat—I'm negotiating for that. I shall wear black shoes, and one of the chaps has got a beret made out of a blanket that I can have."

" What about a suit ? "

Peter grinned. " The Committee have got a phony Marine dress uniform."

" Yes, I've seen it," Stafford said. " It's pretty good."

" Well, it's hidden somewhere—underground, I think—and they won't let me have it until just before we're ready to go. They say it'll fit me, so I'm trusting to luck and hoping that it will."

" And what about your papers ? "

" They're all in hand. We're going to make for Stettin and try to stow away on a Swedish boat. We shall both travel as French draughtsmen and they're forging our Ausweis and Arbeitskarte now. We shall also have a forged police permission to travel and a letter from our firm in Breslau giving us permission to go. We shall say we're going to the Arado Works at Anklam—just north of Stettin."

" You know about the Swedish ships being searched, I suppose ? They use tear-gas bombs and have specially trained dogs."

" Yes, we'd heard about that. We thought of taking forged papers and becoming Swedish sailors when we arrive in Stettin— then we could hang around the docks without looking suspicious. We shall each take a dark blue roll-neck sweater so that we can change from foreign workers to Swedish sailors at short notice."

" Do you know what a Swedish sailor's papers look like ? "

"No, we don't, unfortunately, but there's a chap in the camp who was in the Merchant Service and he's going to rough out an English one for us. We shall more or less copy that in Swedish and hope that we shan't need to use it."

"I still don't like the idea of staying in hotels," Stafford said.

Peter said nothing but looked obstinate. Stafford recognised this obstinacy—the singleness of purpose that had taken the tunnel this far—and he turned to John.

"I agree with Peter," John said. "No one has tried it yet and very few people have got home. Our papers will be good and I think the bolder we are the less suspicious the Germans will be. Besides, it will be October or November before we're out and it's going to be pretty cold sleeping in the open. If we don't get a ship at once—and I don't suppose we will—we'll have to go somewhere at night and I think there's less risk in hotels than in hanging around station waiting-rooms and public lavatories. We've talked the whole thing over and that's what we've decided to do." He said it with finality.

"Perhaps you're right," Stafford said. "I know what it's like to be without a base of some sort. It gets on your nerves, having nowhere to go—no place where you can relax and have a bit of a breather. I've got an address in Stettin. It's a sort of club, but I don't know whether I ought to let you have it."

"Don't you think we're old enough?" John asked.

"It's not that. I've had the address for some time—ever since I was out myself, but I never got as far as Stettin—and the place might have been bust wide open by now. They were Polish and they hid Allied prisoners and airmen who were on the loose. But these places are really more of a danger than a help. The Hun might have rumbled it and be using it as a trap."

"Is it a German club?" Peter asked.

"It's a club for foreign workers. Germans aren't allowed in. But as I say, it might be a trap. I'll give you the address just before you leave the camp. You'll have to commit it to memory. Wouldn't be safe to write it down."

" We'll remember it," John said. " I've never been to a Polish club."

" What's Rowe doing ? " Stafford asked.

" He's going on his own," Peter said. " Going to Danzig—travelling as a Swedish commercial traveller." He smiled now that the need for obstinacy was gone. " He's practising the role already. He's learning to smoke a pipe so that if he's questioned he can gain time by lighting it."

" Well, I wish you luck," Stafford said. " I think you'll make it. Have a drink on me in Shepherd's, will you ? "

" We'll have a drink on you in every pub in town," Peter promised.

CHAPTER EIGHT

Inch By Inch

WHEN THEY reopened the tunnel at the end of seven days they found that the sand on the roof and walls had dried and considerable falls had occurred. It took them another week to clear the fallen sand and to shore the tunnel in the dangerous places.

It was now early October and the long Silesian summer was ending. All through the summer their working had been controlled by the weather. Once the trap was lifted and the workers were in the tunnel it took them all of fifteen minutes to get back to the shaft, close the trap and get ready to be carried in. They could not afford to be caught out by a shower of rain. If it started to rain the vaulters could not continue without arousing the suspicion of the guards. Nor could they run for the shelter of the canteen leaving the vaulting horse to stand out in the rain. The obvious thing was to carry the horse in with them, and they could not do this with the trap open and two men in the tunnel. So they studied the weather carefully and if it looked at all like rain they had to vault without digging. Nearly every time they took the horse out it was only after long discussions on the weather. The nearer they got to the wire the more reluctant they were to risk being caught by the rain. They were also determined to be out by the end of October and as the time passed they began to get dogmatic and short-tempered in their discussions.

Philip was more upset than the other two by a sudden change of plan. They would part in the evening having arranged to vault immediately after breakfast the following morning. Philip would arrive in their room, dressed for digging, only to find that owing to a change in the weather they had decided not to dig. Ten minutes afterwards, if the weather showed signs of clearing, they would decide to start work, and all the vaulters would be assembled at a moment's notice.

It was trying for all of them. They were physically tired after three and a half months of digging and now their nerves were

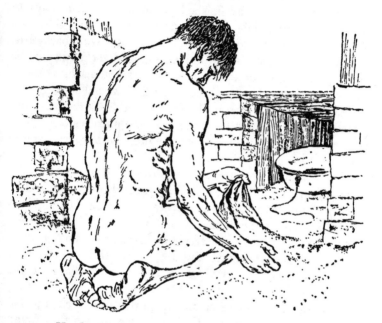

He then tipped the basin over and filled his bags

becoming frayed by continual anxiety and changes of plan. Peter tried to keep cheerful, but fumed inwardly at the delays caused by the more and more frequent showers of rain.

With the new system of digging the tunnel made slow progress. They had enlarged the end of the tunnel to form a " bulge " large enough to allow the man working at the face to rest on his elbows and draw his knees up under his chest. Instead of using the usual wooden toboggan for carrying the sand down the tunnel they used a metal basin eighteen inches in diameter and eight inches deep. The basin was just small enough to fit into the tunnel. Two holes had been drilled in opposite sides of the rim of the basin to take the rope which they had plaited from string off the Red Cross parcels.

When the bulge was finished—it took them four days to remove the extra sand—the tunnel was driven on. One man worked in the tunnel extension, dragging the sand backwards into the bulge. Once in the bulge he pulled the basin up the tunnel, past his feet and over his legs on to his stomach, where he filled it with the sand he had brought back. Two pulls on the rope was the signal for the man in the shaft to pull back the basin full of sand. He then tipped the basin over and filled his bags while the worker in the bulge crawled up the tunnel extension for more sand.

At first they merely threaded the rope through the holes in the rim of the basin. But the holes were raggedly punched through with a nail and soon cut the string, leaving the basin stranded—usually half-way up the tunnel. Then there followed a whispered argument as to who was nearer the basin and whose turn it was to crawl up the tunnel and repair the string. Later they made strong wire hooks with which to attach the basin to the rope.

Up to the time of making the bulge they had been troubled by lack of air in the tunnel. Under the new system they found that sufficient air was pushed up the tunnel by the passage of the basin to supply the man in the bulge. They were now working gradually up towards the surface and it was impossible to remain in the extension for more than a few minutes. If for any reason the basin was not kept moving the shortage of air became dangerous.

After a time they drove the new tunnel so far beyond the bulge that it became impossible to work in the extension and they made a new bulge at the end of the tunnel, filled in the old bulge,

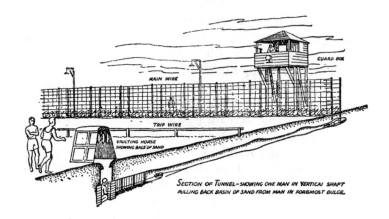

SECTION OF TUNNEL - SHOWING ONE MAN IN VERTICAL SHAFT
PULLING BACK BASIN OF SAND FROM MAN IN FOREMOST BULGE.

lengthened the rope and carried on as before. They made three such bulges before the tunnel was complete.

Try as they might they could not persuade Philip to enter the tunnel in the nude. He insisted on wearing a shirt, shorts and tennis shoes; and for this reason they did all they could to arrange that he remained in the shaft.

It was a feat of some endurance to drag the thirty-odd full basins of sand from the face to the shaft. In addition to this the bags had to be filled and lifted one by one and stacked inside the vaulting-horse. So Peter and John pleaded fatigue and persuaded Philip to allow one of them to work at the face whenever it was his turn to dig.

When they had been digging for some months John became convinced that the tunnel was veering to the left. Peter, who was in charge of the construction, was convinced that the tunnel was straight. They had taken their direction by a home-made compass. After considerable argument they decided to put it to the test.

Peter crawled to the end of the tunnel with the rope of the basin tied to his ankle. He took with him a thin metal poker about four feet long. John sat in the shaft holding the other end of the rope while Nigel sat on the horse apparently resting after an energetic bout of vaulting.

Philip stood gazing out through the wire, hands in pockets, in the hopeless, forlorn and typically Kriegie attitude. Prisoners strolled slowly round the wire. The guards brooded in their boxes. The whole camp wore its usual afternoon air of lassitude.

Peter, lying full length at the end of the tunnel, scooped a deep pit in the floor in front of his face. He placed the end of the poker in the pit and forced it slowly upwards through the roof of the tunnel, using a corkscrew motion to avoid bringing down the roof. It was hard work. Steady trickles of sand fell from the ceiling, covering his head and shoulders. Inch by inch he forced the poker upwards until the end was flush with the ceiling of the tunnel. He scraped the sand away from around the poker and pushed it up still higher. By the sudden lack of resistance he knew that it was through and protruding above the surface of the ground. He gave two tugs on the rope to tell John that he was through. John knocked on the inside of the horse and Nigel, hearing this, sent a messenger across to Philip.

Philip, without appearing to do so, frantically scanned the ground in front of him for the end of the poker. He could not see it.

Peter became impatient and began to move the poker slowly up and down. Then Philip saw it. He scratched his head. Nigel kicked the side of the horse. John pulled the rope and Peter pulled down the poker.

The end of the tunnel was under the wire, but fifteen feet to the left of where Peter had expected it to be.

The following morning Peter, John and Philip walked together round the wire completing their plans for the break.

" We shall have to ' mole ' the last ten feet," Peter said. " We're under the wire now and we've twelve days to go to the end of the month. If we're lucky we shall do another six feet by then. That puts us about three feet outside the wire. There's a shallow ditch about twelve feet beyond the wire and if we can manage to strike that it will give us some cover for the break."

" It's still in the light of the arc lamps," John objected.

"The light from the lamps extends for about thirty feet outside the wire and we can't possibly push the tunnel on as far as that. Besides, the only railway timetable Stafford's got expires at the end of the month and we *must* time the break so that we just have time to leap down to the station and catch a train. If we get out and then have to hang about waiting for a train we stand a good chance of getting picked up right away."

"I agree with Pete," Philip said. "We'll just have to organise a diversion in the huts nearest the wire at the time that we mean to break."

"That won't be too easy," John said. "Who's going to estimate how long it's going to take us to mole ten feet?"

"We'll have to over-estimate it," Peter said. "Then add half as much time again, and if we reach the ditch before the time we've said—we'll just have to lie doggo until we hear the diversion start." He turned to Philip. "Will you organise the diversion?"

"O.K. I'll get that laid on. What about the outside sentries?"

"They don't come on until an hour after dusk. John and I have been sitting up all night watching them. There are two on the side where we are. They each patrol half the wire, meet in the middle, turn back to back and walk to the end. If it's raining they stand under a tree. They walk pretty slowly and when the diversion starts they and the goons in the boxes will be looking inwards towards the noise. We should get past them all right." He spoke confidently, but thought of tommy-gun bullets and the sharp cry in the night when Alan had been shot on the wire. "We shall have to wear dark clothes," he said.

"I'd thought of that," Philip said. "We've just had some long woollen combinations sent in by the Red Cross. If we dye them black with tea-leaves or coffee we could put them on over our clothes. It will keep us clean while we're down there and be good camouflage when we get out."

"John and I thought of going down naked," Peter said.

"*I'm* not going to get caught and dragged off to the cooler without a stitch of clothing. It's all right for you nudists. Besides, my skin's not like yours—it's too white and would show up too much. There's another thing too—I want to go right along that hole to-morrow and have a look at the end. I don't trust you two. I want to make certain it's big enough to take me and all my kit."

" What's all this talk of ' all my kit ' ? " John asked.

" Well, I'm going as a commercial traveller, aren't I ? I shall need a bag of samples and I've got a black Homburg hat I bribed off one of the goons. That will have to go in a box to save it from getting crushed. Then I'm wearing an R.A.F. greatcoat. . . ."

" He'd better go down to-morrow and see how big the hole is," John said.

" Right," Peter said, " but look here, Phil, none of your little games. No widening it while you're down there and saying it fell in. It's quite big enough as it is."

" Let's get this thing straight," Philip said. " You can't go down there naked—you'll have to wear shoes at least in case you have to run. And I wouldn't fancy running through those woods with dogs after me without any clothes on."

" We must remember to get some pepper for the dogs," Peter said.

" Yes, but what about the kit ? "

" I like the idea of the combinations," John said. " We could wear socks over our shoes and black hoods over our heads."

" We shan't be able to wear all our clothes," Peter said. " The hole's not big enough."

" We'll wear our shirts and trousers then," Philip said, " and pack the rest of our kit in kitbags dyed black. We can drag them down the tunnel tied to our ankles."

" We haven't solved the most important problem yet," Peter said.

" What's that ? "

" How to get four people out in the horse."

" Four people ? " Philip sounded excited. " I thought only we three were going ! "

" Yes, but somebody's got to close the trap down after us."

" Do you mean to say that you haven't arranged all that ? "
Philip was even more excited.

" As a matter of fact I never thought we'd get as far as we
have." Peter winked at John. " When we decided to ask you to
come in we never considered how we were going to get out once
the tunnel was finished. We could have got three into the horse
at a pinch, but I'm darned if I can see how we could get four."

" We'll have to draw lots," John said.

Philip nearly choked. " D'you mean to say that you've got
as far as this and never considered how we were to get out ? "

" Did *you* consider it ? " Peter asked.

" I thought you'd got it all fixed."

" We'll have to put the kit down the day before," John said.

" We can't do that," Peter said. " If we put three kitbags in
the tunnel we shan't be able to get down ourselves."

" Then we'll have to make a chamber near the end of the
tunnel large enough to take them."

" That's a week's work in itself," Peter said. " I can't see us
finishing up much outside the wire. We've got to get past the
path where the outside sentries walk and we've got to do it before
the end of the month. Our timetable expires at the end of the
month and after that goodness knows how the trains will run."

" Pray God it doesn't rain much during the next few days,"
Philip said.

" We'll just have to vault in the rain, that's all. The goons
think we're mad already. We'll just have to risk it and hope they
don't get suspicious."

" What train do you and John want to catch ? "

" There's a fast train to Frankfurt at six-thirty p.m. German
time," Peter said. " It's dark by five-thirty and the outside guards
usually come on soon after that. If we break at six o'clock it will
be dark enough and we stand a chance of getting out before the
guards arrive. We don't want to go too early because if they find
the hole and get to the station before the train goes we'll get
picked up."

" That train will do me too," Philip said.

" You're definitely not coming with us then ? " Peter asked. It's just as well, he thought. We'd only row if we all went together. Old Phil's much better on his own. He'll make his plans and he'll stick to them, which is something we'd never do. Ours is the better way though. Keep it fluid. You need less luck our way. And we can do it. . . .

" I'll go on my own," Philip said. " I'll make for Danzig and try to get a boat there."

" We shall get off at Frankfurt," John said. " Take the fast train as far as Frankfurt, spend the night there, and see how things go. We shall most likely make Stettin in two or three short hops. Most likely we shall get off before we get to Stettin station and walk into the town."

" I shall go straight on up to Danzig," Philip said. " I hope to be in Sweden three days after leaving the camp."

" I think you're doing the right thing," Peter said. " The right thing for you. Speaking German and travelling as a neutral, a long-distance fast train is the obvious thing. You should get away with it. Once we get to Frankfurt we shall go by slow local trains."

" I think I've got it ! " John said.

" Got what ? " Peter asked.

" If I go down in the afternoon before roll-call—say about two o'clock in the afternoon—and take the baggage with me, you can seal me down and I'll dig the whole of the afternoon. You can cook my absence at roll-call and then you two come down as soon as you can. Roll-call's at three forty-five, so you'll be down about four o'clock, or soon after. You can take someone out with you— the smallest man we can find—to seal the trap down after you, and then we'll have two hours in which to get ready to break."

" It'll be pretty grim," Peter said, " stuck down there alone for a couple of hours."

" Oh, I shall be all right. I'll put an air-hole up inside the wire where it won't be seen, and mole on quite happily. I should do five or six feet before you come down."

" Don't go and overdo it." Peter knew John's unsparing

energy once he'd set his heart to a thing. He was all energy once he started. Nervous energy and guts. He took more out of himself than he knew. " Remember we may have to run for it," he said. " Don't fag yourself out digging—leave most of it for when we get down there."

" Oh, I'll take it easy," John lied. Peter knew he lied and could do nothing about it.

" That's everything then, is it ? " Philip asked. " I'll go along and see the Committee and fix up the diversion for six o'clock. I want to see about my samples too."

" What are they ? " Peter asked.

" Samples of margarine packed in wooden boxes," Philip replied. " I'll eat them if I get hungry."

CHAPTER NINE

The Break-Out

FOR THE next twelve days they vaulted every day and removed as much sand as they could. They increased the number of bags to fourteen and finally fifteen, although the bearers staggered as they carried the horse into the canteen.

On October the twenty-eighth they made the final bulge at the end of the tunnel. This was as far as they could go. They reckoned that between them they could dig a further ten feet after they had been sealed down. The bulge they made to hold their kitbags while they were digging the last ten feet and finally breaking through to the surface.

They spent the next morning bringing in the last twelve bags and recovering their civilian clothing from their various scattered hiding places round the camp. At twelve-thirty John had his last meal, a substantial meal of bully beef, potatoes and Canadian biscuits and cheese. At one o'clock he went over to the canteen with the camp glee-singing club. He wore his civilian clothes under a long khaki Polish greatcoat. Earlier in the day their baggage had been taken to the canteen, hidden in bundles of dirty laundry.

While John was eating the last of his lunch Peter went along to see the duty pilot. There were two ferrets in the compound. Bother, he thought, they would have to be here now. "Where are they?" he asked.

"One's in the kitchen, the other's hanging around outside the canteen."

Peter thought for a moment. "O.K.," he said. "If any more

come into the compound send a stooge off to Philip. He'll be in the canteen."

He ran across to the S.B.O.; knocked on the door.

" Come in."

He stood in the doorway, panting slightly. " Sir—we're just putting Clinton down and there's a goon hanging round the canteen. I wonder if you could get him out of the way for a few minutes ? "

The S.B.O. smiled and put down his book. " Let me see," he said, " the cooking stove in Hut 64 isn't drawing very well. I'll just stroll over and ask him to have a look at it. He might like to smoke an English cigarette in my room."

" Thank you, sir."

Back at the canteen he found the glee-club singing an old English folk song. John, Philip, Nigel and the vaulters were standing near the door.

" We can't get started," John said. " There's a ferret outside and he keeps walking past and looking in at the window. I don't think he likes the singing."

" It'd be worse without it," Peter said. " There's another next door in the kitchen. The S.B.O. is going to take the one outside away and then we'll get cracking." He looked out of the window. The S.B.O. was walking across the Sportsplatz, a golf club in his hand. Suddenly he appeared to see the ferret and altered course. " Here comes ' Groupy,' " Peter said. " Good man ! "

The group captain exchanged a few words with the ferret and they both walked away across the Sportsplatz.

" O.K.," said Peter. " Let's go ! "

John hurriedly doffed his coat and pulled the long black combinations on over his clothes. He pulled black socks over his shoes and adjusted the hood which was made from an old under-vest dyed black. " It's pretty hot in here," he said.

" You look like the Klu Klux Klan," Peter told him. " O.K.? "

They both crawled under the vaulting-horse, Peter holding a blanket, a cardboard box and twelve empty bags ; John sinister in his black clothes. The three kitbags hung between them suspended from the top of the horse. They both crouched with their backs to the ends of the horse, their feet one each side on the bottom framework. Then the bearing poles were inserted and the horse was raised. Tightly holding the kitbags to prevent them from swaying, they lurched down the steps and went creaking across the compound towards the vaulting-pits.

With a sigh of relief the bearers placed the horse in position and withdrew the poles ready for vaulting.

John crouched in one end of the horse while Peter piled the kitbags on top of him. Peter then spread the blanket on the ground at the other end of the horse and began to uncover the trap. He first collected the grey top layer in the cardboard box and threw the damp subsoil on to the blanket. Feeling round with his fingers he uncovered the bags of sand on top of the trap. He scraped the sand away from the damp wood. As he removed the trap he smelled the familiar damp musty smell of the tunnel. He lifted the kitbags off John's crouching figure and balanced them on top of the trap on the pile of sand. " Down you go," he said, and crouched astride the hole while John dropped feet first into the shaft. " Whew, those clothes stink ! "

" It'll be worse by the time you come down," John said. " It's the dye. Must have gone bad or something."

While John crawled up the tunnel Peter detached the metal basin from the end of the rope and tied one of the kitbags in its place. One by one John pulled the kitbags up the tunnel and put them in the bulge at the end. Peter then replaced the basin and between them they filled the twelve empty bags they had taken out with them.

While Peter was stacking the bags in the body of the horse, John crawled back for his last breath of fresh air. It was the first time he had been in the tunnel wearing clothes and Peter could hear him cursing softly as he struggled to get back. Finally his feet came into view and then his body, clothed and clumsy under the black combinations. Peter crouched inside the horse looking down on him as he emerged. Outside he could hear the shouting of the vaulters and the reverberating concussion as they landed on top of the horse. John straightened up, head and shoulders out of the trap. He had left the hood at the end of the tunnel and his face was red.

" It's pretty hot down there with clothes on."

" Take it easy," Peter said. " For goodness' sake don't overdo it. I don't want to have to carry you once we get outside."

" I'll be all right. You seal me down now and I'll see you later."

" O.K., but for goodness' sake don't make the air-hole bigger than you have to," Peter said.

He watched John's legs disappear down the narrow tunnel and then he replaced the trap. He replaced the heavy bags of sand and stamped the loose sand firmly on top of them. It's burying a man alive, he thought. Then he heard an anxious voice from outside.

" How's it going, Pete ? "

" Five minutes, Phil," he said, and started to hang the twelve bags of sand from the top of the horse. He gathered the blanket in his arms and spread the rest of the sand evenly over the ground under the horse. He sprinkled the dry grey sand from the cardboard box over this and gave Philip a low hail that he was ready. The bearing poles were inserted and he was carried back into the canteen.

As they neared the canteen he could hear the voices of the male voice choir. " He shall set His angels guard over thee . . . Lest thou catch thy foot against a stone. . . ." He grinned widely in the dark belly of the horse.

With a final creaking lurch they were up the steps and inside the canteen. The old horse is falling to pieces, Peter thought. Hope it lasts out this evening.

One end of the horse was lifted and he passed the bags of sand out to Philip. Between them they carried the bags into the band practice room where the choir was going at full blast. " He shall set His angels, there's a ferret outside the window," sang David.

" O.K.," said Peter. " Keep an eye on him. Is Nig in the roof ? "

David nodded his head and continued singing.

" Right. We'll just get these bags to safety in the roof and then we're O.K."

Nigel's anxious face was peering down from the trap door in the ceiling. Peter held out his fist, thumb extended upwards, and grinned. Nigel grinned too, and lowered his arm for the first of the bags.

Roll-call was at three forty-five and Peter and Philip spent the time until then lying on their bunks. For Peter this was the worst moment of all. This waiting after the work had been done. This lying on his bunk while John was down below digging, and at any moment the scheme might blow and their four and a half months' effort be wasted. Once they were outside he felt it wouldn't matter so much. He hardly expected to get back to England. That was looking too far ahead. That was too much in the lap of the gods. Anything might happen once they were outside. Outside the wire they would rely almost entirely on their luck. It was no use making detailed plans of what they would do when they were outside. They could make a rough outline plan of what they wanted to do, but that was all. From the moment they left the end of the tunnel they would have to adapt their policy to the conditions they met. He could not plan ahead a single day.

And so he lay on his back on the bunk and let his mind run over the list of things he was taking with him.

There was the " dog food," a hard cake made from dried milk, sugar, Bemax and cocoa. It had been packed in small square tins from the Red Cross parcels and he intended to wear a girdle of them between two shirts.

Next there were several linen bags containing a dry mixture of oatmeal, raisins, sugar and milk powder. When they ate this it would swell in the stomach and prevent that hollow aching sickness that comes from eating ill-balanced concentrated food.

He had sewn one of these bags into each armpit of his jacket as an emergency ration if he became separated from the attaché case which held the bulk of their food.

The attaché case was already down in the tunnel, at the bottom of the kitbag. He mentally checked its contents : the food, clean socks, shaving gear, a roll-neck sweater, soap, a small packet of paper and pen and ink for minor alterations to their papers, and spare cigarettes and matches.

He got to his feet and checked over his jacket pockets. The wallet which held his papers and German money, a small pocket compass, a penknife, handkerchiefs, his pipe (a German one bought in the town by one of the guards), a length of string, a pencil, a German tobacco pouch, his beret and a comb.

He went out on the circuit. It was no use, he couldn't be still. He walked round, over the tunnel, and thought of John moling away down there, sweating away, not knowing the time, not knowing whether the tunnel had been discovered, out of touch with everyone. John digging away, trying to get as much done as he could before the others joined him.

He checked with Philip on the timing of the diversion for their break, and then walked with Nigel several times round the circuit while they waited for the appel.

" I shall miss you after you've gone," Nigel said. " It's been quite good fun, this vaulting."

" I expect they'll take the horse away when they discover the tunnel," Peter said. He wanted to thank Nigel for all the help he had given, but he knew that he could not do it. To thank him would put the thing on a formal basis and it was beyond that. So they walked, trying to talk naturally, and waited for the roll-call.

At roll-call the Senior British Officer, suitably disguised, took John's place in the ranks and his absence was not noticed.

As soon as roll-call was finished the vaulters assembled at the canteen. Peter's knees felt loose and he did not want to go in the horse. They had taken it out twice already that day and he felt that the third time would be unlucky. It was the first

time they had vaulted after evening roll-call and he was certain
that the guards would be suspicious. As he pulled on the evil-
smelling black combinations he could hear Nigel instructing the
four men who were to carry the horse. He looked at Philip,
unrecognisable in his black hood ; and then at the third man, a
New Zealander called McKay, whom they had chosen as the
lightest man in the camp. He was stripped for lightness and holding the cardboard box for the dry sand to be sprinkled over the
trap after he had sealed them down.

Nigel came in and handed him a bottle of cold tea for John.
" Give him my love," he said, " and tell him to write."

Peter and Philip crawled under the horse, stood one at each
end and held McKay suspended between them. The poles were
placed in position and the horse protestingly started on its last
journey. One of the bearers slipped as they came down the steps
and Peter thought he would drop them. The man recovered his
balance and they went swaying and jerking across the football
pitch.

Once the horse was in position Philip sat on McKay's back
at one end while Peter again removed the trap. As he took out
the wooden boards he listened for sounds of movement in the
tunnel. It was silent. He looked at Philip.

" I'll go up the tunnel and see how John is," he said. " You
fill twelve bags from the bottom of the shaft for Mac to take
back, and then stay down this end. I'll send the sand back to
you in the basin and you spread it along the floor of the tunnel
as you come up."

" Right."

" You'll never get down there ! " McKay looked with wonder
at the narrowness of the shaft.

Peter dropped feet first into the vertical shaft. He slid to his
knees, edging his legs backwards into the back burrow. Stooping
awkwardly in his tight clothing, he managed to get his head under
the lintel of the opening and slipped head first into the tunnel.
He waved his legs in farewell, and squirmed inch by inch along
the hundred feet that had taken them so long to build. Now that

it was finished he was almost sorry. The tunnel had been first in his thoughts for months, cherished, nursed; and now it was finished and he was crawling down it for the last time.

He had brought the torch with him and as he inched along he could see heaps of loose sand dislodged by John's clothing. He noticed all the patches of shoring, strangely unfamiliar in the light but which had been built with difficulty in darkness.

As he neared the end of the tunnel he flashed the torch ahead

Showing how three men were eventually carried. Two are wearing combinations and hoods dyed black to make them less conspicuous when breaking from the mouth of the tunnel. The third man is to replace the trap over the tunnel. The hooks are for bringing in the bags of sand when removed from the tunnel

and called softly to John. He was afraid to call loudly for he was now under the wire and close to the sentry's beat. He passed the bend where they had altered course, and came to the end of the tunnel.

Where he had expected to find John there was nothing but a solid wall of sand.

John must have been digging steadily on and in banking up the sand behind him had completely blocked the tunnel.

Peter bored a small hole through the wall of sand which was

about three feet thick. As he broke through a gust of hot fetid air gushed out and there was John, wringing wet with perspiration and black from head to foot with the dye that had run out of his combinations. Sand clung to his face where he had sweated and his hair, caked with sand, fell forward over his eyes. He looked pale and tired under the yellow light of Peter's torch.

" Where on earth have you been ? " he asked.

" It's only just about four-thirty," Peter said.

" I thought it must have gone six. I seem to have been down here for hours. I thought the roll-call had gone wrong and I'd have to go out alone."

" It's all O.K.," Peter said. " I've got a bottle of tea here." He pushed it through the hole to John. " I'll just send this sand back to Phil and then I'll join you." He pulled the empty basin up the tunnel and sent the first load back to Philip, who filled the empty bags he had brought down and stacked them in the shaft.

As they worked on they found that now the end of the tunnel where Peter and John were working had a certain amount of fresh air from the air-hole under the wire. Philip, with the trap sealed down, had none.

They worked feverishly trying to get as much as possible done before the breaking time. John, in front, stabbing at the face with the trowel and pushing the damp sand under his belly back towards Peter, who lay with his head on John's heels collecting the sand and squirming backwards with it to Philip, who banked it up as a solid wall behind them.

They were now in a narrow portion of the tunnel about twenty-five feet long and two feet square, ventilated by one small hole three inches in diameter.

They were working for the first time in clothes and for the first time without the fresh air pushed up the tunnel by the basin. They were working three in the tunnel and they were anxious about the air. They were working for the first time by the light of a torch, and in this light the tunnel seemed smaller and the

At exactly 6 o'clock they broke through

earth above more solid. The prisoners had been locked in for the night and if the tunnel collapsed now they were helpless.

They all worked fast and steadily. None of them wanted to be the one to break the rhythm of the work.

At five-thirty Peter, who had a watch, called a halt. " We'd better push up to the top now," he whispered. " We've got to be out in half an hour."

John nodded his agreement and began to push the tunnel up towards the surface. It was farther than they had expected and they thought they would never get to the top. Finally, John broke through—a hole as large as his fist—and through it he caught his first glimpse of the stars. The stars in the free heavens beyond the wire.

" I'll break out the whole width of the tunnel," John whispered, " just leaving the thin crust over the top. Then we can break that quickly and there'll be less chance of being seen."

Peter squeezed his arm in reply and squirmed back to Philip to warn him to get ready. On his way back he brought John's kitbag which Philip had tied to his ankle. He then went back for his own. Philip pushed his along the tunnel in front of his nose.

At exactly six o'clock they broke through to the open air, pulling the dry sandy surface down on top of them, choking and blinding them and making them want to cough. As they broke through they heard the sound of the diversion coming from the huts nearest the wire. There were men blowing trumpets, men singing, men banging the sides of the hut and yelling at the top of their voices.

" The silly asses will get a bullet in there if they're not careful," John whispered.

" Go on! Go now!" Peter said. He was scared. It was too light.

Quickly John hoisted his kitbag out of the tunnel and rolled it towards the ditch. He squeezed himself out of the hole and Peter saw his legs disappear from view.

Peter stuck his head out of the tunnel and looked towards the camp. It was brilliantly floodlit. He had not realised how brilliantly it was lit. But the raised sentry boxes were in darkness and he could not see whether the guards were looking in his direction or not. He could not see the guards outside the wire. He lifted out his kitbag and pushed it towards the ditch, wriggling himself out of the hole and rolling full length on the ground towards the ditch. He expected every minute to hear the crack of a rifle and feel the tearing impact of its bullet in his flesh. He gained the ditch and lay listening. The diversion in the huts had reached a new crescendo of noise.

He picked up his kitbag and ran blindly towards the pine forest on the other side of the road where John was waiting for him.

PHASE TWO

CHAPTER ONE

A Night In The Open

ONCE THEY reached the edge of the wood they did not wait for
Philip but walked slowly away from the wire, towards the centre
of the forest. Peter could feel his heart thumping high up inside
his chest, choking him. He wanted to run but forced himself
to walk slowly, feeling with his feet for the dry branches that lay
among the pine needles on the forest floor. His tunnelling clothes
were wet with perspiration and the keen wind cut through them.
He was cold now and anxious to get into the shelter of the forest
where they could dress. Looking backwards over his shoulder
he saw the compound through the trees, floodlit like some giant
circus. There had been no shots and he knew that Philip was
safely away behind them somewhere in the forest.

He stopped and stood looking backwards at the bright lights
among the trees.

" It's a piece of cake," John whispered. " Come on, Pete.
We'll have to move if we're going to catch that train."

But Peter stood for a moment gazing back at the camp that
he hoped never to see again ; the camp that he hated but which
held so many of his friends.

John caught him by the arm and they walked on into the
forest, moving carefully on the loose and noisy ground.

John started laughing under his breath. First giggles and then
long gusts of low, shaking, uncontrollable mirth.

" What's the matter ? " Peter whispered. " What the devil's
the matter ? What the devil are you laughing at ? "

" It's you . . ." John said, " you look like some great bear
mincing along like that. . . ."

Peter was carrying the kitbag baby-like in his arms.

" Let's get out of these combinations," John said. " Let's get cleaned up and look like human beings."

" Not yet. Lay the trail away from the railway station. We'll hide them on the side of the road to Breslau." Peter, too, was laughing, laughing with the release of strained nerves and with the triumph of escape. But he was not yet relaxed. His laughter was brittle, nervous.

They picked their way carefully through the forest until they were out of earshot of the camp. They were trembling now, cold in their thin woollen combinations, cold and tired by the digging; but not feeling tired. Not feeling tired because they were free, outside the wire that had held them for so long.

Ahead of them the pine forest stretched silent and unbroken for miles. It stretched almost unbroken into Jugoslavia. But it was a winter forest. A forest of bare branches and tall silent trees. unfriendly and inhospitable. They had been in the forest before and knew its inhospitality. A short mile away was the railway station, crowded and risky, but holding the promise of a rapid journey to the coast.

They stripped off the black combination suits and the socks from over their shoes. They washed one another's faces with their handkerchiefs and took their civilian jackets, hats and mackintoshes from the kitbags.

At the bottom of the kitbags they each had a small travelling bag. Peter opened his and took out a tin of pepper. He put the clothing together in a heap and sprinkled it liberally with the pepper, holding his nose as he did it.

They put on their mackintoshes and berets and doubled back towards the railway, making straight for the bridge that led to the station. It was a high metal footbridge over the railway line. They crossed it and gained the road on the other side.

" Walk on the right-hand side," Peter said. " Then we shan't be facing the oncoming traffic."

There were several people on the road. A local train had

evidently just pulled in. Hope they're not waiting at the station, Peter thought. Hope the alarm hasn't gone and we don't find a crowd of guards waiting at the station.

"If we're recognised we'll cut and run," he said. "They won't shoot with all these people about. We'll separate. I'll meet you by he water tower in the forest, and we'll walk, or jump goods trains. If they know we're out all the stations for miles around will be watched."

"It's O.K.," John said. "We shan't get caught. If the alarm had gone we'd have heard it. Just look slap-happy. We'll be O.K."

Outside the station it was dark, but inside the booking hall the lights were bright. Peter walked to the timetable on the wall while John joined the queue at the booking office. He had Peter's identity card and police permission to travel.

Peter turned to watch him as he stood in the queue. To him the air force trench coat was glaringly obvious. But the beret and John's lean dark face looked French enough. A young slim figure in a beret and grey-blue trench coat carrying the travelling-bag he had made himself out of a canvas valise. He looked unconcerned as he stood in the queue waiting his turn at the booking-office window; but Peter saw him draw in his underlip and guessed at his feelings as he stood there waiting.

He was at the window now, talking to the girl behind the grille. Peter looked towards the door. It was crowded with people. I'll wait until he gets within about three feet of me and then we'll both charge together, he thought. We'll get through that lot all right. He turned again towards John. He was coming over to him with the tickets in his hand. Peter joined him and they stood together at the barrier waiting for the passengers to leave the platform before they went through.

Peter stood watching the passengers as they came out through the barrier. His heart pounded. He wanted to run. Coming through the barrier was the doctor who had been treating him in hospital. They had talked every day for a week and he was

bound to be recognised. Then he remembered that he had
removed his beard the night before. As the Hauptmann came by,
within a foot of him, Peter stooped and fumbled with the fastener
of his attaché case. When he looked up the Hauptmann had
passed and John was pushing him towards the barrier on to the
platform.

They walked up and down the platform waiting for the train.
They had ten minutes to wait. They walked to the end of the
platform and studied the lie of the land.

" If the alarm goes before the train gets in, we'll jump on to
the line and down that embankment," Peter said. " We'll circle
round the town and if we get separated we'll meet at the water
tower."

" We'll hear the camp sirens all right from here," John said.
" Wait until the last minute in case the train gets in before they
get here." He sounded confident.

" No," said Peter, not liking this confidence, not wanting it to
be too easy. " No—we'll go as soon as we hear the sirens. If they
find out we've gone it'll be no use catching the train. They'll
telephone Frankfurt and catch us there. It'll be better to get
right away from the railway and get into the country."

" We could catch the train and jump it before we got to
Frankfurt."

" It wouldn't be worth it. The train might be late and then
we'd be caught on the platform. If we hear the sirens we'll get
off right away and take to the woods."

" O.K.," John said. " We'll be O.K."

The train was crowded and in darkness. They stood in the
corridor. Peter stood near the door looking out of the window
and listening to the rat-a-tat-tat of the wheels. Every minute is
taking us farther away, he thought. We're going to make it. He
looked round him for John. They had become separated and
John was squeezed in between a burly German soldier and an old
woman. He was leaning back against the side of the carriage with
his eyes closed.

They stood like this all the way to Frankfurt. It was ten-thirty when they arrived and they hurried towards the barrier to see what check there was before the crowd dispersed. The passengers were not being asked to show their papers—they were merely handing in their tickets. Peter walked towards the barrier, but John pulled him back and steered him towards another exit farther away. Peter said nothing but followed him. They passed the barrier and stood safely outside in the spacious booking hall.

" Why did you pull me back ? " Peter whispered.

" That one was for soldiers only, you ass. Come on, let's get out of the station and on to the street." He wanted to get away ; to get Peter away from the bright lights of the station. Away from the danger of the bright lights and the people.

They left the booking hall and walked out into the darkness of the cobbled streets—the strange foreign streets of which they had no experience. In which nothing was familiar, with signposts and shop signs in a foreign tongue. Nowhere to sleep. Strange after the close confinement of the prison camp and exciting to be walking along the streets of a town, fugitives surrounded by enemies and unable to speak more than a few words of the language. Peter stuck close to John and together they made for the centre of the town.

They stopped outside a large hotel. " Let's go in and ask for a room," John said.

Peter hesitated.

" We've got to do it sooner or later," John urged. " It's nearly eleven o'clock and I don't suppose they'll have one. Better do it now, late at night when the porter's tired. We'll see how he reacts."

" It's not worth it," Peter said. " Let's sleep in the country."

" Snap out of it," John said. " We decided against the country months ago. The railway was O.K. and the hotels are going to be O.K. too."

It was a large hotel which would, in England, have been of the Victorian period, but it had been modernised. The walls of the entrance hall were covered in green plastic paint and there was a carpet of modern design on the floor. Several people were sitting in a lounge on the left of the entrance hall.

John went straight up to the hall porter's desk at the far end of the room. He spoke respectfully but with confidence, adopting the role of a member of a defeated nation, but a free worker and not an ex-prisoner of war.

" *Haben Sie, bitte, ein Doppel-Zimmer frei?* "

The porter said something Peter did not understand. John thanked the man and moved towards the door. Peter followed him out on to the street.

" What did he say ? " he asked.

" He said all the rooms were taken."

" I don't like it," Peter said. " We don't even know if foreign workers are allowed to stay in hotels. Did he seem surprised when you asked ? "

" I don't think so. I don't see why foreign workers shouldn't stay in hotels."

" They do some funny things in Germany. They have separate clubs for the foreign workers. I don't see why they shouldn't have separate hotels too."

" We'll try a smaller hotel next time," John said. " Let's go back to the station. The cheaper hotels are usually near the station."

They tried four more hotels and finally found themselves back outside the railway station.

" This is worse than London," John said. " What do we do now ? "

" Let's get out into the country," Peter suggested. " Let's walk out of the town and sleep under a hedge."

They walked for two hours, passing from the industrial city through an area of fine, large houses into the suburbs. They passed through the suburbs and finally came out on to a country lane running between flat fields.

" This is as far as I go," John said.

" We can't sleep here," Peter said. " We must find some sort of cover."

" I'm tired. I must sleep."

" Let's walk a bit more. We're bound to find a barn or something soon."

" I don't care what it is as long as I sleep."

John was finished now. Finished with the digging, the bad air and the strain. They walked on, John stumbling and muttering to himself about sleep. Sleep on a hard bench or even on the gravel by the side of the road. His eyes were pricking as though there were sand under the lids, and his mouth was dry.

They came to a large house standing back from the road, a fine brick house with a high-pitched roof. A typical, angular German farm. There was a notice fixed to one of the brick gate pillars. John stood close to the gate trying to read the notice which was surmounted by a cross.

" It's a Kloster," he said. " A convent. I wonder if they'd give us sanctuary."

" Not in Germany. In France or Holland perhaps, but not in Germany. Imagine an escaping German prisoner going to an English convent and asking for sanctuary. No, it's no use asking for help in Germany. Let's walk on."

They walked on down the road looking for a suitable place to hide up for the night. Finally Peter pointed out a concrete drain running through a deep ditch and passing as a tunnel under the road.

" Let's go down there," he said.

They climbed down the weed- and scrub-covered slope and found a secluded spot hidden from the road above. They opened their bags and ate the sandwiches they had brought with them from the camp.

" To-morrow we start on the dog food," Peter said.

When they had eaten they settled down to sleep. They slept just as they were, in their mackintoshes and their shoes, their heads on their bags, side by side on the rough damp ground.

An hour later Peter woke shivering. He was wearing thick

woollen underclothes, two shirts, a sweater, a naval uniform and a mackintosh ; and he woke shivering. He rose quietly to his feet, afraid of waking John, but John was already awake.

" Let's put my mackintosh on the ground to lie on and put yours over us," John said.

They swung their arms to restore the circulation and did as he suggested. They fell asleep again huddled together for warmth, but they woke later because their backs were cold. So they lay back to back and slept fitfully until just before dawn.

CHAPTER TWO

The Train Check

THEY LEFT their hiding place before it was light and after cleaning one another down they walked back the way they had come, into the town. It was still dark in the streets, but everywhere the German people were hurrying to their work.

As they came into the town they met the early morning trams and by the time they reached the railway station it was almost light. The booking hall was crowded and Peter followed John as he threaded his way towards the notice board. He felt safer as part of this early morning crowd, less vulnerable than when they were walking in the open street.

John stood looking at the board for some minutes, then turned and made towards a less crowded part of the hall.

" There's a train for Küstrin in an hour's time," he said. " It's a local stopping train."

" We'll take that," Peter said. " Let's go and try to get a cup of coffee to warm us up a bit."

" We don't know if it's rationed—but after all we're supposed to be foreigners. Can't be expected to know everything."

" We mustn't go to the Red Cross stalls on the platform," Peter told him. " They're for troops only."

" How do you know that ? "

" Got it off one of the guards in the hospital. Started boasting about our Red Cross and he unbuttoned and told me all about theirs."

The waiting-room was warm and crowded and smelled strongly of German cigarettes. They found a place at one of the tables

135

and sat there awkwardly, not talking. It was difficult to sit there not talking and yet look natural.

Peter looked round him at the people sitting at the tables. They were mostly in uniform and seemed uninterested in the two young Frenchmen sitting silently in the middle of the room. He took out a blue paper packet of cigarettes and offered them to John. John took one and thanked him in fluent French. Peter grinned in outward comprehension, shrugging his shoulders in what he hoped was the French manner.

They had been sitting there for some time before Peter realised that there were no waiters. It was a " help-yourself " counter. John's back was to the counter and he had not seen it. Peter could not speak so he kicked John's foot, but John only smiled reassuringly. Peter picked up a newspaper from the chair next to him and appeared to study it. He took the pencil from his pocket and wrote in the margin NO WAITERS—HELP YOURSELF, and passed the paper to John who tore the margin from the paper, folded it and put it in his pocket. He yawned elaborately and looked at his watch. Then he said something in French and walked over to the counter.

The coffee was ersatz and not very hot. It was made from acorns—the same brand that had been issued in Dulag-Luft. The rations weren't so bad, I suppose, Peter thought. Coming straight from an English standard they seemed foul enough—but by their own standard I suppose they weren't so bad. He looked round him at the workmen and soldiers sitting at the tables. None of them was eating. None of them looked very fit. He looked at John. We look too fit, he thought, although if we were looking for an escaped prisoner in England I shouldn't go for a very fit-looking man. Have to shave soon. He ran his hand under his chin. It'll do. It'll do to-day anyway. Like to clean my teeth too. Daren't go to a wash-and-brush-up place—too intimate. Have to stick it, I suppose. Wonder what John's thinking about ? Looks a bit strained. Wish I could do more to help. Pretty useless not knowing the lingo. Must be a devil of a strain doing all the talking. I'll try to do all the worrying about policy and let

him do the talking. He's good though—looks more French than
the French. Wonder if I look French ? More like an Italian, I
should think. He looked round him at the German people in the
room. They still seemed unsuspicious. He fell to thinking of
the prison camp—wondering what they were doing now—until
John roused him and they went out to buy their tickets for the
train.

Once again Peter stood back from the queue while John
bought the tickets. Peter joined him as he left the queue. They
went upstairs and across a footbridge, without speaking, and
came to the barrier at the end of the platform. John handed the
tickets to the collector.

The collector handed the tickets back and said something Peter
did not understand. John replied in German. The collector
shouted and pointed first to the tickets and then to the destination
board which read KÜSTRIN. John blushed and looked at the
tickets. He turned away, and led Peter to a quiet place away
from the people who were crowding the platform.

" What's the matter ? " Peter whispered.

" They gave us tickets to Berlin instead of Küstrin. It sounds
much the same in German. I'll go and change them."

" No—it'll need too much explanation. Keep them and go
to another grille and buy two more. We've plenty of money."

John looked relieved. " O.K. I was wondering how to cope
with the explanation."

They went back to the booking hall and bought two more
tickets, this time to Küstrin. They got past the ticket collector
who was now shouting at someone else ; and on to the platform.

" Get into a crowded compartment," Peter said, and climbed
into a third-class compartment more like a cattle truck than a
passenger coach. He entered through the door at the end of the
coach. It was a non-smoking section and separated from the rest
of the coach by sliding doors. Through the glass of the sliding
doors he could see that the other part of the coach was overcrowded.

"We'll stay here," he said. "Perhaps no one else will get in."

They sat there until the sliding doors were opened by a German soldier. He shouted loudly and began to push them out of the compartment. If only they wouldn't scream so much I might be able to get what they're talking about, John thought. He scrambled out of the coach and joined Peter, who was already on the platform. The man stood in the doorway shouting after them as they walked down the platform.

"What's wrong now?" Peter whispered.

John drew a deep breath. "That carriage was reserved for Russian prisoners of war. I saw the notice on the side as we got off."

"Definitely not the place for us!"

They climbed into another third-class carriage. This was full of civilians and they stood at one end of the compartment, trying to appear unconcerned.

The train stopped at every station and people got in and out. It seemed to Peter that the journey would never end. At every stop he expected the Gestapo to arrive, and stood in terror until the train began to move again. They did not talk. After a time they managed to get a seat and sat with closed eyes until they got to Küstrin.

They arrived at Küstrin at ten o'clock in the morning. There was no identity card check at the barrier and they left the station and walked into the town. It was a small town, much smaller than Frankfurt, and Peter did not like the look of it.

"It's too small," he said. "We can't walk about here, we shall be noticed. Let's get out of the town and eat our lunch. There won't be any more workmen's trains until this evening and we can't hang about here until then."

They left the station square and walked into the town. It was quiet, sleepy; and they were sure they would be noticed. After nearly two years of imprisonment the town was strange to Peter, frightening. He had not been in Germany before the war and he did not know what to expect.

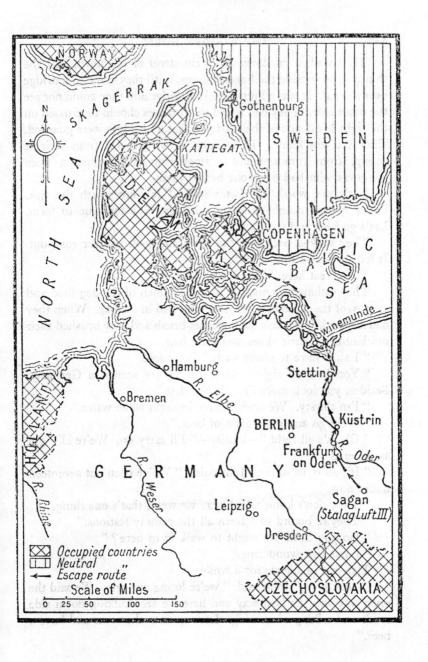

They walked on down the main street of the town, past the thin queues outside the bakers' shops, until they came to a bridge over a canal. It was a hump-backed bridge and they could not see the other side. They had heard that bridges should be crossed on the right-hand side of the road and that all bridges were guarded. They did not know. Their only knowledge was from Kriegie gossip, from rumours and a smattering of information from prisoners who had been out before them.

" It's not worth it," Peter said. " It's not worth the risk. Fancy getting caught crossing a bridge. It's too true to form. Let's go back and try another road."

They walked back into the town and took another road out. It led them to a public park.

" We'll eat here," John said.

They rationed themselves to a cubic inch of the dog food and ate two of the American biscuits John had in his bag. When they had finished, John took out a clothes brush and they brushed their mackintoshes, their shoes and their hair.

" I shall have to shave soon," Peter said.

" You look all right. Razor blades are scarce in Germany. Besides, you look more French like that."

" I'm thirsty. We should have brought some water."

" We'll go and get a glass of beer."

" Oh, it's all right "—hastily—" I'll carry on. We're all right as we are."

" It's all right so far," John said. " We've been out seventeen hours now."

" They don't know which way we went, that's one thing."

" They're bound to inform all the railway stations."

" Do you think we ought to walk from here ? "

" I was just wondering."

They sat in silence for a while.

" Look here," John said, " we're losing our grip. We said the open way was the best way and here we are skulking down side roads and talking of walking. Let's go into the town and have a beer."

" Here comes a policeman," Peter said.

John looked up. A policeman was walking slowly towards them down the path.

" That settles it. Let's go and have that beer ! "

Without appearing to hurry they got to their feet and walked towards the policeman.

" Say something in French just as we pass him," Peter said. " Say something intelligent in case he speaks French."

When they were within a few paces of the policeman John broke into voluble French. Peter tried to look as if he understood. And then they were past. John went on talking and Peter listened for the policeman to turn round ; listened for the hail and the sound of pursuing footsteps. But he didn't turn round and they walked on like that for a hundred yards.

" What did you say ? " Peter asked.

" I couldn't think what to say, so I told you all about a letter I'd had from my Aunt Annette who had bronchitis, and said that my sister Marie was having another baby."

" Good show ! It worked anyway. What shall we do now ? "

" Go into town and have that beer. They serve a coupon-free meal in some of these places."

" Yes, I know, it's called a *Stammgericht*."

They found a café, went in and sat down. It was a large room with heavy, dark wooden tables and chairs. There were four men sitting at a table in the window. They looked like local tradesmen.

Peter and John sat at a table at the other side of the room. It had a red and white check tablecloth and a menu in a wooden holder. A waitress came from a room at the end of the café and stood by their table.

" *Zwei Glas dunkle Bier, bitte*," John said.

" *Zwei Glas dunkles*," she repeated, and went away. She returned shortly with two glasses of beer. It was dark beer in tall glasses, and each glass had a white collar of foam.

" *Danke schön*." John handed her a coin. She groped in the pocket of her apron and handed him several smaller coins which he returned to her.

" *Danke sehr*," she said, and smiled.

John lifted his glass and winked at Peter. " Not bad, what ? " he said when the waitress was out of earshot.

" Not bad." Peter was watching the men in the window. They had stopped talking and were all staring.

Wonder what we've done wrong, he thought. Wonder if foreigners are allowed in here. Wish I knew more about it. It's all this working in the dark. We don't even know if there *are* such things as free French workers. It would be bad enough if we knew what to expect, but working in the dark like this we might barge into anything. Wonder if we can smoke in here. He looked again at the men in the window. One of them was smoking a pipe. He took out his cigarettes and offered them to John, who thanked him in French.

The waitress came in carrying a tray loaded with four large white pottery bowls. They were steaming. She put one in front of each of the men. Peter watched closely. Money passed, but no coupons. This was the coupon-free meal. As she turned away from the table Peter caught her eye. He beckoned and gestured towards the table in front of him. She smiled and vanished into the kitchen.

The *Stammgericht* was a stew made from swedes, potatoes and carrots, but no meat. It was a generous helping, filling and warm. They had two more of the weak German beers and felt more full than they had felt since they had escaped. With a full stomach came renewed confidence.

" What do we do now ? " John asked.

" Better not stay here. It'll look obvious if we stay here too long. Let's walk round the town."

But it was worse in the street. Everyone seems to have something to do except us, Peter thought. Bad enough trying to spend an afternoon in a small English town, but this is getting on my nerves. This is going to be the worst part of the whole show, this trying to look inconspicuous with nothing to do. They tried looking into shop windows ; but all the time the feeling of being watched grew more acute.

" I hate this town," John said. " Let's get out of it."

" No—we mustn't catch a train until it's dark. We've got to stay here until it's dark."

" We've got to do something. These one-street towns give me the willies. What about going back to the park ? "

" Better not do that—we're inviting conversation if we sit

They had stopped talking and were all staring

there. Besides, it's afternoon now and all the women will be there. Much better to stay here."

" I can't stay here," John said. " It's getting on my nerves. We're too conspicuous walking up and down the street."

" Let's look at this objectively," Peter said. " What should we do in England if we had a few hours to waste ? "

" Go to the public library or a museum."

" Or to the cinema. Why not go to the cinema ? "

John grinned. " We escape from a prison camp and the first afternoon out we go to the pictures."

" It'll be safer than the streets," Peter said.

" I bet we're the first escaped Kriegies to go to the pictures."

" That's why we'll get through. Keep it fluid. Do the natural thing. What could be more natural than going to the cinema ? "

They walked towards the cinema, feeling better now that they were doing something, and less conspicuous. There was a queue, and they joined it. The queue was mostly children, with a few women, an old man and some soldiers. They were the only young men in civilian clothes. They stood at the end of the queue hoping that no one would talk to them.

It was not a comfortable cinema and most of the seats were broken. Peter found himself next to a young soldier who sat sleeping, his head fallen forward on his chest. He remembered the cinema in Cambridge. Of how he would go there in the afternoon when he had been flying the night before, and of how empty it would be up there in the balcony with only the chattering of the children in the pit below. Of the soft lighting and the organ music, and of how he himself used to fall asleep as soon as the lights went down and the picture started. Of how the sound of a shot or the sudden scream of the heroine would jerk him into wakefulness, only to fall asleep again to wake finally with a dry mouth and stagger out into the strong afternoon sunshine. And thinking of this he fell asleep until John wakened him when it was time to go for the train to Stettin.

It was nearly dark when they came out of the cinema and they walked quickly to the railway station at the far end of the town.

" What was the film about ? " Peter asked.

" Oh, it was an escapist sort of film—a comedy about a Berlin family on holiday in the Alps. There was nothing about the war in it. I saw you were asleep and was rather frightened you'd wake up suddenly and say something in English."

"I was too tired for that—slept like a log. I feel much better now."

"I could do with a spot of the old bed," John said. "Didn't sleep much last night. I'd like to get my clothes off too. I'm sticky. I'd give anything for a bath and a good night's sleep."

It was a small railway station and John felt conspicuous as he asked for the tickets. Stettin was a Baltic port, a more dangerous destination to ask for. The clerk demanded his papers. He produced his Ausweis and waited nervously.

"Your permission to travel?"

John handed over the rest of his forged papers. He tried to imagine he was buying a ticket in England.

The clerk picked up the papers and glanced at them casually. "*Gut!*" He handed over the tickets.

John took the tickets and his papers and walked away from the ticket office. He could hardly believe it. It had been as easy as that. He joined Peter and they walked up the steps to the platform.

The train was full and again they had to stand in the corridor. There were no lights in the corridor, which was so packed that it would have been impossible for a ticket collector to move down it.

It was a strain to stand there, surrounded by Germans, doing nothing, frightened all the time that they were about to be discovered. It was in the trains, when they could neither move nor speak, that they had time to think.

An hour later they stopped at a large station. Most of the passengers left the train here and a number of them went to the buffet where Peter could see them drinking soup. They were hungry and thirsty, but they stayed in the darkness of the railway carriage rather than brave the lights of the buffet.

When the train started again it was less crowded. They were able to sit on their bags in the corridor; and before long they were both asleep.

They were awakened by the sound of shouting. The typical bullying shouts of a German who has been given authority. It

was the ticket collector, and with him were two of the Bahnhofs
Polizei, the railway police.

John got the tickets ready and watched them work their
way down the corridor, inspecting tickets as they came. In most
cases the ticket collector merely said "*Weiter!*" as he
handed the tickets back to the passengers, but occasionally he
asked for their identity papers which were examined by the
police.

Here we go, Peter thought. He glanced at John who sat white-
faced and silent at his side. Next to him sat an old woman. As
the men approached she showed obvious signs of panic. By
the time the collector reached her she was almost crying with
fear.

"*Ausweis, bitte!*" the ticket collector shouted.

The old woman fumbled in her bag. The ticket collector stood
waiting. She produced a grimy piece of paper. The man handed
it back angrily and shouted again. She said nothing but continued
to offer the grimy piece of paper.

"*Polizeiliche!*" the collector screamed. "*Polizeiliche!*"

The old woman did not reply. One of the Polizei shook her
roughly by the arm. The ticket collector grew red in the face.
"*Polizeiliche!*" he shouted.

The old woman said nothing but sat hopeless on her bag.
The collector said something to one of the policemen who took
the old woman roughly by the arm and began to push her down
the corridor. Peter could hear her whimpered protests as she
was roughly jostled down the corridor towards the guard's van
at the rear of the train.

The ticket collector turned to John, who handed over their
tickets and waited apprehensively for the demand for their papers.
The collector glanced at the tickets and handed them back without
speaking.

When they had gone Peter sat on his bag in the corridor and
broke out in a cold sweat. His knees fluttered and he felt sick.
They had passed the first train check. The old woman had saved
them. Their papers had taken them past the clerks in the booking

offices but so far they had not been inspected by the police. He prayed that their luck would hold.

Just before eight o'clock the train began to slow down. Peter, who was dozing, was awakened by the changing tempo of the rhythm of the wheels. He looked at his watch and wakened John, who was sleeping on his bag in the corner of the corridor.

" We're running in, John. If the train stops outside the station let's get off. There aren't enough passengers aboard to make a crowd. I think it would be safer to jump off outside the station and walk into the town."

" We'll be O.K."

" We might need a special pass to go as far north as this."

" You need a special pass to go anywhere," John told him. " We'll be all right."

" If the train slows down we ought to jump." Peter did not like this confidence in John. It had been easy enough in the camp to talk of travelling openly, but now he was frightened of it.

John got to his feet and dusted his trousers. " O.K.—as you like. That was a pretty good sleep. I feel better now. What about a spot to eat ? "

" We'll go into the lavatory and make some porridge."

In the lavatory at the end of the corridor Peter opened his case and took out a linen bag of dry oatmeal and a small tin. He mixed the oatmeal with water from the tap and handed the tin to John. " I hope the water's all right," he said. " We should have brought some purifying tablets."

" There's a lot of things we should have brought. We'll get by. It's a cinch now. We've done half the journey."

" In terms of miles."

John was feeling happy now and full of confidence. " Let's go right in."

" Not if the train stops. If the train stops we get out."

But the train did not stop and before long they steamed into Stettin station.

There were more people on the train than Peter had thought,

and they were swept towards the barrier by the crowd. John pushed forward to see if there was a paper check. He looked back at Peter and grinned. The passengers were handing in their tickets and passing off the platform without showing their papers. Then they were at the barrier. A quick tightening of the stomach muscles as they came under the lamp—a moment's panic—and they were through the barrier and free to go into the town.

CHAPTER THREE

Nearly Caught

WHEN THEY came out of the railway station it was raining. A cold wind blew in from across the Baltic bringing with it a fine, steady rain that whipped their faces as they stood in the bomb-damaged station square.

" We've got to find shelter of some sort." John buttoned the collar of his mackintosh. " Let's try the hotels. We'd better get in somewhere before midnight. There may be a curfew for foreigners in this town."

" It's Saturday night." Peter was still doubtful about the hotels. " We haven't much hope of getting in."

" We'll have to try," John said. " Unless we stay in the waiting-room until morning."

" No fear ! Waiting-rooms are the most dangerous places. Police check every two or three hours. Why not sleep out again ? "

" It's too wet," John said. " Besides, we must find somewhere to shave. Come on ! "

They stepped out into the driving rain.

Peter shivered. " It's cold."

" Walk fast," John said. " We'll soon get warm."

They walked quickly down the street, past the shells of bombed buildings, gaunt and forbidding in the darkness. There were piles of rubble in the streets and the pavements were uneven and broken where the bombs had fallen.

" Pretty good mess, what ? " Peter said. " I wonder if any hotels are still standing. We could sleep in one of these bombed-out houses."

149

"Too risky. They might think we were looting. Get shot for that in Germany."

The streets were dark and strangely quiet.

"I hope there isn't a curfew," Peter said.

"We'll know when we try the first hotel. Even if there is we can explain that we've just come off the train—though I can't see what reason we can give for getting off here instead of going straight on to Anklam."

"You can say that as it's Sunday to-morrow we thought the factory would be closed. And we thought it would be better to stay for the week-end and go on up to Anklam on Monday morning."

"I doubt if I could say all that in German."

They walked on down the dark wind- and rain-swept street, peering into each doorway as they passed.

"It's this infernal blackout," John said. "It's worse than London."

"I wonder what Phil's doing," Peter said.

"If he hasn't been caught he'll be in Danzig by now—he'd have arrived in Danzig last night. He's either on a boat or in a police cell by now."

"He wasn't equipped for sleeping out."

"No, he won't sleep out. His was an 'all or nothing' effort. He's either on a boat or back in the cells."

Peter laughed. "I bet he's sitting in the hold of some ship eating margarine samples and wondering about us. I don't think he gave very much for our chances."

"That's why he didn't come with us."

"I'm glad he didn't," Peter said. "Three would have been too many. He binds too much. He'd have been binding all the time because it's raining. Remember how he used to bind all the time when we didn't dig because of the rain?"

"We must have been pretty trying," John said.

They stopped outside an imposing stone building with a classical portico and mahogany revolving doors.

"It looks like a club." Peter was doubtful. "It doesn't say it's an hotel."

"Perhaps they don't in Germany. We might as well try anyway."

John pushed his way through the revolving doors. Peter followed, feeling suddenly disreputable and ashamed of his appearance. The carpets were too deep, the air of solid German respectability too strong. He caught John by the arm.

"Let's get out of this," he whispered.

He moved quickly towards the swing doors. John, infected by the sudden panic in Peter's voice, moved with him. They passed quickly through the swing doors and out into the darkness of the street.

"What's the matter?" John asked.

"I don't know. I don't like it. Let's try somewhere else."

"What was wrong with it?" John said.

"I don't know—it seemed wrong somehow. It didn't seem the sort of place foreign workers would stay at. Let's try somewhere else."

"We can't walk round all night looking for hotels."

"All right, we'll try the next one. But I've got a hunch about this place."

"You're always getting hunches—and I'd got my German all ready."

They walked on down the street until they came to a smaller building with a dimly illuminated sign which read " HOTEL."

"That looks all right," Peter said.

John walked in and Peter followed. The lobby had linoleum on the floor and smelled of disinfectant. In one corner was a box for the night porter. The box was empty. In the opposite corner the linoleum-covered stairs rose crookedly to the floor above.

They stood waiting in the middle of the lobby. The place was silent.

"I'll go upstairs," John said.

Peter followed him, not wanting to stay alone in the hall. Not wanting to be left to cope with his lack of German without John. On the floor above was a landing. Opening off the landing were several doors. One was open. There were beds in the room, beds standing in rows, and orderly, as in a barrack room.

" This is no good," Peter said.

He led John quickly down the stairs and out on to the street. They were in the street again and it was still raining. John was growing angry.

" What the . . ." he began, but Peter went on down the street.

" That was too cheap," he said. " It was a sort of doss-house."

" What if it was ? It's a bed and it's dry."

" They're likely to ask questions in a place like that. It's too cheap. They're likely to have police checks and goodness knows what. It's the sort of place they look for deserters in. We want a more expensive place." He was shivering.

" You said that last place was too expensive. We can't afford to be choosey."

" We've *got* to be choosey. That's just what we've got to be. If the place is too cheap it's dangerous because it's liable to police checks—and if it's too luxurious it's dangerous because we're conspicuous. We've got to find a quiet, respectable family hotel."

" Then we'd better ask a policeman," John said angrily.

" We might do worse than that."

" Don't be silly ! "

They were both angry now. Angry and tired, frightened and wet to the skin. Angry and bewildered because they hadn't imagined it would be like this ; angry because they were suddenly without a plan and outside the routine they had known so long.

Presently they were at the bottom of the hill, walking along the main street towards the centre of the town. They had tried several hotels, but they were all full.

" It's no good," John said at length. " It's Saturday night. Let's walk out of the town and find somewhere to sleep."

" O.K." Peter said it with relief. " We'll find a hotel to-morrow," he added. " We'll find somewhere dry to kip down to-night. A railway arch or something."

" Which way shall we go ? "

" Let's go south. If we go north it's the sea, and east and west we go along the coast."

He took the small compass from his pocket and studied it by the light of his torch.

" We'll go down to the Square," he said, " and take the main road going south."

They walked down a long, straight, concrete road with a cemetery on one side and large brick buildings on the other.

" If the worse comes to the worst we can sleep in the cemetery," John said.

" It'll be locked. They always lock cemeteries at night."

" We can climb over."

" It's not worth it. We might be seen climbing over. It's not worth the risk. I don't suppose it would be very comfortable anyway."

" No, but it would be quiet."

They walked on past the cemetery, past the large buildings, until they came to an area of small suburban houses.

" This looks like going on for miles," John said.

" I wish we knew if there was a curfew."

" Even if there is, I don't expect it's until midnight. What time is it now ? "

Peter looked at his watch. " Eleven-thirty."

" Well, we've got half an hour before midnight. We'll push on and see what we come to."

And all this time they were walking down the long, straight, concrete road, with the rain slanting down, running down inside their collars, soaking their trouser legs, falling, bouncing back off the pavement, steady, continuous, drumming rain.

When they had been walking for some time Peter saw a policeman approaching them, tall, jack-booted and wearing a sword.

He was on the opposite side of the road, but when he saw them he started to cross.

" I'll talk French," John said. " Be listening to me, but look at him as you go past."

" Let's run."

" No—look at him. We'll be all right." He began talking fast in French.

They went on as they were. The policeman crossed the road to intercept them. He's going to stop us, Peter thought. What shall we tell him ? What excuse can we give for walking out here at this time of night ?

" Tell him we're going to visit friends," he whispered, but John went on talking in French.

They were abreast of the policeman now and Peter looked at him. He half stopped as though to accost them, and John let fly a torrent of excited French. He waved his hands and hunched his shoulders. He's wonderful, Peter thought. What a man ! Good old John. And they were safely past the policeman and he hadn't stopped them. But he had stopped. Peter could not hear his footsteps and imagined him standing there watching them and wondering whether to turn and follow.

" Turn down here," he said.

It was a side street. They turned down out of the policeman's sight. Peter quickened his pace.

" I think he's following," he said. " I don't think he likes the look of us."

They were at the end of the street. It was a cul-de-sac and there was no way out.

" We've had it now ! " John said.

" Through the garden—quick ! "

Peter glanced over his shoulder. The policeman was standing at the top of the road watching them.

" Look as though we're going into the house." Peter walked into one of the front gardens where he was hidden from the policeman's sight.

" He's coming down the road," John said.

Peter tried the gate leading to the back garden. It was locked.

" Give me a hand."

John stooped and locked his hands. Peter put a foot in them and caught the top of the gate. He hauled himself up and put

"*He's coming down the road,*" *John said*

down a hand for John. Then they were standing, trembling, on the far side of the gate.

"We can't go back," John said.

"Let's climb over the fences into the next street."

"O.K., but look out for dogs."

There was a low fence at the end of the garden. They climbed it and found themselves ankle deep in newly turned earth.

"It's allotments," John said.

"Find a path and cut along behind the houses."

They found a path and followed it along the fence. It was dark and quiet and slippery, and there seemed no way out.

"We'd better sleep here," Peter said.

"What? Among the cabbages?"

"No—in one of these air raid shelters." He had stopped behind one of the gardens and pointed to a covered trench near the fence. "Let's crawl in there and sleep."

"It'll be dry at least," John said. "I'm wet through."

They climbed the fence again and crawled into the air raid shelter. It was a trench. W in plan and about four feet deep. It was so built that it was difficult to lie down and impossible to stand up. The rain had seeped in and formed a thick slime of mud on the bottom of the trench.

"A typical goon effort," John said.

"Uncomfortable—but I expect it's safe enough."

"I don't only want safety. I want sleep. Let's go and find a more comfortable one."

They tried several and finally found a wooden shed with earth banked up at the sides and the top covered with turf. Inside was a bale of straw. As an air raid shelter it was useless. As a hide-out for the night it was just what they were looking for. They took off their mackintoshes and their boots and socks.

"I could do with a drink!" Peter said.

"Put out the old tin and collect some rain-water."

"I will. I'll put it out now and then we'll have a drink for to-morrow morning." He rummaged in his bag for the tin. "What about a spot of porridge?"

"It'll take too long to collect the water. I'll have a piece of dog food. What I want most is sleep."

Peter took out the dog food and cut two pieces about two inches square. He cut it by the light of the torch shielded in John's hands. The air raid shelter looked warm and comfortable in the dim light. "We could live here for days," he said.

"We've got to have a base in town. This is too far out. We must get somewhere where we can wash and shave, otherwise we'll begin to look like tramps. Respectability's the thing. My jacket's soaked. Are you taking yours off or leaving it on?"

"I'm leaving mine on—it'll dry quicker like that. We'll burrow down in the straw and they'll dry on us."

"I hope we wake before it's light. Don't forget we've got to get out of this place."

"The policeman will be gone by then," Peter said. "We'll wake up all right. I give us about three hours and then we'll be awake shivering."

"Not me!" John said. "I'm really sleeping to-night."

He burrowed down into the straw and Peter heaped more on top of him. Presently they were both asleep.

CHAPTER FOUR

The Chase In The Docks

WHEN PETER awoke it was still dark. At the moment of waking he thought he was back in his bunk in the prison camp and he put up his hand to rearrange the rolled-up shirt under his head. Then he felt the straw, and he was fully awake and remembering where he was. He fumbled in his jacket pocket for the torch and, shielding the light under the jacket, he looked at his watch. It was five forty-five. He flashed the torch over John. He was sleeping like a child, one hand under his head and his hair falling forward over his face.

Peter rose quietly and opened the door of the air raid shelter. It had stopped raining and there was a keen wind. He looked up at the sky. It was paling slightly in the east and scattered remnants of cumulus cloud chased one another across the horizon. A few stars showed in the full zenith of the sky and the air smelt good and clean.

Well, this is our second free dawn, he thought. He looked carefully all round him—at the backs of the houses and then at the allotments behind. Not a light showed. In the distance he could hear the faint clanking of a shunting train and suddenly close at hand a cock crowed loudly. It's Sunday morning, he thought, perhaps people won't be getting up so early. We'd better get moving though. We must find somewhere to get a shave. And then a meal.

He stooped to where he had left the tin. It was half-full of water. He went back into the shelter and mixed some dry oatmeal with the water in the tin. He shook John gently by the arm.

158

" *On appel, mein Herr,*" he said. " *On appel, bitte, mein Herr!* "

John grunted and rolled over.

" Come on, wake up, John ! "

John opened his eyes.

" Come on, John, time to get cracking. I've made some porridge."

John grunted again. He ran his fingers through his hair and groaned. " I've got a mouth like the bottom of a parrot's cage."

" It's a lovely morning. Eat some porridge and we'll get out of here before anyone else is about."

" I'm stiff ! " John said. " I can hardly move. I think I've got rheumatism."

" Nonsense—you've been sleeping too heavily, that's all. Here's your breakfast. Leave half for me."

John began to eat slowly. " I'm hungry enough, but this stuff takes some getting down."

" You'll be all right once you get it inside you," Peter assured him.

John ate half the porridge and handed the tin to Peter. " Is that all we get ? "

" I've got some biscuits but I thought I'd save them until we can get a drink."

John put on his collar and tie and then his socks and shoes. He got to his feet and stumbled towards the door. Peter collected his things together and joined him outside in the garden.

" Shall we go back the same way ? " John asked.

" I was just thinking. There must be a way out other than through the garden. We don't want to be seen climbing over the gate. Let's walk down behind the houses."

They walked back along the path behind the fence at the bottom of the gardens until they came to an alleyway between two of the houses. This led them out on to the main road.

" If we don't find anywhere we'll come back here to-night," Peter said.

"We shan't need anywhere," John told him. "We'll get a ship. This is going to be our lucky day."

The sun was shining as they came into the city and the streets were clean and sparkling in the freshness of the morning. Early workers were hurrying to and fro and the first tramcars were grinding their way up the steep hills of the town.

"Where do we go from here?" John asked.

"Let's go down to the docks and have a look at the shipping."

They walked down the steep cobbled street until they came to the docks. There was a sea breeze and the air was full of the sea. There were ships in the harbour, some of them wearing their wartime coat of grey paint, others painted black and red and white, brave and toylike in the sun. As Peter and John drew nearer they could see that most of them were flying the German flag.

They did a quick tour of the docks, walking fast to avoid suspicion, but they saw no neutral shipping. Most of the bigger ships lay moored away from the quayside. The smaller boats were berthed alongside the quays but these were obviously fishing vessels and no use to them.

"This isn't what I expected," Peter said. "I expected to find them at the side of the docks." He realised then that he had not really thought of the escape beyond the railway. He had always thought of the docks as being the objective. Getting to the docks had been as good as getting home to him. Now they were there, and the difficulties were just beginning. From now on they would have to make their plans as they went along.

"They've got to load and unload sometime," John told him.

"Perhaps the best thing would be to hang around a bit and see what happens."

"Better not hang around the docks too long. That's just where they'd expect to find us. Let's take a walk round the town and get the lie of the land. We'll try a few more hotels and get a room for a couple of nights. What we want is a headquarters. Then we can take our time and make our plans."

They walked up into the town, this time through the shopping centre, with the shops shut because it was Sunday and the streets crowded with people. It was strange to be free to walk through the streets again. To look into shop windows and see the cars and motor buses with their wood burners attached to the luggage carrier or towed behind on two-wheeled trailers. It was strange to be among people who had a purpose in life, who had somewhere to go, who were not just passing the time until the next roll-call or waiting for the soup to arrive.

Three hours later they again found themselves down by the docks. All this time they had been searching for a place to stay. Everywhere they had been told that the hotel was full.

"This is a dead loss," John said. "I feel inclined to stow away on one of these fishing boats and trust to luck."

"We mustn't be in too much of a hurry," Peter told him. "It's taken us four and a half months to get as far as this. We don't want to throw it all away in a few minutes and get marched back to the camp after being out for a couple of days. This is all new to us and it's worth giving it some thought. We must get out a plan of campaign. Here we are in Stettin and we want to get to Sweden. We've a little German money, good papers—we've proved that—and fairly good civilian clothes. We speak a little German and we have some food."

"Yes," John said, "and we've nowhere to sleep to-night and there's most likely a curfew for foreign workers. We've got to be safely stowed away somewhere by the evening. Most of the ships in the docks seem to be German. Even if they were Swedish, I don't see how we could get out to them."

"The only way is to meet the sailors ashore," Peter said. "Contact the crew ashore and arrange with them to get us on the ship." It seemed simple to him as he said it, merely a matter of speaking a few words and perhaps the exchange of a little money.

But John was reluctant. He wanted to keep the thing as small as possible. To talk to complete strangers was making the thing too big—spreading the risk. "I don't like to," he said.

" But you said yourself we can't just wander aimlessly around. We've worked to a plan so far and now we've got as far as we planned."

" O.K.—we'll see what we can do. But if we have no luck by the afternoon we must organise somewhere to sleep before it gets too late. We don't want to get picked up on the streets after the curfew."

" Come on, snap out of it—we'll be all right."

Peter had been holding back because he was without a plan. But now he could see it clearly—to meet some of the seamen ashore. To make their arrangements to stow away safely—away from the docks. Not to go dashing into things, but to work slowly towards their objective.

They walked along the quays, looking at the men now and not at the shipping. There were Polish workers with the large " P " on a brassard worn on the arm, Ukrainians and Lithuanians with " OST " stencilled on their clothes, and scores of Frenchmen wearing an odd assortment of military uniform. In addition to these—all of whom were prisoners working under armed guard—there were the seamen of all the occupied nations, some in civilian clothes and some in the uniforms of their companies.

As they walked along one of the quays they came to a group of haggard men, stooping, thin and weary, with their feet tied in rags and the tattered remnants of green uniform hanging from their backs. By their queer spiked cloth helmets and ragged appearance Peter knew them to be Russians. These men were barely alive, too weak almost to lift the picks and shovels with which they were supposed to work. They moved slowly, eking out their meagre strength, never smiling, doomed to slavery until the war was over.

So long as they kept on the move and were not obviously loitering they felt safe enough in this polyglot crowd and moved slowly among them, trying to learn as much as they could about the docks.

" If we get caught again," John said, " we could try to pass as Frenchmen. If we get returned to this sort of thing it won't be so bad. Far better than being in a British camp. Look at the chance these chaps have of getting away."

" Let's have a word with one of them," Peter said.

" I've told you before, I don't like to talk to them. They'll know I'm not one of them by my accent, and it's dangerous."

" We shan't get anywhere unless we take some sort of risk," Peter said. " We've got to speak to them sometime."

" Yes—but not in the docks."

" The docks are as safe as anywhere else if you get them alone. Pick one that's walking on his own and ask him."

" Ask him what ? "

" Just speak to him in French and ask if he can tell you where to stay for the night."

" Supposing he starts to yell."

" He won't yell. We'll go down some dark side street off the docks and stop one there and ask him."

" All right," John said. " But I don't like it."

" I don't like it either, but we've got to take the risk sometime."

" All right, I'll try. You stand behind him while I'm talking and if he yells sock him behind the ear."

" I'll sock him behind the ear all right. I'll clock him with the tin of dog food."

They went down one of the quiet roads leading off the docks and accosted some of the more obvious Frenchmen who came along. In every case the man looked at them nervously and hurried on without speaking.

" What's the matter ? " Peter asked.

" They know I'm not a Frenchman. I expect they think I'm a German—a sort of ' agent provocateur.' This seems to be hopeless. I wish I knew exactly what these fellows are. They're French all right, but they don't seem to be prisoners of war."

" Let's try this one." Peter indicated a short, olive-complexioned man of about thirty years of age walking slowly towards them down the street. He wore a beret like themselves and a leather jerkin. Round his neck was a brightly coloured handkerchief.

"He's the last one," John said. "I'm frightened of some of the others coming back with the Gestapo."

He spoke to the Frenchman. Peter stood on one side, ready to go to his assistance if necessary. There was a quick exchange of fast-sounding French and the Frenchman pointed down the road. He appeared to be giving minute instructions with many extravagant gestures and emphasis, and finally shook John warmly by the hand. John said something to him and the Frenchman looked at Peter, smiled and called, "*Salut!*"

Peter grinned, wondering what it was all about. The Frenchman again shook hands with John, slapped him on the back, waved to Peter and walked on down the road.

"What did he say?" Peter asked.

"I think he guessed what we are. I didn't tell him, but I think he knew. He gave me an address—the Hotel Schobel. He advised me not to stay there more than two days, because, if you do, they have to send your papers in to the police."

"Where is it?"

"Down by the docks. It's not a very posh place, but he says that they usually have some rooms free."

"O.K.," Peter said, "let's go there."

They found the Hotel Schobel in a road leading off one of the docks. It was a large building, old-fashioned and shabby. The entrance hall had a tiled floor and a lavish display of carved woodwork and uncleaned brass.

They were greeted by the proprietor, a stout German with a close-cropped bullet head and half-spectacles, smoking a large curved pipe; a German of the last generation.

John began his carefully rehearsed German. "*Haben Sie ein Doppel-Zimmer . . . ?*"

Yes, apparently the proprietor had a double room. He pulled a bunch of blue forms from a drawer in his desk and handed them to John.

Peter pressed forward to see what John was writing. To his surprise the forms were printed in German, French and English. They filled in two of the forms, taking care to print in the continental manner they had practised in the camp. MARCEL LEVASSEUR, Peter wrote, BORN LILLE, 17 JULY 1914, EMPLOYED BY METALHUTTENWERK DR. HOFFMAN & CO., BRESLAU. NORMALLY RESIDENT IN LILLE.

John wrote, MARCEL CONDE, BORN PARIS, 2 OCTOBER 1921, EMPLOYED BY METALHUTTENWERK, BRESLAU. NORMALLY RESIDENT IN PARIS.

They produced their Ausweis to prove this and were asked to show their police permission to be in that town. John showed the form giving them permission to travel to Anklam and explained that they wanted to stay in Stettin for two nights so as to arrive in Anklam on Tuesday morning. The proprietor asked for his money in advance. And then they were free to go to their room.

It was a large room, the walls covered with floral wallpaper. A wardrobe stood against the wall opposite the door and a grotesque dressing-table filled the space in front of the single window. There was a double bed surmounted by floral drapes and a tiled stove like the outside of a public-house. In one corner, incongruously, stood a white wash-basin with chromium-plated hot and cold taps.

" Well, here we are," John said. " The first thing I'm going to do is wash."

He took off his clothes and crossed to the wash-basin. From ankles to wrists his body was black from the dye off the combinations he had worn in the tunnel. He turned on the hot water tap.

" It's a snare and a delusion," he said.

" What is ? " Peter was unfastening his bag.

" This basin. The hot water doesn't work."

" There's a war on, you know. I don't suppose they've got any coal."

" Oh, well, we'll have to manage in cold."

He took a piece of Red Cross soap from his bag and began to wash. Peter lay on the bed watching him.

" Why do you think those forms were printed in French and English ? " Peter asked.

" Oh, they had them before the war, I expect, and they're still using them."

" No wonder the Germans have an inferiority complex. Just imagine if English hotels had registration cards printed in German."

" They wouldn't have. English is an international language."

" Our menus are printed in French."

" Yes, but that's to kid ourselves. Not to help foreigners. That's just to kid ourselves that the cooking's good."

" What couldn't I do to a Chateaubriand steak ! " Peter said. He lay on his back on the bed as he had so often done in the prison camp, conjuring up his ideal meal. " A Chateaubriand steak garni, with spinach and French mustard, followed by green figs in syrup."

" Oh shut up ! " John said. " Make some porridge."

" Or a grilled Dover sole swimming in butter. Or even a good mixed grill."

" Shut up ! " John was standing on his towel furiously scrubbing at his legs. He looked very young standing there, thin and young and graceful against the background of floral wallpaper.

And suddenly Peter realised that John was near to breaking point. That talking to these Frenchmen had taken the last of his nervous strength. He cursed himself for a selfish fool. He had been pushing John harder than he should. " You don't want any more porridge," he said. " We'll get washed and go out and get a couple of beers and a Stammgericht."

" O.K.—but don't talk about food. I feel as though I haven't eaten for years."

" You've hardly eaten for forty-eight hours. I had a meal just before I left. I've got a spot of chocolate—how about that ? "

" Yes, please," John said, and ate it there and then standing on his towel by the wash-basin.

While John finished washing Peter slit open the lining of his mackintosh and took a waterproof bag from under the armpit. He opened it and took out a map which he spread out on the bed. With the map were a Swedish sailor's identity card and some German money.

" It's the Freihafen we want," he said, studying the map. " If we cross over the second bridge from the railway station it'll bring us straight to it. That's where the Swedish ships will be— if there are any. The dock we were in this morning was all wrong. If we get no joy at the Freihafen we'll go on to Reiherwerder coaling station and see if there's any chance of stowing away on a coaling barge."

" Is the club marked on the map ? "

" Yes—Number Seventeen Kleine Oder Strasse. But we won't use that except as a last resort. Remember what Stafford said. It's too dangerous."

The Freihafen was protected by an eighteen-foot diamond mesh wire fence with three strands of barbed wire running along the top. There were arc lamps over the wire and armed guards at the gates. The place looked like a prison camp.

They walked slowly round the outside of the docks. There were wooden buildings inside the wire but between them they could see the hulls and the funnels of the ships.

Suddenly John caught Peter by the arm.

" Look—a Swedish ship ! " Peter could see the black hull of a ship with the yellow cross and *Sverige* painted on her side.

" We'll get on board to-night," John said. " We'll come back after dark and climb aboard."

" There's bound to be a watchman on board," Peter said.

" It'll be one of the crew. They wouldn't have a German watchman in a guarded dock."

" I don't like it," Peter said. " I'd much rather try and get hold of one of the crew ashore. It's sticking our necks out to go into a place like that."

" We wouldn't be here if we hadn't stuck our necks out.

Besides we can't speak any Swedish and if we've got to talk to the crew it's going to be much safer in the ship than out here surrounded by goons. Anyway, she might be gone by to-morrow."

Peter allowed himself to be persuaded. He still did not like the idea of climbing into the docks, but as John said, they had to take some risks. By avoiding all unnecessary risks they might remain free, but they would not be getting anywhere.

They made a careful inspection of the fence and chose a spot where a railway siding ran close to the wire. It was half-way between the two arc lamps and by climbing on to the truck which stood on the siding they would be able to reach the top of the fence.

" Now we've got to find an exit," Peter said. " We may want to come back."

They chose a shed standing near the wire. It was directly in the light of the arc lamps but it was the only means of getting out of the docks.

They spent the afternoon at the cinema. The film was a story of ancient Germany called *Paracelsus* and to Peter, whose lack of German made it difficult for him to follow, it was not exciting. He sat there dreading the evening. Dreading the risk of climbing into the guarded docks, but seeing John's point of view. Seeing that unless they took the risk they would never get out of Germany.

They came out of the cinema and went straight down to the docks. There was a sentry patrolling the railway siding outside the wire. They walked down the road past the siding and stood, apparently in conversation, watching the sentry. He was doing a steady beat up and down the siding, his rifle slung from his left shoulder.

" Next time he turns his back we'll slip in behind the truck," John said, " and climb on top. We'll wait for him to come up again and then next time he turns away we'll nip smartly down into the docks."

" We'll go and have a look at the place where we're going to climb out first," Peter said. "If there's a sentry there we'll call it off. We may want to come out in a hurry."

They walked round the outside of the fence to the shed but they could see no more German soldiers.

"It's O.K.," John said. "He's guarding the railway siding, not the dock."

Peter felt committed; but he said nothing.

They climbed the fence carefully, one at a time, taking their feet slowly from the wire to stop it twanging. The fence was slack and when they reached the top it swayed so that the one who stood on the ground had to hold it still for the other. The noise of the climbing ran along the fence and they were frightened that the sentry would hear.

Peter had been dreading this the whole afternoon. But once he was over the fence and inside the dock and creeping in the darkness towards the quay where they had seen the Swedish ship, he felt a completeness that he had rarely felt before. An aloneness, an awareness of himself as a vulnerable entity, a feeling that came only when he was hunted. It was not only the danger of the thing. He had not felt like this when, as a member of an air crew, he had been stalked by night fighters. It was more animal than that. It was nearer to the earth. And as he crept forward in the darkness towards the black bulking outline of the shipping in the docks, he felt a thrill of pleasure in the game that he was playing and an added awareness of the clean air blowing in from the sea.

When they reached the quay the Swedish ship had gone. At first they thought they had come to the wrong quay and they cast round looking for her. They took a bearing on a large German vessel they had seen from the road and realised that they were in the right quay; but the ship had sailed.

It was dark in the docks and they had to use a torch to read the names on the counters of the ships. They had explored two of the quays and were about to move on to a third when they saw

a light jerking towards them across the open ground at the end
of the quay.

Peter saw it first. " Look out, we've been seen ! " And he
ran towards the sea end of the quay.

There was a whistle and shouting, and lights flashed out in
front of them from the end of the quay. He caught John's arm
and turned sharply to the right between two warehouses and out
on to the other side of the quay where they crouched behind some
barrels. He was panting now and wishing they had never come
into the docks. John lay beside him, panting too. And then they
heard the sudden yelping of the dogs.

We've had it now ! Peter thought.

John gripped him by the arm and nodded away towards their
left. A German soldier with a storm lantern was passing them,
walking towards the sea end of the quay.

" That's the light we saw."

" Let's cut away towards the left—towards where we came
in."

They came out from behind the barrels and crept down the
side of the warehouse towards the main part of the docks. Suddenly
there was a guttural " *Halt!* " behind them. They started running
together, running fast, expecting all the time to hear the rifle
crack and feel the impact of the bullet in their backs. There were
more shouts now and the dogs yelped again.

They were running side by side and running hard, making
for the open part of the docks, away from the confinement of the
quays. They came round the corner of the warehouse going fast
and crossed over some railway lines.

Peter was panting in earnest now. There was a pain in his
side and the air felt like cold water as it went down into his lungs.

Then John was in front, running easily. He turned sharply
to the left into a dark alley between two of the warehouses. They
came to a concrete railway platform raised some eighteen inches
above the level of the ground. John dived under it and Peter
followed, full length on the dry earth under the concrete and
panting, panting so that he felt his chest would burst. They lay

A German soldier with a storm lantern was passing them

there panting and spent, drawing the cold burning air into their lungs and expelling it quickly to snatch more.

They lay for some time listening to the sound of the German soldiers searching the docks. Several times they heard voices loudly at the end of the alley where the platform was. But the searchers did not go down and the sound of voices grew fainter and finally ceased altogether.

They lay under the platform for an hour and a half before they considered it safe to come out. Then they came out from under the platform and stood listening. They were cold now that the sweat had dried on them and stiff from lying on the cold ground.

" Let's make our way towards the fence," Peter suggested. " We'll follow the railway down. There's bound to be a gate where it enters the docks."

They followed the railway, walking now. Walking softly on the sleepers and slowing down as they came to a branch in the line. There was an arc lamp over the points, but they did not see the sentry until they were right on top of him. Then they stopped dead. He was standing just to one side of the railway line, looking at them as they came down the line.

" Walk on," John whispered, and walked on down the line, ignoring the sentry.

" *Halt!* "

They stopped and the sentry came towards them.

" *Ausweis, bitte.* "

They took out their wallets and handed him the papers. He looked at them. Studying them closely as a man will who does not read easily. He was middle-aged and looked stupid. As they stood there Peter could smell the German soldier smell. The smell of ersatz soap and German tobacco. The smell of German sausage and sauerkraut. The man put the papers back into the wallets, creasing them with his thick fingers as he pushed them in. Hope to God he doesn't ask for our dock passes, Peter thought. But the sentry, apparently satisfied, handed back their wallets. He said something in German and John replied.

" *Ach so ?* " said the sentry, and laughed.

And then they were past him and walking on down the railway line.

" What did he say ? " Peter asked.

" He was suspicious at first. He asked what all the shouting was about and I told him someone had fallen in the sea and they were trying to get him out. Then he seemed amused—perhaps it was my accent. I think we'd better get out of here."

" It was a darn' sight easier getting into this place than it's going to be getting out," Peter said. " I bet they've got guards posted outside by now."

" I don't think so—it doesn't mean that they thought we were escaped prisoners. They may have thought we were Frenchmen doing a spot of pilfering. If they've scared us off I expect that's all they worry about."

" I hope you're right."

They went on down the railway line until they came to the fence. Everything was quiet now. But they were not taking any chances. They lay listening for ten minutes before Peter spoke.

" Creep up to the fence and when I say ' Go ' we'll both climb up together. If we're seen, go like blazes when you get to the other side and I'll see you back in the hotel."

They crept quietly up to the fence.

" O.K.? "

" Yes."

" Go ! "

They covered the short distance to the fence in a few paces and began to climb. Climbing quickly and as silently as possible. Expecting every minute to hear shots from the guards inside the wire. But the shots did not come and they got safely down on the other side and ran two blocks before they felt it was safe enough to stop and talk.

" So much for the docks ! " Peter said.

" We were just unlucky."

" Unlucky be damned ! We were lucky not to be shot. We were lucky enough to get out of there without being caught."

CHAPTER FIVE

The French Workers

PETER AWOKE to see John standing fully dressed by the wash-basin. He was wearing Peter's blue mackintosh and a beret pulled down over his eyes.

" Where are you going ? " Peter asked.

" I'm not—I've been."

" Where ? "

" Down to the docks."

" What on earth for ? "

" I thought I'd go and have a look round."

" Then you're a fool. Supposing you'd got caught. I shouldn't have known where you were."

" I left a note for you," John said mildly.

" Why didn't you wake me up and tell me you were going ? "

" I woke up and couldn't get to sleep again. You were sleeping pretty soundly and I didn't want to wake you. I lay there thinking for a bit and decided that the best time to contact the Frenchmen was in the early morning, just as they were going to work, before it was light."

" Why didn't you wake me ? I'd have come with you."

" Well—as a matter of fact," John looked embarrassed, " I thought perhaps I'd have more success if I went alone. I lay in bed wondering why they all seemed so scared when I spoke to them and I came to the conclusion that (*a*) the Air Force mackintosh I was wearing looked too much like the German ' Feld grau,' and (*b*) the fact that you were hanging around in the background made them suspicious. So I thought I'd just go down in your mackintosh and put it to the test."

" I think you might have told me. I'd have worried if I'd known. Did you have any luck ? "

" I'll just get back into bed and then I'll tell you all about it." John undressed again and got into bed beside Peter.

" It's too cold out. I'm not getting up again until ten o'clock."

" What happened ? "

" Well, it was just as I thought. I got down to the French camp in the docks just as they were all streaming out to go to work. I tagged on to a chap who was all alone and walked down the road with him. I didn't tell him I was English, just said ' Good morning ' and walked along beside him. I asked him where the Swedish boats were berthed and he confirmed that it *is* the Freihafen. I asked him where the Swedish sailors go in the evening and he said either the club in Kleine Oder Strasse or the cafés down Grosse Lastadie Strasse. He didn't think there are any neutral ships in the Freihafen at the moment. You need a dock pass to get into the Freihafen. He showed it to me—it's on a pink card."

" Does he work in the docks ? "

" They all work in the docks in that camp. They unload the ships."

" What did he say about the curfew ? "

" There's no curfew for foreigners in this town. But all the French workers who live in the camp have to be in by ten o'clock."

" Did he give you any suggestions ? "

" No, he wasn't a bit helpful really. He answered the questions I put to him, but that's all. When I didn't ask him questions there were awkward silences. These chaps don't speak my sort of French. I had to repeat each question about six times and even then I'm not sure I understood the answer. But there's a chap in their camp who speaks English. He said if we go along there to-night he'll have him there to meet us."

" Now we're getting somewhere ! What time ? "

" He said to go along any time after eight o'clock. He showed me where the hut is. We're to climb in over the back fence."

" Do you mean we're to climb into the camp ? "

" Yes."

" Well I'm darned ! We nearly got shot climbing into the docks last night—now you want to go climbing into a prison camp."

" It's the safest place to talk," John said. " Safer than talking in a café."

" You said that about the docks."

They both lay silent for a while, warm and comfortable in the large bed, secure behind the shut window, listening to the noise of the traffic in the street below.

" Is it very closely guarded ? "

John smiled. " They're not guarded at all. There's an old civilian gatekeeper who books them in and out of the camp, but apart from that they can come and go as they please."

" We'll go along to-night and have a look at it," Peter said. " Let's get up now and go and find that coaling station at Reiherwerder. There might not be a fence round that."

Reiherwerder coaling station lay about four kilometres outside the dock area and according to the map could be reached by tramcar. They followed the tram track out. There were docks and coaling stations all along the road, approached by narrow lanes running off the main road. At the entrance to each lane was a swing gate and a watchman's hut.

It was a grey morning and they walked quickly to keep warm. There was little traffic, but they passed several foreign workers with the yellow letter " P " on a diamond-shaped patch sewn on to their jackets. There were girls too, heavy peasant girls, in wooden clogs and blue overalls with the word " OST " printed on them in yellow letters. They were laughing as they walked, in scattered groups, towards the coal yards.

" I don't like the look of this," Peter said. " I don't think we'll get much joy here."

" We'll push on," John said, " we'll see what it's like at Reiherwerder."

Half a mile up the road they were stopped by a level crossing.

A long train of empty coal trucks was steaming slowly into the docks."

" That's the way to get in ! " John said. " Come up here after dark and jump one of these trains. It'll take us right into the coaling station."

Peter did not reply, while they waited for the train to pass. He was afraid of John's impetuosity. To jump a coal train. To leave the safe guise of a French worker and become an escaping prisoner. To be committed. To go in with no way out. To take the final step that might lose the whole game. They were safe now, part of the crowd. To jump a train would be to break away from the crowd, become conspicuous.

The train clanked slowly by.

It would be too easy. Stretch out a hand, a quick jump and you were in. But once in, you were committed. Someone might see you. You had made the move that would commit you for the rest of your time. It wasn't worth it.

" Look here, John, let's not rush our fences. We're quite safe as long as we take things quietly. We could live here for weeks— as long as the money lasts."

" That's all very well, but we're not getting anywhere. There's no point in just living here. The object of the exercise is to get to Sweden."

" I couldn't agree with you more. Surely our best plan is to talk to some more Frenchmen and find out more about these places before we start climbing into them."

" And tell half Stettin what we're doing ! That's a risk, if you like. I think it's risky talking to anyone."

" Not as risky as climbing into places. Just suppose we were French workers, as we pretend to be. Even then we'd be breaking the law by going into the coaling station. By not breaking any laws we could stay here as long as we like."

" Yes, but where's it getting us ? "

" Nowhere at the moment, I admit. But we've only been here a day and I don't think we should go charging into things. After all, we've got plenty of money and time's no object."

" Then what have we come to Reiherwerder for, anyway ? "

" Now you're just being silly."

" I'm not being silly. We decide not to use the Freihafen again, so we come out here. We find a good way of getting in here, and you want to cry off."

" I don't want to cry off. I just want to be certain about it."

" How can you be certain about it—how can you be certain about anything here ? "

" We can be more certain after talking to the French. After all, they've been here longer than we have. We wouldn't have found a hotel if it hadn't been for a Frenchman."

" That's true. We were lucky that time. He might just as easily have given us away."

" That's true, too."

" Then what are we arguing about ? "

" I don't know. Let's push on to Reiherwerder." Peter suddenly realised that they had been arguing heatedly in English, their voices rising as their tempers rose. His last words had been spoken as the clanking of the train died away in the distance, and the high English words rang across the street.

" Come on, John," he muttered in a low voice. " Sorry if I lost my temper."

Before they came to Reiherwerder they had to cross a bridge. On the far side was a barrier guarded by a German soldier. They stood for some time watching people crossing the bridge.

" It's all boloney about crossing bridges on the right-hand side," Peter said. " They cross on both sides."

" Yes—what's more, if you go across in a tram you get over without having to show your papers."

" You'd have to show them to the conductor when you buy your ticket," Peter said. " It's not worth it. Let's go back and try a few cafés in the town. Then this evening we'll go and have a look at that French camp. Look—there's a Frenchman over there. Go and have a natter to him."

" You're always wanting me to natter to Frenchmen. What do you want me to ask him ? "

" I'd do it myself if I could, but you know I can't speak French." Peter felt the helplessness of his position. " Ask him if he knows where we can find some Swedish sailors."

They crossed the road and John spoke to the Frenchman. Peter listened, not understanding. Then a tram came along and the Frenchman got on to it. Peter moved after him but John held him back.

" What did he say ? "

" He spoke a sort of argot I couldn't understand. Perhaps my French isn't as good as I thought it was. Either he didn't understand me or he was too scared to talk. I didn't want to get on the same tram in case he wanted to carry on the conversation in front of the Germans."

" Never mind. We'll go back into the town on the next tram and go round a few of the cafés. When it's dark we'll have a look at the French camp."

They spent that afternoon exploring the cafés round the docks. Frightened to stay too long in any one place, they went from café to café, having one drink in each and passing on to the next. Everywhere they felt conspicuous, felt all the time that people were watching them, that their clothing was not right, that they were doing something which made them stand out from the other customers.

As it grew dark it became more difficult. They could not see inside the cafés before they entered. After stumbling into one full of German soldiers they decided that it was time to go to the French camp.

It had been easy getting into the camp. They had no difficulty in finding the hut and now they were standing in a room full of Frenchmen and smelling again the odour of captivity.

There was a silence when they came into the room. A sudden silence and then a resuming of the conversation in a lower key.

A closer drawing-together of the men round the table and some laughter and loud remarks from the men on the bunks against the wall.

John's contact of the morning was there. When he saw them he rose to his feet, mumbled a few words and went out through a door at the back of the room.

"Where's he gone?" Peter asked.

"To fetch the chap who speaks English, I expect."

Peter looked round him at the familiar scene. The room was very like the one they had lived in. Here, perhaps, the smell was stronger than he had known it—that unmistakable, unforgettable, compounded prison smell. The room was dirtier and showed less ingenuity and improvisation; but it was the same room, the same bunks, the same wooden clogs under the bunks.

But the men in the room were not the same. Peter felt the resentment all around him. He did not feel among friends. The Frenchmen were eating and as they ate they watched. A dozen pairs of eyes watched them as they stood by the stove waiting for the contact to return.

"I wish that chap would hurry up," Peter said.

"Not a very promising bunch, are they?"

So they stood, simulating indifference until the English-speaking Frenchman came to take them to his room.

The men in this room were more polite. They stood when John and Peter entered and offered them coffee and black German bread. Peter in return produced a packet of French cigarettes.

The English-speaking Frenchman was half-way through his meal and excused himself in broken English, explaining that he was the camp barber and had to cut hair after the others returned from their work. He was a thin, sharp-featured man of about thirty-five. He looked cleaner than the others and wore a collar and tie.

The barber's English was not as good as the contact had led them to suppose. When Peter asked him in English about the Swedish ships and sailors he did not understand and John had to ask most of the questions in French. While they were speaking

A dozen pair of eyes watching them

in English the other Frenchmen were silent; but when John spoke
in French they all replied together at such a speed that Peter
found it difficult to follow.

The French were apparently delighted that the English
prisoners had escaped. For the escape they offered their felicita-
tions and their admiration. But as for helping them—it was too
bad. They would have liked to help—but the Germans. They
would be shot if they were caught. It was too bad.

When John asked the barber about the Swedish ships and
whether he could make a contact for them among the Swedish
sailors, he replied that he himself did not work in the docks. But
he had friends in the docks and he would find out from them.
He sounded confident, but he also made it sound too simple.
The whole time they were talking there was an atmosphere of fear.

It seemed to Peter that the French were anxious to get rid of them. That their presence was an embarrassment and a danger.

They finally gave it up as hopeless. The more they talked the less promising it seemed to be. They traded cigarettes for black German bread and asked the barber to tell all the other French workers that there were two escaped English prisoners in Stettin and that they could be approached through him. They offered a reward to anyone who would help them.

They got safely out of the camp and walked back towards the town.

"So much for the French," Peter said. "They're a dead loss."

"Oh, give 'em a chance," John said. "At least we know we can get bread for cigarettes now. And if they tell the others we may find someone who's got the guts to help us."

"They certainly didn't seem too keen. They're not even guarded."

"They couldn't go anywhere if they did escape," John said. "Not much point in going back to France. Besides, they've been subject to German propaganda for years now."

"They've got their beer and cigarettes. They're just sitting pretty waiting for the war to end."

"There are bound to be some good types," John said. "I expect they're all in the underground movement and lying low. They'll make contact when they get to hear about us."

CHAPTER SIX

Things Get Complicated

JOHN LAY in bed watching Peter shaving in front of the mirror over the wash-basin. He finished shaving and began to wash himself all over with a face-cloth he had cut from the tail of his shirt.

" What's the programme for to-day ? " John said.

" We'd better go and have another look round the docks, I suppose."

" I thought you decided against climbing into the docks."

" I don't mean climb in—I mean mark down a few cafés for this evening. You can't see what you're doing in the dark."

" Are we going to start all that café-stalking again ? "

" It's the only thing to do, John. We made one contact last night but that's not enough. We've got to get every Frenchman in the town working for us."

" I don't like it," John said.

" It's safe enough. We won't tell 'em where we live. We'll just make a rendezvous like you did with the last chap. We're bound to strike oil sooner or later."

" Better make it sooner then. The money won't last for ever. We've got to move out of this hotel to-day. We can't go on like this."

" Shall we go back to the air raid shelter ? "

John pulled the sheet up round his ears. " We'll find another hotel all right. We've got enough money for three or four more days. What have we got for breakfast ? "

" I've got enough porridge for one more meal. And there's the bread we got from the French last night."

" Let's go down and have breakfast in the hotel."

" Too risky. No sense in running into trouble."

" Come on, Pete—a hot drink will do us good."

" It's not worth risking it for a cup of coffee."

" Come on, Pete—we'll take down some of the bread and eat it with the coffee. Start the day with something warm inside us. Things will look entirely different after a cup of coffee."

" We'll go and see what it's like. If there are many people there it won't be worth risking."

When John was ready they went down to the dining-room on the ground floor. There was an empty table with a banquette seat in the corner. They sat on the seat with their backs against the wall. A waitress came over to them and John ordered coffee. She brought a pot of coffee and two cups. John poured the coffee and they knew at once by the smell that it was made from acorns.

John took the bread from the side pocket of his coat. It was wrapped in a copy of the *Völkischer Beobachter*. Peter looked round quickly to see if they were being watched. There was an old lady at the next table and on the far side of the room an elderly couple were studying the morning paper. In the middle of the room a middle-aged man who looked like a commercial traveller was writing in an exercise book. Except for the heavy smell of German cigarettes and an occasional " *Heil Hitler!* " from the foyer they might have been in some provincial hotel in England.

They sat there eating the bread and drinking the ersatz coffee. Peter relaxed and sat back on the seat. They were fooling them all along the line. He glanced casually towards the door and stiffened suddenly as he saw the German military uniforms in the foyer.

There was no other door out of the room. What he had always feared was to be in a room with only one door. He had dreamed of it in the camp. A room with only one door, and the Germans there.

The two German officers gave a perfunctory " *Heil Hitler!* " as they entered the room. They made straight for the table where

Peter and John were sitting. As they approached Peter felt his stomach contract and the piece of bread he was eating stuck in his throat. Always that sudden contraction of the stomach and the desire to run. The exhilaration came afterwards. First the blind, unreasoning panic to get away. Only after that came the exhilaration and the trembling at the knees.

But the two officers were not looking for them. They were an oberst and a major and both carried black briefcases. The major was wearing jackboots and spurs and had a scar from the left eye to the corner of his mouth. He carried an ornamental dagger from chains at his waist and on his collar he wore the red artillery flash. The oberst was more quietly dressed. He was in slacks and carried no dagger, but he wore the insignia of the Knight's Cross of the Iron Cross.

What do we do now? Peter thought. Do we stand up when they get here? Do we speak to them? Do we " Heil Hitler " ? Is it done for foreign workers to eat at the same table as German officers? And he went on eating his bread. There was nothing they could do. They could not walk out leaving their coffee and bread on the table. They just had to sit there and take it as it came and trust that their luck would hold.

The Germans sat down at the table. They both had thick colourless skin and closely cropped hair. Peter felt the revulsion that he always felt when he was close to a German officer. The oberst wore pale-blue spectacles and his mouth was small and tight. He ordered coffee and began to talk to the major.

Peter glanced at John out of the corner of his eye. He looks young, he thought, we're O.K., we'll be O.K. We'll just sit here for a minute and then we'll get up and walk out.

The major opened his briefcase and took out a bundle of papers. He put on a pair of rimless spectacles and began to explain the papers to the oberst. Listen, John, Peter thought, this may be important. He grinned inwardly. Don't be an ass. Colonels don't discuss military secrets in cafés in front of foreign workers.

They finished their coffee. John looked at Peter and raised his eyebrows. They rose without speaking and left the hotel.

" What were they talking about ? " Peter said. " Was it important ? Could you get any of it ? "

" I couldn't follow it very well. It was some educational scheme, I think. They were talking about the Hitler Jugend and the Hitler Mädchen."

" Preparing for the next war, I expect," Peter said.

They tried several dockside cafés that morning, including one that the French barber had told them was run by a Communist. This was a low, square room with a door opening directly on to the street. It was full of seamen and dockside workers who were sitting at round metal tables drinking dark beer out of tall glasses. In this café there were no pictures of the Fuehrer, nor did the customers give the Nazi salute on entering and leaving.

They chose a table in a corner where they could talk without being overheard. In the more crowded cafés they could not talk in English. They had to sit in silence the whole time ; and if they wanted to talk they had to go into the lavatory, and there was usually somebody in the lavatory. But in this café they could talk comfortably and they sat in the corner sipping their beer and watching the people at the other tables.

Peter sat watching the two Frenchmen who were sitting at a table in the opposite corner of the room. They were young and their dark hair and olive skins looked warm and vital compared to the Germans around them. They sat with their heads close together in argument. They look just like us, Peter thought. We must look exactly like that when we're whispering together. I wonder what they're talking about. The more he watched the more suspicious the two French boys seemed. They each had a bundle tied up in coloured cloth and the one facing the room cast nervous glances round him as he spoke.

" Just look at those two frogs behind you," Peter said. " Move over here so that you can see them without turning round."

John moved over next to him. " They do look a bit furtive, I think I'll saunter over and have a word with them."

Peter watched him as he crossed the room. He's as young as they are, he thought, and looks as French.

John was standing by the table now, looking down. The two Frenchmen had stopped talking and looked scared. He sat down with them at the table and Peter saw them grow less scared. He saw John pull his Kriegsgefangener identity disc from his pocket and show it to them across the table. I won't join them, he thought, I'll stay here and watch, and if they get too suspicious-looking I'll go and warn them.

But John refused to allow it to look like a conspiracy. He took out a packet of cigarettes and leaned back in his chair. He called a waiter, ordered more beer and then when he had finished he bade the Frenchmen farewell and rejoined Peter.

"I scared them out of their lives," he said. "They were planning to stow away in a Swedish ship and I went up and leered and asked them if they could put me in touch with any Swedish sailors. They thought I was a member of the Gestapo who was just playing with them before he ran them in. They were scared stiff."

"I thought they looked pretty scared."

"They were scared stiff. They live in a camp about ten miles outside Stettin and they come in as often as they can with all their luggage wrapped in a bundle, ready to stow away. They really thought they'd got it that time."

"Were they any help?"

"Not really. They don't know any more about it than we do—rather less if anything. They've been trying to stow away for six months now. Money is their difficulty. They said a pal of theirs saved up forty marks, which was the price asked by a Swedish sailor, and the fellow took it and handed him over to the Germans."

"What a dirty thing to do."

"They know who he is and they say the next time he comes to Stettin he'll get a knife in his back—that's if he ever comes here again. He won't if he's got any sense."

"Where do they try to stow away?"

"Reiherwerder. They've got passes. They know a chap who works down there. Apparently they work alternate day and night shifts and when he's on nights he lets them have his pass during the day. They reckon they can stow away in a collier."

"I wonder if we could get hold of one of the passes."

"I've fixed that. They're going to bring a couple along to-morrow. We can't keep them for long, but I thought perhaps you could fake a couple of them up. They don't look very elaborate affairs."

"I should be able to." Peter was eager to take some of the work off John's shoulders. "I brought some Indian ink with me and one of the rubber stamps. We should be able to fake something up all right."

"Good show. I'll go down to the coaling station with one of the passes to-morrow afternoon while you make a couple of copies at the hotel."

"If we've got a hotel by then."

"We'll find one all right. We'll go and find one now. And then we'll go and make a few more contacts."

They went to several more cafés before they booked a room. They were now living on two cups of acorn coffee for breakfast, vegetable stew at midday, and a square inch of dog food before they went to bed. On some days they had managed to buy another plate of stew or potato salad in the evening.

This was the fifth day of their freedom and they were running short of money and food. They had eaten the last of the oatmeal and were saving two of the tins of dog food to eat on board the ship. Although they wore warm clothing they were always cold; the cold came from inside, it was a coldness that only food would warm. The constant strain of living in the heart of an enemy city was beginning to tell on their nerves, nerves that had been almost at breaking point during the long anxious weeks before the tunnel broke. They found themselves arguing over the most obvious decisions. They had a long argument before deciding to spend their precious marks on the cinema. But it was warm in the cinema and they had not sufficient food to keep them warm. It was dark and in the darkness they felt safe. In the cinema they could relax and drop for a moment the constant guard upon their actions and their tongues. And they came out again rested and ready to start once more on their circuit of the cafés.

" We've got two tentacles out," Peter said. " The barber and the two boys. They cover two of the camps. What we want tonight is a chap from another camp. If we go on long enough we'll have our feelers out in every camp in Stettin."

" It's too slow. Money's getting short and if I don't get a square meal soon I shall faint on you in the street. Where are we going to sleep to-morrow night ? We haven't had much luck with our contacts so far."

" We're doing pretty well, if you ask me. We're dry, clean and shaved—and we've still got some money left."

" It won't last us long. If we don't strike oil soon we'd better get out of here and jump a goods train up to Danzig."

They walked on for some time in silence.

" Let's go and have a look at that club," John suggested.

" It wouldn't be open yet, would it ? "

" I don't know. What time do these clubs usually open ? "

" I don't know."

There was a short silence.

" Where did you say it was ? " John asked.

" Seventeen Kleine Oder Strasse."

" Let's go and have a look at it."

They walked down a steeply cobbled street on their right and came out on the Bollwerk. There was a watery moon rising above the river and the streets shone wetly where they were lit by the shaded street lamps. They followed the river for a hundred yards and then turned to the left again. Kleine Oder Strasse lay on their right hand, a narrow winding alley cutting darkly between the houses. They followed the alley down until they came to Number Seventeen, a tall house without lights in the windows. On the right-hand side of the door was a notice which read, NUR FUR AUSLANDER.

"Doesn't look very glamorous," Peter said. "You'd most likely have to show your papers as you go in. Doesn't it say 'Foreigners Only' on that notice?"

"Yes."

"It's too dangerous. We were told not to go there except in dire need. And you could hardly call this dire need. It's nearly a year since Stafford got that information about this place and the Gestapo are bound to have got on to it by now. They've probably got one of their own people in the place as a spy."

John looked again at the face of the dark house with the abrupt and unequivocal sign.

"What about going in and having a look round?" he suggested.

"It's not worth it. You'd most likely have to show your papers as you went in."

Once again they started on their round of the cafés. At the first three they drew a blank. In each case the French were too near the Germans. It would have been impossible to talk to them without being overheard.

They went back to the café where they had met the two French boys. It was still uncrowded and they sat where they had sat before facing the café and watching the seamen, dock-workers and unidentifiable Germans who seemed to stand on street corners all day wearing nautical caps and smoking pipes.

"Not a very promising bunch," John said.

"That fellow looks all right." Peter indicated a thin, wild-eyed Frenchman who was leaning forward haranguing the other men at his table. His eyes were alight with enthusiasm and he seemed to be urging them to do something against their will.

"Wait till he goes to the lavatory," John said. "I'll talk to him and you stand behind him in case he yells. He's the last one I'll try. If he's no good I'm finished for the night."

"O.K. I'll fix him if he yells."

But the man did not go to the lavatory. He looked at his watch, excused himself and made for the door.

" After him ! " Peter said, and they left their beer on the table and followed him out on to the street.

They caught him in the street just before he turned the corner and Peter heard John say, " *Pardon, M'sieur, nous sommes prisonniers de guerre anglais. . . .*" But the Frenchman took him by the arm and hurried him back into the café before he could say more.

Peter followed them in and they sat at the table where they had been sitting before. The Frenchman was pale and still gripped John by the arm. The men who had been sitting with him before he left the café turned and watched them as they sat down. The Frenchman spoke to John in a fast whisper.

Why must he look so furtive ? Peter thought. Why does he have to make the whole thing look like a conspiracy ?

" He wants to see your Kriegie disc," John said.

Peter took the Kriegsgefangener identity disc from his pocket and handed it to the Frenchman, who took it and rubbed his hands together, the disc between his palms.

" *Mon Dieu, il fait froid! On gèle ce soir*," he said, and shivered theatrically, cupping his hands and blowing into them, surreptitiously peeping at the disc as he did so.

He'll get us all arrested if he goes on like this, Peter thought.

The Frenchman handed back the identity disc under the table, carefully looking round the room before he did so. By this time most of the customers were eyeing them with curiosity and Peter began to feel uncomfortable. The Frenchman was talking to John in a low voice, his mouth hidden behind his hand.

" He wants to take us to another café," John said. " He says he can put us in touch with some Swedish sailors there."

" He'll put us all in jail if he's not careful. What does he want to act like that for ? "

" He says he's a member of the Underground. But I can't understand half of what he says. He says that the café he wants to take us to is ' sympathetic.' "

"O.K.," Peter said. "Let's get out of here."

Sympathetic, he thought, they're all sympathetic. Why can't they talk without looking furtive all the time ? Those two boys looked furtive enough but this chap looks like a stage villain. Perhaps they always look like that. Perhaps it's me. Perhaps I'm getting nervy. Perhaps they don't look furtive at all. Or perhaps the Germans are used to it and don't notice it. Anyway, I don't like it, it frightens me.

When they came to the café the Frenchman led the way in and Peter and John followed. This was brighter than the other cafés and there were women. The Frenchman chose a corner seat and ordered beer. John tried to pay for it but the man pushed the money away. "*Gardez les sous*," he said, and began to talk.

The French was too fast for Peter and he looked round the room. It was a cheerful place and there was some music. A seedy-looking young man in a stained dinner-suit was playing a piano. There were some German soldiers and they each had a girl. It was light and the people looked happier than they had in the other cafés. It smelled of food, good meat food, and there were tablecloths on the tables.

The door opened and four German soldiers came in. They looked enormous as they came in the door and Peter realised how difficult it would be to get out of the place. There was only one door and even if one soldier was standing there it would be impossible to get out. He looked round for the lavatory. It would be as well to have another exit. There was a door in the corner marked HERREN and he crossed over and went in. It was the usual affair with a small window opening on to a lane at the back of the café. He made certain that the window would open and went back to the table.

"There's a window in the bog," he told John. "If anything happens we can get out that way."

"Good show." John turned again to the Frenchman.

Peter leaned back in his chair. A woman sitting at the next table smiled at him. She had red hair and her smile was an invitation. He was alarmed. He leaned towards the other two, assuming an interest in their conversation. The Frenchman was about to leave. As they stood to shake hands a waitress passed their table. The Frenchman stopped her.

"My friends are Swedes," he said in loud German. "They are lonely in this town. If any Swedish sailors come in this evening show them to this table, please." And then he left the café.

The fool! John turned to Peter, but it was too late. The red-headed woman was sitting at their table talking earnestly to him in a language that was neither French nor German. Peter sat there looking frightened, obviously wondering what to do. He played his trump card. He rose to his feet. "*Ich bin Ausländer*," he said with dignity, "*nicht verstehen*," and walked with determination towards the lavatory.

The woman turned to John, addressed him in the same language.

"I do not speak Swedish," John said in German.

"But your friend said you were Swedes."

"My friend you were speaking to is Swedish. I am French."

"He did not sound Swedish," the woman said.

"He is very drunk."

The woman began a long apology for speaking to them without an introduction. She was heavily made up and was about to cry.

"My friend is not well," John said. "Please excuse me."

When he got to the lavatory Peter had locked himself in. He knocked the "V" sign with his knuckles and Peter opened up.

"How was my German?"

"Awful," John said.

"She's German, isn't she?"

"Yes, but she speaks Swedish—I don't know how much, but she speaks it all right. She started off in Swedish, but I interrupted her and told her I was a Frenchman. I told her you were a Swede but you'd gone to the lavatory to be sick."

"I've opened the window," Peter said. "Lock the door—

we'd better get out of here." He stood on the lavatory seat and thrust his head and shoulders through the window. John heard him grunting, then he wriggled back, red in the face. " We'll have to go feet first," he said. He swung on the water pipe and managed to get his legs out of the window. He landed with a thud in the street below.

John followed, giggling. " I wonder what they'll do when they find the door locked."

" Break it down, I expect. We won't go back to that place."

" You can say that again," John said.

CHAPTER SEVEN

The French Are Suspicious

THEY ROSE early the following morning and kept their appointment with the French boys who brought the two dock passes. They spent the rest of the morning in fruitless wandering round the dockside cafés. After the episode of the Swedish-speaking German woman they were more cautious in their attempts to make contact with the Swedes. The lack of food and constant strain were having their effect. They fluctuated between extremes of caution and recklessness and as their moods did not always coincide they spent most of the time urging one another in opposite directions.

When they had eaten their midday Stammgericht they managed to book a room for one night at the Hotel Sack. This time they explained that they were returning to Breslau from Anklam, and were accepted without question.

It was a modern hotel and steam-heated. After they had been shown to their room John took one of the passes they had borrowed from the French boys and set out for the coaling station. Peter stayed behind in the hotel bedroom to make copies of the other pass.

He locked the door and took a flat tin box from his travelling-bag. Inside the box were bottles of red, black and Indian ink, a camel-hair brush, a razor blade, two mapping pens, a small metal ruler and a stamp cut from a rubber heel.

He made a careful study of the pass. It was a piece of thin pale pink cardboard about the size of a playing card. In the left-hand top corner was the photograph of the holder ; it was roughly the same size as the photographs on their Swedish passes. To the right of the photograph was the superscription. Below these in black German-gothic lettering was the usual list. Name, age, sex, height, eyes, hair; followed by the signature of the Chief of Police. In the left-hand bottom corner was the well-known imprint of the swastika-carrying eagle. Peter noted with satisfaction that all the particulars had been filled in with pen and ink —he did not feel capable of reproducing typescript accurately. It was not the shaping of the letters but the intensity of the ink that he found difficult to reproduce. The only way was to trace it through carbon paper and he had forgotten to bring any.

He took a sheet of thick paper almost as stiff as the cardboard on which the pass was printed, and cut two pieces of the right size. He cut them carefully with the razor blade and metal ruler on the mirror from the dressing-table; absorbed now in what he was doing and forgetting the ultimate aim of his work. He would be absorbed for the rest of the afternoon and would finish the job with aching eyes and stiff shoulders; but rested and in some way renewed by the intensity of his work. It had been the same in the prison camp when he had been painting scenery or a water-colour. Then he had realised suddenly that an afternoon had passed with him absorbed and unaware that it had gone.

He gave the two pieces of paper a wash of clear water and left them to soak. He mixed a thin solution of red ink and water in one of the tooth glasses and washed this on carefully; giving them three washes before he was satisfied that they were nearly enough the colour of the pass. He left them to dry, flat on the glass above the radiator.

While the pieces of paper were drying he took some tracing paper and carefully traced out the spacing of the lettering on the pass. He did not trace the actual lettering; it was too small for that. He was experienced enough to reproduce the German print freehand and with enough accuracy for it to pass for the real thing at a quick glance.

When the two pieces of paper were perfectly dry he pricked

out the tracing through the tracing paper and started on the lettering. He wrote slowly, taking only sufficient ink on the pen to draw one stroke, and writing with the paper resting on the sheet of glass so that there would be no indentation made by the nib and the ink would stand up proudly. It was careful, finicky work and he only stopped to turn on the electric light or refill his pipe.

When at last he leaned back, yawned and looked at his watch, it was nearly ten o'clock.

They were not a good job. They were not nearly up to the standard of their other papers. But they would do. He removed the two photographs from the Swedish sailors' passes and stuck them on to the new ones with paste made from dog food.

Then he lay on his bed and fell asleep.

When John left the hotel there was a fine drizzle of rain falling and he buttoned his mackintosh tightly round his neck. The cloth beret he was wearing gave no protection to his face and as he screwed his eyes against the driving rain he cursed the nation that had adopted such idiotic headgear. It was cold and he would rather have stayed with Peter in the warmth of the hotel bedroom. But he had to get to Reiherwerder and carry out his inspection before it grew too dark, so he thrust his hands into the pockets of his mackintosh and bowed his head before the rain.

As he walked down to the tram stop he realised why so many escaping prisoners seemed in a way relieved when they were caught and brought back into the camp. None of them seemed to suffer deeply from the disappointment of being caught. And now, huddled in his thin mackintosh against the cold and driving rain, he thought of the warmth and companionship of their room in the camp.

Now he was alone, even away from Peter. He had been alone in the prison camp, in the cooler, but this was different. He felt vulnerable and slightly lightheaded as he walked down the rain-swept street ; an exaggerated facet of that mood which had haunted him ever since they had crawled from the narrow tunnel into the lesser darkness of the forest—a feeling of unreality, of too-good-to-be-true. He felt like an exotic bird escaped from a gilded cage, prey to the hardier natives. My heart is like a singing bird. He pulled himself together, grinned. A turtle-dove—a turtle-dove in a turtle-neck sweater.

When he got down from the tram the rain had turned to snow, and warmly, in that short time between dusk and the official black-out, a light was shining from the porter's hut at the entrance to the coaling station. He showed his pass and the sentry let him through. He walked quickly through the gate, past the sudden glow of warmth and light from the porter's hut, into the desolation of the dock. There huge mounds of coal loomed on either side of him and as he came out on to the quay he saw the coal tips standing gauntly against the solidness of the sky.

There were no ships berthed alongside the quay, but a short distance away to his right he saw a group of prisoners wearing the long tunics and characteristic cloth helmets of the Russians. Near them stood the German sentry, his heavy-booted and long-skirted silhouette barely visible through the driving snow.

Not much future there. He turned to his left. He had his back to the wind now and could see more comfortably. Ahead of him was a large timber building and to one side of it the smoke-blackened funnel of a steamer.

He walked on down the quay and as he came to the small shed he saw that it was a kitchen. There was a straggling line of men at the open door, each man holding a mess tin in front of him. They were Russians, and in the fading light of the afternoon their faces looked thin and pinched, wolfish under the mangy fur and grotesque ear-flaps of their helmets. Very few of them had coats and some were without shoes. Their rag-bound feet seemed to melt into the mud and slush in which they stood. As he passed them he saw one of the Russians pour half of his portion of soup into his companion's cup. And he walked on towards the steamer at the quayside feeling a glow inside him, an echo of the warmth that had come to him from that line of tattered men.

When he reached the quayside he found that the ship was

German. He decided that had she been Swedish he could have climbed aboard. He hung around for some time anxious to find out whether a sentry was posted in the docks. The prisoners had finished work now and the guards were marshalling them into lines to march them back to the huts. It was foolhardy to hang around any longer and he left the docks and caught a tram back into the town.

He made for the café where he had arranged to meet the Frenchman who had left them so abruptly at the mercy of the Swedish-speaking German woman. I'll tell him off for that, he thought. It's no good being sarcastic. I couldn't manage that in French. I'll tell him how dangerous it was. I'll tell him not to be so furtive too.

The Frenchman was sitting at a table near the door. When he saw John he motioned him to a table some distance away.

Here we go again, John thought. More games of hide-and-seek. He sat down and ordered a beer.

The Frenchman had half a glass of beer in front of him and he was smoking a cigarette. He did even this furtively, drawing swiftly at the cigarette and glancing round the café between draws. He did not look at John but kept glancing towards the door. John lit a cigarette and sat waiting for some sign from the Frenchman. He was growing angry now. What the devil was the fellow playing at ?

When the Frenchman got up and went out John followed him into the street. The Frenchman led him out on to the Bollwerk down the first turning on the left and up past the club in Kleine Oder Strasse. They turned to the left at the top of the hill and the Frenchman disappeared into a doorway at the end of the street. I wonder if he wants me to follow, John thought. I wonder if it's a trap. And then he laughed at himself. There would be no point in laying a trap. They could have picked him up at the last place if they'd wanted to. So he went in.

It was a " Wirtshaus," very like an English pub. There was the same heavy wooden panelling and long mahogany counter

with the etched mirror behind it. The Frenchman was sitting
with three other men in the far corner of the room. He was
sitting forward, talking in a low voice and casting sidelong glances
round the room. I shan't stay here long, John thought, my nerves
won't stand it. He joined the Frenchman at the table.

When the Frenchman had introduced him to the other men
he began to make excuses. He explained they were members of
a Communist group and were engaged on very dangerous work.
He hinted at sabotage and mentioned that the Germans had placed
a price on their heads.

" I could not speak to you in the café. We were being watched.
We are safe here. The publican is a member of the Party."

" Then you cannot help us," John said.

The Frenchman shrugged his shoulders. " We each have our
job to do. Yours is to escape and return to England. Mine——"
He shrugged his shoulders again. " But we have some money.
Would you like some money ? "

" We are short of money," John said. " We also have need
of food. Food is of more importance to us than money. If you
could give us some ration cards we should be grateful."

" We cannot give you ration tickets. We live on the black
market. But we can give you food."

He called the Gastwirt and ordered sandwiches. When they
arrived John split them in two and put half in his pocket.

" For your breakfast ? " the Frenchman asked.

" For my friend."

" Then we will repeat the order."

While John was eating they discussed his plans. When they
heard how he and Peter were living they suggested that it would
be better for them to get into a French camp. They told him that
it would be quite safe living in a French camp ; but they did not
offer to take him into theirs. They warned him against staying
in a certain hotel where the proprietor spoke fluent French, and
advised him that a café called the Café d'Accordion was the best
place to contact Swedish sailors.

He left them as soon as he could and made his way to the

Café d'Accordion. Entering through the low swinging doors, he stumbled down three steps and found himself in a long low room filled with tobacco smoke and the sound of talking. There was singing too, the first he had heard in any café in Germany, and in one corner a pianist was accompanying a hunchback in gipsy costume who played an accordion. Most of the conversation seemed to be in French, although occasionally he could pick out the sing-song tones of Scandinavia. Next to the piano a girl in a tight sweater and a black skirt was sitting on the knee of a man in a seaman's jersey. She had one bare arm round his neck and was drinking a glass of wine.

As John came into the room he realised the hunchback was playing " J'Attendrai." This isn't real, he thought, this is Hollywood. This is a scene in Montmartre. This is a film setting for *The Rat*.

He ordered a glass of wine, leaned with his back against the bar and looked at the people in the room.

" J'Attendrai." . . . He thought of his room in Oxford and the houseboat on the Thames. The portable gramophone and a record of Jean Sablon's. That tune had so many memories for him. He thought of that long summer on the Thames. Of Janet and going ashore at Shepperton. Drinking beer at the Anchor when they were both learning to drink and didn't like it much. His brother home from Sandhurst ; and drinking pints. Janet poling a punt under the green shade of the willows, the water dropping from the pole in a cascade of diamonds and himself lying in the punt and watching her. His mother making tea over the Primus stove. And, always, somewhere in the background, the gramophone playing " J'Attendrai."

Then he saw the English-speaking barber. He was sitting at the back of the room behind a table full of glasses of beer.

He saw John and beckoned him across to the table. John took his wine over and sat with them.

" At last I have found you," the barber said. " This is Pierre. We have searched the town for you."

" Have you heard of a ship ? " John said.

" This is Pierre," the barber said. " I think that he will help you."

John shook hands with Pierre ; noticing how, as always before, the French were known only by their first names. Nor did they ask him for his name or any proof of his identity.

Pierre said, " I have a friend who is going to Sweden in a Danish boat. He leaves to-morrow. I do not know how he is going or why. When I heard from our friend here that there were two English prisoners in Stettin trying to get out of Germany, I approached my friend and asked him for his help. If you will come with me now you can meet him and perhaps he will help you."

" Where is he ? " John asked.

" I will take you to him."

" Is it far from here ? "

He shrugged his shoulders. " Not far. But I will take you there."

" I should like to tell my friend where I am going."

" I am afraid that is not possible."

" Very well. I will go with you."

" Good," Pierre said. " That way is better. Do not walk with me but follow close behind. I will take you to my friend."

It was a typical prison camp hut and it smelled strongly of French tobacco. The walls were covered with pictures torn from magazines and on one of the walls were painted the words VIVE DE GAULLE.

" Rest here," Pierre said, and went out through a door at the back of the hut.

John sat on one of the wooden stools and wondered what would happen next. The man had led him by devious routes but he guessed that he was in the camp they had visited two nights ago.

A short while later Pierre returned, accompanied by two other men. They were big men and one of them was armed with a thick stick. The man with the stick stood by the door.

" What is your name ? " the other asked in French.

" John Clinton. I am a British officer."

" He looks like a stool pigeon," the man with the stick said. " He has the accent of a Boche."

" It might also be the accent of an Englishman," the first one said. " André will be here in a minute. He will know."

There was a short silence.

" He has the look of a Frenchman," the man with the stick said.

" You cannot tell by appearances, Raoul. All men look alike these days."

" He is certainly not French." This was Pierre, who till then had been silent.

" Of course I'm not French," John said. " I told you, I'm British."

" We have to prove that," Raoul told him. " Do you know what will happen if we find that you are not British ? "

" I tell you I *am* British ! "

The man shut one eye and drew a forefinger across his throat. " You will be found floating in the dock. No one will know how you came there. We had a stool pigeon before, did we not, Pierre ? "

" André will know," Pierre told him.

There was a long silence while John wished himself well out of this " cloak-and-dagger " atmosphere. It was melodramatic, but it was also dangerous. Then footsteps were heard treading lightly on the path outside.

" Here is André," Raoul said.

André's face was pale and his brown eyes burned darkly. He looked ill and walked with a stoop. As he entered the hut Pierre took him to one side and whispered in his ear.

He looked at John and came towards him across the room.

" Do you speak French ? " He said it in broken English.

" A little."

" Good. It is important that I speak fast. I leave for Sweden to-morrow. There is an organisation. But first I must have proof of your identity."

"I have my identity disc here." John began to unfasten his coat.

"I regret that is not sufficient. What is your name?"

"John Clinton."

"Your age?"

"Twenty-three."

"Are you a soldier?"

"Yes."

"What rank?"

"Captain."

"What camp were you in?"

"Stalag Luft Three."

"What regiment were you in?"

"I cannot tell you that."

"You do not trust me. It is right that you should not. But I must have proof of your identity. When did you escape from the camp?"

"Last Friday."

"When were you captured?"

"December 17th, 1942."

"Where?"

"Africa."

"Were you in a tank?"

"No. I was on a motor cycle."

"What make?"

"B.S.A."

"Were you wounded?"

"In the arm."

"Show me."

John began to remove his coat.

"No. Do not show me. You look tired. Two years is a long time to be a prisoner of war."

"I was only there for one year."

"Of course."

There was a silence. They stood facing one another. How can I help him, John thought. How can I prove that I'm what

I say I am ? It must be damn' difficult for them, but how can I trust them ?

"What are your mother's christian names ?" André asked.

"Mary Elizabeth."

"What does your father call her ?"

"Betty."

He suddenly slapped John

"Have you a garden ?"

"Yes."

"What flowers grow in it ?"

"Roses, lupins, pansies, geraniums."

"Have you a car ?"

"Yes."

"What make ?"

"Morris."

" Horse-power ? "

" Ten."

" Do you know London ? "

" Fairly well."

" What is the name of the statue in Piccadilly Circus ? "

" Eros."

" What is it famous for ? "

" Its flower-sellers."

" That is good. One more thing." He suddenly slapped John lightly across the face.

" What the devil . . . ! " John began.

All the Frenchmen laughed.

" I am sorry," the man called André said. " You have passed the test." He turned to the short man. " He is British all right. I, André, can vouch for that."

" Good," Pierre said. " Now we can get down to business. First, you must eat."

CHAPTER EIGHT

The Cafe d' Accordion

PETER WAS dreaming he had been caught in the tunnel. A fall of sand had pinned him to the floor and he was struggling to get free. It was dark and hot and the sand was smothering him. There was sand in his eyes, in his ears and in his nose. He was swallowing sand with every breath. And the more he struggled the more the sand kept pouring down from the roof. Someone was digging down to save him. It was John. He knew it was John and kept calling to tell him where he was. He could hear the thumping of the spade as John dug furiously away to save him before he suffocated. If only he could keep the sand away from his mouth he would be all right. He pushed his hands away from his face, clearing the sand away, pushing hard against the force of the onrushing sand. . . .

Then he was in the hotel bedroom in Stettin. The sand was the pillow smothering his face and the weight of the sand was the weight of the heavy German quilt he had pulled over himself. The sound of John digging was a gentle thumping on the door. As he crossed the room to open the door he looked at his watch. It was ten-thirty.

" What did you lock the door for ? " John asked. " Afraid of the goons ? "

" I locked it while I was working on the passes. I must have fallen asleep."

" How did they go ? "

" I don't know—haven't looked at them since I finished." He crossed the room and picked up one of the passes. " Not bad. Not bad at all, though I say it myself. What do you think ? " He handed them to John.

"They're the right colour anyway. It's a pity we shan't have to use them."

"Why? What happened? Come on—you're tired—sit down and tell me about it." He dragged up the chair for John and sat himself on the bed. "Now tell me about it."

"Wait a minute. I've got something for you first." John pulled out the now rather dirty sandwiches. "Sorry I couldn't get any paper to wrap them in."

"Where did you get these?" Peter asked through a mouthful of bread-and-sausage.

"That furtive chap gave them to me. He gave me some money too. Apparently he's a saboteur or something and that accounts for all that ' cloak-and-dagger ' stuff."

"They're good sandwiches anyway. Here, have one."

"It's all right, I've had mine. I had a meal in a French camp too." He told Peter everything that had happened since he had left the hotel.

"That Café d'Accordion sounds a pretty good joint," Peter said.

"Yes—not bad. Beer's good too. Thought we might go there to-morrow night."

"What about that chap Pierre? Won't he be looking out for us?"

"We can't depend on them," John said. "They talk so much. I rather think it's all talk. It's no use sitting back and depending on them."

"Where shall we sleep to-morrow?"

"The Frenchmen told me to stay here, but I'd rather not. I don't altogether trust them. Besides, we only booked for one night and it would rouse suspicion to stay longer. Then there's the money question. What about trying another night in an air raid shelter?"

"I'm game," Peter said. "It can't be long now. We're bound to strike oil sooner or later."

The following morning they stayed in bed as long as they

dared. Now that they knew the French were helping them it was becoming more and more difficult to fill in the time. Every moment they spent on the streets was dangerous, yet they could not stay too long in the hotel for fear of arousing the suspicions of the proprietor.

They stayed in bed until lunchtime. It was raining again and they wanted to keep themselves dry for the night, when they might have to sleep in their clothes. Then they got up, had a bath in the wash-basin and walked down to the Café d'Accordion. It was closed.

" Have they been shut down, d'you think ? " John asked. " It was a pretty blatant sort of joint."

" Oh, I expect they only open in the evenings. Let's go and get a Stamm and come back later on."

The café was crowded, but they managed to find a table for two. They had been eating in these places every day that they had been in Stettin and Peter was no longer dependent on John for his peace of mind. Now as always John did the talking and when he had ordered the beer and the Stammgericht he went to the lavatory to wash, leaving Peter to guard the table.

He had been sitting there for some time, day-dreaming. At first he did not realise that he was being addressed. Then he looked up and saw the angry German face glaring down at him. " *Ich bin Ausländer, nicht verstehen.*" He was about to say it when he realised that the German was asking him if the other chair was occupied. Nothing could have been more plain. The man was standing one hand resting on the back of the chair, his eyebrows raised in interrogation.

What shall I say ? Peter thought. Where's John ? The blighter will sit down if I don't say something. He smiled brightly. " *Das ist besetzt,*" pointing to John's chair ; " *Das ist frei,*" pointing wildly across the café.

Then John came back.

" Some goon wanted your chair," Peter said.

" How did you stave him off ? "

" Oh, I explained that the chair was occupied and suggested that he sat somewhere else. He seemed quite a decent chap. Had quite a conversation with him as a matter of fact."

After lunch they walked round the docks again. The docks they had come to know so well. Down the Bollwerk where the river Oder flowed dark and sluggish and the gulls wheeled and swooped in the sky, jeering and shrieking at them because they were earthbound and looking at them with yellow staring eyes as they swooped by in the perfect freedom of their flight. Past the motor torpedo-boats, E-boats and ships' pinnaces lying waiting to dash out to the destroyers moored by Swinemünde. Past the Café d'Accordion still dark and closed, over the bridge and out opposite the gates of the Freihafen. There they found no neutral shipping and although they walked round several times they could not pick out the Swedish flag.

When it began to get dark they returned to the café where they had met the French boys. They sat quietly sipping their beer and watching the other people in the room.

Peter was thinking of the Frenchmen. Were they really any use ? Was it worth the risk of hanging around or would it be better to make for Danzig ? Phil had gone to Danzig and was probably in Sweden by now. They were getting too involved with the French. Perhaps John was right. Perhaps it would have been better to have kept it to themselves.

He found that he was looking at a man who sat at the next table. He had seen the face before. Noticed it several times, but almost subconsciously. It suddenly seemed that the man had been in every café they had used. The face had cropped up time and again, but he had not consciously noticed it before.

It had caught up with them at last. It had been too good— too easy. Now that they were face to face with it he was almost relieved. It had been the uncertainty more than the danger that had got him down. He leaned over to John.

" See that fellow who's just come in ? "

" Which one ? "

" That one. Sitting near the radiator."

" What about him ? "

" He's following us."

" Nonsense."

" He is. He's been in nearly every café we've been in."

" Why should he follow us ? If they wanted to pick us up they'd do it without following us."

" I don't know why," Peter said. " But he *is* following us."

" Easily find out. Drink up and we'll go to another café."

They finished their beer and without looking at the man they got up and left. They walked quickly down the street and went into another café. They ordered more beer and sat watching the door. The man did not come in.

" Imagination," John said. " Let's go back to the other place."

" No. Have a beer here."

" We'll go back afterwards then. No good being uncertain about it."

When they got outside it was quite dark. They turned to the right of the door and started back towards the café where the man was.

" He's behind us," Peter said. " He must have been waiting outside."

John looked round quickly. " Yes, that looks like the same chap. What are we going to do ? "

" We can't talk to anyone while he's with us. If he is following us it's to catch the French who are helping us. We'll have to drop him somehow."

" Let's go to the place where we climbed out of the window."

" We can't do it again. They'd be on us as soon as we walked in. I don't suppose they've repaired the lock yet anyway. Have to drop him somehow else. Let's separate."

" O.K.," John said. " Where shall we meet ? "

" Better not the Café d'Accordion in case we haven't managed to drop him. I'll see you outside the hotel at "—he looked at his watch—" nine-thirty."

" Right. We won't walk towards him. When we get to the next crossroads I'll go right and you go left. He may hesitate and then we stand a chance of losing him straight away. If we don't it's up to the one he follows."

They walked on at the same pace until they reached the corner. Then they separated and began to walk fast. Peter turned to the left as soon as he could and then to the right and out on to the Bollwerk. There were a number of people about and he walked fast, threading his way between them and not looking back. Mustn't let him think I know I'm being followed. If he knows that they'll arrest us right away. He slowed down and began to fill his pipe. He filled it carefully and patted his pockets as though looking for matches. Pretending not to find any he turned and walked back the way he had come. As he turned he saw the figure of a man slip into a doorway.

He walked past the doorway without looking. He walked back to a café where he knew there was a permanent light burning on the counter for customers to light their cigarettes. He lit his pipe at the flame and came out of the café. He came out fast and turned in the direction he had been going in the first place, hoping to catch a glimpse of the man who was following him.

This time he did not see him and he walked on down the Bollwerk. He crossed the bridge by the railway station and came out on to the road leading to Reiherwerder. There was a tram at the stop, just about to start. He ran the last hundred yards and caught the tram as it was gathering speed. The conductor caught his arm and shouted at him in German. He looked back but he could not see the man who was following.

He stood on the platform of the tram for two stops. At each stop there was a car close behind them and he thought it might be a car commandeered by his pursuer. At the third stop there was no car ; so he got down off the tram and crossed the road. He caught the next tram going back into town. But he did not get off at the Bollwerk. He went right on into the town and made for the Hotel Sack where he stood waiting for John. I'd better not walk about, he thought. I'm safer standing still.

Punctually at nine-thirty he saw John coming down the street.

" He followed you," John said. " I stopped to light a cigarette and saw him chasing you down the road. Did you drop him all right?

"Yes. I jumped a tram and gave him the slip. What do we do now?"

"Let's get out of this. The quicker we get out of here the better. Let's jump a train up to Danzig."

"Seems a pity to waste all the contacts we've made. I thought we were getting somewhere at last. If we go up to Danzig we'll have to start all over again."

"All right—we'll go up to the Café d'Accordion first," John said. "I don't fancy sleeping out to-night and we might be able to pick something up there. If we don't have any luck we'll go straight up to the goods yard and get right out of the place."

The Café d'Accordion was full as ever. They ordered their drinks and stood by the bar, sizing up all the likely people there. Standing next to Peter was a man of his own age, a merchant seaman. He was drunk, rolling drunk, and he gabbled a mixture of German, French and English. He was trying to sell a boiler suit.

"How much?" John said in English. "*Wieviel?*"

The man turned round and stared at him solemnly.

"How much?" he said. "I spik English, I spik German, I spik Dutch. I spik French, I spik all languages. . . ." He stumbled forward and recovered himself. "I tell you how much." He pulled John forward and whispered drunkenly in his ear. "I pinch 'em from a raumboot." He flung an arm affectionately round John's shoulders. "I pinch 'em from a raumboot tied alongside my dredger. Now I sell 'em, see? I spik English, I spik American, I spik . . ."

"What sort of boat are you from?" John spoke in English, but quietly.

The sailor did not want to talk quietly. "I spik English, I spik German . . ."

Suddenly, he went out. Out like a light, flat on his face on

the floor, down among the feet of the people at the bar. In falling
he knocked a glass of beer from John's hand and it fell on top
of him, soaking the back of his jacket and his hair.

Peter pulled John to one side.

" Don't get mixed up in it," he said.

Someone had pulled the sailor to his feet and taken him away
into a corner. Peter could still hear him shouting, " I spik
Swedish, I spik Russian, I spik German . . ."

" What is he ? " he whispered.

" Swedish, I think," John said.

" He's too drunk. Keep clear of him."

" O.K."

A waitress came by with a tray full of glasses of beer. As she
passed, a young Frenchman put his arm round her waist and
began to speak in burlesque German.

" *Ach, mein Liebe*," he said. " *Ach, mein Liebling, mein
Liebschen.*"

She threw off his arm angrily.

" That's our man ! " Peter said.

John looked at him. He was about twenty-five, tall and
powerful-looking, with a dark face and brown angry eyes, a wide,
full mouth, straight nose and tousled hair. He wore a scarf round
his neck and his jacket was too short in the sleeves. He was sitting
slouched back in his chair, a cigarette dangling from the corner of
his mouth, just drunk enough to do and say as he pleased. He
looked as though he usually did as he pleased. A man to help
you if he thought he wanted to help you. Not a man to be
frightened to help you.

" I'll wait until he goes to the lavatory," he said.

When the Frenchman went out to the lavatory John followed.
Presently they both came back into the room. John beckoned
Peter over to the Frenchman's table and introduced him as René.
He spoke no English, but Peter could tell by his voice he was
going to help them. There was no doubt in that voice. It was a
friendly, excited voice.

René called for a round of drinks and John told him the story of their stay in Stettin. He told him about the man who had been following them, because they did not want him to run any risks that he did not know about.

"You must come back to my camp," René said. "The air raid shelter is not safe. It is not safe to walk about the streets now. You must hide away until we can find you a ship. I know the barber—the English-speaking Frenchman, as you call him. He is a good man. He will find you a ship. In the meantime I and my friends will look. You must come with us. We will feed you and look after you until you can get away."

John turned to Peter and quickly translated what René had said. Thank God, Peter thought, thank God. At last, after all this time, we've found the man we're looking for. He smiled at René and René smiled back and raised his thumb.

Then Peter glanced at the door, the quick, furtive glance round that he had laughed at in the Frenchmen but had unconsciously acquired himself. And in that quick glance he saw the man who had been following them.

He was standing with his back to the counter, watching them and drinking a glass of beer.

Peter felt a sudden anger, an anger against the fate that had lured them on with every promise of success only to let them down at the last minute. A thought flashed through his mind to murder the man, to kill him and throw his body into the sea. And then commonsense came to his rescue and a fatalism that had grown in him since he had been taken prisoner. They'd had a good run for it. The only thing was to submit now and go back quietly. There was no use in struggling against it. There was a time to struggle and a time to submit. They'd had a good try and now if they were lucky they would go back to the prison camp— to try again. It was always a matter of luck and the dice were so heavily loaded against the escaping prisoner. Once you were out of the camp it was all luck and they'd had it all with them for a time. And now it had turned against them. But he felt sick. He felt sick inside him with a desperate desire to go back in time. To turn back the clock and not make the mistakes that had brought the Gestapo on their track. He turned to John and tapped him on the knee.

" That chap who followed us is by the bar."

John was talking to René and René was smiling. John said something quickly in French, but René did not stop smiling. He looked at the man by the counter and his smile grew broader.

The man's cool, Peter thought. He hasn't turned a hair. And he felt a sudden increase of faith in the man who sat there wearing the broad grin.

René got up and crossed over to the man at the bar. He said a few words and the man immediately left the café.

" What did you say to him ? " John asked when René came back.

René laughed. " That is the barber's brother. He has been following you to see that you do not get into trouble. Now we should return to the camp."

CHAPTER NINE

They Meet Sigmund

THEY HAD some miles to walk before they got to René's camp, but they walked them cheerfully. This was no longer aimless walking. It was not walking because they dared not stay in one place, because they felt hunted and if they walked they felt less hunted. It was not walking round the docks, round the town, in search of Frenchmen whom they hardly expected to meet, and frightened all the time they would be stopped and their papers demanded. It was not walking because they were hungry and cold, and if they walked they felt less hungry and less cold. It was walking to get somewhere. It was walking openly and fast and they were cheerful because of that.

As they walked René explained why they had been followed. The man was a member of an anti-German organisation—part of the organisation to which the man who was going to Sweden belonged. Apparently André had not been completely satis-fied with the result of the interrogation and so they had been followed; at first because André was suspicious, later for their own safety.

John asked him about the organisation and he told them its real object was to preserve the morale of the French prisoners. It was not for action. They carried out a little negative sabotage; but the main purpose of the organisation was to unite the prisoners in their hatred of the Boche and to keep alive the spirit of France.

"At the moment we can do nothing," René said. "We are powerless. But when the British invade, when the British drop us arms, then we shall rise."

When they reached the camp they went in through the gate, this time openly. It was larger than the other, built as a labour camp and not as a prison. There was barbed wire, but as a gesture rather than as a defence. The huts were clean and dry; but they had the same smell, the same compounded smell of prison life. There were ten beds in René's room, ten lockers, and a table and some stools.

When Peter and John had been introduced they were given food, black German bread and lard-like margarine.

They did not talk much. They were tired. Soon after they had eaten the Frenchmen suggested that they should go to bed. They shared René's bed and he shared with another man. It was almost good to be back on the hard prison bed again; back in the live darkness of the crowded room, the friendly sound of sleeping men, and the sudden-glowing cigarettes.

They were awakened early in the morning, before it was light, when the Frenchmen dressed to go to work. They shared their breakfast of bread and margarine and ersatz coffee and were lighting their cigarettes when they heard footsteps outside. René tried to get them hidden under the beds, but before they could move the door burst open and a man stood panting inside the room.

It was the barber and when he could speak he spoke in French. He sat on the nearest stool and mopped his brow with a handkerchief.

John turned to Peter. " He's fixed up for a boat to take us to Copenhagen."

" Copenhagen ? That's in Denmark."

" Yes."

" That's occupied by the Germans."

" I know."

" What's the use of that ? "

" Well, it's somewhere."

" We haven't any Danish papers. Or money."

" We haven't any German left—so that's no argument. And

we do stand a chance of getting help from the Danes. Besides, it'll be easier to get to Sweden from Denmark than from here."

Peter thought it over. As usual John was all for going. All for going there and then; taking the risk and getting out of Germany. But Peter was cautious. He wanted to be certain they were not jeopardising the ground they had already won. The longer they stayed out of the camp the more cautious he became, the more he wanted to hang on to what they had—even, sometimes, at the risk of not getting any farther.

He stood there undecided and the Frenchmen stood there in silence wondering at the delay.

"We can live here now," Peter said. "Why not stay here until we can get a boat to get us all the way?"

"We can't live on these chaps for ever!" John was growing impatient, not seeing the cause of Peter's doubt, not thinking about what they would do in Denmark, but thinking of getting there, of taking decisive action and getting out of the country.

"We can get in touch with the Resistance in Denmark," he said.

"What do we do until then?" Peter asked. "Sleep in the fields?"

"Well, I'm for going." John was growing angry now, and obstinate.

"Ask them more about it. Ask them if the crew are staying in Denmark and if we can stay with them when we get there.'

John turned to the barber and spoke to him in French. The barber shrugged his shoulders as he replied.

"He doesn't know," John said. "He says the organisation have arranged it. That's all he knows. He's come to take us to meet one of the crew."

"We ought to make certain. It's taken us long enough to make this contact, and now as soon as we've made it you want to go dashing off to Denmark. Getting caught in Denmark is no better than getting caught in Germany. It's no use dashing off after the first red herring that comes along."

"How do you know it's a red herring? I should think it's

pretty easy to get across from Denmark into Sweden. We might find it easier to steal a small boat there. Anyway, it's better than going up to Danzig."

" O.K. Let's meet him and see what he has to say."

John turned again to the Frenchman and then to Peter.

" We're to meet him in an hour's time outside the Café d'Accordion."

An hour later they were awaiting the arrival of the Danish sailor. They did not wait outside the door of the café, but farther down the road where they could watch the meeting-place.

They waited for ten minutes after the agreed time, but the sailor did not come. They began to feel alarmed and were about to return to the camp when they were accosted by a young man wearing a neat blue overcoat. He looked like a student.

" Good morning." He said it in passable English.

" Good morning," Peter said.

" I have come to take you aboard my ship. I have one spare pass. I can take one of you and return for the other."

" What happens when we get to Denmark ? " Peter asked, feeling ungrateful as he said it.

" When you get to Denmark you will be all right."

" Where shall we stay ? How soon can we get to Sweden ? "

" When you get to Denmark you can easily reach Sweden from there. People go from Denmark to Sweden all the time. From Germany it is not so easy."

" He's right, Pete." John wanted to stir him. Wanted him to see the advantage of this as he himself saw it, clearly and without alternative.

" Where will you hide us in the ship ? " Peter asked and John stood by feeling embarrassed. He felt embarrassed as he had felt when he had gone shopping in Exeter with his aunt and she, after years in India, had haggled with the shopkeeper. Had tried to beat down the price that was as fixed and unassailable as the ancient town itself.

" They'll hide us all right," he said. " They'll know where to put us."

" We sail this afternoon," the Dane said.

" We'd better go, Pete."

" Who's going first ? " Peter asked, accepting it grudgingly. " You can if you like."

" No fear ! " John said. " You go first." He turned to the Dane. " I'll wait here for you." To Peter, " You'll only get into conversation with someone if I leave you here alone."

They had no difficulty in getting into the docks. The Dane made Peter walk in front of him, alone through the gate into the dock, and then caught up with him and said, " Follow me, but do not come too close. Follow me up the gangplank and do not look at anyone. Do not come too close. If I stop to talk to anyone walk past us and slow down until I come."

Peter followed him down the quayside, openly and in daylight where they had gone before furtively and in the dark. They came to the quay where the Danish ship was berthed. She was called the *S. I. Norensen.* There was a gangplank down and on the other side of the quay Russian soldiers were loading a ship under the supervision of a German guard.

The Dane walked up the gangplank, crossed the deck and vanished down a companionway. Peter followed and found himself in the forecastle. The Dane motioned him to a seat without speaking and went out again by the companionway.

Peter sat in the dark cabin waiting for the Dane to return with John. He looked round him at the triangular cabin, lined with two-tier bunks. The apex of the triangle was the bows of the ship. At the base of the triangle was a cast-iron stove and a long table ran down the centre between the bunks.

He wanted the ship to be at sea. To feel the roll and lurch of it and to know that it was taking them away from Germany. He crossed to one of the portholes and looked out on to the docks. The German sentry had his back to the ship and was watching the Russians. John and the Dane were walking unconcernedly along the quay. It's going to be O.K., he thought, we're going to make it.

Then John and the Dane were in the forecastle and the three of them stood round the cast-iron stove warming their hands.

"You will be home soon," the Dane said. "You will be home for Christmas maybe."

Peter looked at John. Home for Christmas. What had been a dream was becoming real. What had seemed a fantastic shot against long odds was now a possibility. And the nearer they came to winning through the more nervous he became. They were now in someone else's hands. They had no decisions to make until they were ashore again. Just do as they were told and ride it out. Ride it out patiently while the others did the thinking. And were the others competent? Their necks were at stake. All their necks were at stake now except his and John's, but he did not like trusting them. While he and John went their own way, while they stayed alone and worked together, he did not mind. If they lost it they lost it themselves and had no one to blame for it. At first it had been John who had wanted to go alone, John who had not wanted the contact with the French, who had not wanted to accept the risk involved in speaking to them in the streets; he had wanted to go on alone, to stow away or steal a boat, but to travel alone and not depend on the French.

But now it was both of them. They had done what they could. They had gone as far as they could go alone. They had depended on the French and now they were depending on the Danes. They could do nothing about it now. They could just ride it out and leave the decisions to others. And he was nervous because of this.

Then Larensen came in. Larensen was the crew boss and had been ashore. He was a big man. Big, dark and fleshy with a stubble of black beard and a face that showed red and fleshy through the stubble. His eyes were blue and bloodshot and he smelled of schnapps. He was drunk, affectionately drunk.

"You boys will be all right now. I'm Larensen, see?" He spoke English with an American accent. "Call me Olaf. I see

you all right. I'm de head man around here. I send Sigmund
for you, see? I fix everything. You don't have to worry now."

He turned to John. "You an aviator?"

"No," said John, "I'm in the army."

"In the army, eh?" He pulled a bottle of schnapps from his
coat pocket. "You boys like a drink, eh?" He took out the cork
and wiped the top of the bottle with his hand before offering it
to John. "What do you do before the war?"

John took a drink from the bottle before replying. "I was
at the university."

"A professor, eh?" He turned to Peter. "He's too young
to be a professor."

"He was a student," Peter explained.

"He was a professor," Larensen said.

"All right," Peter said, "he was a professor."

The rest of the crew came in one by one and then they were
all there. They did not seem surprised that there were strangers
in the forecastle. They came in one by one until there were five
of them. Five young men, almost boys, dressed in cheap smart
suits and overcoats. As they came in they each took a drink from
the bottle of schnapps. They changed from their smart clothes
into sweaters and overalls and became at once men and more
dependable. Sigmund, the man who had brought them aboard,
altered most with the change of clothes. He wore a heavy knitted
Scandinavian sea jersey and assumed authority with it.

When the crew had changed they sat round the table in the
forecastle drinking schnapps while the cabin boy fried eggs and
bacon on the cast-iron stove. Peter sat there with his back against
one of the bunks drinking schnapps from the bottle and smelling
the bacon as it was cooking. One of the crew gave him a cigarette,
but he could not smoke. His stomach was turning over and he
was nearly sick from the smell of the frying bacon and the sound
of sizzling and spluttering in the pan.

It's quite true, he thought, your mouth does water. He sat
there trying to talk to Larensen until the boy placed a plate of
eggs and bacon on the table in front of him. He passed it to John

and Larensen cut them thick slices of white bread from the loaf on the table. Then his plate came up and Larensen sat watching them as they ate, eating quickly and thoroughly and wiping their plates with bread when they had finished.

" You boys were hungry, eh ? " Larensen went to a cupboard at the end of the forecastle and came back with a large piece of cake on a plate. " Made from eggs," he said. " Our last cargo was of eggs. Eggs for Germany." He made a short explosive sound with his lips.

They slept on the bunks while the crew made the ship ready for sea. About two o'clock Larensen woke them with tea and sandwiches and told them that the Germans were coming to search the ship before she sailed. He sat opposite them at the small forecastle table while they ate the food. His two mahogany-coloured, dirt-grained and calloused hands rested on the edge of the table. One of the fingers of his right hand was missing.

" You boys eat good ! " he told them. " Presently you go down in the bilge. We put in for an inspection first thing in the morning. We have another search at Swinemünde and that's the last of Germany. After that we go straight to Copenhagen."

" Are there many Germans in Copenhagen ? " Peter asked.

" Sure, hundreds. You ask Sigmund all about the Germans. He'll tell you. He's a fire-eater. He wants to eat all the Germans there are. He wants to throw 'em all into the sea. He's a dangerous guy."

" Is he one of the crew ? "

" He's a contact man for the underground organisation. He sails with us as a deckhand. He sails with us too long now. Soon he will be caught. He takes might' big risks, that feller."

Larensen slid aside a panel in the apex of the triangle that was the forecastle. Behind the panel was a small cubby-hole formed in the extreme bows of the ship. It was just large enough to hold the two of them and smelled of paint and sea-water. The walls were the steel walls of the ship, and they were cold and water condensed and dripped from them.

They squeezed into the cubby-hole and Larensen passed them

a wooden box to sit on, a torch, a bottle of water, an empty bottle and a metal funnel.

"You may be there some hours," he said. "Don't shine the torch if you hear voices and don' speak unless I open the door. The Germans will come down here but they won' use tear gas in the fo'c'sle. I give 'em a drink, see? I give 'em a drink in the fo'c'sle, so you keep very quiet. If you make a noise "—he drew his hand across his throat in a cutting gesture—" and don' smoke, or you cough. I fix 'em, see? I fix 'em good. If the dog comes down here I fix 'im too. I got pepper to fix 'im. I fix 'im good."

He replaced the panel, leaving them in the darkness of the cubby-hole. John shone the torch and they settled themselves to wait. It was cold and in spite of their mackintoshes and heavy woollen underwear they shivered.

They stayed there for several hours, unable to talk and apprehensive of every step on the deck above. Once they heard the sound of military boots and the whining of a dog and then German voices shouting on the quay. Then there was silence. They began to feel stiff and were tempted to tap on the panel in front of them. They had filled the empty bottle and the cold was becoming unbearable. Waves of coldness came from the wet steel hull, numbing their limbs and deadening their minds.

Escape is all coldness, Peter thought. Coldness and waiting. It's heat sometimes in digging and in running away. But mostly it's coldness and hunger and hanging about waiting.

They heard the Germans come below into the cabin. They heard the unnecessarily loud voice of Larensen talking German and the laughter and the sound of a glass against a bottle. And the heavy dragging movement as the soldiers eased themselves into the seat that ran along underneath the bunks.

Peter sat there riding it out. He had forgotten the cold now and the fact that his bladder was full. He was listening for the sound of the German voices and for the sniffing of the dogs. He thought he heard it once but he could not be certain. They had put out the torch and through the darkness he could feel John's

tenseness as he crouched down beside him, listening to the voices
in the cabin on the other side of the wooden partition.

Then he heard them leaving, heard the triumphant note in
Larensen's voice as he saw them out of the forecastle, heard their
feet trampling across the deck and heard Larensen come back
into the cabin and squeeze past the seat to remove the panel.

"I gottem," he said. "I fixed 'em. We have something to
eat now, then I hide you down below. The German guard, look,
look, here! See?" He took them over to a porthole. There was
a German soldier standing at the bottom of the gangplank. "When
we sail he come with us as far as Swinemünde. We drop 'im off
at Swinemünde and then you can come up here. But now you
have something to eat and then go down below, eh?"

He got them more sandwiches of dry bread and bacon and
led them down through a trap door in the floor of the forecastle
on to the deck below, down through another trap door, forward
and down through another trap door; and forward again into
the bilges where the anchor chain was stored.

"Be careful of the chain," he said. "Keep away from that
chain when the anchor goes down. It goes down at Swinemünde.
When the anchor goes down you know you won't have to wait
long." He left them a storm lantern and the fat bacon sandwiches
and went back up the ladder. They could hear the trap doors
banging as he climbed into the forecastle.

They found a canvas sea-anchor in a corner and made themselves a bed. It was cold in the bilge, colder than it had been in
the cubby-hole, but they could move and stamp their feet and
beat their arms across their backs to keep them warm. Peter ate
his share of the sandwiches and fell asleep.

Some time later he was wakened by the slowing-down of the
engines and they knew that they had reached Swinemünde. They
crouched in a corner as far away as they could from the anchor
chain. Then the engines died and the anchor went down, the
chain plunging and kicking like a wild animal as it crashed around
in the small compass of the locker. It stopped and they heard the
gentle lap, lap of the waves against the hull. It was deathly silent

in the locker after the thump of the engines and the clatter and the bang of the running anchor chain.

This is the last check, Peter thought. If we pass this one we get to Denmark.

They lay on the hard canvas of the sea-anchor listening to the lapping of the water and imagining the pilot and the guard leaving the ship, and the captain taking over. They could hear nothing but the lapping of the water on the hull and an occasional thump that they thought might be the pilot boat pushing off.

Then the anchor came up and the engines started again. And they began to move and they knew that they would get to Denmark.

CHAPTER TEN

The Danish Resistance

PETER WOKE suddenly and completely. It was quite dark. He reached for the torch in the side pocket of his mackintosh and flashed it on his wrist. His watch had stopped. He sent the thin beam of light cutting across the darkness of the locker. John lay sleeping with his head on his arm, his long lashes dark over his cheeks and a slight smile on his unshaven face.

They had been sick during the night. Peter shifted his weight uncomfortably on the hard canvas. His mouth tasted foul and his lips were dry and cracked. They had been sick until they had fallen asleep from sheer exhaustion. The lamp had burned itself out and it had been dark. Peter had been sick before, he had been sick on the sea and in the air. But he had never been as sick as this. The sea had been rough and the water in the bilge had swished and rolled, filling the locker with the smell of all the refuse of the years.

It had not been so bad while they had the storm lantern. But when the oil ran out and they were left in the darkness, unable to see one another but hearing the groans and falling cascades of one another's sickness, then the locker had become a black, damp, tossing, stinking hell.

He heard footsteps on the deck above and Larensen came down the ladder bringing with him a jug of coffee and some sandwiches. He was sober now and told them that there was no longer any danger of their being boarded.

" I had to leave you boys in the locker," he said, " because of the coast patrol. You been sick, professor ? "

John looked at Peter. " He wants to know if we've been sick."

An hour later Sigmund came down with a lantern and took them up to the forecastle. " You will be more comfortable here," he said. " You can sleep in the bunks for the next two nights and then you will have to go down in the bilges again. It is not very comfortable down there, I think."

" It's not too bad," John said. " We're not used to the movement yet."

" It will get worse," Sigmund said. " We get very rough crossings at this time of the year. It will be better when we are among the islands."

" Where shall we go when we get to Copenhagen ? " Peter asked.

" You will either be hidden in the town or you will come with me to the Resistance. It will depend on the sailors. Sometimes our boats have to hide because of German patrols. We must wait until we reach Copenhagen before we know. It will be arranged. You are with us now. It is for Mr. Olsen to decide."

" Who's Mr. Olsen ? "

" There is no such person as Mr. Olsen. It is the name we give to the leader of the Resistance. I do not know his real name. I do not wish to talk about the Resistance."

They spent the rest of the day sitting in the forecastle playing cards, sleeping and eating the eggs and bacon that Larensen cooked on the small cast-iron stove. As Sigmund had predicted, the weather worsened as the day passed and by the evening the ship was rolling so much that the two passengers were glad to climb into their bunks.

The next day was just as rough. They could not eat breakfast but lay in their bunks waiting for the time to pass. Now they had time to think about the future. To Peter, sick as he was, it seemed that in Denmark they would be little better off than they had been in Germany. In Denmark they would be in the hands of the Resistance Movement. They would act without knowing the cause or the meaning of their actions. They would merely do as they were told, without knowing or considering the wisdom of what they did. He decided to cut their stay in Denmark as short as possible.

During the next two days Sigmund told them of the German occupation of Denmark. How at first the Germans had been " correct," hoping to make a peaceful conquest of the country, taking their food for the German army and using only a small part of that army as a force of occupation. But the Danish people had refused to co-operate. There had been clashes in the streets at night. Some German soldiers had been killed. Hostages had been taken and a curfew declared. Now, no Danes were allowed out of their houses after eight o'clock at night and many of the younger people had withdrawn to the country where they waged guerrilla warfare against the Germans.

" We are mostly students," Sigmund told them. " Only those who can no longer work in the open live in the country. The life of a contact man is not long. After a few trips he becomes known to the Jerries. Then it is a matter of luck whether he is recalled before he is sent to a concentration camp or shot. I have had luck. This is my last journey. When I reach Copenhagen I shall go to the country."

In the morning of the third day Sigmund, who had been up on the bridge, came down to the forecastle.

" We have had a code radio from Mr. Olsen ! " he said. " The Jerries are waiting to arrest me when we get to Copenhagen. Mr. Olsen is sending a small boat out to pick me up before we get in. We shall alter the ship's log so that my name is not there. You will come with me."

" Where shall we go ? " Peter asked.

" To the country. It seems there has been much trouble in Copenhagen. Many have been arrested. There will be much to do."

" How will they take us off in a small boat ? " Peter asked.

" It will be difficult. The captain has been given a rendezvous.

The ship docks early to-morrow morning. During the night we shall meet the boat and she will take us off. If we miss her, we are all finished. For myself, I shall go overboard during the night and try to swim to the shore. It will be better than a concentration camp."

"We could take a lifeboat," John suggested.

"That we cannot do. They would see that a boat was missing and shoot the captain. We shall not appear on the books and it will not involve him. But we cannot take a boat."

They spent the rest of the day and the night waiting anxiously for the boat. The wind was rising and they were both sick again.

Before daybreak the engines slowed down and they went on deck. There was a heavy sea running and it was raining. The wind breaking the tops of the waves sent a fine spray of salt water sweeping across the ship. The rain was slanting down as a solid sheet ; but the sea spray was horizontal, a fine stinging horizontal spray of drenching wetness. The sky was a few feet above the sea, solid and black, and the wind howled through the rigging as the ship nosed down into the sea.

"It's a bit rough !" Peter shouted. "Never get a small boat out in this."

They stood by the rail, the spray stinging in their faces, straining their eyes for a sight of the boat.

"I don't like it," John said. "We'll never swim in this."

The ship was rolling in the sea like an old tub. In the faint light of the early morning they could see the white-crested waves riding past them, breaking and blowing and spraying in the wind. At one moment the ship was poised forty feet in the air and in the next she was sinking down, down, as though she would never rise again. But she did rise, shaking the sea from her decks and wallowing on, her engines barely giving her steering way.

"There she is !" Sigmund shouted.

Peter had just time to see a red star shell curve down into the sea. "They'll have the coastal patrol on us !" he said.

As he spoke there was a swoosh behind him and a rocket went

rushing up into the night. There was an answering star shell from the boat and then they could see her tossing like a cork on the waves.

" We will have to jump," Sigmund said. " They will not get alongside in a sea like this." He went down to the forecastle and returned with three lifebelts. " Wear these. We will jump one by one. Do not jump until you see they have picked up the man before you. You go first ! " he told John.

The boat came round to their lee side. She carried a small searchlight which she played on the water between them.

" Over you go ! " Sigmund ordered.

John held his nose and jumped. He fell into the water between the ship's side and the boat and was hauled on board as the boat fell rapidly astern. Presently she was up with them again.

" You next ! " Sigmund said.

Peter climbed the rail and stood looking down on the black sea. Choosing the moment when the ship was in a trough he jumped far out from the side of the ship towards the boat.

The sea was not cold at first. But then the coldness gripped him. He struck out for the boat, wildly, his lungs full of salt water, terrified and clumsy. They had some difficulty pulling him into the boat. Then he was lying in the bottom of the boat and someone was forcing brandy between his teeth.

Sigmund joined them in the bottom of the boat. The engine was put to " full ahead " and they were plunging and bouncing towards the shore.

They came to the land at first light. The wind had abated slightly but there was a fast sea running and the sky was low and angry. It was a bleak and desolate coastline, great black cliffs rising from the grey sea with a surf line that showed white and angry at their base.

The two men who were the boat's crew sat silent as she plunged and quivered to the pounding sea. The three passengers lay wet and shivering under a pile of blankets in the well.

As they came to the shore, Sigmund spoke in Danish to the man who was steering.

John held his nose and jumped

The man replied, also in Danish. He was a quiet man, bleached and tanned by the sea.

"They have caught Mr. Olsen," Sigmund said. "The Jerries have caught Mr. Olsen." He said it as though it meant the end of the Resistance.

"How?" Peter asked. He did not care much about Mr. Olsen at the moment. He was cold and sick and he wanted to get to the shore.

"The Jerries raided the farm where he was staying. They have put him in prison."

They came round in a wide sweep in the bay and ran into a narrow fjord where there was a strip of white beach and a steep path to the top of the cliff. They could smell the seaweed as they came in, strong and heady in the early morning freshness, and the gulls soared and swooped above them, screaming and turning their heads to watch the boat as she ran in to the rough jetty at the bottom of the cliff.

The steersman spoke again to Sigmund.

"We must go quickly," Sigmund translated. "There are bicycles at the top of the cliff. These men will hide the boat. There are German patrols. We must not waste time."

They climbed the steep path to the top of the cliff, their clothes hanging damply to them as they climbed By the time they reached the top they were warm, and steam rose from them as they stood looking at the orderly countryside.

It was a toy landscape. A landscape of neat houses, trim fields and well-kept roads. There were no hedges, but wooden fences and earthen walls.

Three bicycles stood at the top of the path, chained together and fastened by a padlock which Sigmund unlocked with the key given to him by the boatman. "We will ride fast. It is getting late."

He led them inland down the smooth tarmac roads, riding oddly on the right-hand side of the road. They were queer heavy bicycles, with thick tyres and upturned handlebars, but it was better than walking and the rush of the wind was drying their clothes. Then the sun came out, weakly at first but growing warmer, and the blood moved in them and for the first time since leaving Germany they felt free.

Sigmund led them at a fast pace. He led them for several hours, past hamlets and villages without stopping; shouting greetings to the villagers, but pressing on all the time, urgent, anxious to get to the Resistance and hear the news of Mr. Olsen.

Peter was not urgent. The sun was shining and he was reluctant to involve himself in the troubles of the Resistance Movement. He wanted to get away. The Resistance was a side issue, an incident in the main scheme of the escape, and he wanted to make that incident as short as possible. His clothes were dry now and he was enjoying the ride across the strange and lovely countryside.

The storm had passed, leaving a sky of clear blue against which the faint streaks of high cirrus floated like silver smoke. The roads were straight and lined with trees, and in the villages the houses were painted pink and white and pale blue, and huge beech trees with their bare branches guarded the quiet streets.

They stopped outside one of the villages, at a small farm which lay back off the road.

" This is the headquarters," Sigmund told them. " Wait here till I report."

He handed his bicycle to John and knocked at the door. DIT DIT DIT DAH, the V sign.

A woman came to the door. She was an old woman, dressed in peasant costume. Her face was brown and red and her hair was tied in a coloured handkerchief.

Sigmund came back to the road again. " They have gone. We must ride some more miles."

They mounted their bicycles again and rode on. Peter was not interested in the countryside any more. He was stiff and saddle-sore and he wanted to get to wherever they were going as soon as possible. He was hungry and thirsty and his clothes were irritating where the salt had dried in them.

The new headquarters was in a large farmhouse. Of brick this time, with a thatched roof and huge old-fashioned chimneys.

There was a sentry standing at the gates, a young man wearing British battledress trousers, a sweater and sea-boots. On his head he wore a black cap with a shiny peak to it and he was armed with a Thompson sub-machine-gun and a revolver in a leather holster which he wore tied cowboy-fashion to his leg.

Sigmund spoke to him in Danish. The sentry saluted and stepped to one side as they went in through the gate.

They entered the farmhouse and found themselves in a low room with a stone floor and a heavy beamed ceiling. There was a large tiled stove at one end of the room and in the centre a long trestle table at which three men were sitting. The room was like an armoury. Service rifles stood in wooden racks against the far wall and beneath them were boxes of ammunition and open trays full of hand grenades. To the left of the rifles stood a small table on which was a grey British transmitting and receiving set. On the table where the men were sitting lay four Browning machine-guns.

The men looked up as the three of them came into the room. They were all armed.

Sigmund spoke to them in Danish. He spoke fast. Peter heard the letters R.A.F. repeated several times.

The men stood up. Their faces had brightened as Sigmund spoke.

" R.A.F.," the man at the head of the table said in un-accustomed English. " You are welcome to our country. It is good to see the R.A.F."

" This is Carl," Sigmund said. " He is Mr. Olsen's second-in-command."

Carl was a tall man in his late forties. Grey and thin but with keen eyes and steady hands.

" You are welcome," he said again.

" Thank you," Peter said. He looked at the other two men. They were both young. They looked like students. He walked over to the table. " Browning guns!" He took up one of the guns, holding its well-known shape, brown and slightly oily, in his hands.

" It will not fire," Carl said.

Peter turned the gun over. " Number one stoppage," he said. " We ought to be able to fix that."

The men watched Peter as he stripped the gun. It was good to see the stripped gun coming to pieces in his hands, to see the clean and oiled parts placed in neat rows on the wooden table. He stripped the gun down to the breech block.

" Bad luck. Broken firing pin."

" You can fix it ? " Carl asked.

" Not unless you have a spare breech block," Peter told him.

Carl crossed to a pile of sacking in the corner of the room and returned with a Browning gun, its barrel bent and twisted by fire.

" Where did you get them ? " John asked.

" From a crashed R.A.F. bomber," Carl said. " We got there before the Germans did. All the crew were dead. We gave them a military funeral. They are buried in the local churchyard. We got the guns and the ammunition away."

Peter was stripping the damaged gun. " Good show ! " he said. " The breech is O.K. We can fix the gun for you all right."

" That is good," Carl said. " We have made stands for them. We shall use them against the Germans."

They had eaten their meal, all sitting together at the long table and eating the roast goose and vegetables from the farm, with weak Danish beer and good white bread made by the farmer's wife. Carl had taken Sigmund to another room, leaving the four young men sitting at the table. The Danes spoke good English and the talk had been of their weapons. They carried an assortment of Danish, German and Finnish arms, but these were the first Browning guns they had seen and they were keen to know how they were fired.

" There are right- and left-hand feeds," Peter explained. " They're made that way to fit into the gun turrets. To change them over you do this." He showed them how to adapt the feed of the guns.

" How do you load them ? " one of the Danes asked. He was a tall, fair-haired youth with spectacles, and they called him Hans

"First you make up the belt"—Peter showed them how to fit the cartridges together to form the belt—"always keeping the smooth side of the clip to the same side of the belt. The belt you found in the aircraft will be composed of assorted rounds in the following order : armour-piercing, incendiary, explosive, solid and tracer." Saying this, he was carried back to a small wooden hut on an airfield in England. There was the sound of revving engines outside the hut, and inside a class of bored navigators were half-listening to the instructor who, parrot-fashion, ran through the patter from the armament manual.

"You'll use the bullets you need for the particular job you're doing," he continued. "The tracer won't be much good, but the incendiaries should be very useful for sabotage work." He showed them how to tell the type of bullet by the colour of the roundels on the base of the cartridges.

"What of the cooling of them ?" the second student asked. He was a short young man with a mop of dark curly hair. He looked Jewish.

"You'll have to fire it in short bursts. They're air-cooled and were designed to fire in the air. They'll be all right if you fire short bursts as you would with a Tommy-gun. Otherwise they'll jam."

"We shall use them in the raid on the jail," Hans said. "If we had known how to work them earlier they would not have caught Mr. Olsen. We shall rescue him to-night."

"How was he caught ?" John asked.

"After a raid," the Jewish one told him. "It was a good raid, a raid on a transformer in Copenhagen. We got away by lorry and threw spikes on the road as we flew. It was a good raid and we all got away."

"It was after this raid that they caught Mr. Olsen," Hans said. "He was seen by one of the Schalburg Corps who recognised him and informed the Jerries."

"The Schalburg Corps ?" John asked.

"A section of the Danish Nazi Party. They were organised to counteract the activities of the Resistance Movement. Being Danes, they are more dangerous to us than the German military.

They are traitors and between us there is war to the death. The fight between us and the Schalburg Corps is worse than that between us and the Germans. It is hard now to think of one's life before the Germans came. I have been fighting now for more than a year. My mother and sister are in Copenhagen but I have not been to my home for a year. I cannot see my mother or the Germans would take her. My brother has been sent to a concentration camp in Germany."

"My father was shot," the Jew said. "They shot him because he was a Jew. My mother got away and is in Sweden."

"We got five hundred Jews to Sweden last month," Hans said.

"How do you take them?" Peter asked. This was what he wanted. What he had been waiting for.

"In small boats. We take them over the Straits at night."

"What about the German patrols?"

"We dodge them. We know the waters and use the wind. I enjoyed doing that. We were entertained well in Sweden."

"Can you get us across like that?"

"We will see Carl," Hans said. "He is in charge while Mr. Olsen is not here. But first we have to rescue Mr. Olsen."

That afternoon Sigmund took them by train to Copenhagen. "I am taking you to my sister," he said. "You must do exactly as she says and make no noise. If I should not return for you, you must wait there until one of us makes contact with you. On no account must you leave the flat."

He walked them by a roundabout route through a maze of similar streets and stopped outside a block of flats. He rang one of the bells and went in through the swing doors and up the concrete stairs. Peter and John followed him to one of the flats on the third floor landing.

The door was opened by a tall, fair girl. She looked frightened. Sigmund spoke to her in Danish and she closed her eyes. Her face went white but she smiled and motioned them into the room.

CHAPTER ELEVEN

The Last Enemy

IT WAS a small room with modern furniture, plain cream walls and green plants in boxes under the window and trailing from small shelves fixed to the wall. It was quiet and there was an air of feminine order about it. Peter felt strange and uncouth in this room—the first private room he had entered for a year. He felt that he was bringing dirt and danger into this girl's flat, and he did not like it.

Sigmund had not introduced them. He had spoken in Danish to the girl, warned them again not to leave the flat and had gone ; leaving them standing awkwardly, facing the frightened girl across the table.

The girl's fear was obvious. She was tall and fair, and now her face was pale. Her large eyes betrayed her fear. It was a fear that was new to Peter and it disturbed him.

John spoke first. " It's good of you to have us here." A stock opening gambit which sounded lame as he said it.

The girl said something in Danish.

" She doesn't speak English," Peter said.

John tried again in French, but the girl still replied in Danish and shook her head. He tried German, but she still could not understand. So they stood there awkwardly. Standing because the girl was standing and hoping that she would sit.

Peter took a chair and placed it behind her. She smiled and they sat on opposite sides of the table.

The girl seemed helpless with fear. Peter wondered whether she was frightened of them or of the danger they had brought with them. This was difficult. What could they do? There was a wireless set standing in the corner of the room. He pointed to it and said "England?"

The girl nodded. She took a portable gramophone from a shelf and put on a dance record. Then she crossed to the radio and tuned in, very faintly, to England. It seemed a well-worn routine. In Germany, among the French, it would have been furtive. Here, encircled by the girl's fear, it seemed a reasonable precaution.

Peter and John crouched down, ear to the loudspeaker, while the girl played dance music on the gramophone. It was the B.B.C. —the calm, unemotional voice of an announcer reading the news. England seemed very near to them then. Very near and very real.

When the news was finished the girl put on her hat and coat. She traced her finger round the dial of her watch to tell them that she would be gone for an hour.

While she was away they washed themselves and shaved. Then they fell asleep in their chairs, sitting one each side of the electric fire.

In the evening she woke them with cups of apple-leaf tea.

"Even if she doesn't speak English she knows the good old teatime," John said.

She had brought a Danish-English dictionary with her. She told them to take off their shoes so that their footsteps could not be heard in the flat below. She played the radio to drown their conversation. She played the radio all the time, so that they began to feel nervous if it was not playing.

The girl was frightened all the time. Every time a door opened, or she heard footsteps on the pavement below, she started nervously in her chair and only relaxed when the footsteps had died away in the distance.

This fear was new to Peter. In the camp the prisoners had not been afraid of the Germans. You might be shot escaping, but that was a risk of war. In escaping he had not been frightened like this. That had been the hot, exhilarating fear of excitement. This was the cold, pervasive fear of the Gestapo, the fear of informers, the helpless fear of the civilian under military rule. This girl's fear was of torture, of whips and the horror of the concentration camp. The fear of being taken away to an unknown but imagined fate.

It was infectious. For the first time since leaving the camp Peter began to regret its security, began to admit their danger in being outside the camp. He wanted to get away from this girl, away from the fear in which she lived.

He helped her wash the teacups in the small kitchen and went back into the lounge where John was trying to get the B.B.C. on the radio.

" That kid's scared," Peter said.

" So am I," John told him. " I'd much rather be outside than cooped up like this."

" I don't like being involved with these people," Peter said. " If we're caught on our own we're caught and it's all clear-cut. And we know what's coming to us. But if we get caught with a crowd like this there's no knowing where we'll end up."

" It's a risk we've got to take. I don't like it any more than you, but we've got to trust them, I suppose."

" It's not that I don't trust them. I don't like not knowing what's going on. It's depending on someone we don't know that frightens me. What happens if the raid goes wrong and they're all arrested or killed ? "

" They'll be all right," John said. " Sigmund will come back for us. Be in Sweden before we know where we are."

" Hope to God you're right—I hope he comes soon. Can't stand much more of this hanging around."

They slept that night in the flat and the following morning Sigmund returned. One of his hands was bandaged.

" How did it go ? " John asked.

" It was O.K.," Sigmund said. " We got Mr. Olsen all right. We killed several Jerries."

" What have you done to your hand ? "

" It is a bullet wound. It was a good raid. Now we go. We

shall try to get you away to-night. We must go now to meet
Larensen."

" How shall we go ? " Peter asked.

" We shall go in the same ship. She docked last night. Now
I am to take you on board again. She will pass down the Swedish
coast on her way back to Germany and arrangements will be
made to put you ashore."

" How will they do it ? " Peter asked.

" It will be arranged," Sigmund assured him. " When they
enter neutral waters they take a Swedish pilot aboard and drop
him again when they leave neutral waters. Arrangements will be
made for you to go ashore with the pilot."

" How shall we get into the docks ? " Peter asked.

" That also has been arranged. You will use the passes of
two of the crew. The same was done for a prisoner called Rowe.
He was taken from Danzig in a Swedish ship."

Peter turned to John. " Phil ! He beat us to it."

" That was the one you were telling me about," Sigmund
said, " the one who escaped with you ? "

" He followed us out," Peter said. " We never thought he'd
make it."

" I bet he thinks we're back at Sagan," John said. " I bet
he's written to us already."

" We'll see him soon." Peter grinned. " That'll shake 'im."

" We have to go now," Sigmund told him.

They all stood up.

" Thank your sister for us," Peter said. " Tell her we think
she is very brave."

Sigmund spoke with his sister.

" She thanks you," he interpreted, " and wishes me to tell
you that she is not brave. She is glad to help those who are
fighting to liberate our country. But she is frightened all the
time."

" Tell her she's not the only one," Peter said. " Tell her we're
scared too."

Sigmund translated, and the girl smiled her disbelief. She

held out her hand and they left her watching them from the top of the narrow stairs.

Whenever Peter saw Sigmund in his shore-going clothes he lost faith in him. Sigmund on board ship and Sigmund ashore were two different people. Afloat, in his narrow trousers and thick natural-wool jersey, he was strong. A man of rough sympathy to be depended on because he was not seasick. But ashore, in his white collar and cheap blue tie, walking uncomfortably in tight shoes, he was frightening. Peter had no faith in Sigmund ashore. He had no faith in Larensen either.

They had their lunch in a large café in the centre of Copenhagen. It was crowded. They were handed menu cards as large as foolscap and ate oysters, chicken and ice cream. While they ate, a dance band played English dance tunes and the crooner sang the words in English.

But all the time they were nervous. There were German soldiers sitting round them and they could not talk. They had meant it to be a celebration for Philip, but it was not a celebration. It was too soon to celebrate.

Then they went to meet Larensen. Sigmund took them down into the dock area past the wooden fishing vessels and down among the high walls of the warehouses. As they were walking they heard a muffled explosion to the north of the town.

" Do you hear ? " Sigmund said.

" Yes. What was it ? "

" Sabotage."

" How do you know ? "

" That was the power station. We had arranged to blow it up to-day."

Peter and John walked on in silence. If it were so it was tremendous. They found it hard to believe.

Then they saw Larensen. Even from that distance they could see he was drunk. He was reeling along the pavement and there was a woman with him, supporting him.

As soon as he saw them he began to shout. " Hey, professor ! Hey, Peter ! "

He came towards them shouting in English and waving his arms.

Peter said, " Sigmund, can't you keep him quiet ? "

" I will go to talk with him," Sigmund said.

They slowed down and watched him as he hurried forward. They saw him stop in front of Larensen and reason with him. Sigmund, his coat open and a new brown felt hat respectably on his head, reasoned with Larensen, fleshy and confident, dressed in dirty sea-going clothes, a scarf knotted round his throat and his woman clinging to his arm. They saw Larensen fling his free arm round Sigmund's shoulders and the three of them walk up the road staggering with the weaving of Larensen's progress and trying to keep him quiet.

" Hey, Peter," he called. " Professor, come here ! " And he laughed and hugged Sigmund round the shoulders.

" Let's get out of this," John urged.

" We'd better talk to him," Peter said.

Larensen was calling out again. " Hey, professor ! Professor. You meet my wife, eh ? We all have a drink, then I take you on board. I fix, eh ? "

" This is awful ! " John said.

Peter hurried forward and spoke to Larensen. " Shut up, or I'll hit you ! "

" What for ? "

" Talking in English like that—you must be crazy ! "

Larensen flung his arm round Peter's neck. " You wouldn't hit old Larensen ? " He still spoke in English. " You wouldn't hit old Larensen who helped you out of Germany ? " He was maudlin now. " That's no way to treat a pal, eh, professor ? " He turned to John. " That's no way to treat a pal, is it, professor ?"

" Shut up," Peter repeated.

" Come and have a drink," Larensen insisted. " All go and have a drink. This is my wife." He chucked her under the chin with a large, dirty hand and winked at John. " Prima, eh ? I got plenty of money. All go and have a drink."

He began to walk down the road, his wife and Sigmund supporting him.

"This is awful!" John said.

"We'd better follow them," Peter told him. "I expect they're going on board soon."

"The sooner we get on board the better. I'd hate to get caught now through that chap getting drunk."

"We'll have to keep him quiet somehow. As long as we can keep him away from the goons we're all right. We'll stay with them and keep him quiet. He scares me stiff."

They followed the other three down the street and when Larensen turned into a café they followed him in. They all sat on a long seat in a small private room at the back of the café. It was a red plush-covered seat with broken springs and in front of the seat was an old, dark wood table with a strip of brightly coloured cloth across the centre. The room was divided from the front part of the café by a bead curtain and Peter sat with his back against the wall so that he could see through the curtain and out into the café.

If any soldiers come in and Larensen starts talking English I'll knock him out, he thought. He measured the distance to Larensen's jaw and decided on the exact spot to hit him.

A woman brought glasses of beer on a tray and Larensen spoke in English again.

"I bring my wife to England. I do one more job and then I bring my wife to England."

"One more job?" John asked.

"Yes, one more trip. Then I take a rest." He took a long pull at the glass of beer and leaned back on the narrow seat.

"We bring some Frenchmen next time," Sigmund said.

"Frowg-aiters!" Larensen said. "Goddam frowg-aiters. They got plenty guts, those fellas."

"What do they do when they get here?" John asked.

"They try to get to England," Sigmund said, "to join the French army there. First they go to Sweden. I do not know what happens after they leave Denmark."

"We get 'em out of Germany," Larensen said. "We feed 'em good. You boys hungry?"

"No thanks," Peter said. He did not want Larensen to order anything. He did not want Larensen to do anything but keep quiet.

"You boys are hungry," Larensen said. He called the woman from the front of the shop and ordered food and beer.

Peter sat drinking the beer and eating the food that the woman had brought. He felt more helpless than he had felt since they first escaped from the camp.

Larensen sat watching them eating, beaming with a vast proprietorial grin. "That's right, you boys. Eat good. We have more eggs and bacon when we get back to the ship."

"What time are we going back to the ship?" Peter asked.

"When it gets dark," Sigmund told him. "About six o'clock."

"What shall we do with Larensen until then?" Larensen was talking to his wife in Danish.

"He is quite safe."

"But it's all so open," Peter said. "You talk English openly in the street. We hear an explosion and you calmly tell us it's the power station. Even the band in the café at lunchtime was playing English songs."

"The Danes have never been beaten." Sigmund said it seriously. "We are occupied but we are not beaten. We are combined against the Germans. They cannot arrest us all."

"They can have a good try," Peter said.

"No. They cannot arrest us all. They need us for our food. That is why we have the curfew at eight o'clock. There were too many Germans killed in the street at night. Denmark has not been ravaged like the rest of Europe because the Germans want our food. But Denmark is fighting. We have our traitors but not more than other countries. There are still Germans killed in the street at night."

"It would be the same in England," John said.

"Yes," Sigmund agreed. "I think it would be the same in England."

Larensen was quiet now. He was occupied with his wife. The others ignored him, thankful for the silence.

During the afternoon Sigmund went down to the docks to arrange for their embarkation. He returned some time later with bad news.

" The Jerries are in the docks," he said. " There is special caution because of the rescue of Mr. Olsen. I have been told to take you away from Copenhagen. We are to take a small boat from a village a few miles from here."

" What shall we do with Larensen ? " Peter asked. Larensen and his wife were sleeping.

" Leave him. He will be too noisy. Come, let us go."

They left the café and walked up into the town, where Sigmund bought tickets for the electric railway and they sat silently watching the Danish countryside grow dim in the fading light.

" The place where we are going is on an island," Sigmund told them. " The island is approached by a bridge. On the bridge there may be a sentry. I shall not be much use because of my hand. You must deal with the sentry."

Peter looked at John. All the time they had been escaping they had avoided violence. No escaping prisoner used violence unless he was within sight of freedom. The stake was too high.

" Shall we be sure of getting away once we reach the island ? " Peter asked.

" Absolutely ! " Sigmund said.

" Must we go to the island ? " John asked. " Can't the boat pick us up from the mainland ? "

" That is impossible. The sentry must be silenced, otherwise he will give the alarm. We should be stopped by the patrol boats. This is the only way it can be done."

Peter looked at John. " How are you fixed for Commando work ? "

" I did the old battle course," John said. " We'll manage all right. We'll pick up a couple of bricks on the way out."

" I'd rather have a sandbag."

" We'll use a sock," John said. " Fill it with earth."

They left the train at a small wayside station and set out for the bridge. On the way they each took off one sock and filled it with gravel from the side of the road.

They walked on down the road without speaking, their feet brushing up the dead leaves as they walked, stirring the sweet odours of late autumn. From across the fields came the faint tang of burning wood and above them the last few dead leaves rustled in the light wind. Peter felt as he used to feel before flying on a raid, a mixture of fear and anticipation. This night-stalking was new to him and he did not know how he would react.

" There it is ! " Sigmund said.

He had stopped dead in the road and was holding Peter by the arm. Ahead of them they could see the break in the trees where the gorge was, and the stark outline of the bridge.

" We'll creep along in the ditch," Peter whispered.

" While you fix the sentry I will go to the boats," Sigmund told them. " When you have fixed him, cross the bridge and I will be waiting for you. You will see the boats on the right-hand side of the road. The other guards are at the far end of the island beyond the boats. Be silent."

They climbed down into the ditch and crept towards the bridge, their footsteps deadened by the leaves.

When they reached the bridge they stopped. The ditch ended short of the bridge and a steel railing took its place, naked in the moonlight and without cover.

" We'll never get to the bridge without being seen," Peter whispered.

John put his mouth close to Peter's ear. " I'll go back along the ditch and attract his attention. I'll try to get his back to you, and you hit him."

" O.K."

John crept back along the ditch. When he was out of sight of the sentry he got up on to the road and walked slowly towards the bridge. He came within sight of the sentry, walking slowly in the middle of the road and staggering slightly as he walked.

" *Halt! Wer ist dort?* " It was the sentry's challenge.

" *Hilfe!* " John said, staggering and holding his hand to his side.

Peter, hiding in the ditch, saw the sentry bring his rifle to the ready, peering down the road. The sentry took a step forward. " *Wer ist dort?* " he repeated.

John staggered on until he was opposite where Peter crouched in the ditch. The sentry took another step forward.

" *Hilfe!* " John groaned. He sank to his knees as though he were exhausted.

The sentry walked slowly towards him with his rifle, bayonet fixed, held in front of his body.

John moaned and fell forward, his hands on the ground in front of him.

The sentry was standing over him now, his back towards Peter. This is it, Peter thought. He scrambled from the ditch, slipping in the soft earth as he sprang. The sentry heard him, turned ; and in that instant John threw himself at the man's knees.

The sentry raised his rifle and clubbed down at John's head as Peter's sandbag caught him across the shoulders. The sock was too big, too full of earth. It hit the sentry equally across the rim of his helmet and the collar of his coat.

Peter flung himself forward, clutching the sentry round the neck and bringing him crashing down on top of him. He wriggled like an eel, squirming out from under the German and going for his throat, to stop him crying out. He got his fingers round the man's neck, but it was a big neck, fleshy, and he could not feel the windpipe.

The German grunted and groped wildly for the revolver at his belt. Then he felt Peter's fingers at his throat and forgot the revolver, kicking hard with his three-quarter boots and clawing at Peter's face with his fingernails. He was fighting for his life now.

Peter fought in a cold fury, his whole strength going in one gigantic effort to stop the man from crying out. His fingers

John threw himself at the man's knees

slipped from the sweat on the man's neck and he felt him getting away. Then he was at the neck again. He felt the man's hands tearing at his face, his heels drumming on the metal of the road. He was on top of the man now, sitting astride him, his fingers on his windpipe, pressing, pressing, pressing. . . .

The man's struggles grew weaker. Peter felt the body grow slack and without resistance. He sat there for some time, pressing his thumbs into the man's neck, making sure that he was unconscious. Then he relaxed. He got to his feet. His knees were trembling and his face was sore where the man's nails had gouged the flesh.

The body of the sentry was sprawled in the road, head flung back at an unusual angle, mouth open as though he still struggled for breath.

John lay where he had fallen. His hair was matted with dark blood. Peter loosened his collar and lifted him to a sitting position. He took him in his arms and dragged him to the side of the road. John moaned as he put him down. Then he opened his eyes and put his hands to his head.

" What happened ? "

" He hit you on the head with his rifle," Peter said.

" Where is he ? "

" Over there."

He helped John to his feet and they walked slowly across the bridge towards the boats. Peter, quiet and shaken and still trembling at the knees.

As they left the bridge they heard a low shout ; and there was Sigmund standing by one of the boats.

" It needs three of us," he said. " It is stuck on the mud."

They waded into the shallow water and began to heave the boat into deep water. It scraped harshly as it slipped across the mud and they expected every minute to hear the sound of a rifle shot or the challenge of a sentry. They pushed the boat into deeper water and clambered aboard.

" I will steer," Sigmund told them. " You get the sail up and then lie in the bottom of the boat."

Peter and John hoisted the sail. There was a light offshore wind which heeled the boat over as Sigmund tacked along the shore.

Peter lay in the bottom of the boat, smelling the strong smell of fish and salt water and listening to the sound of the low waves slapping against the sides. He wiped his hands on his trouser legs and tried not to think of the sentry. They would be in Sweden by the morning.

It was cold in the bottom of the boat. He shivered in his sweat-soaked clothes.

CHAPTER TWELVE

The Welcome Home

SOME WEEKS later, having met Phil in Sweden, they were flown to England. They landed at an airfield in the Midlands and it was raining. It was four o'clock in the morning and they were not expected.

After a delay of two hours they were taken before the station intelligence officer. He was wearing tartan trews and could not have been less interested. He took their ranks, names and numbers. The German officer who had interrogated Peter when he was captured had been more polite.

" Can we get anything to eat ? " John asked.

The officer was flustered. He had been asleep when they had landed and he was not yet fully awake. " You'll find something in the airmen's mess. I'll have you called in the morning. Your train goes at seven-thirty."

In the airmen's mess they were given cold bacon and potatoes on enamel plates. The corporal in charge was worried because they had not brought their own knives and forks.

They found three empty beds in a crowded dormitory and fell asleep. Half an hour later Peter was awakened by a batman. " The major wants to see you, sir."

" But I've just seen him."

" He told me to call you again, sir."

Peter began to put on a dressing-gown.

" I should advise you to dress properly, sir. The major's apt to object if you're not properly dressed."

Peter had been ordered about for so long now that he took

it calmly. Soon he was standing in front of the major's desk. This time the major had a captain with him. Intelligence. Peter thought he looked a pretty dim type.

The captain asked Peter's rank, name and number.

"You've just had them."

The major mumbled something about losing the papers. He looked too old to be up at that time of the morning. Peter felt sorry for him. He gave him his rank, name and number.

"How long were you a prisoner?" the major asked.

Peter told him.

"What was it like?" He seemed to be making conversation, making up for getting him out of bed. Peter wondered what to say. He could describe the damp barrack blocks, fetid and close from overcrowded living, the rows and rows of two-tier bunks, the scuffing of wooden clogs on damp concrete as the bearded and dirty Kriegies queued up for the midday ration of cabbage water. He could describe the circuit, the crowd of lonely figures, shoulders hunched, eyes on the ground, mooching slowly round; refusing to acknowledge the existence of the wire, self-contained figures, lonely in spite of the proximity of a thousand like them. But what could he say of the companionship, of the humour, of the fierce joy of baiting the Hun? What could he say of the home that each man had made of his bed space, the rough shelves above the beds, the few books, the photographs, the sudden generous gifts when the giver had so little to spare? Of how each man was stripped bare in front of his fellows and was accepted for what he was rather than for what he had. What could he say of the decency and humour of the average man? Words could not convey what he felt about that queer, unhappy, glorious, quarrelling, generous, indomitable, scruffy family that he had left behind.

"It wasn't so bad in some ways," he said. "The chaps were pretty good."

"How did the Germans treat you?" the major asked.

He could tell of Alan, shot through the belly as he climbed the wire; starvation rations, solitary confinement, the stupid, petty restrictions. He could tell of the kindly tolerant guards with families at home and their fear of the Gestapo and the Russian front. Of the bullying braggart of a Feldwebel who was nothing but a lout and could have been born in England as easily as in Germany.

"They weren't too bad," he said. "There were some decent ones."

"I hear you had a golf course," the captain said.

A golf course. . . . Peter was angry at first. He looked at the smug non-prisoner face. A golf course. He remembered the earnest ragged Kriegies knocking home-made balls round the huts with clubs made from melted-down metal water-jugs. He turned to the major.

"I'd like to turn in now, sir. We're leaving early in the morning. By the way—could you let us have any money?"

"You should have been given English money before you left Sweden," the major said.

"We've only got Swedish money."

"We've no machinery for giving you English money here." The major was getting flustered again.

There was a short silence. The intelligence captain spoke.

"Do you have a cheque book?"

"Don't be silly—we've just come from a prison camp!"

The captain turned to the major; he had solved the problem. "I think we can trust them, sir. After all, they *are* officers."

THE END

Escape Alone

by

DAVID HOWARTH

Contents

AUTHOR'S NOTE

I HEARD the bare bones of this story during the war, soon after it happened, and I mentioned it briefly in my book *The Shetland Bus*. All that I knew about it then was based on a report which was written in a Swedish hospital by a man called Jan Baalsrud. It was a graphic report, but Baalsrud was very ill when he wrote it, and it left a lot unsaid. One could see that there was much more in the story, some things which Baalsrud had forgotten and others he had never known, although he played the main part in it. But it was not until ten years later that I had a chance to talk it all over with him, and persuade him to come with me to the far north of Norway where it happened, to try to find out the whole truth of it.

Now that I have found it out and written it down, I am rather afraid of being accused of exaggeration. Parts of it are difficult to believe. But I have seen nearly all the places which are mentioned in this book, and met nearly all the people. Not one of the people knew the whole story, but each of them had a most vivid recollection of his own part in it. Each of their individual stories fitted together, and also confirmed what Baalsrud himself remembered. Some minor events are matters of deduction, but none of it is imaginary. Here and there I have altered a name or an unimportant detail to avoid offending people; but otherwise, I am convinced that this account is true.

CHAPTER ONE

LANDFALL

EVEN AT the end of March, on the Arctic coast of northern Norway, there is no sign of spring. By then, the polar winter night is over. At midwinter, it has been dark all day; at midsummer, the sun will shine all night; and in between, at the vernal equinox, the days draw out so quickly that each one is noticeably longer than the last. But the whole land is still covered thickly with ice and snow to the very edge of the sea. There is nothing green at all: no flowers or grass, and no buds on the stunted trees. Sometimes there are clear days at that time of year, and then the coast glitters with a blinding brilliance in the sunlight; but more often it is swept by high winds and hidden by frozen mist and driven snow.

It was on that coast, on the 29th of March, 1943, that this story really began. On that day a fishing-boat made landfall there, six days out from the Shetland Islands, with twelve men on board. Its arrival in those distant enemy waters in the third year of the war, within sight of a land which was occupied by the Germans, was the result of a lot of thought and careful preparation; but within a day of its arrival all the plans which had been made were blown to pieces, and everything which happened after that, the tragedies and adventures and self-sacrifice, and the single triumph, was simply a matter of chance; not the outcome of any plan at all, but only of luck, both good and bad, and of courage and faithfulness.

That particular day was sunny, as it happened, and the twelve men watched it dawn with intense excitement. It is always exciting to make the land after a dangerous voyage; the more so when one's ship approaches the land at night, so that when the daylight comes a coast is revealed already close at hand. In that landfall there was an extra excitement for those men, because they were all Norwegians, and most of them were about to see their homeland for the first time since they had been driven out of it by the German invasion nearly three years before. Above all, there was the supreme excitement of playing a dangerous game. Eight of the twelve were the crew of the fishing-boat. They had sailed it safely across a thousand miles of the no-man's-land of ocean, and had to sail it back when they had landed their passengers and cargo. The other four were soldiers trained in guerrilla warfare. Their journey had two objectives, one general and one particular. In general, they were to establish themselves ashore and spend the summer training the local people in the arts of sabotage; and in particular, in the following autumn they were to attack a great German military airfield called Bardufoss. In the hold of the boat, they had eight tons of explosives, weapons, food and arctic equipment, and three radio transmitters.

As the day dawned, they felt as a gambler might feel if he had staked his whole fortune on a system he believed in; except, of course, that they had staked their lives, which makes a gamble even more exciting. They believed that in a Norwegian fishing-boat they could bluff their way through the German coast defences, and they believed that with their plans and equipment they could live ashore on that barren land in spite of the arctic weather and the German occupation; and on these beliefs their lives depended. If they were wrong nobody could protect them. They were far beyond the range of any help from England. So far, it had all gone well; so far, there was no sign that the Germans were suspicious. But the gleaming mountains which they sighted to the southward, so beautiful and serene in the morning light, were full of menace. Among them the German coast watchers were posted, and soon, in the growing light, they would see the fishing-boat, alone on the glittering sea. That morning would put the first of the theories to the test, and that night or the next would bring the boat and its crew to the climax of the journey: the secret landing.

At that time, in 1943, that remote and thinly populated coast had suddenly had world-wide importance thrust upon it. Normally, in time of peace, there is no more peaceful place than the far north of Norway. For two months every summer there is a tourist season, when foreigners come to see the mountains and the Lapps and the midnight sun; but for the other ten months of the year, the people who live there eke out a humble livelihood by fishing and working small farms along the water's edge. They are almost cut off from the world outside, by the sea in front of them and the Swedish frontier at their backs, and by bad weather and darkness, and by the vast distance they have to travel to reach the capital of their own country or any other centre of civilisation. They live a hard life, but a very placid one. They are not harassed by many of the worries which beset people in cities or in more populous countrysides. They take little account of time.

But when the Germans invaded Norway in 1940, the thousand miles of Atlantic seaboard which fell into their hands was the greatest strategical asset which they won; and when Russia entered the war, the far northernmost end of the coast became even more important, and even more valuable to Germany. The allied convoys to the Russian arctic ports, Archangel and Murmansk, had to pass through the narrow strip of open sea between the north of Norway and the arctic ice; and it was from north Norway that the Germans attacked them with success which had sometimes been overwhelming. Bardufoss was the base for their air attacks and their reconnaissance, and the coast itself provided a refuge for submarines and a safe passage from German harbours all the way to the Arctic Ocean.

As soon as the Germans had installed themselves on the northern coast, their position was impregnable. It was a thousand miles from the nearest allied base, and the country could not have been better for defence. A screen of islands twenty miles wide protects it from the sea, and among the islands are innumerable sounds through which defending forces could manœuvre by sea in safety. The mainland itself is divided by a series of great fjords, with mountainous tongues of land between them. Beyond the heads of the fjords is a high plateau, uninhabited and mostly unsurveyed, snow-covered for nine months of the year; and across the plateau, marked by a cairn here and there among its deserted hills, is the frontier of Sweden, which was a neutral country then, entirely surrounded by others under German occupation. To attack the Germans in arctic Norway with any normal military force was quite impossible. Every island and every fjord could have become a fortress ; and if the Germans had ever found themselves hard pressed in northern Norway, they could have reinforced their position by occupying Sweden, which would not have been to the advantage of the Allies.

In these circumstances, the voyage which had come to its end on that March morning had a possible importance out of all proportion to the size of the expedition. Great hopes of its outcome were held in London. Only four men were to be landed, but they were quite capable, with a little luck, of putting the air base at Bardufoss out of action long enough for a convoy to have a chance of getting through undetected ; and the time was also ripe for the training of local people. The great majority of Norwegians up there would have gladly taken some positive action against the Germans, and would have done it long before if they had had any weapons and any instructions on how to set about it. Once the training was started, it would grow like a snowball.

The only reason why nothing of the kind had been done in north Norway before was that it was so difficult to get there. Small parties of men on skis could get over the mountains across the border from Sweden, and a radio transmitter had been taken in that way and was installed in the town of Tromsö. But a saboteur's equipment was much too bulky and heavy to carry across the mountains, or to smuggle past the Swedes. The only way to take it was by sea.

By that time, a great many landings had been made in the southern part of Norway by fishing-boats fitted with hidden armament, which sailed from a base in Shetland, and the resistance movement down there was well supplied and flourishing. But none of these boats, up till then, had tackled such a long and risky journey as the one to the north of Norway. The boat which had just accomplished it had come from the Shetland base. Its name was the *Brattholm*. It was 75 feet long, and had a single-

cylinder engine which gave it a speed of eight knots. Its appearance had been carefully preserved, so that it looked like any
Norwegian fishing-boat, and it had false registration numbers
painted on its bows. But it was armed with seven machine-
guns hidden on mountings on deck, and each of its passengers
had his own spare machine-gun stowed somewhere where he
could get it in a hurry.

The date when it sailed from Shetland, in the third week in
March, had been a compromise which was not entirely satisfactory for anybody. The skipper and crew of the boat had to make
up their minds between sailing in the depth of winter, when they
would have the cover of the arctic night but would also have to
weather the arctic storms, or in the late spring or early autumn,
when the weather would probably be rather more moderate but
the German defences, and their air patrols in particular, would
have the advantage of daylight. On the whole, from the skipper's
point of view, it would have been better to go earlier than March,
because his boat was sound and fit to stand up to any weather.
But the passengers also had to be considered. If they had been
landed in the worst of the winter weather they might not have
been able to keep themselves alive after they got ashore.

But still, the choice of March had been justified in so far as the
voyage had been a success. The weather had not been bad. The
little boat had felt very conspicuous to the people on board it as
it slowly steamed northwards day after day, but it had only been
sighted once, by a German aircraft about three hundred miles
from land; and this aircraft, which was probably on a weather
reconnaissance flight and not really concerned with stray fishing-
boats, had only circled round and then flown away.

So it seemed that whatever happened when they were sighted
from the shore, at least the shore defences could not have been
warned about them, and would have no reason to guess that the
humble boat they saw in front of them had crossed a thousand
miles of the Atlantic. But it still remained to be seen whether the
coast watchers would be deceived by *Brattholm's* innocent
appearance. It had worked often enough farther south, but on a
new bit of coast there was always the risk of infringing some
local fishing regulation and so giving the game away. For all

that the crew or the passengers knew, they might be pretending to fish in the middle of a minefield, or an artillery range, or some other kind of forbidden area, because nobody had been able to tell them before they left Shetland exactly where these kind of defences were.

At the tense moment of the dawn, all the four passengers were on deck. Wars often bring together people of very different character, and these four were as varied in experience and background as any four Norwegians could have been. Their leader was a man in his middle forties called Sigurd Eskeland. As a young man, he had emigrated to South America, and he had spent most of his adult life in the back of beyond in Argentine running a fur farm. On the day when he heard on the radio that Norway had been invaded, he got on his horse and left his farm in the hands of his partner, and rode to the nearest town to volunteer by cable for the air force. The air force turned him down on account of his age, but he worked his way to England and joined the army instead. He got into the Commandos, and then transferred to the Linge Company, which was the name of the military unit which trained agents and saboteurs for landing in occupied Norway. Long ago, before he went abroad, he had been a postal inspector in north Norway, so that he remembered something about the district he had been assigned to.

The other three men were very much younger. There was a radio operator called Salvesen, who was a member of a well-known shipping family. He had been a first mate in the Merchant Navy when Norway came into the war; but after a time that defensive job had begun to bore him, and when he heard of the Linge Company he volunteered to join it as an agent.

The other two were specialists in small arms and explosives, and they were close friends who had been through a lot of queer experiences together. Both of them were 26 years old. One was called Per Blindheim. He was the son of a master baker in Ålesund on the west coast of Norway, and in his youth he had served his time on the bread round. Superficially, he was a gay and very handsome young man in the Viking tradition, tall and fair and blue-eyed; but hidden beneath his boyish appearance and behaviour, he had a most compelling sense of justice. When the Russians attacked Finland, it seemed to him so wrong that he threw up his job and left home to join the Finnish army. When the World War began and his own country was invaded, he hurried back and fought against the Germans ; and when the battle for Norway was lost, he set off for England to begin it all over again, escaping from the Germans by way of Russia, the country against which he had fought a few months before.

The other one of this pair of friends, and the fourth of the landing party, was Jan Baalsrud. To look at, Jan was a contrast to Per ; he had dark hair and grey-blue eyes, and was of a smaller build altogether. But he had the same youthful quality, combined with the same hidden serious turn of mind ; a depth of feeling which neither of those two would show to strangers, but one which all four of the men must have needed to carry them through the hardships of their training and bring them to where they were.

Jan had been apprenticed to his father, who was an instrument maker in Oslo, and had only just started his career when the invasion came. He had fought in the army, and escaped to Sweden when there was no chance to fight any more. By then he had discovered a taste for adventure, and he volunteered as a courier between Stockholm and Oslo, and began to travel to and fro between neutral Sweden and occupied Norway, in the service of the escape organisation which the Norwegians had founded. Luckily for him, he was caught and arrested by the Swedes before he was caught by the Germans. They sentenced him to five months' imprisonment, but after he had served three months of his sentence he was let out and given a fortnight to leave the country.

This was easier ordered than done ; but he got a Russian visa and flew to Moscow, where he landed inauspiciously among Russian celebrations of German victories. However, the Russians treated him well and sent him down to Odessa on the Black Sea ; and it was while he was waiting there for a ship that he first met Per Blindheim, who was on the same errand. The two travelled together to England by way of Bulgaria, Egypt, Aden, Bombay, South Africa, America and Newfoundland. When they got to London, the first of the sights that they went

to see was Piccadilly Circus ; and while they were standing looking rather glumly at this symbol of their journey's end, and
wondering what was going to happen next, Jan saw in the crowd
an English officer he had known in Stockholm. This man
recruited them both forthwith for the Linge Company, and there
they found a job which fulfilled all their hopes of adventure.

These, then, were the four men who stood on the deck that
March morning at the climax of a year of preparation. They had
trained together in the highlands of Scotland, doing forced
marches of thirty and forty miles with packs across the mountains,
living out in the snow, studying weapons and underground
organisation, doing their quota of parachute jumps, and learning
to draw and cock an automatic and score six hits on a half-man-
sized target at five yards, all in a space of three seconds ; finally
learning all the vulnerable points of airfields ; and incidentally,
enjoying themselves tremendously. They were tough and
healthy, and elated at the imminence of danger ; and very
confident of being able to look after themselves, whatever the
dawn might bring.

CHAPTER TWO

THE FIGHT IN TOFTEFJORD

ON THAT sort of expedition it was useless to make a detailed plan, because nobody could foresee exactly what was going to happen. The leader always had a degree of responsibility which few people are called upon to carry in a war. The orders he was given were in very general terms, and in carrying them out he had nobody whatever to advise him. His success, and his own life and the lives of his party, were in his own hands alone.

As leader of this party in north Norway, Eskeland had a specially heavy load to carry. From the south, or from any country from which a lot of refugees had escaped to England, a fund of information had been collected about German dispositions and the characters and politics of innumerable people, and the information was always being renewed. The leader of an expedition could be told, in more or less detail, whom he could trust and whom he should avoid, and where he was most likely to meet enemy sentries or patrols. But information about north Norway was scanty. A good many people had escaped from there, but the only route they could follow was across the mountains into Sweden, where they were interned. Many of them were content to stay in internment and wait for better times ; and even those who made the effort to escape again, and managed to pass on what they knew to the British intelligence services, had usually been held by the Swedes for a matter of months, so that all that they could tell was out of date. Eskeland had been given the names of a few people who were known to be sound, but beyond that very little could be done to help him. Once he left Britain, he could only depend on his own training and wit and skill.

He had been as thorough as he possibly could be in his preparations. Ever since he had known he was to lead a landing from a fishing-boat, he had pondered in a quiet way over every emergency he could foresee. On the high seas, the skipper of the boat was in command, and out there the problems had been comparatively simple. The boat might have been overcome by stress of weather, which was a matter of seamanship; or its one single-cylinder engine might have broken down, which was a job for the engineers; or it might have been attacked by aircraft, which would have been fought with the boat's own "Q-ship" armament. But now that it had closed the coast, he had to take charge, and now anything might happen and an instantaneous decision might be needed. For the present, the boat's first line of defence was for its guns to be kept hidden, so that it seemed to be innocently fishing. But once they got into the constricted waters of the sounds among the islands, they might meet a larger ship with heavier armament at short range at any moment, and then the boat's armament would be nothing but a hindrance. They might still bluff their way out as a fishing-boat, but they could not hope to fight an action at two or three hundred yards. Apart from anything else, a single shot in their cargo might blow them all to pieces. The only way they could prepare for that kind of encounter, as Eskeland foresaw it, was to hide every vestige of war-like equipment and to lure the enemy ship to within pistol shot. Then, by surprise, there was a chance of boarding it and wiping out its crew.

During the past night, as *Brattholm* approached the coast, Eskeland and his three men had begun to prepare for this possible crisis. They had cleaned and loaded their short-range weapons, Sten guns and carbines and pistols; and they had primed hand-grenades and stowed them in convenient places, in the wheelhouse and galley, and along the inside of the bulwarks, where they could be thrown without warning on board a ship alongside. In case it came to close quarters, he and his three men had all put on naval uniform, although they were soldiers, so that the Germans would not be able to identify them as a landing party.

But even while they made these preparations, they all knew

that although with luck they might be successful in that sort of hand-to-hand action, they had very little chance of getting away with their lives. Between themselves and safety there were the thousand miles of sea which they had crossed. They might hope to kill or capture the entire crew of even a larger ship ; but unless they could do it so quickly that no radio signal could be sent, and unless it happened in such a remote place that nobody heard the gunshots, all the German defences would be alerted ; and then, it was obvious, *Brattholm* at eight knots would not get very far. The only hope of escape then, and it was a small one, was to scuttle the ship and get ashore.

Eskeland had provided for this too. The three radio transmitters in their cargo were a new type still graded top secret, and they also had a few important papers : ciphers, maps, and notes about trustworthy people and German defences. They all understood quite clearly that they had to defend these things with their lives. It went without saying. It was one of the basic rules which they had been taught. Ever since they had entered enemy waters, the papers had been stowed in an accessible place with matches and a bottle of petrol ; and a primer, detonators and fuses had been laid in the eight tons of high explosives in the hold. The transmitters were on top of the primer. There were three fuses. One had a five-minute delay, for use if there seemed to be a chance to destroy the ship and cargo and then to get away. The next was thirty seconds, and the last was instantaneous. Each of the twelve men on board was able to contemplate soberly the prospect of lighting the instantaneous fuse, and they understood the circumstances in which they were to do it ; if they had tried a hand-to-hand fight with a German ship, for example, and been defeated. The main point was that the Germans should not get the cargo.

Eskeland should have felt satisfied with these preparations as he approached the coast ; they were intelligently conceived, and carefully carried out. But on that very day a change of plan was forced upon him, and he was reminded, if there had been any doubt about it, how sketchy his information was. They had intended to land on an island called Senja, about forty miles south-west of the town of Tromsö ; but as they approached it,

steaming peacefully through the fishing zone, they sighted a
trawler coming out towards them. They altered course to the
eastward, waiting to see what was going to happen. The trawler
reached the open sea at the outer edge of the islands, and then
it turned back on its track and went into the sounds again. As
it turned, they saw a gun on its foredeck. It was a patrol ship,
where no patrol ship had been reported.

At that stage of the expedition, it was their job to avoid trouble
rather than look for it, and there was no sense in trying to land
their cargo on the one island, from all the hundreds in the
district, which they now knew for certain was patrolled. Their
disguise had worked so far. They had been seen, and passed as a
fishing-boat. The sensible thing to do was to choose another
island ; and after a discussion, they agreed upon one a little
farther north. It is called Ribbenesöy. It is due north of Tromsö,
thirty miles from the town. On the chart of it, they found a little
bay on the north-east side which seemed to offer good shelter,
and one of the men who had been in that district before remembered the bay as a remote and deserted spot. At about midday
on the 29th of March, they set course towards it. Its name is
Toftefjord.

It was late in the afternoon by the time they reached the
skerries which lie scattered in the sea for seven miles off the
shore of Ribbenesöy, and began to pick their way among them.
In bad weather the passage which they used is impassable. There
are thousands of rocks awash on either side, and the whole area
becomes a mass of spray in which no marks are visible. But on
that day the sea was calm and the air was clear. They sighted
the stone cairns which are built as seamarks on some of the biggest
rocks, and passed through into sheltered water. They steamed
below a minute island called Fuglö, which rises sheer on every
side to a black crag a thousand feet high ; they skirted the north
shore of Ribbenesöy, a steep, smooth, gleaming sheet of snow
which sweeps upwards to the curved ice-cornice of a hill called
Helvedestind, which means Hell's Peak ; and as the light began
to fade they crept slowly into Toftefjord, and let go an anchor
into clear ice-blue water.

When the engine stopped, Toftefjord seemed absolutely silent.

After six days of the racket and vibration of a Norwegian fishing-boat under way, the mere absence of noise was unfamiliar; but there is always a specially noticeable silence in sheltered places when the land is covered thickly with snow. All familiar sounds are muted and unresonant. There are no footfalls, no sounds of birds or running water, no hum of insects or rustle of animals or leaves. Even one's own voice seems altered. Even without reason, in places hushed by snow, the deadening of sound seems menacing.

Yet the appearance of Toftefjord was reassuring. They stood on deck when the work of coming to anchor was finished and looked round them, talking involuntarily in quiet voices. It was almost a perfect hiding-place. To the south and west and east it was shut in by low rounded hills. The tops of the hills were bare; but in the hollows by the shore, the twigs of stunted arctic birch showed black against the snow. To the north was the entrance of the bay, but it was blocked by a little island, so that one could not see into it from outside. *Brattholm* was quite safe there from observation from the sea, and she could not be seen from the air unless an aircraft flew almost overhead.

The beaches showed that the bay was always calm. On the rocks and islands which are exposed to the sea, there is always a broad bare strip of shore where the waves have washed the snow away; but there in the land-locked fjord the snow lay smooth and thick down to the tidemark. There were no tracks in it. Close inshore, the sea itself had been frozen, but the ice had broken up and was floating in transparent lumps around the ship. The air was cold and crisp.

Yet the place was not quite deserted. At the head of the bay, below the hill, there was a barn and a very small wooden house. Close by, on the beach, there were racks for drying fish. There was nobody to be seen, but there was smoke from the cottage chimney.

The first thing to be done, when the ship was at anchor, was to find out who lived in that cottage, and whether they were likely to cause any difficulties or danger. Eskeland and the skipper changed out of their naval uniforms into fishermen's clothes and rowed ashore. Perhaps they wanted to be the first to land in Norway. It was always a moment of unexpressed emotion.

They soon came back, saying there was nothing to worry about. There was a middle-aged woman with her two children, a boy of about sixteen and a girl who was younger. Her husband was away at the cod fishing in the Lofoten islands, and she did not expect him back for several weeks. Eskeland had told her that they had stopped to make some engine repairs. There was no reason why she should be suspicious, and there was no telephone in the house. It would be quite easy to keep an eye on her and the children. She had told him, incidentally, that no Germans had ever been in Toftefjord. In fact, she herself had never seen a German. Her husband had had to hand in his radio set to the authorities, and her nearest neighbours were two miles away. She was quite out of touch with the world and with the war.

The landing party and the crew had dinner in relays, leaving a watch on deck. They were very cheerful. For one thing, it was the first good dinner they had had on board, not only because it is difficult to do much cooking in a fishing-boat at sea, but also because the cook had been seasick and Jan Baalsrud, who had deputised for him, had had rather limited ideas. The landing party were happy also because the voyage was successfully ended, and they could really get to work. For soldiers, a sea voyage is always tedious ; they are usually pleased to get out of the hands of sailors.

While they ate, they discussed the coming night. When the four men of the sabotage group had started to prepare themselves for the expedition, they had divided between them the enormous territory they were to cover, and each of them had studied his own part of it in detail. But by changing the landing place from Senja, they had put themselves farther north than any of the districts they knew best. However, Eskeland remembered a little about Ribbenesöy from his days as a postal inspector, and he had taken the precaution of learning the names of a few reliable people in the neighbourhood. One of these was a merchant who kept a small general store on the south side of the island. Eskeland had never met him, but his name was on a list in London of men who could be trusted. His shop was only a few miles away, and they decided to make a start that night by going to see him and asking him about hiding their cargo. Experience in the southern part of Norway had shown that shopkeepers were often more adept than anyone else at providing a temporary hiding-place for stores. Most shops had outhouses and back premises which in war-time were nearly empty. Cases of weapons had often been stacked among cases of groceries. A shopkeeper was also a likely man to tell them where they could get a local boat to take them into Tromsö, where they would find their principal " contacts."

So Eskeland set off, as soon as it was dark, in *Brattholm's* motor dinghy. He took the ship's engineer with him to look after the motor, and another man who had been added to the crew as an extra hand because he knew the district. They steered out of the bay and followed the shore of Ribbenesöy to the eastward, through the sound which separates it from the next island of Hersöy, and then back, close inshore along the south side of the island. They saw the shop and a few buildings near it, and a wooden jetty, silhouetted against the afterglow in the western sky. There was a light in the shop, and another on board a boat which was lying, with its engine running, a few yards off the end of the jetty.

As they approached the jetty, they passed close to the boat. It was a small fishing craft with two or three men on board. It would have seemed strange to pass it without a word, and besides, a small local fishing craft was one of the things they wanted. So they hailed it and told the men the story they had prepared : that they had engine trouble and wanted a lift to Tromsö to get some spare parts.

The men were sympathetic, and only mildly inquisitive, as fishermen would naturally be. They talked all round the subject, in the infinitely leisurely manner of people who live on islands. They asked what make of engine it was, and what horse-power, and what spare parts were needed. They recommended a dealer in Tromsö, and suggested ringing him up in the morning and getting him to send the parts out in the mailboat, which would probably be as quick as going to fetch them, and certainly cheaper.

They asked what the herring fishing was like, and where the *Brattholm* was bound for.

Everyone who lives under false pretences gets used to receiving perfectly useless advice with patience and cunning. Eskeland and the engineer, in this unrealistic conversation across the dark water, answered the questions carefully one by one, until a chance came for them to put the one question in which they were interested.

" I suppose you couldn't take us into Tromsö ? "

This started a long explanation of how they were waiting there for a man to bring them some bait which they had paid for already, so that they could not afford to miss him, and they said all over again that they could not see any sense in going all the way to Tromsö for spares when there was a telephone up in the shop. But they told Eskeland that if he was really set on wasting money by going there, the shopkeeper had a boat and might take him in.

Eskeland thanked them and left them, understanding perhaps that to a man who lives in the outer islands Tromsö is a very distant city, and a journey there is not a thing to be undertaken lightly. At least, he had learned that the shop at the head of the jetty was really the one he wanted.

The shopkeeper was in bed when they got to the house ; but when they knocked he came downstairs in his underclothes and took them into the kitchen. They apologised for coming so late, and told the same story again. But with him, they only told it as a means of introduction, to make conversation till he felt at ease with them and they could tell him the true reason for their visit. While they were talking, they slipped in questions about the Germans. No, he said when they asked him, the Germans had really been no trouble out there on the islands. They had never been ashore. He saw their convoys passing in the channel south of Ribbenesöy, and they had been out laying minefields. And of course they sent out notices which had to be stuck up everywhere : " Contact with the enemy is punished by death." There was one downstairs in the shop. He had heard stories about how they behaved in Tromsö, but as for himself, he had never had anything to do with them.

Carefully feeling his way, Eskeland began to broach the
subject of his cargo, and his need to go to Tromsö. The shopkeeper was willing to take one or two men to town in his boat.
Eskeland offered to pay him a substantial sum of money for his
help. It was the size of this sum which first impressed on the
shopkeeper that he was being asked to do more than hire out a
boat. He looked puzzled ; and then, because it would be unjust
to involve a man in what they were doing without giving him an
idea of the risks he was running, and because the man had such
an excellent reputation, Eskeland told him that they had come
from England.

At this, his expression changed. At first he was incredulous.
One of them gave him a cigarette, and he took it and lit it ;
and the English tobacco seemed to convince him that what they
said was true. Then, to their surprise, they saw that he was
frightened.

He began to make excuses. He couldn't leave the shop. It
wasn't fair to leave his wife alone in the house these days. There
were the animals to attend to. Fuel for the boat was difficult
to come by.

Slowly and reluctantly, they had to admit to themselves that
it was useless to try to persuade him. An unwilling nervous
helper would be a danger and a liability. Yet they could not
understand how a man who had been so highly recommended
could be so cowardly in practice. The vast majority of Norwegians, as everybody knew, would have been delighted by a
chance to do something against the Germans. They puzzled
over his behaviour, and told him they were disappointed in
him.

" But why did you come to me ? " he asked plaintively.
" What made you think I'd do a thing like that ? "

They told him they had heard he was a patriot ; and then
the truth came out, too late, and they saw the mistake which they
had made. The man told them he had only been running the
shop for a few months. Its previous owner had died. His
name was the same, so there had been no need to change the
name of the business.

There was nothing left to do then except to impress on him as clearly as they could that he must never tell anyone what they had told him. He promised this willingly, glad to see that they had accepted his refusal. In his relief, he even recommended two other men who he thought would give them the help they needed. Their names were Jenberg Kristiansen and Sedolf Andreasson. They were both fishermen, and they lived on the north shore of the island, beyond Toftefjord. He felt sure they would be willing.

Eskeland and his two companions left him then, with a final warning that he must never mention what he had heard that night.

They went back to their dinghy, annoyed and slightly uneasy. There was no reason to think that the shopkeeper was hostile, or that he would do anything active to harm them. Not one man in a thousand would go out of his way to help the Germans. But many Norwegians of the simpler sort were prone to gossip, and any man whose own safety was not at stake was potentially the nucleus of a rumour. It was a pity, but the risk so far as they could see, was small, and without entirely recasting their own plans there was nothing much they could do about it. It was sheer bad luck that the one man they had selected from the lists in London should have died, and even worse luck that another man with the same name should have taken his house and business. But it could not be helped. At least, he had given them new contacts.

They set off back towards Toftefjord, to tell the rest of the party what had happened. On the way, they were overtaken by the fishing-boat which had been lying off the jetty of the shop. Its crew had got their bait and were on their way to the fishing-grounds. They took the dinghy in tow; but just before they came to the mouth of Toftefjord the skipper shouted that they had forgotten a rope, some part of their fishing gear, and that they had to go back to the shop to fetch it. He cast the dinghy off. Eskeland went on into Toftefjord, and saw the fishing-boat turn round and steam away.

What happened when the skipper and crew of the fishing-boat got back to the shop will never exactly be known. The shopkeeper had gone back to bed, but they called him out again, and this time his wife joined them to hear what was going on. He said he was feeling sick and giddy. He thought it was due to the cigarettes the strangers had given him. His brother was one of the crew, and he and the skipper plied him with questions about the strange boat and the three unknown men. Before very long, the shopkeeper had told them everything.

It was probably during this conversation that a new and appalling fear struck him. Was it possible that the three men were German agents sent to test him? He had heard people say that the Germans sent men about in the islands, dressed in civilian clothes, to do that very thing: to say that they came from England, and then to report anyone who offered to help them. What was more likely than that they should pick on him, a merchant, a man with a certain standing in the community, and one who had only recently set up in business? He was thankful, now he came to think of it, that he had refused to help them. And yet, had he been careful enough? He racked his brains to remember exactly what he had said about Germans. He felt sure he had been indiscreet. There had been something about minefields. That was probably secret. Of course, he said to the others, the only way to make sure of his position, the only safe thing to do, was to report what the men had told him. Supposing they were German agents, it would not be enough only to have refused to help them. They would be waiting now to see if he reported them. If he didn't, they would get him anyhow.

The three men discussed this dilemma for an hour. The shop-keeper's wife listened in distress at his agitation. His brother was in favour of doing nothing. It would be a bad business, he admitted, if the men were Germans; but on the other hand, if he reported them and it turned out that they had really come from England, it would be far worse. The trouble was, it was impossible to be sure; but on the whole, he thought it was right to take the chance.

With this decision, after a long confusing argument, the skipper and the shopkeeper's brother left for the fishing again. The shopkeeper himself went back to bed, still feeling sick and dizzy. He could not sleep. He knew what it meant to be dis-loyal to the Germans, or rather, to be caught at it : the concentra-

tion camp for himself and perhaps for his wife as well ; the end
of the little business he had begun to build up ; the end of
everything. He lay there imagining it all. But to make sure of
his safety was so easy. There was the telephone downstairs in
the shop. And yet, if they were really Norwegians, and had really
come from England, and the neighbours got to know he had
told the Germans, he knew very well what they would say, and
he knew what his customers would do. Those men had sounded
like Norwegians : not local men, but they spoke Norwegian
perfectly. But of course there might be Norwegian Nazis, for all
he knew, who would do a job like that for the Germans. And was
it possible to come in a fishing-boat in March all the way from
England ? That sounded an unlikely story. Perhaps the best
thing would be to get up and go over to Toftefjord and speak to
them again and see if they could prove it. But then the Germans
were too clever to do anything by halves ; they would have their
proofs all ready. How could he tell ? How could he possibly
find out ?

The shopkeeper lay all night, sick with fear and confusion.
Towards the morning, the last of his courage ebbed away. About
seven, he crept down to the shop, and picked up the telephone.
He had thought of a compromise. He asked for a man he knew
who had an official post in the Department of Justice.

In Toftefjord, when Eskeland had told the others about the
two merchants with the same name, they agreed that there was
nothing to be done. The man had promised not to talk, and short
of murder they could not think of any way of making more sure
of him than that. So Eskeland set off again, not very much dis-
couraged, to see the two fishermen the shopkeeper had recommended.

This time he got the answer he expected. There was no point
in telling these men the story about spare parts. By then, it was
about three o'clock in the morning, and even in the Arctic,
where nobody takes much notice of the time of day, people would
not expect to be woken up at such an hour with any ordinary
request. He did not ask them to go to Tromsö either. Most of
the first night was already gone, and the most urgent need was

to get the cargo ashore so that *Brattholm* could sail again for Shetland.

The two fishermen agreed at once, enthusiastically, to hide it in some caves which they knew. Eskeland did not tell them the whole story. He did not mention England, but left them with the impression that he had brought the cargo from the south of Norway, and that it contained food and equipment for the home forces to use when the tide began to turn. But the two men did not want to be told any more about it. If it was anti-German, that seemed to be good enough for them. They said they would come to Toftefjord at half-past four on the following afternoon to pilot *Brattholm* out to their hiding-place, so that everything would be ready for unloading as soon as it was dark.

It was daylight by the time the dinghy got back to Toftefjord. Eskeland and the men who were with him were tired, not merely by being out all night, but by the long hours of careful conversation. When they came aboard, they found that Jan Baalsrud, the only one of the landing party who had not been either to the shop or the fishermen, had been at work all night checking over their small arms again. As an instrument maker, Jan loved the mechanism of guns and always took particular care of them ; and like Eskeland, he had been a little worried about the shopkeeper.

They made breakfast, and talked about the shop again. It was only two hours' steaming from Tromsö, somebody pointed out, for any kind of warship ; so if they had really had the bad luck to hit upon a Nazi and he had reported them, they would surely have been attacked by then. Dawn would have been the obvious time for the Germans to choose. But dawn was past, and Toftefjord was as quiet and peaceful as before. They agreed in the end that the landing party should stay on watch till ten o'clock. If nothing had happened by then, it really would look as if that particular danger was over ; and then the landing party would turn in and leave some of the crew on watch till the fishermen came at half-past four.

The morning passed. The only thing which was at all unusual was the number of aircraft they could hear. There was the sound of machine-gun fire too, from time to time. It was all out at sea.

But none of the aircraft flew over Toftefjord. It sounded as though there was a practice target somewhere beyond the islands, and that seemed a possible explanation. The air forces at Bardufoss must have somewhere for training, and the sea or the outer skerries would be a likely place. As the day went by, the men began to relax. By noon, they were reassured. Eskeland and his party went below to sleep, leaving half of the crew on deck.

A shout awoke them: "Germans! Germans!" They rushed for the hatch. The men on watch stood there appalled. Two hundred yards away, coming slowly into the fjord, there was a German warship. As the last of the men reached the deck, it opened fire. At once they knew that the aircraft were on patrol stopping the exits from the sounds. There was no escape for *Brattholm*. Eskeland shouted "Abandon ship! Abandon ship!"

That was the only order. They knew what to do. Somebody ran up the naval flag to the mizzen head. The crew leaped down into one of the boats and cast off and rowed for shore. The German ship stopped and lowered two boats. Troops piled into them and made for the shore a little farther north. Jan Baalsrud and Salvesen poured petrol on the cipher books and set them all on fire, and cast off the second dinghy and held it ready in the lee of the ship out of sight of the Germans. Eskeland and Blindheim tore off the hatch covers and climbed down among the cargo and lit the five-minute fuse.

With her boats away the German ship began to approach again. It was firing with machine-guns and a three-pounder, but the shots were going overhead. The Germans meant to capture them alive: they were not expecting much resistance. Eskeland called from the hold: "Jan, hold them off." Jan took a submachine gun and emptied the magazine at the German's bridge. The ship stopped for a moment, and then came on again. Eskeland jumped up from the hold, calling to the others "It's burning," and all of them climbed down into the dinghy, and waited. They knew the drill: to wait till the last possible minute hidden in *Brattholm's* lee before they started to try to row away.

Eskeland sat looking at his wrist-watch, with his arm held steadily in front of him. One of the others held on to the side of *Brattholm's* hull. Two were ready at the oars. One minute had gone already. They could not see the German ship from there. They could hear it approaching the other side of *Brattholm*, firing in bursts at *Brattholm* and at the crew in the other dinghy. Per Blindheim said : " Well, we've had a good time for twenty-six years, Jan." Eskeland said : " Two minutes." Jan could see the crew. They had got to the shore. Two were still in the dinghy with their hands up. Three were on the beach. One was lying in the edge of the water. One was trying to climb the rocks, and machine-gun bullets were chipping the stones above him and ricocheting across the fjord. Eskeland said : " Three minutes." The German landing party came into sight, running along the shore towards the place where the crew had landed, jumping from rock to rock. When they got near, the firing stopped, and for a few seconds there was no sound but the shouts of German orders. " Three and a half," Eskeland said. " Cast off."

They began to row, keeping *Brattholm* between them and the Germans. In that direction, towards the head of the fjord, it was two hundred yards to shore. But the German ship was very close, and it was much bigger than *Brattholm*. Before they had gone fifty yards they were sighted, and at this point-blank range the Germans opened fire. The dinghy was shot full of holes and began to sink. But the German ship was slowly drawing alongside *Brattholm*, and the last quarter of a minute of the fuse was burning down, and the fascination of watching the trap being sprung blinded them to the miracle that so far they had not been wounded.

The ship and *Brattholm* touched, and at that very moment the explosion came. But it was nothing, only a fraction of what it should have been. Only the primer exploded. The hatch covers were blown off and the front of the wheelhouse was wrecked, but the German ship was undamaged. There were shouts and confusion on deck and for a few seconds the firing stopped. The ship went full speed astern. *Brattholm* was burning fiercely. In that momentary respite, the men in the dinghy rowed for their lives, but the ship swung round till its three-pounder came to bear. Its first shot missed the dinghy. And then the whole cargo exploded. *Brattholm* vanished, in the crack of the shock wave, the long roar in the hills, the mushroom of smoke streaked with debris and blazing petrol. Eskeland was blown overboard. Jan leaned out and got him under the arms and hauled him on to the gunwale, and the German gunner recovered and a shot from the three-pounder smashed the dinghy to pieces. They were all in the water, swimming. There were seventy yards to go. The Germans brought all their guns to bear on the heads in the water. The men swam on, through water foaming with bullets, thrusting the ice aside with their heads and hands.

All of them reached the shore. Jan Baalsrud stumbled through the shallows with his friend Per Blindheim beside him. As they reached the water's edge Per was hit in the head and fell forward half out of the water. With a last effort, Jan climbed a rocky bank and found cover behind a stone. As he climbed he had been aware that his leader Eskeland had fallen on the beach and that Salvesen, either wounded or exhausted, had sunk down there unable to make the climb. He shouted to them all to follow him, but there was no answer. A bullet hit the stone above his head and whined across the fjord. He was under fire from both sides. He looked behind him, and saw the Germans who had landed. Four of them had worked round the shore and crossed the hillside fifty yards above him to cut off his retreat. He was surrounded.

At the head of the fjord there is a little mound, covered with small birch trees. Behind it the hills rise steeply for about two hundred feet. A shallow gully divides them. Within the gully the snow lies deeply, a smooth steep slope only broken by two large boulders. The patrol came floundering down the hill, pausing to kneel in the snow and snipe at Jan with rifles. Caught between them and the fire from the ship he could find no cover. But to reach him the patrol had to cross the little dip behind the mound, and there for a moment they were out of sight. He got up and ran towards them. He could not tell whether they would come over the mound, through the birches, or skirt round it to the left. He crept round it to the right. He had been wearing rubber sea-boots, but had lost one of them when he was swimming, and one of his feet was bare. He heard the soldiers crashing through the brittle bushes. Soon, as he and the patrol each circled round the mound, he came upon their tracks and crossed them. It could only be seconds before they came to his. But now the foot of the gully was near and he broke cover and ran towards it.

They saw him at once, and they were even closer than before. An officer called on him to halt. He struggled up the first part of the gully, through the soft sliding snow. The officer fired at him with a revolver and missed, and he got to cover behind the first boulder in the gully and drew his automatic.

Looking back down the snow slope, he watched the officer climbing up towards him with three soldiers following close behind. The officer was in Gestapo uniform. They came on with confidence, and Jan remembered that so far he had not fired a shot, so that they possibly did not know that he was armed. He waited, not to waste his fire. Beyond the four figures close below him, he was aware of uproar and confusion, shouting and stray shots in the fjord. As he climbed, the officer called to Jan to surrender. He was out of breath. Jan fixed on a spot in the snow six yards below him. When they reached there, he would shoot.

The officer reached it first. Jan squeezed the trigger. The pistol clicked. It was full of ice. Twice more he tried, but it would not work, and the men were within three paces. He ejected two cartridges, and it fired. He shot the Gestapo officer twice and he fell dead in the snow and his body rolled down the slope over and over towards the feet of his men. Jan fired again and the next man went down, wounded. The last two turned and ran, sliding down the snow to find cover. Jan jumped to his feet and began the long climb up the gully.

For a little while, it was strangely quiet. He was hidden from the fjord by one side of the gully. The snow was soft and deep and difficult, and he often slipped with his rubber boot. With all his strength, he could only climb slowly.

Above the second boulder, for the last hundred feet, the gully opened out into a wide snow slope, perfectly clean and white and smooth, and as soon as he set foot on it he came into sight of the German ship behind him.

In his dark naval uniform against the gleaming snow up there he was exposed as a perfect target for every gun on the warship and the rifles of the soldiers on the beaches. He struggled in desperation with the powdery snow, climbing a yard and slipping back, clawing frantically with his hands at the yielding surface which offered no hold. The virgin slope was torn to chaos by the storm of bullets from behind him. Three-pounder shells exploding in it blew clouds of snow powder in the air. He could feel with sickening expectation the thud and the searing pain in his back which would be the end of it all. The impulse to hide, to seek any refuge from this horror, was overwhelming. But there was nowhere to hide, no help, no escape from the dreadful thing that was happening to him. He could only go on and on and on, choking as his lungs filled with ice crystals, sobbing with weariness and rage and self-pity, kicking steps which crumbled away beneath him, climbing and falling, exhausting the last of his strength against the soft deep cushion of the snow.

He got to the top. There were rocks again, hard windswept snow, the crest of the hill, and shelter just beyond it. He dropped in his tracks, and for the first time he dared to look behind him. The firing died. There below him he could see the whole panorama of the fjord. Smoke hung above it in the sky. The German ship was at the spot where *Brattholm* had been anchored. On the far shore, a knot of soldiers were gathered round the crew. Nearer, where he had landed, his companions were lying on the beach, not moving, and he thought they were all dead. All round the fjord there were parties of Germans, some staring towards him at the spot where he had reached the ridge and disappeared, and others beginning to move in his direction. In his own tracks before his eyes the snow was red, and that brought him to full awareness of a pain in his foot, and he looked at it. His only injury was almost ludicrous. It was his right foot, the bare one, and half his big toe had been shot away. It was not bleeding much, because the foot was frozen. He got up and turned his back on Toftefjord and began to try to run. It was not much more than ten minutes since he had been sleeping in the cabin with his friends, and now he was alone.

CHAPTER THREE

HUNTED

IF JAN had stopped to think, everything would have seemed hopeless. He was alone, in uniform, on a small bare island, hunted by about fifty Germans. He left a deep track, as he waded through the snow, which anyone could follow. He was wet through and had one bare foot, which was wounded, and it was freezing hard. The island was separated from the mainland by two sounds, each several miles wide, which were patrolled by the enemy, and all his money and papers had been blown up in the boat.

But when a man's mind is numbed by sudden disaster, he acts less by reason than by reflex. In military affairs, it is at moments like those that training is most important. The crew's training had been nautical, the sea was their element, and when their ship disappeared before their eyes and they were cast ashore without time to recover themselves and begin to think, their reaction was to lose hope and to surrender. But Jan had been trained to regard that barren hostile country as a place where he could live and work for years. He had expected to go ashore and to live off the land, and so, when the crisis came, he turned without any conscious reason to the land as a refuge, and began to fight his way out. If his companions had not been wounded or overcome by the icy water, no doubt they would have done the same thing, although none of them knew then, as they learned later, that any risks and any sufferings were better than surrender.

For the moment, his thoughts did not extend beyond the next few minutes. He thought no more than a hunted fox with a baying pack behind it, and he acted with the instinctive cunning of a fox. It served him better, in that primitive situation, than the complicated processes of reason. On the southern slopes of the island there was less snow. Here and there, where the rocks were steep, he found bare patches, and he hobbled towards them and crossed them, leaving no track, laying false trails, doubling back on the way he had come, jumping from stone to stone to leave the snow untrodden in between. But there was no cover. Wherever he went, he could be seen from one part of the island or another; and as the shock of the battle faded and his heart and lungs began to recover from the effort of his climb, he began to believe that although he had escaped, it could only be minutes before the Germans ran him down.

Running blindly here and there among the hills, hampered by his wounded foot, he had no idea how far he had come from Toftefjord, and before he expected it he found himself facing the sea again. Below him on the shore there were some houses and a jetty, and from Eskeland's description he recognised the shop. He had crossed the island already. He remembered that the shopkeeper had a boat, and he thought of trying to steal it. But the water in front of him was wide and clear, and the Germans would be over the hill behind him at any moment. He knew he could not get out of sight in a boat before they came.

He went on, down to the shore a little way from the jetty. There at least there was a narrow strip of beach which was free of snow, and he could walk along it, slowly and painfully, without leaving any tracks at all. He turned to the left, away from the shop, back towards Toftefjord. He felt intolerably lonely.

There were two little haysheds by the shore. He wanted to creep into one and hide there and burrow in the hay and get warm and go to sleep. They were obvious hiding places. But even as he began to think of it, he knew they were too obvious. They were isolated. He pictured himself hidden there in the dark, hearing the Germans coming along the beach, and their expectant shouts when they saw the sheds, and himself trapped in there while they surrounded him. The very uselessness of the haysheds impressed upon him that there really was no hiding place for him in that dreadful island. If he stayed on the island, wherever he hid he would be found.

As he scrambled along the beach he was coming nearer, though he did not know it, to the sound which Eskeland and the others had passed through on their way to the shop. It is called Vargesund, and it is full of rocks, in contrast to the wide open waters to the north and south. The largest of the rocks is about half an acre in extent. As soon as Jan saw this little island, he knew what he had to do, and for the first time he saw a gleam of hope. He hurried to the edge of the water, and waded in, and began to swim again.

It was only fifty yards to the rock, and in spite of his clothes and his pistol and his one sea-boot, he had no difficulty in swimming across. But when he dragged himself out of the mixture of ice and water, and climbed over to the far side of the rock, the effect of this second swim began to tell on him. He had to begin to reckon with the prospect of freezing to death.

There was a minute patch of peat on top of the islet, and someone had been cutting it. He got down below the peatbank and started to do exercises, keeping an eye on the hills of the main island. His bare foot was quite numb, although running had made an unpleasant mess of the raw end of his toe. He took off his sea-boot and moved his one sock from his left foot to his right. It seemed a good idea to have a boot on one foot and a sock on the other. He stamped his feet, crouching down below the bank, to start the circulation and try to ward off frostbite.

It was only a very short time before the Germans came in sight, and for the next two hours he watched them, at first with apprehension, and then with a growing sense of his own advantage. They came slowly, in straggling line abreast, pausing to challenge every stone, with a medley of shouts and orders and counter-orders ; and Jan, watching them critically in the light of his own field training, remembered one of the many things he had been told and had only half believed : that the garrisons of that remote part of Norway were low-grade troops whose morale was softened by isolation and long inactivity. Gradually, as he watched their fumbling search, he began to despise them, and to recognise beneath that formidable uniform the signs of fallibility and even fear. They were probably clerks and cooks and bat-men, dragged out unwillingly at a moment's notice from comfortable headquarters billets in the town. He could guess very

well what they would think of having to hunt a desperate armed
bandit among ice and rocks and snow.

It was dusk when the first party of them came along the beach,
but he could see them clearly because they were using torches
which they flashed into dark crevices. They passed his island
without a glance behind them out to sea. So far, it seemed not
to have crossed their minds that he might have swum away.

When it was dark, the confusion increased. They were
scattered in small groups all over the hills. Each group was
signalling to others with its torches. Men were shouting their
own names, afraid that their friends would mistake them for the
bandit. Now and then a single shot echoed from hill to hill.
That could only mean that nervous men were firing at fancied
movements in the dark. Slowly it dawned on Jan, with a feeling
of intense elation which gave him new strength and courage, that
for all their numbers, they were afraid of him.

That opportunity to study the German army at its worst was
worth months of military training, because after it he never again
had the slightest doubt that he could outwit them till the end.

At the same time, he was becoming more aware of the dangers
of his natural surroundings. A human enemy, however relentless
and malevolent he may be, has human weaknesses ; but nobody
can trifle with the Arctic. In immediate terms, Jan knew that
if he stayed where he was in his wet clothes, he would be dead
before the morning.

Of course, there was only one alternative : to swim again.
He could swim back to Ribbenesöy, among the Germans, or he
might conceivably swim on across the sound, to Hersöy, the
next island to the eastward. One way or the other, he had to find
a house where he could go in and get dry and warm. He had only
seen two houses on Ribbenesöy, the shopkeeper's and the one
in Toftefjord, and both of them were out of the question. He
knew from the chart that there were others farther west, but by
that time they were probably full of Germans. Across the
sound, on Hersöy, he had seen a single lonely house, but he had
no idea who lived there.

He looked at Vargesund, and wondered if it was possible. In
fact, it is 220 yards across, but it was difficult for him to guess

its width in the darkness. The far shore was only a shadow between the shining water and the shining hills. The surface of the
sound was broken here and there by eddies : the tide had begun
to set. In health and strength he could easily swim the distance ;
but he could not judge the effects of the tide and the cold and his
own exhaustion. He stood for a long time before he made up his
mind. He did not want to die either way, but to drown seemed
better than to freeze. He took a last look behind him at the
flashing torches of the soldiers, and stumbled down the rocks
and waded in and launched himself into the sea again.

It is a mercy that the ultimate extremes of physical distress
often get blurred in memory. Jan hardly remembered anything
of that third and longest swim, excepting an agony of cramp,
and excepting the dreadful belief that he was just about to die ;
an experience most people encounter once or twice in a lifetime,
but one he had had to face so many times on that single day. It
was after he had given up any conscious struggle, and admitted
his defeat, and was ready to welcome his release from pain, that
some chance eddy swept him ashore on the farther side and rolled
his limp body among the stones, and left him lying there on his
face, groaning and twisted with cramp, and not able to move or
to think of moving.

Seconds or minutes or hours later, in the mists of half-
consciousness, there were voices. There were footsteps on the
beach, and the clink of stones turning. He wondered with a
mild curiosity whether the words he could hear were German or
Norwegian, and from somewhere outside himself he looked
down with pity on the man who lay beaten on the shore and the
people who approached him ; because if they were German, the
man was too weak to get away. But slowly his dim enfeebled
brain began to accept a fact which was unforeseen and strange on
that day of death and violence. They were children's voices.
There were children, coming along the beach and chattering in
Norwegian. And suddenly they stopped, and he knew they had
seen him.

He lifted his head, and there they were, two little girls, holding
hands, wide-eyed with horror, too frightened to run away. He
smiled and said : " Hallo. You needn't be afraid." He managed

to turn round and sit up. "I've had an accident," he said. "I do wish you could help me." They did not answer, but he saw them relax a little, and he realised that when they had seen him, they had thought that he was dead.

Jan loved children; he had looked after his own young brother and sister after his mother died. Perhaps nothing in the world could have given him strength of mind just then, except compassion : the urgent need to soothe the children's fear and make up for the shock which he had given them. He talked to them calmly. His own self-pity and despair had gone. He showed them how wet he was, and made a joke of it, and they came nearer as their fright gave way to interest and wonder. He asked them their names. They were Dina and Olaug. After a while he asked if their home was near, and whether they would take him there, and at the idea of bringing him home and showing their parents what they had discovered they brightened up and helped him to his feet. The house was not far away.

There were two women there, and the rest of their children. They exclaimed in horrified amazement at the frozen, limping, wild dishevelled man whom the little girls led in. But the moment he spoke to them in Norwegian their horror changed to motherly concern and they hurried him into the kitchen, and took him to the fire and brought him towels and put the kettle on.

Of all the series of acts of shining charity which attended Jan in the months which were to come, the help which these two women gave him on the first night of his journey was most noble, because they knew what had happened just across the sound, and they knew that at any moment, certainly by the morning, the Germans would be pounding on their door. They knew that their own lives and the lives of all their children would hang on a chance word when they came to face their questioning. Yet they opened their door at once to the stranger in such desperate distress, and cared for him and saved his life and sent him on his way, with no thought or hope of any reward except the knowledge that, whatever price they paid, they had done their Christian duty. Their names are Fru Pedersen and Fru Idrupsen.

The first thing Jan did was to warn them all that the Germans were after him, and that when they were questioned they must

say that he came in carrying a pistol and demanded their help by
force. He brought out his pistol to emphasise what he said. As
soon as he had made quite sure that they understood this, and
that even the children had a clear idea of what they should do and
say, he sent two of them out as sentries, and told them to warn
him at once if they saw a boat coming into the sound.

Fru Idrupsen, it turned out, was the woman from Toftefjord.
She had run to the hills with her children when the shooting
started, and she had seen most of what happened from the top
of the island. She had rowed across the sound to take refuge
with her neighbours. Fru Pedersen had a grown-up son and
daughter and two young children. Her son was out fishing, but
she expected him back at any minute. Her husband, like Fru
Idrupsen's, was away for the Lofoten fishing season and would
not be home till it ended.

All the time Jan was talking, the two women were busy with
the practical help which he needed so badly. They gave him food
and a hot drink, and helped him to take off his sodden clothes.
They found him new dry underclothes and socks and a sea-boot
Herr Pedersen had left behind, and they hung up his uniform to
dry, and rubbed his feet and legs till the feeling began to come
back to them, and bandaged the stub of his wounded toe.

Twice while they worked to revive him, the sentries came running in to say that a boat was coming. Each time Jan pulled on
his steaming jacket and trousers and the sea-boots, one his own
and one Herr Pedersen's, and gathered together everything which
belonged to him and ran out of the house and up into the hills.
But each time the boat passed by.

Between these alarms, he rested and relaxed. That humble
Norwegian kitchen, with the children gathered round him speaking his native tongue, was more homely than any place he had
seen in the three years he had been abroad. The warmth, and
the sense of homecoming, and the contrast of family life after the
fearful tension of the day, made him drowsy. It was difficult to
remember that outside in the darkness there still were ruthless
men who would shoot him on sight, and wreck that home if they
found him there, and carry the children off to captivity and
the mothers to unmentionable torment. Such violence had the

quality of a dream. And when he dragged his mind back to grapple with reality, Jan found himself faced with a doubt which often came back to him later : ought he to let such people help him ? Was his own life worth it ? Was he right, as a soldier, to let women and children put their lives in such terrible danger ? To save them from the consequence of their own goodness, ought he not to go out, and fight his own battle alone ? But for the moment, these questions went unanswered, because he was not fit to make any such decision. Fru Pedersen and Fru Idrupsen had taken him in hand, and they treated him as an extra child.

When he had been there half an hour or so, the eldest son of the Pedersen family came home. He had heard the explosion in Toftefjord, but he did not know what had happened. They told him the story, and as soon as he had heard it he took it as a matter of course that a wounded survivor should be sitting in his mother's kitchen while the Germans scoured the islands round about. As his father was not at home, it was up to him to get Jan away to safety. He began to debate the question of how to do it.

The first thing was to rest. For one thing, there was no knowing when Jan might get another chance, and for another it would be madness to go out in a boat while the Germans were still there. And after that, the boy said, when he had rested, he ought to get away from the islands altogether, to the mainland. Any island, however big it was, might be a trap, not only because you might find your retreat cut off, but also because everyone on an island knew everyone else's business. If he stayed another day in Hersöy, everyone would know he was there. But on the mainland, if they did come after you, you could always go on a stage farther ; and gossip did not spread there quite so fast. Altogether, he would be safer there. Besides, that was the way to Sweden.

This was the first time Jan had paused to think of an ultimate escape. Up till then, it had only been a matter of dodging for the next few hours, and he had still thought of north Norway as his destination. That was where he had set out for, and he had arrived; and although he had lost his companions and all his equipment, he had not admitted to himself that the whole expedition was a

failure. He still hoped to do part of his job there, at least, as soon
as he had got his strength back and shaken off the Germans. But
the people who lived there, as he now began to see, all thought
at once of Sweden for a man in such serious trouble. It was a
difficult journey, but not a very long one; about eighty miles, in
a straight line; if you could travel in straight lines.

The trouble was, the boy went on, he only had a rowing-
boat himself, and they could never row to the mainland. Just
south of them was the sound called Skagösund, which was two
miles wide. On the other side of that was Ringvassöy, an island
about twenty miles square, and south of that again you had to
cross Grötsund itself, which was the main channel into Tromsö
from the north and was four miles wide and full of patrol boats.
The best he could do himself was to row Jan across to Ringvassöy
before the morning. But he knew a man there called Jensen
who was all right, and he had a motor-boat and was meaning to
go into Tromsö some day soon. His wife was the midwife over
there, and he had a permit and was always moving about with his
boat. He could easily put Jan ashore on the mainland.

Jan listened gratefully as this plan unfolded. He was glad for
the moment to have everything thought out for him, and was
ready to fall in with any idea which would take him away from
Toftefjord.

When it was all decided, and he was resting, the eldest son of
the Toftefjord family went out in his boat to see what had
happened at his home, and to find out for Jan if there was any
sign of the rest of his party. He was away for a couple of hours.
When he came back, Jan knew for certain that of all the twelve
men, he was the only one who was not either killed or captured.
Toftefjord itself was quiet. There were still parties of Germans
searching the distant hills. The slopes of the fjord were littered
with scraps of planking. The boy had found the remains of a
petrol barrel, and seen an ammunition belt hanging in a tree.
But there was no one, alive or dead, on the beaches. The German
ship had left. It was steaming slowly up the north side of the
island, using a searchlight. Jan's friends, or their bodies, must
have been taken aboard it. Eskeland and Per Blindheim and all
the others were gone, and he could never expect to see any

of them again. There was nothing he could do except to go on alone.

He left the house on Hersöy very early in the morning, well before it was light. Fru Pedersen and Fru Idrupsen watched him go and brushed aside his thanks, which could certainly not have been adequate for what they had done. The boy took him down to his boat and they got aboard and pushed her off into the sound. Jan felt fit again and ready for anything. They turned to the southward and began to row, past the place where he had landed from his swim, past the shop, and then out across the open water, heading for Ringvassöy, with Toftefjord astern. Everything was peaceful.

CHAPTER FOUR

SEA-BOOTS IN THE SNOW

IN MOMENTS of calm, Jan often thought about his family, as all soldiers of all armies think in war. So far as he knew, they were still in Oslo : his father, and his young brother Nils, and his sister. His sister's name was Julie, but none of them ever called her that because they thought it was old-fashioned ; they had always gone on calling her Bitten, which was the nickname he had invented for her when he was eight and she was a baby. When his mother died, he had been sixteen, Nils ten, and Bitten only eight ; and so he had suddenly had to be very much more grown up than he really was ; he had had to take care of the children when his father was at work, and even shop and cook and wash for them for a time till his aunt could come to the rescue.

They had always been a closely united family, both before and after that disaster, until the morning just after the invasion when his orders had come and he had left home on an hour's notice. But somehow a special affection had grown up through the years between himself and Bitten. Young Nils was a boy and an independent spirit who had always been able to stand on his own feet ; but Bitten had turned to him more and more for advice, and he had become very fond of her, and proud of her, and deeply interested in her growing-up.

Perhaps this big-brotherly affection had been the deepest emotion in Jan's life, when fortune landed him in Toftefjord when he was twenty-six. At any rate, leaving Bitten had hurt more than anything when the time came. He had tried to make the break as quick and painless as it could be when he knew he had to do it. He had waited around that morning till he knew

she would be coming home from school, and he had met her in
the street on his way to the station just to tell her he was going.
She was fifteen then, and he had never seen her since. For the
first few months, while he was in Norway and Sweden, he had
been able to write to her sometimes, using a false name so that if
the letters got into the wrong hands she would not get into
trouble for having a brother who was still opposing the Germans
after the capitulation. In his letters he had begged her to stay
on at high school, not to be in a hurry to get a job ; but he had
never known if she had taken that advice. While he was in
prison in Sweden he had had a few letters from her, sending him
press cuttings about netball games she had played in. It had made
him smile to think that she wanted him to be interested in netball
when he was just beginning a prison sentence ; but it had also
made him very homesick. Since he had left Sweden and started
his journey to England, he had never heard of her at all. That
was nearly three years ago. She would be eighteen now : grown
up, he supposed. He sorely wished that he knew if she was
happy.

Sitting in the boat that early morning, as the boy from Hersöy
rowed him across the sound, Jan had every reason to think of his
family. It had always been on his mind since he started to train
as an agent that he would have to be careful to protect them from
reprisals if anything went wrong. Now that capture and death
were so close to him, he had to remind himself of the one and
only way he could protect them : to refuse to be captured, and
to die, if he had to die, anonymously. He had nothing on him
to identify him or his body as Jan Baalsrud, and that was as it
should be : if the worst came to the worst, the Germans would
throw him into a grave without a name. His father and Nils
and Bitten would never know what had happened to him. He
would have liked them to know he had done his best ; but to
leave them in ignorance was the price of their safety.

Something the boy said brought this forcibly to his mind. The
boy meant to take him to Jensen's house and introduce him and
make sure that he was safe ; but Jan had to ask him to put him
ashore out of sight of the house and leave him. He explained the
first principle of any illegal plan : that nobody should know more

than he needs. It was a pity that the boy and his family knew Jan was going to Jensen, but there was no need for Jensen to know where he came from. You might trust a man like your brother, he said, but it was no kindness to burden him with unnecessary secrets, because no man alive could be certain he would not talk if he was caught and questioned. What your tongue said when your brain was paralysed by drugs or torture was not a mere matter of courage; it was unpredictable, and beyond any self-control. Jan himself would be the only one who knew everyone who helped him; but he had his pistol, and he solemnly promised this boy, as he promised more people later, that he would not let them catch him alive. So the two of them parted on the shore of Ringvassöy, and the boy backed his boat off and turned away into the darkness, leaving Jan alone.

Jan owned nothing in the world just then except the clothes he was wearing, and a handkerchief and a knife and some bits of rubbish in his pockets, and his pistol. He had navy blue trousers and a sweater and Herr Pedersen's underclothes, and a Norwegian naval jacket, a warm double-breasted one with brass buttons and a seaman's badges, though he had never been a seaman, and was not even very sure if he could row. The jacket had the Norwegian flag sewn on its shoulders, with the word NORWAY in English above it. He had lost his hat. He was amused at the odd footprints which his two rubber boots left in the snow, one English and one Norwegian. There was something symbolic there, if you cared about symbols.

There were a dozen houses in that part of Ringvassöy, but he easily picked out Jensen's. The lights were on, and there were voices inside. He hoped that might mean that Jensen was making an early start on his trip to Tromsö. He went to the back door, and hesitated a moment, and knocked. A woman opened the door at once, and he asked if Jensen was at home. No, she said, he had left for Tromsö the morning before, and would not be back for two or three days.

At this disappointing news Jan paused for a moment uncertainly, because he did not want to show himself to people who could not help him. He would have liked to make an excuse and go away; but he saw surprise and alarm in her face as she noticed his uniform in the light of the lamp from the doorway.

" I'm in a bit of trouble with the Germans," he said. " Have you got people in the house ? "

" Why, of course," she said. " I have my patients. But they're upstairs. You'd better come inside."

That explained the lights and the voices so early in the morning. He had not made allowances for what a midwife's life involves. He went in, and began to tell her a little of what had happened, and what he wanted, and of the danger of helping him.

Fru Jensen was not in the least deterred by danger. She had heard the explosion in Toftefjord, and already rumours had sprung up in Ringvassöy. The only question she asked was who had sent Jan to her house, and when he refused to tell her and explained the reason why, she saw the point at once. She said he was welcome to stay. She was very sorry her husband was away, and she herself could not leave the house at present, even for a moment. But there was plenty of room, and they were used to people coming and going. He could stay till the evening, or wait till Jensen came home if he liked. He would be glad to take him to the mainland. But she could not be sure how long he would be away, and perhaps it would be risky to try to ring him up in Tromsö and tell him to hurry back.

" But you must be hungry," she said. " Just excuse me a moment, and then I'll make your breakfast." And she hurried upstairs to attend to a woman in labour.

Jan felt sure he would be as safe in her hands as anyone's. He could even imagine her dealing firmly and capably with Germans who wanted to search her house.

But he was still much too close to Toftefjord. If the Germans really wanted to get him, it would not take them long to turn Ribbenesöy inside out: they had probably finished that already. And the obvious place for them to look, when they were sure he had left the island, was where he was now, on the shore of Ringvassöy which faced it. Their search would gradually widen, like a ripple on a pond, until they admitted they had lost him ; and until then, at all costs, he must travel faster than the ripple.

When Fru Jensen came back and began to lay the table, he told her he had decided to move on. She did not express any feeling about it, except to repeat that he was welcome to stay if he wanted to ; if not, she would give him some food to take with him. She began to tell him about useful and dangerous people all over her island. There were several ways he could go : either by sea, if he happened to find a boat, or along either shore of the island, or up a valley which divides it in the middle. But if he went up the valley, she warned him, he would have to be careful. People in those remote and isolated places were inclined to take their politics from the clergyman or the justice of the peace, or the chairman of the local council, or some other such leader in their own community ; they had too little knowledge of the outside world to form opinions of their own. In the valley there happened to be one man who was a Nazi, or so she had heard ; and she was afraid a lot of people might have come under his influence. If a stranger was seen there, he was certain to hear of it ; and although she could not be sure, she thought he might tell the police. Of course, most of Ringvassöy, she said, was quite all right. He could go into almost any house and be sure of a welcome. And she told him the names of a lot of people who she knew would be happy to help him.

It was still early when Jan left the midwife, fortified by a good breakfast and by her friendliness and fearless common sense. He wanted to get away from the houses before too many people were about ; but it was daylight, and it was more than likely someone would see him from a window. It was a good opportunity to be misleading. He started along the shore towards the west. In that direction, he might have gone up the valley or followed the coastline round the west side of the island. But when he was out of sight of the last of the houses, he changed his direction and struck off into the hills, and made a detour behind the houses to reach the shore again farther east. He had made his plans now a little way ahead. The next lap was to walk thirty miles to the south end of the island.

It looked simple. He remembered it pretty clearly from the map, and during his training it would have been an easy day. He knew that maps of mountains are often misleading, because even the best of them do not show whether a hill can be climbed or not ; but he was not prepared for quite such a misleading map as the one of that part of Norway. In the normal course of events, nobody ever walks far in the northern islands. The natural route from one place to another is by sea. The sea charts are therefore perfect; but the most detailed land map which existed then was on a scale of about a quarter of an inch to a mile, and it made Ringvassöy look green and smoothly rounded. No heights were marked on it. There were contours, but they had a vague appearance, as if there had been more hope than science in their drawing. One might have deduced something from the facts that the only houses shown were clustered along the shores, and that there was no sign of a single road; but nothing on the map suggested one tenth of the difficulty of walking across the island in the winter.

Jan had arrived there in the dark, and if he had ever seen the island at all, it was only in that momentary glimpse when he had come over the hill from Toftefjord with the Germans close behind him. So he set off full of optimism in his rubber boots; but it took him four days to cover the thirty miles.

He was never in any immediate danger during that walk. The only dangers were the sort that a competent mountaineer can overcome. Once he had disappeared into the trackless interior of the island he was perfectly safe from the Germans until he emerged again. But it was an exasperating journey. It had new discomfort and frustration in every mile, and the most annoying things about it were the boots. Jan was a good skier; like most Norwegians, he had been used to ski-ing ever since he could walk: and to cross Ringvassöy on skis might have been a pleasure. Certainly it would have been quick and easy. But of course his skis had been blown to pieces like everything else; and there can hardly be anything less suitable for deep snow than rubber boots.

He had started with the idea of following the shore, where the snow would be shallower and harder and he would have the alternative of going along the beach below the tidemark. But on the very first morning he found it was not so easy as it looked. He soon came to a place where a ridge ran out and ended in a cliff. He tried the beach below the cliff, but it got narrower and narrower until he scrambled round a rock and saw that the cliff face ahead of him fell sheer into the sea. He had to go back a mile and climb the ridge. It was not very steep, but it gave him a hint of what he had undertaken. The wet rubber slipped at every step. Sometimes, where the snow was hard, the climb would have been simple if he could have kicked steps ; but the boots were soft, and to kick with his right foot was too painful for his toe. He had to creep up slowly, one foot foremost, like a child going upstairs. But when the snow was soft and he sank in it up to his middle, the boots got full of it, and came off, and he had to grovel and scrape with his hands to find them.

At the top of the ridge, when he paused to take his breath, he could see far ahead along the coastline to the eastward; and there was ridge after ridge, each like the one he was on, and each ending in a cliff too steep to climb.

He started to go down the other side, and even that was painful and tedious. Down slopes which would have been a glorious run on skis, he plodded slowly, stubbing his toe against the end of the boot, and sometimes falling when the pain of it made him wince and lose his balance.

But still, all these things were no more than annoyances, and it would have been absurd to have felt annoyed, whatever happened, so long as he was free. He felt it would have been disloyal, too. He thought a lot about his friends as he floundered on, especially of Per and Eskeland. He missed them terribly. Of course he had been trained to look after himself, and make up his own mind what to do. In theory he could stand on his own feet and was not dependent on a leader to make decisions for him. But that was not the same thing as suddenly losing Eskeland, whom he admired tremendously and had always regarded as a bit wiser and more capable than himself, someone he could always rely on for good advice and understanding. And still less, in a way, did his training take the place of Per, who had shared everything with him so long. Jan knew his job, but all the same it was awful not to have anyone to talk it over with. As for what was happening to his friends, he could not bear to think about it. He would have welcomed more suffering to bring himself nearer to them in spirit.

In this mood, he forced himself on to make marches of great

duration : 24 hours, 13 hours, 28 hours without a rest. But the distances he covered were very short, because he so often found himself faced with impassable rocks and had to go back on his tracks, and because of the weather.

The weather changed from one moment to another. When the nights were clear, the aurora glimmered and danced in the sky above the sea. By day in sunshine, the sea was blue and the sky had a milky radiance, and the gleaming peaks of other islands seemed light and insubstantial and unearthly. The sun was warm, and the glitter of snow and water hurt his eyes, though the shadows of the hills were dark and cold. Then suddenly the skyline to his right would lose its clarity as a flurry of snow came over it, and in a minute or two the light faded and the warmth was gone and the sea below went grey. Gusts of wind came whipping down the slopes, and clouds streamed across the summits ; and then snow began to fall, and frozen mist came down, in grey columns which eddied in the squalls and stung his face and hands and soaked him through, and blotted out the sea and sky so that the world which he could see contracted to a few feet of whirling whiteness in which his own body and his own tracks were the only things of substance.

In the daytime, he kept going in these storms, not so much for the sake of making progress as to keep himself warm ; but when they struck him at night, there was no question of keeping a sense of direction, and one night he turned back to take shelter in a cowshed which he had passed four hours before.

He stopped at two houses along the north shore of the island, and was taken in and allowed to sleep ; and oddly enough it was his wounded toe which he found was a passport to people's help and trust. Rumours had gone before him all the way. It was being said that the Germans had started a new search of every house, looking for radio sets, which nobody was allowed to own. Everyone had already guessed that this search had something to do with what they had heard about Toftefjord, and as soon as they learned that Jan was a fugitive, they jumped to the conclusion that the Germans were searching for him. And indeed, if the search was a fact and not only a rumour, they were probably right. This made some of them nervous at first. Like the shopkeeper they were frightened of *agents provocateurs*, and Jan's uniform did not reassure them; it was only to be expected that a German agent would be dressed for his part. But the toe was different. The Germans were thorough, but their agents would not go so far as to shoot off their toes. When he took off his boot and his sock and showed them his toe, it convinced them; and he slept soundly between his marches, protected by men who set faithful watches to warn him if Germans were coming.

Always they asked who had sent him to them, and some of them were suspicious when he would not tell them. But he insisted, because he was haunted by the thought of leaving a traceable series of links which the Germans might " roll up " if they found even one of the people who helped him. Such things had happened before, and men on the run had left trails of disaster behind them. To prevent that was only a matter of care. He never told anyone where he had come from, and when he asked people to recommend others for later stages of his journey, he made sure that they gave him a number of names, and did not tell them which one he had chosen. Thus nobody could ever tell, because nobody knew, where he had come from or where he was going.

The last stretch of the journey was the longest. Everyone he had met had mentioned the name of Einar Sörensen, who ran the telephone exchange at a place called Bjorneskar on the south side of the island. All of them knew him, as everyone knows the telephone operator in a country district, and they all spoke of him with respect. Bjorneskar is opposite the mainland, and if anyone could get Jan out of the island, Einar Sörensen seemed the most likely man. But if he refused, on the other hand, or if he was not at home, it would be more than awkward, because the south end of the island was infested with Germans, in coastal batteries and searchlight positions and patrol boat bases, defending the entrance to Tromsö. Bjorneskar was a kind of cul-de-sac. The shore on each side of it was well populated and defended, and Jan could only reach it by striking inland and going over the mountains. It would be a long walk, and there was no house or shelter of any kind that way; if there was no help when he got to the other end, it was very unlikely that he could get back again.

But some risks are attractive, and he liked the idea of descending from desolate mountains into the heart of the enemy's defences.

It was this stretch of the march which cost him 28 hours of continuous struggle against the wind and snow. Up till then, he had never been far from the coast, and he had never been able to see more than the foothills of the island. The sea had always been there on his left to guide him. But now he entered a long deep valley, into the barren wilderness of peaks which the map had dismissed so glibly. Above him, especially on the right, there were hanging valleys and glimpses of couloirs, inscrutable and dark and silent, and of snow cornices on their crests. To the left was the range of crags called Soltinder, among which he somehow had to find the col which would lead him to Bjorneskar.

Into these grim surroundings he advanced slowly and painfully. Here and there in the valley bottom were frozen lakes where the going was hard and smooth; but between them the snow lay very deep, and it covered a mass of boulders, and there he could not tell as he took each step whether his foot would fall upon rock or ice, or a snow crust which would support him, or whether it would plunge down hip deep into the crevices below. Sometimes a single yard of progress was an exhausting effort in itself, and he would have to pause and rest for a minute after dragging himself out of a hidden hole, and look back at the ridiculously little distance he had won. When he paused, he was aware of his solitude. The whole valley was utterly deserted. For mile upon mile there was no trace of life whatever, no sign that a man had ever been there before him, no tracks of animals, no movement or sound of birds.

Through this solemn and awful place he walked for the whole of a night and the whole of a day, and at dusk on the third of April he came to the top of the col in the Soltinder, four days after Toftefjord. Below him he saw three houses, which he knew must be Bjorneskar, and beyond them the final sound; and on the other side, at last, the mainland. He staggered down the final slope to throw himself on the kindness of Einar Sörensen.

He need never have had any doubt of his reception. Einar and his wife and his two little boys all made him welcome, as if he were an old friend and an honoured guest. Their slender rations were brought out and laid before him, and it was not till he had eaten all he could that Einar took him aside to another room to talk.

To Einar's inevitable question, Jan answered without thinking that he had heard of his name in England, though he had really only heard it the day before. At this, Einar said with excitement, " Did they really get through to England ? " Jan knew then that this was not the first time escapers had been to that house. He said he did not know whether they had reached England or only got to Sweden, but at least their report had got through.

After this, there was no limit to what Einar was willing to do. Jan felt ashamed, when he came to think of it later, to have decieved this man on even so small a point. But the fact is that a secret agent's existence, whenever he is at work, is a lie from beginning to end ; whatever he says is said as a means to an end, and the truth is a thing he can seldom tell. The better the agent is, the more thorough are his lies. He is trained with such care to shut away truth in a dark corner of his mind that he loses his natural instinct to tell the truth, for its own sake, on the few occasions when it can do no harm. Yet when, through habit, he has told an unnecessary lie to a friend, it would often involve impossible explanations to put the thing right. So Jan left Einar with the belief that whoever it was he had helped had got somewhere through to safety.

They sat for an hour that night and talked things over. Einar thought Jan should move at once. His house was the telegraph office as well as the telephone exchange, and people were in and out of it all day ; and there were German camps within a mile in two directions. As for crossing the sound, there was no time better than the present. It was a dirty night, which was all to the good. The patrol boats ran for shelter whenever the weather was bad, and falling snow played havoc with the searchlights. The wind was rising, and it might be worse before the morning. While they were talking, Einar told Jan that all his friends from the *Brattholm* had been either killed in the battle, or executed by the Germans afterwards.

CHAPTER FIVE

THE AVALANCHE

ABOUT MIDNIGHT Einar went to fetch his father, Bernhard Sörensen, who lived in the house next door. The old man was in bed. Einar called to him from the bottom of the stairs, and when he woke up and asked what the matter was, he said, " Come out, Father, I want to talk to you." He was not sure if he ought to tell his mother.

Bernhard, who was 72 at that time, came down and listened to Einar's story, leaving his wife upstairs. When he had heard it all, he went back to his bedroom and began to put on his clothes. Fru Sörensen asked him here he was going.

" We've got to take the boat out," the old man said. " There's a man who wants to cross the sound."

" But now, at this time of night ? " she asked him.

" Yes," he said.

" It's a terrible night."

" So much the better. We'll go down to Glomma and cross with the wind. Now, don't worry. He must get across, you see. It's one of those things we mustn't talk about."

When he was ready he left her, with no more reassurance than that, to the traditional role of women in a war. She spent an anxious night at home, waiting for Bernhard, to whom she had then been married for fifty years.

But he was enjoying himsef. Jan had been worried at asking a man of his age to cross the sound on such a night of wind and snow. It was a row of ten miles across and back. But Bernhard laughed at his fears. When he was a young man, he had rowed to the Lofoten fishing and back every year, and that was two hundred

58

miles. He did not think much of the rising generation. " In my day," he used to say, " it was wooden ships and iron men, and what is it now ? Iron ships and a lot of wooden men. Why, do you know," he said, as they went down to the boathouse at the water's edge, " do you know, there was a young fellow taken to hospital sick only the other day. And do you know why he was sick ? Because he'd got his feet wet. Yes," he chuckled, " taken to hospital because he'd got his feet wet. I've had my feet wet for over seventy years. Come along, boy. Across the sound is nothing. We'll swindle the devils out of one corpse, eh ? "

The old man's good humour was catching, and Jan himself was elated at the prospect of reaching the mainland. The news of the fate of his friends had not shocked him very deeply in itself. Like everyone who took part in that kind of operation, they had all left England with a small expectation of life, and death loses its power to hurt when it is half-expected. Besides, he had thought of them as dead ever since he had seen them lying on the beach in Toftefjord. It distressed him more to learn they were captured alive and had lived for another three days, because for their own sakes and from every point of view it would have been better if they had been killed in action.

But apart from the matter of emotion, the story had a minor lesson to teach him. Hitler himself had just issued an order that everyone who took any part in this kind of guerrilla action was to be shot, whether he was in uniform or not. They had all known this before they left England ; but if the order was meant to be a deterrent, it was accepted as a compliment. So far as Jan knew, this was the first time since the order was made that a crew had been captured, and he had still had a half-formed belief that a uniform might give some protection. He was still dressed as a sailor himself ; but now it seemed rather absurd, on the face of it, to try to cross Norway in such a conspicuous rig. But to change it was easier thought of than done. It had been simple enough to swap underclothes with the Pedersen family, but it was different to ask someone to give him a whole civilian outfit when he had nothing to give in exchange and no money to offer. But anyhow, when he came to think of it carefully, it could not make very much difference. The Germans knew he was still at large, and he could never pass himself off as a local civilian without his civilian papers. If he kept out of sight of the Germans, his uniform did not matter, and if he came to close quarters with them, he would have to fight it out whatever clothes he was wearing. In the middle distance, the uniform might be a disadvantage; but on the other hand, he thought to himself, it was warm.

But at the particular moment when they got into the boat and took up the oars, the naval uniform was an embarrassment, because Einar and Bernhard took it for granted that he was a naval rating, and he felt that he ought to offer to row. He had rowed before, but only on lakes when he was trout fishing; and when he tried one of the heavy sweeps in the high sea which was running off Bjorneskar, all he managed to do was to knock the tops off the waves and splash the old man who was sitting astern. He had to make the lame excuse that he was too tired, and Bernhard took over, probably not surprised to find that the navy was not what it had been.

Bernhard referred to the Germans as devils. Devil is one of the few serious swear words in the Norwegian language, but he used it with a lack of emphasis that made it rather engaging. It was as if he could not bring himself to utter the word German. " You see the point of land over there ? " he would say to Jan. " That's Finkroken. There are seventy devils there with cannons and searchlights. We'll give them a wide berth. And down there ahead of us, that's Sjursnes. That's where the patrol boats lie. A whole company of devils there too. But don't you worry. They won't get you this time, boy. We'll swindle them. We'll steer between them." And he chuckled with joy, and heaved on his massive oar.

Jan was more than content to leave it to Einar and Bernhard to get him across the sound. This was the second consecutive night he had been without sleep, and he had been on the go all the time. He was too tired to take any notice of the flurries of snow and spindrift, or the steep seas which bore down on them out of the darkness to starboard, or of the searchlights which endlessly swept the sound and sometimes appeared as a dazzling

eye of light with a halo round it when a beam passed over them.
Einar and his father were sure they would not be seen, so long
as the snow went on falling, and they were not bothered about
the patrol boats, although they were crossing their beats. " No
devils at sea on a night like this," the old man said. " There's
not a seaman among them."

Jan did not care. The mainland was close ahead, and Einar
had given him the things which he coveted most in the world
just then : a pair of ski-boots and skis. In an hour or so, he
would finish with boats and the sea, and enter a medium where
he would feel at home. Among the snow mountains on skis he
would be confident of outdistancing any German. He could go
where he wished and depend upon no one. Even the Swedish
frontier was only sixty miles away : two days' journey, if all
went well ; and the Germans had lost his trail. He needed
one good sleep, he thought, and then he would be his own
master.

It was about three in the morning when Bernhard and Einar
beached the boat on the southern shore. Jan jumped out thankfully. The others could not afford to wait. To take advantage of
the wind on the way back home, they would have to row close
under the devils' gun battery at Finkroken. They thought they
could bluff it out if they were seen, so long as they were not too
far away from home, but it would be better not to have to try.
So as soon as Jan was ashore with his skis, they wished him luck
and pushed off and disappeared : two more to add to the list
of chance acquaintances to whom he owed his life.

There were small farms along the water's edge just there, with
houses spaced out at intervals of two hundred yards or so. The
people who owned them pastured sheep and cattle on the narrow
strip of fertile land between the sea and the mountainside, and
eked out a living by fishing. The Sörensens knew everyone who
lived there, and had said he could go safely to any of the houses.
They had specially mentioned a man called Lockertsen. He lived
in a farm called Snarby, which was a little larger than the
rest, and he had a thirty-foot motor-boat which might come in
useful.

Jan would glady have set off there and then without making

further contacts. He felt guilty already at the number of people he had involved in his own predicament ; and besides, this series of short encounters, each at a high pitch of excitement and emotion, was exhausting in itself. He longed to be able to sleep in barns without telling anyone, and take to the hills again each morning. But before he was fit to embark on a life like that, he had to have one long sleep whatever it cost him, and that night he could only count on a few hours more before the farms were stirring. He reluctantly put his skis on his shoulder and went up through a steep farmyard to the house which was nearest. He crept quietly round the house till he found the door, and he tried the handle. It opened. As it happened, this was Snarby.

Fru Lockertsen said afterwards it was the first night she had forgotten to lock the door since the occupation started. In ordinary times, of course, nobody thought of keys in a place like that ; it was not once in a year that a stranger came to the door. But now, when you could always see a German patrol ship from the front windows of Snarby, you felt better at nights behind a good lock ; and when she was woken by blundering footsteps in the kitchen, the first thing she thought was that some German sailors had landed. She prodded her husband and whispered that there was somebody in the house, and he listened, and dragged himself out of bed, and went to see what was happening.

Lockertsen was a big heavily-built man like a polar bear. He was a head taller than Jan and looked as though he could have picked him up and crushed him ; and probably that is what he felt inclined to do. He was intensely suspicious. Jan told him his story, and then told it all over again, but every time he told it Lockertsen had thought of new doubts and new questions. He simply refused to believe it, and Jan could not understand why. But the fact is that Jan was so sleepy that he hardly knew what he was saying. His explanation was muddled and unconvincing, and the way he told the story made it sound like a hastily-invented lie. The only thing that was still quite clear in his head was that he must not say where he had come from. Somebody had brought him across from Ringvassöy, he insisted ; but he refused to say who it was and could not explain why he refused to say it. To

Lockertsen one naval uniform was probably much the same as another, and Jan had obviously landed from the sound ; and the only navy in the sound was German. It seemed much more likely that he was a German deserter. Even the toe would have fitted that explanation. Everyone had heard of self-inflicted wounds.

The argument went on for a solid hour, and it only ended then because Jan could not talk any longer. His speech had got slow and blurred. He had to sleep. It was a pity, and he was resentful that the man did not believe him. But he was finished. He had taxed his endurance too much, and left himself without the strength to get away. Let him report him if he liked ; there was nothing more to be done about it. He lay down on the rug in front of the kitchen stove. He heard Lockertsen say : " All right. You can stay there till half-past five." At that, he fell deeply asleep.

Lockertsen spent the rest of the night pacing up and down the kitchen and trying to puzzle things out, and stopping from time to time to look down at the defenceless, mysterious creature asleep on his floor. Many of the doubts which had afflicted the shopkeeper came to him also, and they were strengthened for him by the fact that the stranger had come from a place where he knew there were Germans. But Lockertsen was a man of different calibre. He had plenty of courage. He was only determined to get the truth out of Jan, if he had to do it by force. He was not going to act one way or the other until he was sure.

Some time while Jan was sleeping the big man went down on his knees on the hearthrug and searched through his pockets. There was nothing in them which gave him a clue, and Jan did not stir.

He had said he could sleep till 5.30 ,and at 5.30 he shook him awake. The result of this surprised him. Jan was subconsciously full of suspicion, and leapt to his feet and drew his automatic and Lockertsen found himself covered before he could move.

" Take it easy, take it easy," he said in alarm. " Everything's all right." Jan looked round him and saw that the kitchen was empty, and grinned and said he was sorry.

"You can't lie there all day," Lockertsen said. "The wife'll be wanting to cook. But I've made up my mind. You can go up in the loft and have your sleep out, and then we'll see what's to be done with you."

Jan gratefully did as he told him; and when he woke again in the middle of the day, refreshed and capable of explaining himself, Lockertsen's distrust of him soon disappeared. Fru Lockertsen and their daughter fed him and fussed over him, and Lockertsen himself grew amiable and asked him where he was going. Jan answered vaguely, "Over the mountains," and Lockertsen offered to take him part of his way in the motor-boat if that would help him.

Jan's idea of where he was going was really rather vague. By that time, by a process of subconscious reasoning, he had decided to make for Sweden. He knew he ought to tell London what had happened. At headquarters they would soon be expecting signals from his party's transmitter, and they would already be waiting for *Brattholm* to get back to Shetland. In a week or two they would give her up as lost, and when no signals were heard they would probably guess that the whole party had been lost at sea. No one would ever know, unless he told them, that he was alive, and sooner or later, in the autumn perhaps, they would send another party. It would really be stupid for him to try to work on alone when nobody in England knew he was there. Any work he could do might clash with a second party's plans. The proper thing for him to do, he could see, was to get into Sweden and fly back to England and join the second party when it sailed.

To go to Sweden was a simple aim. If he kept moving south, he would be bound to get there in the end. But nobody he had met had had a map, even of the most misleading sort, and he could only plan his route from recollection. He was now on the very end of one of the promontories between the great fjords which run deep into the northern mountains. To the west of him was Balsfjord, and to the east Ullsfjord and then Lyngenfjord, the greatest of them all, fifty miles long and three miles wide. All the promontories between these fjords are high and steep. The one between Ullsfjord and Lyngenfjord in particular is famous for

its mountain scenery : it is a mass of jagged peaks of fantastic
beauty which rise steeply from the sea on either side. Away from
their shores, these promontories are not only uninhabited, they
are deserted, never visited at all except in summer and in peacetime by a few mountaineers and by Lapps finding pasture for their
reindeer. Along the shores there are scattered houses, and roads
where there is room to build them.

Jan's choice of route was simplified by the fact that Tromsö
lay to the west of him, and the farther he went that way the
thicker the German defences would become. Apart from that,
he had to decide whether to keep to the fjords and make use of
roads when he could find them, or to cut himself off from all
chance of meeting either friend or enemy by staying in the
hills.

Lockertsen's advice was definite. On the shores of the fjords
he would run the risk of meeting Germans, which would be
awkward ; but to cross the mountains alone at that time of year
was, quite simply, impossible and suicidal, and nobody but a
lunatic would try it.

They talked all round the subject several times. Jan listened
to everything that Lockertsen suggested, intending as usual to
take the advice which suited him and forget about the rest. In
the upshot, Lockertsen said he would take him in his motor-
boat that night as far as he could up Ullsfjord, and land him on
the far shore, the eastward side. There was a road there which ran
up a side fjord called Kjosen and crossed over to Lyngenfjord
through a gap in the mountains. Then it ran all the way to the
head of Lyngenfjord ; and from there there were both a summer
and a winter road which led to the frontier. It was true that the
road itself might not be much use to him. It ran through several
small villages on the fjord, which would be sure to have garrisons.
Beyond the end of the fjord, the summer road of course would
be buried in snow and the winter road, which crossed the frozen
lakes, was certainly blocked and watched by the Germans. But
at least this was a line to follow, and it skirted round the mountains.

Jan hated the thought of putting to sea again, but the lift he
was offered would put him twenty miles on his way, and he ac-

T.G.E.S.   L

cepted it. When it was dark, he said good-bye to Fru Lockertsen and her daughter and went down to the shore again. Lockertsen rowed him out to the motor-boat, which was lying at a buoy, and a neighbour joined them. There was fishing gear on board, and Lockertsen and the neighbour meant to use it, when they had landed Jan, to give themselves a reason for the journey. They started her up and cast off, and put out once more into the dangerous waters of the sound.

Jan made them keep close inshore, so that if they were suddenly challenged by a German ship he could go over the side and swim to land. So they crept up the sound under the shadow of the mountains. But nothing happened; they slipped safely round the corner into Ullsfjord, and in the early hours of the morning they put Jan ashore on a jetty at the mouth of Kjosen.

Neither Lockertsen's warning, nor the maps and photographs he had studied, nor even the fame of the Lyngen Alps had quite prepared Jan for the sight which he saw when he landed at Kjosen. It was still night, but ahead of him in the east the sky was pale ; and there were the mountains, a faint shadow on the sky where the rock was naked, a faint gleam where it was clothed with snow. Peak upon peak hung on the breathless air before the dawn, immaculate and sublime. Beneath their majesty, the enmity of Germans seemed something to be despised.

He saw the road, beside the shining ribbon of the fjord ; it was the first road he had seen in all his journey. He put on his skis with a feeling of exaltation and turned towards the frontier. The crisp hiss of skis on the crusted snow and the rush of the frosty air was the keenest of all possible delight. He knew of the danger of garrisons in the villages on the road, and he knew that the largest of them was only five miles ahead, but at that time and in that place it seemed absurd to cower in fear of Germans. He determined to push on and get through the village before the sun had risen or the people were awake.

The name of the village is Lyngseidet. It lies in the narrow gap between Kjosen and Lyngenfjord. In peace, it is a place which cruising liners visit on their way to North Cape. From

time to time in summer they suddenly swamp it with their
hordes of tourists ; the people of the village, it is said, hurriedly
send lorries to Tromsö for stocks of furs and souvenirs, and the
Lapps who spend the summer there dress up in their best and
pose for photographs. In war-time it was burdened with a
garrison of more than normal size, because it is the point at which
the main road crosses Lyngenfjord by ferry.

Jan expected to find a road block on each side of it, and
probably sentries posted in the middle, but on skis he felt sure
he could climb above the road to circumvent a block, and to
pass the sentries he relied on his speed and the remaining darkness.

He came to the block, just as he had foreseen. It was a little
way short of the head of the fjord at Kjosen. There was a pole
across the road, and a hut beside it which presumably housed a
guard. He struck off the road up the steep hillside to the left.
As he had thought, on skis it was quite easy ; but it took longer
than he expected, because there were barbed-wire fences which
delayed him. One of his ski bindings was loose as well, and he
had to stop for some time to repair it. When he got down to the
road again a couple of hundred yards beyond the block, it was
fully daylight.

He pushed on at top speed along the road. He knew it could
not be more than two or three miles to the village, and he ought
to be through it in ten or fifteen minutes. It was getting risky,
but it was worth it ; to have stopped and hidden where he was
would have wasted the whole of a day, and the thought of the
distance he might cover before the evening was irresistible. There
was a little twist in the road where it rounded a mass of rock, and
beyond it he could already see the roofs of houses. He turned
the corner at a good speed.

Fifty yards ahead was a crowd of German soldiers. They
straggled across the road and filled it from side to side. There
was not time to stop or turn and no place to hide. He went on.
More and more of them came from a building on the left : twenty,
thirty, forty. He hesitated for a fraction of a second but his own
momentum carried him on towards them, and no challenge came
to halt. They were carrying mess tins and knives and forks. Their

uniforms were unbuttoned. He shot in among them, and they stood back to right and left to let him pass, and for a moment he looked full into their faces and saw their sleepy eyes and smelled the frowsty, sweaty smell of early morning. Then he was past, so acutely aware of the flag and the NORWAY on his sleeves that they seemed to hurt his shoulders. He fled up the road, expecting second by second and yard by yard the shouts and the hue and cry. At the turn of the road he glanced over his shoulder, and they were still crossing the road and going into a house on the other side, and not one of them looked his way. A second later, he was out of sight.

The road went uphill through a wood of birch, and he pounded up it without time to wonder. After a mile he came to the top of the rise. The valley opened out, and ahead he saw the village itself, and the spire of the church, and the wide water of Lyngenfjord beyond it, and the road which wound downhill and vanished among the houses. He thrust with his sticks once more, and began a twisting run between the fences of the road. He knew he would come to a fork at the bottom, in the middle of the village. The left-hand turning ran a little way down Lyngenfjord towards the sea and then came to an end ; it was the right-hand one which led to the head of the fjord and then to the frontier. He passed the first of the houses, going fast. The church was on the right of the road and close to the water's edge. There was a wooden pier behind it, and down by the churchyard fence where the road divided a knot of men was standing.

A moment passed before he took in what he saw. Two or three of the men were soldiers, and one was a civilian who stood facing the others. Behind them was another pole across the road, and one of the soldiers was turning over some papers in his hand.

About five seconds more would have halted him among them at the roadblock, but there was a gate on the right which led to a garage in a garden and it was open. He checked and turned and rushed through the gate and round the garage and up the steep garden and headed for some birch scrub behind it. There were shouts from the crossroad, and as he came out into view of it again beyond the garage two or three rifle shots were fired, but he reached the bushes and set himself to climb the mountain-side.

In Toftefjord when the Germans were behind him, he had been afraid, but now he was elated by the chase. With a Norwegian's pride in his skill on skis, he knew they could not catch him. He climbed up and up, exulting in the skis and his mastery of them and hearing the futile shouts grow distant in the valley down below. He looked back, and saw a score of soldiers struggling far behind him up his trail. He passed the treeline and went on, up on to the open snow above.

Up there, he met the sunshine. The sun was rising above the hills on the far side of Lyngenfjord. The water below him sparkled in its path, and in the frosty morning air the whole of the upper part of the fjord was visible. On the eastern side and at the head he could see the curious flat-topped hills which are the outliers of the great plateau through which the frontier runs ; and far up at the end of the fjord, fifteen miles away, was the valley called Skibotten up which the frontier road begins. To see his future route stretched out before him added to the joy he already felt at having left the valley and the shore : he was almost glad of the accident which had forced him to grasp the danger of taking to the hills. And seeing the fjord so beautifully displayed below him had brought back his recollection of the map. There had been a dotted line, he now remembered, which ran parallel to the road and to the shore. This marked a summer track along the face of the mountains ; and although it was the same map as the one of Ringvassöy, and the track had probably been put in from hearsay and not surveyed, yet if it had ever been possible to walk that way in summer, it ought to be possible now to do it on skis in snow. At least, there could not be any completely impassable precipice, and so long as the fjord was in sight he could not lose his way.

He stopped climbing after about 3000 feet, and rested and looked around him. The pursuit had been given up, or fallen so far behind that he could not see or hear it ; and up there everything was beautiful and calm and peaceful. At that height he was almost level with the distant plateau, and he could see glimpses here and there beyond the fjord of mile upon mile of flat unbroken snow. But on his own side, close above him, the mountains were much higher. He was on the flank of a smooth conical hill with the Lappish name of Goalesvarre, and its top was still 1500 feet above him; and behind it the main massif of the Lyngen Alps rose in a maze of peaks and glaciers to over 6000 feet.

It was not until he rested there that he had leisure to think of his fantastic encounter with the platoon of soldiers. At first it had seemed incredible that they should have taken no notice of him and let him pass; but when he came to think it over, he saw that it was typical of any army anywhere. It was like the search in Ribbenesöy: one expected the German army to be more fiendishly efficient than any other, but it was not; or at least, not always. He could imagine a British or Norwegian platoon, or an American one for that matter, shut away in a dreary post like that, with nothing whatever to do except guard a road and a ferry where nothing ever happened. With one section on guard at the roadblock, the others, to say the least of it, would never be very alert, and just after reveille they would not be thinking of anything much except breakfast. If someone in a queer uniform came down the road, the guard must have let him through, they would say, and that was the guard's funeral. The officers would know all about it, anyway, whoever he was. Nobody would want to make a fool of himself by asking officious questions. And the uniform itself, Jan reflected, would have meant nothing to them in a foreign country. Probably none of them knew that the word NORWAY was English, any more than you would expect an English soldier to know the German word for Norway. For all they knew or cared, he might have been a postman or a sanitary inspector on his rounds; anything was more likely, far inland, than meeting an enemy sailor on skis. Sooner or later, one of them might mention it to an n.c.o., who might pull the leg of the corporal of the guard next time he saw him, and by the evening perhaps it would come to the ears of the platoon commander, who certainly would not want to report it and would spend a lot of time questioning his men to prove to himself that it was really nothing important.

But of course the guard on the roadblock in Lyngseidet was a more unfortunate encounter. They certainly knew he was up to something illegal, because he had run away, and they knew fairly exactly where he had gone. That incident was bound to be reported, at least to battalion headquarters. He could not be sure if they had seen the uniform, or whether headquarters would put two and two together and guess that the man who had been been seen in Lyngseidet was the one who had escaped in Toftefjord. It depended how many other people in the district, for one reason or another, were on the run. At the worst, it meant they had picked up his trail again, and if they thought it was worth it, they might put extra patrols in the country he had to pass through. He wondered how badly they wanted to catch him.

In any case, the best thing, as ever, was speed : to travel faster than they would think he could possibly travel. And now he had the means to do this, because people who do not know much about skis can often hardly believe the distance an expert can go on them in the course of a day. The Germans would not know much about them unless they were Bavarians ; and even people who ski in the Alps are inclined only to think of ski-ing downhill, and going uphill by lifts or even railways. Cross-country ski-running, uphill and down, is a particularly Norwegian activity, and a Norwegian skier on holiday, or merely on a journey, thinks nothing of fifty miles a day.

So Jan set off with confidence, and even with a certain amount of pleasure, in anticipation of the run. He imagined himself staying at about 3000 feet, following the contour along the fjord and keeping the water in sight. But of course no mountainside, even the side of a fjord, is quite so regular and simple. He had only gone a few miles along the slope of Goalesvarre when he found a side valley in front of him which ran deep into the mountains. As he approached it and the head of it opened up, he saw the smooth snow surface of a glacier in it, and even the glacier was below him. Rather than try to cross it, he went right down to the valley bed below the ice and climbed up it again on the other side.

Beyond the valley there was another minor hazard of a different kind. The side of the fjord became steeper, and finally sheer. To get past this cliff he might have gone over the top ; but it was very high, and to the right of it, on the inland side, there was a col which seemed a more sensible line for the summer track to follow. It looked as though it would lead back to the fjord five miles or so beyond. So he headed for the col, and very soon he lost sight of the fjord.

By then it must have been about eleven o'clock in the morning, and he had covered something like twenty miles since he left the boat at Kjosen. It was good going, and everything looked promising; but it was just before he reached the col that the weather changed again.

It came over the high summits on his right, first the white wisps of clouds like flags on the highest peaks, and then the stray gusts of wind and the darkening of the sky. The sun went in, and the snowfields lost their sparkling clarity and detail and became monotonous and grey, and the air at once struck chill. And then the snow began to fall, softly at first but more heavily minute by minute as the wind increased and the clouds descended. With the same abruptness that he had seen in Ringvassöy, the storm swooped downward and enveloped him in a whirling white impenetrable wall.

It had happened before, and it gave him no cause to be alarmed, because all the sudden storms he had seen in the last few days had been short and had ended as suddenly as they had begun. It was annoying, the more so now that he had skis. In his rubber boots the storms had not made much difference to his speed. He had plodded on all through them. But now he could not make use of his extra speed. He could hardly see five yards in front of him, and any slight downward grade might lead to a sudden drop. He had to be able to stop at any moment, and on slopes which he might have run at full speed he now had to check, and creep down circumspectly. It was not only slow, it was twice as tiring.

Nevertheless, he pressed on, hoping and still expecting to see the lightening of the cloud which would be the sign that the squall was passing and that a few minutes more would bring sunshine again with the snowcloud whirling away towards the fjord.

But no sign came. On the contrary, the wind went on increasing. It was getting worse than anything he had experienced before, and as hours passed he had to admit to himself that this was not merely a squall. It was useless to rely upon its ending. He ought to act as though it might last for days. That meant that he must find shelter, and to find it he must get down to the fjord again.

But before he had come unwillingly to this decision, a new aspect of storm began to be manifest. The surface of the lying snow began to creep, first in whirls and eddies, and later in clouds which forced him to shut his eyes and put his hand over his mouth to keep the driving snow-powder out of his throat and lungs. When the very surface he stood on began to move, there was nothing stable left for his eyes to be fixed upon; when he stood still, the snow silted into the tracks which he had made, and then it was only by the wind that he could have any idea which direction he had been going. Each little slope which faced him then became a new problem in itself. Each one which he saw from the bottom vanished into the shifting mists a few feet above his head, and each of them might be the foot of a great mountain or the whole of a tiny mound. From the top of a slope he could not tell whether it was five feet in height or a thousand. He only knew that somewhere about him the surface plunged down in sheer chasms to the fjord waters three thousand feet below, and that somewhere it rose three thousand feet above him to the soaring crags he had seen in the light of the dawn.

He guided himself by the wind, keeping it on his right. The right side of his body was coated with ice; it matted his hair and his week-old beard, and his right hand grew numb. He had tried to keep on in the direction he had been going when the storm came down, because he believed it would lead him to lower ground. But after some hours he began to doubt even the wind. He would sometimes have sworn that he had travelled for fifty yards in a straight line, and yet the wind which had been on his right swooped down on him from ahead. It seemed to be eddying down from the higher mountains, perhaps following valleys which he could not see. He stood still to test it, and even while he stood still it changed direction. Without the wind to guide him, he was lost.

Some time during that day he stopped and tried to dig himself into the snow to wait for the abatement of the storm, because he despaired of finding the way out of the mountains. But as soon as he crouched down in the little hollow he scraped out, the cold attacked him with such violence that he knew he would die there if he rested. He had often read that if you lie down and sleep in a blizzard you never get up again. Now he knew it was true : it would not take very long. He got up and put on his skis and struggled onwards, not caring much any more which way he was moving, but moving because he did not dare to stop. Towards the end of the day his wandering became quite aimless and he lost all sense either of time or space.

One cannot say whether it was the same day or the next that he first perceived a continuity in the slope of the mountain. He was going downhill. By then he had devised a plan for descending slopes which had probably already saved his life. When he came to a void, he gathered a big snowball and kneaded it hard and threw it in front of him. Sometimes, above the sound of the wind, he heard it fall, and then he went on ; but more often it vanished without any sound at all, and he turned aside and tried another way. Now, edging cautiously down a slope and throwing snowballs, he saw rock walls both to right and left of it. It was a watercourse. He knew it was possible, or even likely, that it led to the top of a frozen waterfall and that he was running a serious risk of stepping on to the ice of the fall before he could see it. But at least it was something to follow which must lead in the end to the sea. He crept down it with infinite caution, testing every step for hidden ice. He saw little bushes and knew he was getting low. And then, directly below him, there was a square block which loomed dark in the snow. He ran joyfully down the last few yards towards it, because he thought it was a house. But it was not. It was only an enormous isolated rock. But it had a hollow underneath it, like a cave, and he squeezed in there, lying down because it was not high enough to crawl. As soon as he lay down, in shelter from the wind and snow, he went to sleep.

That rock is the first identifiable place which Jan came to on that journey. It stands in a narrow valley called Lyngdalen. It is only about ten miles in a perfectly straight line from Lyngseidet, where the road black was : but nobody knows where or how far he had been before he got there.

At the rock he made a mistake which was nearly fatal. There is an acute bend in the valley just there. As he approached it, down the northern side, the valley led on in two directions, one only a little way to the left and the other equally little to the right. Downstream was to the left, and that way the valley ran without any hazard straight down to Lyngenfjord, five miles below. To the right the valley led gently up to the foot of the highest mountain in north Norway, the peak of Jaeggevarre, 6200 feet high. In clear weather, the choice is obvious ; in fact, Jaeggevarre towers over the upper valley and closes it with a sheer bastion 3000 feet high and three miles long. But in storm, when neither the mountain nor the valley walls were visible, the place was a trap. A great moraine nearly closes the valley at that point. The summer river passes it through a gorge. But in winter the gorge is full of snow, and the immediate foreground of the valley floor slopes down to the right, upstream. When Jan woke up and crept out of the crevice below the rock, the storm was still raging. He saw nothing except the foreground, and he put on his skis again and set forth, downhill, towards the right, away from Lyngenfjord and all possible help or safety, into the very heart of the highest hills.

He was beginning to suffer from exposure by then, and one cannot deduce how long he had been stormbound, or whether it was night or day. When one's body is worn by a long effort at the limit of its strength, and especially when its function is dulled by cold, one's mind loses first of all its sharp appreciation of time. Incidents which are really quite separate become blended together; the present and the immediate past are not distinct, but are all part of a vaguely defined present of physical misery. In a person of strong character, hope for the future remains separate long after the past and present are confused. It is when the future loses its clarity too, and hope begins to fade, that death is not far away.

Jan's mind was certainly numbed and confused by then, but so far he had not the slightest doubt about the future, and he was still thinking clearly enough to use the common sense of the craft of mountaineering. Now that he had found what he knew was

a river valley of considerable size, he did not expect any trouble
in following it to the sea ; and so he was astonished and baffled
when he found the ground rising in front of him again. He had
come to what he thought was a frozen lake, though in fact it is
only a level part of the valley floor, and he followed what seemed
to be the shore of it, with the valley wall above him on his right.
He came to the end of it expecting to find its outflow ; but there
was still a steep slope above him, and he could not see the top.
He went right round the lake till he came back to the moraine
where he had started ; and there for the second time he missed
the snow-filled gorge. Search as he might, he could not find the
outlet. He seemed to be in the bottom of a bowl, with the lake
on his left as he circled round it and unbroken snow-slopes always
on his right. There was nothing for it except to give up the hope
of going on downhill. He had to start climbing again.

His choice of direction then, if it was not at random, was
probably governed by the light. In the thickest of cloud and
snow one sometimes has an impression of greater darkness where
a steep rock face is close above. The sides of Lyngdalen may have
thrown extra darkness, and so may the sharp bend downstream
in the narrow valley. But upstream Jaeggevarre stands farther
back, and in that direction there is less to obscure the light. Jan
may have concluded that this was south, or that it was really the
lower reaches of the valley. At all events, he began to climb that
way. He went up diagonally, hoping and expecting all the way
to find an easing of the gradient and a sign that the valley went
on beyond. Very soon he lost sight of the bottom, but although
he climbed on and on, he could not see the top. He was on a
slope of snow which in his restricted vision seemed eternal ; on
his left it vanished into invisible depths, and on his right it merged
in the cloud above. In front of him and behind him, it was exactly
the same : his ski tracks across it disappeared a few seconds after
he had made them. It was a world of its own, dizzily tilted on
edge, full of the tearing wind, with himself for ever at the centre
and the farthest edges diffuse and ill-defined.

Suddenly with lightning speed the snow slope split from end
to end and the snow below his feet gave way. He fell on his side
and snatched at the surface, but everything was moving, and the

snow fell upon him and rolled him over and over. He felt himself going down and down, faster and faster, fighting with roaring masses of snow which were burying him alive. It wrenched and pounded his helpless body, and choked him and battered him till he was unconscious. He fell limply in the heart of the avalanche and it cast out his body on the valley floor below. Down there he lay still, long after its thunder had echoed away to silence.

CHAPTER SIX

SNOWBLIND

THE NEXT summer, somebody passed that way and found the broken pieces of Jan's skis, among the massive blocks of melting snow which were all that was left of the avalanche. They were at the foot of the icefall of the unnamed glacier under the east face of Jaeggevarre. One can guess what he had done. He had started his final climb up the valley wall, but had traversed on to the icefall without knowing it. When one can see a little distance, the snow on ice looks different from the snow on rock; but if one can only see a yard or two one cannot tell what is underneath. The snow on the steep ice at that time of year would have been very unstable, ready to fall by itself within a week or two, and Jan's weight and the thrust of his skis were enough to start it. The scar of the avalanche stretched from top to bottom of the icefall. Jan himself must have fallen at least three hundred feet.

To start an avalanche is apt to be fatal, but it did not kill Jan. Luck was extraordinarily kind to him again. Of course nobody knows how long he lay there unconscious; but when he came to, his head was out of the snow, so that he could breathe, and most of his body was buried, which had possibly saved him from freezing to death; and none of his bones was broken. To be alive was far more than he had any right to expect, and so the other results of his fall can hardly be counted as bad luck. One of his skis was lost and the other was broken in two places; and the small rucksack with all his food had disappeared; and he had hit his head and could not remember where he was trying to go. He dug himself out of the snow and stood up, and unfastened the broken bit of ski and dropped it there, and wandered away on foot, utterly lost, with no plan and no notion of where he was going ; in fact, without any coherent thoughts at all, because he had concussion of the brain.

After the avalanche, Jan had no sense of time, and hardly any awareness of the reality of what happened. He never stopped walking, but as his body froze slowly and ice formed in the veins of his feet and hands and crept inch by inch up his legs and arms, his mind became occupied more and more by dreams and hallucinations. But the length of this ordeal is known : he was four days and four nights in the mountains from the time when he passed through Lyngseidet. The storm lasted for nearly three days, and then the snow stopped and the clouds lifted and the mountains were clear ; but Jan knew nothing of that, because by then the glare of the snow had scorched the retina of his eyes and he was blind.

One has to imagine him, both in the dark and the daylight, and both in the mists of the storm and the clear air which followed it, stumbling on unable to see at all. He never stopped because he was obsessed with the idea that if he lay down he would go to sleep and die ; but all the time he was in snow between knee-deep and waist-deep, and towards the end of the time he fell down so often full length on his face in the snow that he might be said to have crawled and not to have walked.

His movements were totally aimless. This is known because his tracks were found here and there, later on in the spring. For the most part, he probably stayed in the valley of Lyngdalen, but at least once he went over a thousand feet up the side of it, and down again in the same place. He was deflected by the smallest of obstacles. There were boulders sticking up out of the snow, and when he ran into them head-on he turned and went away ; not round the boulder and on in the same direction, but away at an angle, on a totally different course. There were birch bushes also, in the bottom of the valley, and among them he wandered hither and thither for days, crossing his own tracks again and again and blundering into the bushes themselves so that he got tangled in them and scratched his face and hands and tore his clothes. Once he walked round and round a small bush for so long that he trod a hard deep path in the snow, which was still to be seen in the summer : one can only suppose that he thought he was following somebody else's footsteps.

But he himself knew almost nothing of this. Because he was blind, he believed that the mist and falling snow went on all the time, and he could not reckon the nights and days which were passing. All that he knew of reality was pain in his legs and arms and eyes, and cold and hunger, and the endless, hampering, suffocating wall of snow in front of him through which he must force his way.

On one of the mountains he came to, there were hundreds of people, marching with bare feet which were frozen and they were afraid of breaking them, because they were quite brittle.

He knew it was a dream, and he wrenched himself awake because he was terrified of falling asleep, but when Per Blindheim began to talk to him it was more real than reality, and he swung round joyfully and called " Per, Per," into the darkness because he could not see where he was. But Per did not answer him, he went on talking to Eskeland. They were talking together somewhere, and a lot of the others were with them too, but they were not listening to him. He shouted louder, " Per ! Eskeland ! " and began to run after them, afraid that they would miss him in the night. And then they were close, and he was thankful to be with them all again. But they were talking together among themselves, quite cheerfully as they always did, and they never spoke to him. He called them again and again to tell them he could not see, but he could not make them hear him. They did not know he was there. And it came back to him that all of them were dead. Yet they had been talking together before he lost them, and he was the one who could not make himself heard. He began to believe that the dream was reality, and that he was the one who was dead. Stories of death came back into his mind. It seemed likely that he had died.

But in the same thought which made it seem so likely, he knew it was fantasy that he was still determined not to die, and to this end he must keep going, on and on, until something happened : something. He could not remember what it was that he had hoped would happen.

As he was going through the woods, he came to a trapdoor

in the snow, and he tried to open it by the iron ring. But he was feeling very weak, and it was too heavy for him. It was a pity, because of the warm fire inside it, but he had to give it up. But whenever he turned his back on it to go away, somebody slipped out of the forest and opened it and got inside and shut it again before he had time to stop him. It was unfair that they kept him shut out in the cold and darkness while they all enjoyed the lights and gaiety inside. They always waited till he turned away, and then they were too quick for him. They must have been watching him and waiting for their chance.

It was the same when he found the mountain with windows in it, except that that time he never saw them go in. But they all climbed up to the door at the top so easily. Nobody would help him, and he tried and tried but always slipped down again to the bottom so that he was the only one left who could not do it. But perhaps it was nobody's fault; perhaps the explanation was that they could not see him. That would be logical if he was dead. But he shouted I am still alive and alone out here in the snow, it's all a mistake. The windows went away and the mountain turned into a little mound of snow, and he was scrabbling feebly at its sides.

It was the same too when he came to the log cabin. Stupidly, he was not looking where he was going, and he hurt himself again when he blundered into it. But as soon as he put out his hands and felt the rough logs he knew what it was although they never told him, and he started to feel his way along the wall, round the corner, hoping they would not see him before he found the door. It seemed a long way to the door, but he found it, and felt for the latch. But that time it opened, and he fell inside.

CHAPTER SEVEN

MARIUS

HANNA PEDERSEN was having dinner with her two boys, Ottar and Johan, when the door burst open and the dreadful thing stumbled into the room and groped blindly towards the table. They jumped to their feet and backed away in horror. She nearly screamed, but she put her hand to her mouth and stifled the impulse because of the children. She managed to whisper, "Ottar, go and fetch your uncle," and the elder boy slipped out of the room.

"What do you want?" she said. "Who are you?" But Jan's answer was incoherent, and he collapsed on the floor. She overcame her terror and revulsion enough then to creep near him and look at him closely to see if he was somebody she knew.

It would have been hard to tell. When he lay still like that on the floor, one would have thought he was a corpse dug out of the snow. He was caked with ice and frozen dirt and dried blood. His hair and his beard were solidly frozen and his face and hands were bloated and discoloured. His feet were great balls of compacted snow and ice. His eyes were tight shut, screwed up with the pain of snowblindness. He tried to speak again as he lay there, but she could not understand anything he said. Distracted with fright she took the smaller boy and ran to the door to meet her brother.

Her brother's name was Marius Grönvold. He lived in the next house, and when he heard the boy's anxious frightened story he ran across to see what had really happened. He pushed past his sister and took a single look at Jan. It was enough to show him that they would have to take measures quickly, whoever this man was, if they were to save his life. He had two other sisters who lived nearby, Gudrun and Ingeborg, and he sent the children to fetch them. They both hurried in, and between them all they set to work to bring Jan back to life. They built up the fire, and fed him with hot milk from a spoon, and got off the worst of his clothes and wrapped him in blankets, and lifted him on to a bed. Marius took a sharp knife and carefully cut his boots to pieces and peeled them off. His socks also had to be cut up and taken off in strips, revealing horrible feet and legs in an advanced stage of frostbite, with the toes frozen stiffly together in a solid block of ice. Everyone there knew the first-aid treatment for frostbite : to rub it with snow. The three sisters started then and there to try to save his feet, taking the ice-cold limbs between their hands and kneading the brittle flesh. Jan paid no attention to what they did, because he could not feel anything in his legs at all. He seemed to be slipping off into sleep or unconsciousness.

When the ice began to thaw on the jacket, Marius saw, to his amazement, that it was some kind of uniform, and he had also seen that Jan was armed with a pistol. That meant he was either a German or some sort of Norwegian Nazi, or else someone so actively anti-German that his presence in the house was like dynamite. Whether Jan was going to live or die, Marius simply had to know who he was : everything he did to try to save him, or even to dispose of his body if he failed, would depend on that answer. He asked him where he came from, and when he bent down to hear what Jan was trying to say, he heard the name Overgaard, which is a place at the head of the fjord. He knew that was a lie, because he had seen Jan's tracks and they came from the opposite direction ; and the fact that he tried to tell a lie was reassuring, because a Nazi would be too powerful to have any need to do so.

Marius had heard about Toftefjord and suspected the truth already. He sent the women out of the room, and when they had shut the door he said : "Listen to me. If you're a good man, you've come among good people. Now, speak out." Jan told him then, in a halting whisper. Marius heard him out, and took his resolve at once. "Don't worry," he said, "we'll look after you. Go to sleep." Jan asked him what his name was, and

he told him Hans Jensen, which is the same as to say John Jones.
He asked where he was, and this Marius told him truthfully : in
the hamlet of Furuflaten, where the valley of Lyngdalen reaches
Lyngenfjord. In the three days since the avalanche, all Jan's
wandering had carried him seven miles. Marius also told him
that it was the 8th of April, late in the afternoon.

When he was satisfied that he had got the truth, Marius called
his sisters in again and told it to them in whispers. They went
to work again, looking at Jan with new pity at what they had
heard, but with a desperate anxiety for themselves and the
children. Nobody whatever must hear of it, Marius had said ;
and they could hear him saying the same thing, again and again,
to the boys.

He came back to the bed when he had made sure that the
children understood him, and looked down at the ghastly face
on the pillow. He was trying to think ahead. He was also
beginning to see the explanation of some strange events which
had happened since the storm. The Germans had suddenly
searched every house in Furuflaten. They had been through his
own house and his sister's from top to bottom. They were
looking for radio sets, they had said ; but everyone had thought
at the time there was something more behind it, because the place
had been searched thoroughly enough for radio sets before. And
for the first time, in the last few days, there had been motor-boats
patrolling on the fjord, which did not fit in with the radio story.
Now, Marius knew what they were searching for. There was the
object of all the activity, lying at his mercy on his sister's children's
bed.

Jan's luck was still good when it took him to that door.
Marius Grönvold was a very unusual man. He was in his early
thirties then, still a bachelor, a short strong stocky man with the
face of a peasant and an extraordinarily alert and well-stocked
mind. His occupation in those days was typical of this contrast :
he ran a small farm, and also wrote for the Tromsö paper. His
hobbies were politics and Norwegian literature. He knew the
Norwegian classics well, and could recite in verse or prose for
hours together, and often did so to entertain himself or anyone
else who would listen ; and he was already a leading member of

the local Liberal party, and well on his way to becoming the most
prominent citizen in those parts : the sort of man, one might say,
who was destined from birth to become a mayor or the chairman
of the county council. With these politics and his love of Norwegian history and culture, it went without saying that he was a
member of the local resistance group in Lyngenfjord, which was
a branch of the one in Tromsö.

To speak of a resistance movement in a place like Lyngenfjord
might be a little misleading. There was an organisation, but there
was hardly anything it could do. There had never been time
when Norway was invaded to call up or train the people in those
far-off northern areas. The battle had been fought and lost before
they had had a chance to go and take part in it. Ever since then,
they had been entirely cut off from the world outside the German
orbit. Their radio sets had been confiscated, and the papers they
read were censored by the Germans. All that they ever heard of
the fight that was going on from England was in occasional
whispered scraps of clandestine news passed on from mouth to
mouth from somebody who had hidden a radio somewhere or
seen a copy of an illegal newspaper. Yet men like Marius resented
their country's enslavement as deeply as anyone : even more
strongly perhaps because they had not done anything themselves
to try to stop it. It lay heavily on their consciences that they had
not been soldiers when soldiers were needed so badly, and that
brave deeds were still being done while they could not find any
way to test their own bravery. Their organisation was really a
kind of patriotic club. None of its members had any military
knowledge ; but at least they could talk freely among themselves,
and so keep up each other's resolution, and help each other not
to sink into the belief that the Germans could win the war and
the occupation go on for ever ; and they knew they could count
on each other for material help as well if it was ever needed.

This was the background of Marius's thoughts while he
worked on Jan's feet and fed him and kept him warm. The
problem which Jan had brought with him was not a mere matter
of a night in hiding and a little food. Probably Jan still thought,
if he thought at all, that after a good sleep he would get up and
walk away ; but anyone else who saw him could tell he would

be an invalid for weeks, and that walking was the last thing he would do. Marius, turning things over in his mind, could see no end to the problem in front of him, except capture. Furuflaten was a tiny compact community of a few hundred people ; and it was on the main road and convoys of German lorries passed through it day and night, and it had a platoon of Germans quartered in its school. He could see the German sentries on the road when he looked out of his sister's window. He could not think how he could keep Jan's presence secret. Even to buy him a little extra food would be almost impossible. Much less could he see how he could ever nurse him back to fitness and start him off on his journey again. But there was never the slightest doubt in his mind that he was going to try : because this was his challenge ; at last it was something which he and only he could possibly do. If he could never do anything else to help the war, he would have this to look back on now ; and he meant to look back on it with satisfaction, and not with shame. He thanked God for sending him this chance to prove his courage.

Jan was restless and nervous. He kept dozing off into the sleep which he needed so badly, but as soon as he began to relax, he roused himself anxiously. It was a symptom of his feeble mental state. He felt terribly defenceless, because he could not see. He was afraid of being betrayed ; but if he had been in his right mind and able to see Marius's honest worried face, he would have trusted him without the slightest qualm.

Marius, in fact, was watching over him with something very much like affection : the feeling one has towards any helpless creature which turns to one for protection. He had already promised his protection in his own mind, and in the best words he could think of, and it upset him that he had not succeeded in putting Jan's fears to rest. He wanted to find some way to soothe him and make him believe in his friendship ; and on an impulse, when the women were not listening, he took hold of Jan's hand and said very emphatically and clearly : " If I live, you will live, and if they kill you I will have died to protect you." Jan did not answer this solemn promise, but its sincerity had its effect. He relaxed then, and fell asleep.

He slept so deeply that even the massaging of his hands and

legs did not disturb him. His legs were the worst. Marius and his sisters worked on them in turns for the whole of that night and the following day, trying to get the blood to circulate. Quite early, they invented a simple test to see how far up they were frozen. They pricked them with needles, starting at the ankles and working upwards. When they began, the legs were insensitive up to the knees. Above that, the needle made them twitch, although even this treatment did not disturb Jan's sleep. But as they rubbed the legs, hour by hour, they came back to life, inch after inch, and showed a reaction lower and lower down. Jan did not wake at all during the first night and day after he came in. When he did, even his feet were alive, and he woke with a searing pain where they had been numb before. Hanna Pedersen gave him a little food, and then he went to sleep again.

Although their efforts seemed to be succeeding, Marius and his sisters were all afraid that there might be some better treatment for frostbite which they had never heard of ; and so it happened that the first time Marius invoked the organisation was to ask for a doctor's advice. He went first of all to Lyngseidet : a journey of twenty minutes by bus, which covered the whole of the distance which had taken Jan four days. His object there was to talk to the headmaster of the state secondary school, whose name was Legland. There were two reasons for seeing him : one was that he was the member of the organisation who had direct contact with the leadership in Tromsö ; and the other was that most of the people of Lyngenfjord were in the habit of going to him when they were perplexed or in trouble. Herr Legland was a patriarch, revered by all his neighbours. The more intelligent of them, in fact, had all been his pupils, for he was an old man by then, and his school served the whole of the district. It was from him that Marius had learned his love of literature as a boy, and he regarded him as the wisest man he knew. Besides, he was a patriot of the old uncompromising school of Bjornsen and Ibsen. To him, the invasion of Norway was a barbarous affront, a new dark age. His school buildings in Lyngseidet had been requisitioned as a billet for German troops : a symbol of the swamping of the nation's culture by the demands of tyranny.

When Marius sought out this shrewd old gentleman and told

him his story, he gave his approval of what Marius and his family
had done, and he agreed with what he proposed to do. It went
without saying that he would give his help. At the bottom of all
the ideas which Marius had thought of up to then was the
difficulty, and the necessity, of keeping Jan's presence secret from
the people of Furuflaten. It was not that there was anyone really
untrustworthy there; but there were plenty of gossips. As soon
as it leaked out at all, the whole village would know about it as
fast as exciting news can travel; and then it would only be a
matter of time before the Germans found out about it too.
Nobody would tell them; but living right in the centre of the
place, in the school, they had a good idea of what went on there.
They only had to keep their eyes open; it was a most difficult
place for keeping secrets. The houses are widely spaced on each
side of the river which runs out of Lyngdalen, and along the road
which runs close beside the shore. There are hardly any trees,
and from the middle one can see almost every house and most of
the ground between them. It would only need a few too many
neighbours calling at Marius's house, out of curiosity or with
offers of help, for the Germans on watch at the school, or
patrolling the road, to notice that something unusual was
happening.

From this point of view, to get a doctor to come and look at
Jan would be very risky. Marius's house was the farthest up the
valley, and the farthest away from the road. The doctor would
have to leave his car on the road and go on skis for half a mile,
all among the houses; and of course as soon as he had gone, they
would have everyone up there kindly inquiring who was ill. If
the worst came to the worst, they would have to try it; but at
present all they needed was advice and some medicine, if there
was any medicine that was any good.

This meant sending a message to Tromsö. If they asked the
local doctor, or got a prescription made up at the local dispensary,
they would have to say who it was for, and have two or three
outsiders in the secret; but in Tromsö inquiries like that could
be made without anyone knowing exactly where they came from.

Luckily, the road to Tromsö was still open, though as soon
as the spring thaw set in it would become impassable for two or

three weeks. To send a private car would be difficult, because the driver would have to give a good reason for his journey at every road block he came to ; but people had noticed that the Germans never bothered much about a bus. If it was one which ran a regular service on the road, so that they knew it by sight they usually let it through without questioning the driver. One of the local bus drivers was a member of the organisation. Marius and Legland asked him to do the job and he agreed. One of the bus company's buses was put out of action, and the driver set off in another to fetch a spare part to repair it.

The arrival of this man in Tromsö was the first indication the leaders had had that there was any survivor from Toftefjord. Legland sent the driver to Sverre Larsen the newspaper editor, whose right-hand man Knudsen had been deported. Naturally, his message was only verbal. Larsen did not know the driver, and the organisation was still more than usually wary and on edge. Larsen refused to commit himself, and told the driver he could come back later in the day. But as soon as he had gone, he set about checking the man's credentials through the organisation's chain of command ; and by the time he came back he had made sure that he was not a German agent, which he very well might have been, and had already consulted a doctor and a chemist about frostbite. Both of them said there was nothing to be done which had not been done already except to alleviate the pain, and the chemist had made up a sedative. Jan got the first dose of it that evening.

In the meantime, Marius had moved Jan from his sister's house and hidden him in a corner of his barn. He knew it would not make any difference where he put him if the Germans came up to his farm to search, but at least the barn was safer from casual visitors and family friends. These were a constant worry. Jan had come to the house on a Saturday. On a fine Sunday in spring the people of Furuflaten are in the habit of ski-ing a little way up the valley by way of a constitutional ; and that Sunday the valley was full of Jan's tracks, which led in the end, plainly enough for anyone to see, up to Hanna Pedersen's door. For anyone to go about on foot was unheard of, and foot tracks instead of ski tracks were the very thing to set people talking.

To forestall inquiries, Marius went out and inspected his farm early that Sunday morning, leaving his skis at home, and mixed up his own footsteps with Jan's. He thought out some story to explain why he had done such an eccentric thing. It was a thin story, but good enough to put people off the idea that the tracks had been made by a stranger. They would merely think that the man of the house had taken leave of his senses.

At that stage, the Grönvold family were the only people in Furuflaten who were in the know : Marius, his three sisters and the two small boys, and Marius's mother. Hanna's husband was away at the fishing, and Marius had the added worry of having no other man in the family to talk to. His sisters never relaxed their efforts to nurse Jan back to health ; but women in the far north are not often consulted by men in matters of opinion, and Marius could not help being aware that Jan's sudden arrival had been a serious shock to them all. His mother, in particular, was far from strong, and he was seriously troubled by the strain which it put on her. In fact, it must be a terrible thing for an elderly woman to know that her family is deeply involved in something which carries the death penalty for them all if they are caught. At one moment near the beginning she was inclined to oppose the whole thing, though of course she had no clear idea of the only alternative ; but Jan had told Marius by then about his father and sister in Oslo, and Marius put it to her from Jan's father's point of view. " Suppose I was in trouble down in Oslo," he said, " and you heard that the people there refused to help me." In these simple terms she could see the problem better. It made her think of Jan as a human being, a Norwegian boy very much like her own, and not just as a stranger from a war which she had never quite understood. She gave Marius her consent and blessing in the end. Yet it is doubtful whether she ever quite recovered from the nervous tension of the years after Jan arrived there : for the strain did not end when Jan finally went away. Till the very end of the war the risk remained that some evil chance would lead the Germans to discover what she and her children had done. In the upside-down world of the occupation, the Pharisee was rewarded, and the good Samaritan was a criminal. People who acted in accordance with the simplest of Christian ethics were condemned to the life of fear which is only normally lived by an undiscovered murderer.

The two boys were a further worry. To send them to school every day when they knew what they did was a heavy responsibility to put upon children. Some children of ten can play a secretive role in a matter of life and death as well as anyone older ; but to go on doing it for long will wear them down.

Jan lay for nearly a week in the barn. For four days he was never more than semi-conscious ; and that was just as well, because he could not have moved in any case, and when he did rise out of his drugged sleep the pain of his feet and hands and his blinded eyes was bad. But he was certainly getting better. Towards the end of the week his eyesight was coming back. He began to see the light of the barn door when it was opened, and then to recognise the faces of the people who came to feed him. By that time, also, it looked as if his feet would recover in the end, though he was still a long way from being able to stand on them or walk. Most important of all, his brain had got over the concussion, and his power of thought and his sense of humour had come back : he was himself again. He and Marius began to find they had a lot in common. Their experience and background could hardly have been more different within a single nation : one the arctic farmer and country-bred philosopher, the other the town technician ; one cut off from the war, the other entirely immersed in military training. But Jan's sense of comedy was never far away, and Marius, though he was a serious-minded man, was irrepressible when he was amused. He listened to Jan's stories of England and the war with the greed of a starving man who has an unexpected feast spread out in front of him, and when Jan told him about the many ridiculous aspects of army life, it made him laugh. When Marius laughed, it was as if he would never stop. It was an odd infectious falsetto laugh which started Jan laughing too ; and then Marius, squatting beside him in the hay in the darkened barn, would rock with renewed merriment and wipe away the tears which poured down his cheeks, and they had to remind each other to be quiet, in case anyone heard the noise outside.

But although there were these moments when Marius enjoyed

Jan's company, he remained a most serious danger as long as he stayed on the farm. There was an alarm every time someone was sighted climbing the hill from the village, and every time the Germans in the schoolhouse made some slightly unusual move. He had to be taken away from there as soon as he was fit enough to go, and Marius had thought of a place to put him.

The opposite shore of Lyngenfjord is steep and uninhabited. There had once been a farm over there : just one in a stretch of eight miles. But it had been burnt down a long time before, and never rebuilt. One small log cabin had escaped the fire and was still standing. It was four miles from the nearest house, either along the shore or across the water, and so far as Marius knew, nobody ever went there. If any safe place could be found for Jan, that seemed the most likely. The name of the farm had been Revdal.

To get Jan across there was more than Marius could manage with only the help of his sisters, because he would have to be carried all the way down to a boat and out of it again at the other side ; and so at this stage he began to bring in other members of the organisation from the village. He chose them on the principle that no two men from one family should be mixed up in the affair, in case something happened and another family besides his own was entirely broken up. In the end, he let three of his friends into his secret : Alvin Larsen, Amandus Lillevoll and Olaf Lanes. All of them had known one another since they were children. When he told them about it, one by one, they all offered eagerly to help.

They agreed to make the move on the night of the 12th of April. In the fortnight since Toftefjord, the nights had got quite a lot shorter : uncomfortably short for anything illegal. To avoid disaster, the first part of the journey would have to be planned with care and carried out without the least delay. This was the half-mile from Marius's barn to the shore.

Marius had lived there all his life, but it was a new experience for him, as it would be for most law-abiding people, to plan a way out of his own home which he could use without being seen. It was extraordinarily difficult. Jan would have to be carried on a stretcher, and the two sides of the valley set limits to the routes which could be used, because they were both too steep to climb. On the other hand, the triangle of gently sloping ground between them was in full view of the houses, and the paths which crossed it led from door to door. There were two principal dangers, the German garrison in the school and the sentry who patrolled the road. But what worried Marius almost more than these was the thought of meeting a series of neighbours and having to stop to give endless explanations. To carry a man on a stretcher through one's own village in secret at dead of night is a thing one cannot explain away in a casual word or two.

Marius made a reconnaissance, looking at his home from this unfamiliar point of view. There turned out to be only one possible route, and that was the river bed. The river, which is called Lyngdalselven after the valley, runs down through the middle of the village and under the road by a bridge about two hundred yards from the shore. It has a double channel, one about fifty feet wide which carries the normal summer flow, and another much wider flood channel which only fills up during the thaw in spring. That mid-April, the thaw had not yet begun, and the whole of the river was still frozen. The flood channel has banks about fifteen feet high, and Marius found that close below them, on the dry bed of the river, one was fairly well hidden from view. There was one snag about it. The nearest of all the houses to the channel was the schoolhouse where the Germans lived. It stands within three or four paces of the top of the bank. But even so, it still seemed that this was the only way. Looking out of the schoolhouse windows the troops could see almost every inch of the valley mouth. The only place they could not see was the foot of the bank immediately below their windows.

When dusk began on the night which they had chosen, they all assembled in the barn. Two men were to go with Marius and the stretcher. His sister Ingeborg had volunteered to go ahead of it to see that the way was clear. Another man was to climb to the top of a high moraine on the other side of the river, where he could watch the sentry on the road. A rowing-boat with a sail had already been hauled up on the beach at the river mouth. Jan had been wrapped in blankets and tied to a home-made stretcher, and they had a rucksack full of food and a paraffin cooker to leave

with him in Revdal. They waited nervously for the long twilight
to deepen till it was dark enough to go. It was after eleven when
Marius gave the word.

It was a breathless journey. For once, they could not use their
skis. To ski with a stretcher down steep slopes among bushes
in the dark could only end in disaster, at least for the man on the
stretcher. But to carry their weight on foot in the deep snow was
exhausting work, even for such a short distance. They started by
climbing straight down to the river, and when they got to the
bottom of the bank without any alarm they put Jan down in the
snow for a few minutes and rested. The lookout left them to
cross the river and go up to his point of vantage, and Ingeborg
went ahead to see what was happening at the school, and to tread
out a path in the snow. It was very quiet, but there was a light
southerly breeze which hummed in the telephone wires and stirred
the bare twigs of the bushes ; it was not much, but it helped to
cover the sound of their movements. When they had got their
breath they bent down and picked up the stretcher and set off
down the channel towards the school.

It soon came in sight. There were lights in some of the
windows which cast yellowish beams on the trodden snow outside
it. One of them shone out across the river channel, but close in,
right under the wall of the building, the steep bank cast a shadow
which looked like a tunnel of darkness. The stretcher bearers
approached it, crouching as low as they could with their burden,
keeping their eyes on Ingeborg's footsteps in front of them in
case they should stumble, and resisting the impulse to look up at
the lights above them. When they came to the fence of the play-
ground, they crept closer in under the bank. In an upward glance
they could see the edge of the roof on their right, and the beam
of light lit up some little bushes on their left, but it passed a foot
or two over the tops of their heads. The troops in the school
were not making a sound, and the men were acutely conscious
of the faint squeak and crunch of the snow beneath their tread.
The silence seemed sinister. It made the thought of an ambush
come into their minds. But in thirty seconds they passed the
school : and there was the road, fifty paces ahead of them.

This was the place they had feared. With the school behind

them and the road ahead, there was nowhere for four men to hide themselves. It all depended on luck : how long they would have to wait for the sentry, and whether a car came past with headlights. But Ingeborg was there, behind a bush at the side of the road, where she had been lying to watch the sentry, and she came back towards them and pointed to the right, away from the river bridge. That was the way they wanted the sentry to go, the longest leg of his beat. At the same moment, there was a tiny spark of light on the top of the moraine ; the watcher there had struck a match, and that was the signal that the sentry was nearly at the far end of the beat and would soon be turning round. It was now or never : they had to go on without a pause. They scrambled up on to the road. For a few seconds they were visible, dark shadows against the snow, from the school and the whole of the beat and a score of houses. Then they were down on the other side, among bushes which gave them cover as far as the shore. The worst of the journey was over.

When they had hauled the boat down the beach and bundled Jan on board it, they rowed off quietly for a couple of hundred yards, and then set the lugsail and got under way, with the breeze on the starboard beam and a course towards the distant loom of the mountains across the fjord, under which was the cabin of Revdal.

CHAPTER EIGHT

THE DESERTED FARM

WHAT JAN came to know as the Savoy Hotel, Revdal, was not very commodious, but the first two days he spent there were the happiest and most peaceful of the whole of his journey, a short fool's paradise: if one can use the word happy about his state of mind, or the word paradise about a place like Revdal. The hut was ten feet long and seven feet wide, and you could stand upright under the ridge of the roof. It was built of logs, and it had a door but no window. The only light inside it when the door was shut came through chinks in the wall and the roof, which was covered with growing turf. On one side, it had a wooden bunk, and the rest of the space in it was filled with odds and ends which seemed to have been salvaged, long before, from the ruins of the burnt-out farm. There was a small, roughly hewn table, and some pieces of a wooden plough, and some other wooden instruments which Jan could not imagine any use for, and an elaborate carved picture frame without any glass or picture. Everything was made of wood, unpainted, even the latch and hinges on the door, and it was all worn with years of use, and white and brittle with age.

As they carried him up there from the boat, he had had a glimpse of its surroundings. It stands about ten yards back from the shore, in a small clearing which slopes up to the forest of little twisted trees which clings to the side of the mountain. He had seen posts and wires in the clearing, which looked as if someone still came there to cut and dry the crop of hay, which is a precious harvest in the north. But there was no sign that anyone had been there for the past eight months of winter, and it was very unlikely that anyone would come for another three months, until

July. Under the towering masses of snow and rock the solitary deserted little hut looked insignificant and forlorn, and even smaller than it really was. From a distance one would have taken it for a boulder, three-quarters covered by snow. There was no landing-place to draw attention to it, only the lonely beach. A stranger might have sailed along the fjord ten times and never seen it.

They put Jan in the bunk, and put the food and the paraffin stove on the table within his reach. Marius hesitated a little while, as if there should have been something else he could do for Jan, but there was nothing. He promised to come back two or three nights later to see him, and Jan thanked him, and then he went out and shut the door and left Jan alone there in the dark. For a few minutes Jan listened, hoping to hear the crunch of the boat on the beach as they pushed it off; but inside the hut it was absolutely silent. When he was sure they had gone away, he spread out his meagre belongings round him, and settled down on the hard boards of the ancient bunk. He was as contented as he could be. He had everything he wanted: time, and a little food, and solitude. He could lie there as long as he liked, not much of a burden to anyone, until his feet got all right again. Very soon he drifted off to sleep.

He had had a capacity for sleep, ever since the avalanche, which seemed to have no limit, and there was nothing to wake for in Revdal except to eat. Sometimes when hunger did wake him there was daylight shining through the holes in the roof: sometimes there was not, and he groped for his matches and ate by the dim blue gleam of the paraffin cooker. But whether it was day or night outside no longer had any interest for him.

When he was awake, he daydreamed, about Oslo before the war, his family, his football club at home where he had been president, the adventures which he had packed into the three years since he left home, and about his friends in the training camp in Scotland, and about his own ambitions and hopes for the time when the war was over. It had been a long journey and a very strange one all the way from his home and his father's instrument makers' workshop to this bunk and this hut and this desolate arctic shore; but he never thought then that it would

end there. Some time, he would get up and go out of the door
and begin all over again. And meanwhile, time was passing, and
that was all that mattered ; because time, he believed, was the
only thing which could cure his feet and give him the strength
to tackle the last twenty-five miles to Sweden.

But Marius, back in Furuflaten, was not so optimistic. He
felt troubled in his mind at having left Jan all alone : he would
much rather have hidden him somewhere where he could have
kept an eye on him day and night. But he consoled himself by
thinking that he had done it more for his family's sake than for
his own, and also that it was in Jan's own interest to be in a
place which the Germans were very unlikely to search. He
believed, just as Jan did, that in time he would get fit again, but
he thought it might be a very long time ; and he knew, although
Jan did not, how difficult it was going to be to keep him supplied
with even the barest necessities of life across at Revdal. He would
never have grudged him anything, neither time nor danger, nor
money while his savings lasted out ; but he was very much afraid
that keeping things secret, which was so difficult already, would
become impossible if it had to go on very long. If people noticed
him going off two or three nights a week in a boat towards the
uninhabited side of the fjord, there was no credible explanation
he could give ; and besides, there was always the chance that the
Germans might yet make some sudden swoop which would
prevent him from crossing at all. They might come and arrest
him, and in case they did, he would have to find somebody who
could not be connected with the affair but who could take over
his responsibilities when he was gone. Otherwise, Jan would be
left there till he starved. What it came to, in fact, was that there
might be a crisis at any time ; and therefore there ought to be a
plan to get Jan over the frontier if the crisis came before he could
go on his own feet.

Marius went to Herr Legland again, and they had a long
discussion. They agreed that apart from being safer in Revdal,
Jan was better placed there for an attempt on the frontier. If he
had tried to go straight from Furuflaten, there would have been
valleys to cross, and the main road ; but from Revdal one only
had to climb straight up for 3000 feet and one was right on the

plateau. Once one was up there, there was no road or habitation whatever before the frontier, and the ski-ing was straightforward. But if Jan needed help on the journey, it would have to come from one of the settlements on the other side of the fjord.

Marius may have felt disappointed at the idea that he might have to hand Jan over to somebody else, but he had to agree that if it came to a dash for the frontier, he could not be of any help. For one thing, he had never been up on the plateau ; and besides, there was no knowing how long the journey might take. It would certainly not be less than four days, and if he was away from home for as long as that, everybody would know it. But on the other hand, there was at least one settlement on the other side where there was no German garrison at all. The men from there would know the plateau, or at least the part of it near at hand, and it would be much easier for them to disappear for a few days.

When Marius had reluctantly agreed with this conclusion, Herr Legland undertook to send a warning to people he knew on the other side that an escort might be needed for the frontier. He meant to arrange a meeting place and a code-word for the operation in case it had to be undertaken in a hurry.

The name of the settlement they had in mind is Mandal. It lies in a deep valley which penetrates for twenty miles into the plateau, and it has a population of six or seven hundred. It is much more cut off from the world than Lyngseidet or Furuflaten. There is no road to it, and not a single pass through the mountains to give access to it by land. It can only be reached by climbs which are always dangerous in winter, or else by a sea voyage of ten miles from Lyngseidet. But even there the organisation had its contacts.

As soon as they began to think about Mandal, it brought them up against a problem which had already been causing both of them some worry, the problem of money. If Mandal had to come into it, the whole business of rescuing Jan was going to cost more than Herr Legland or Marius could possibly find out of their own pockets or their neighbours'. One is apt to forget that this sort of activity needs money, but it does : or at least, it did in north Norway. People like Marius were glad to stretch their own rations to feed Jan, and to sleep with a blanket less on their own beds, and to give him their clothes; but sooner or later he was sure to need something which neither of them possessed themselves. Then there would be only one option: either to go to somebody who could supply it, and let him into the secret so that he would give it for nothing, or else to buy it. The things Jan was most likely to need, the simple necessities of life, were rationed, and a lot of things he might possibly need could not be bought at all except at black market prices; and of course a man who was willing to sell on the black market was the last sort of person one would want to know about Jan. The only safe way to get what was needed would be to pay the price which was asked, however high it was, and not tell anybody. Jan had already had the last of all the brandy and cigarettes that Marius could lay his hands on, and he needed more; or to be accurate, he needed brandy, to keep him going in the cold, and cigarettes were the only luxury he could enjoy. If Mandal came into it too, there was going to be the question of diesel oil for boats. There was a telephone in Mandal, but all telephones were tapped. The only way to tell the Mandal men what was happening would be to get a motor-boat and go there, and if the owner of the boat could not give a proper reason for the journey, the fuel would have to come from the black market too.

There was also the question of paying people for the time they spent on a job of this kind. Marius was his own master and could afford to take time off to look after Jan, and so could the other Furuflaten people. But a lot of men around there, especially in a place like Mandal, lived from hand to mouth, and if they lost a few days' work it really meant less to eat for their wives and children. That might not prevent them from helping, but the organisation's principle was that nobody ought to suffer real financial hardship for anything he was asked to do. The state paid its soldiers, and the organisation expected to do the same. Certainly if anyone had to be asked to take Jan across to Sweden, he would have to have his income made up for the days he was away. One way and another, the whole operation might cost much more than the resources of Lyngseidet and Furuflaten could afford.

Luckily, Herr Legland had to go into Tromsö, and he

promised Marius he would take care of this question of finance. Thus for the second time news reached the city of what was happening in Lyngenfjord. Legland went to Sverre Larsen, whose father, the dismissed owner of the newspaper, was an old friend of his. He arrived on a Saturday evening, and told Larsen the whole story from beginning to end, except that he left out all the names of people and places. He had reckoned that he must have a fund of £150 for urgent expenses which he could already foresee. Without it, or the certainty of being able to get it quickly, he would not feel he could ask anyone to go to the frontier.

Larsen accepted the request without any question. It was the kind of thing which the Tromsö merchants expected to pay for. But it was a stern test of his organisation to find the money in cash on a Saturday night. If Legland had come at a time when the banks and offices were open, it would only have taken a few minutes. As it was, Larsen himself put in all the money which he happened to have in the house, and then went the rounds of his friends in the organisation. By Sunday morning he had collected it all, in varying sums from a lot of different people, and Herr Legland took it home, with his money worries set at rest for the time being. But as things turned out, this was only the very beginning of the expense of saving Jan's life. Before the end, it cost £1650 in cash, besides the labour and goods which were given freely by hundreds of people ; and the whole of this sum was contributed by business houses and individuals in Tromsö who regarded him as a symbol of the battle against the Germans.

Marius kept his promise to go back and visit Jan. Two nights after he had left him at Revdal, he set off again and rowed across the fjord, taking a new stock of food and some bottles of milk. Jan was still in the bunk, exactly as he had left him. He was cheerful, and the rest was doing him good. He had been amusing himself by pulling out the moss which had been used to caulk the joints between the logs of the wall of the hut, and rolling it in newspaper to make cigarettes. Marius swore that before next time he would find him something better to smoke than that. Meanwhile, he cooked up some fish for him, and when he had eaten it they both had a look at his feet. They seemed to be getting on all right, and they talked things over in the hope that Jan would be able to put on skis again before very long.

They had already agreed that Jan ought not to know anything about the organisation. Although his prospects looked a little brighter than they had a week before, both he and Marius knew in their heart of hearts that so long as he could not walk his chance of avoiding being captured in the end was really very small. So Marius still called himself Hans Jensen, and Jan did not know any names at all for the other people he had seen, or anything about the activities in Lyngseidet or Tromsö. He had to be content not to know who was helping him, but just to be grateful for the help when it arrived.

However, Marius did tell him that night, in order to keep his spirits up, that people in Mandal were being asked to stand by in case their help was needed ; and he explained the geography of the surrounding mountains and the plateau, so that Jan would have it clear in his head if they had to take sudden action. It is not very far across the mountains from the hut at Revdal into the valley of Mandal : only about five miles on the map, though it involves the climb of 3000 feet up to the plateau level and down again. If Jan needed help when the time came, Marius meant to come to Revdal and lead him up the climb ; and he would arrange for the Mandal men to come up from the other side and meet them on top, so that they could take over there and escort Jan southwards across the plateau till he came to the frontier.

It was encouraging for Jan to know that some positive plans had been made to get him away, and Marius left him that night in good humour and quite contentedly resigned to another two days of solitude and darkness.

It was very soon after Marius left, not more than a few hours that Jan's feet began to hurt. It was nothing much at first, only a slight increase in the pain which had been going on ever since they were thawed. It came and went, and sometimes, that early morning, he thought it was imagination. But by the time when sunlight began to come through the holes in the roof, he was sure that something was happening. He struggled out of his blankets, when it was as light as it ever got in the hut, and unwrapped his feet. The sight of them alarmed him. They had changed visibly since the night before when Marius was with him. Now, his toes seemed to be grey, and although his feet as a whole were more painful than they had been, the ends of his toes were numb and cold, as if he had pins and needles. He rubbed them, but it only made them hurt more, and the skin began to peel off them. The toe which had been wounded had begun to heal, but the scar had a dark unhealthy look.

He rolled himself up again in the blankets and lay there uneasily, wondering what it meant. He did not know what had gone wrong, or what he ought to do to try to stop it. For the first time since he had met Marius, he began to feel lonely. It had seemed so easy to say he would wait for another two days alone, but now he regretted it. He wanted very much to have someone to talk to about his feet. He knew that the thirty-six hours he still had to wait before he could hope to see Marius were going to pass very slowly.

They turned out to be infinitely worse than he expected. The pain grew with appalling quickness, hour by hour. It grew so that sleep became out of the question and he could only lie there staring into the darkness and counting every minute till Marius might arrive, moving his legs in hopeless attempts to find a position which would ease them. The pain spread up his legs in waves, and sometimes seemed to fill his whole body like a flame so that when it receded it left him sweating and trembling and breathless.

In the second dawn, when the light was strong enough, he unwrapped his feet again. After the night he had just survived, what he saw then did not surprise him. His toes were black and swollen, and a foul-smelling fluid was oozing out of them, and he could not move them at all any more.

He was shocked and bewildered, with nobody to appeal to for advice or comfort. When the pain was at its worst, he could hardly think at all. When it eased, he lay there, wondering what Marius would do : whether he would take him back to Furuflaten, or whether there was any doctor who would take the risk of coming to Revdal. He wondered whether there was anything that even a doctor could do, without taking him to hospital. He thought he had either got blood poisoning or gangrene. Either of them, he imagined, would spread farther and farther up his legs. If he had been in hospital, he thought, they would have given him injections and stopped it before it got too far; but there in Revdal, without any kind of medical equipment, he could not think of anything to do. He wondered whether he ought to agree to go to hospital if he got the chance, and soon made up his mind that he should not. In hospital, the Germans would certainly get him in the end, and all kinds of people might get themselves into trouble on his behalf. He knew it might be tempting to agree if the pain went on, so he took a firm and final decision there and then, in case he was not in a fit condition to decide when the moment came; he would not go to hospital whatever happened. He tried to think of the worst that could possibly happen, so that this resolve would never weaken, and after all, the worst was only death. He put all his faith in Marius. Marius would know what to do: he would either take him to a doctor or bring a doctor to Revdal; or if he could not do either of those things, he would get advice and borrow medicine and come and doctor him himself. This thought kept him going all through the second day.

At long last the evening came. The little shafts of light inside the hut began to fade, and the darkness he had longed for all day set in. Marius could not begin to row across till it was dark, so that an hour and a half of night must pass before he could be expected. But long before that, Jan lay and listened for the footsteps outside the door, and the cheerful greetings which Marius always gave him before he came in, so that he would know it was a friend who was coming. The minutes of the night dragged on and on till the first light of the dawn, and Marius did not come.

A period of time began then which Jan remembered, after it ended, with the utmost horror. It was the first time that he sank into absolute despair of coming through alive, and he had not really resigned himself yet to dying: at least, not to dying the lingering, lonely agonising death which seemed to be all he could expect. At first, he waited for each night with the hope of hearing Marius; but as each night passed and nothing happened the hope slowly died within him. After five days, he could only believe that Marius and everyone who knew he was there had been arrested and shot, and that he was quite forgotten by the world, condemned to lie in the desolate hut till the poisoning killed him, or till he wasted away through starvation. Revdal, which they had chosen because it seemed safe, had turned into a trap. He was walled in by the barren mountain which hung over him, and by the sea and the miles of lonely shore on either side. He could not believe any more that he would ever get up and go across to the door and open it and go out into the fresh air to start on his journey again. He knew his own feet would never carry him to the nearest friendly house, and he knew that so much of his strength had ebbed away that he would never be able to swim or even to crawl there.

So day followed day, each merged into another by the mists of pain. On one day, he was aware of the sound of wind, and of snow sifting through the holes in the walls and beneath the door. On another, when he put out his hand to feel for the food on the table, he found it was all gone. On all of them, when he fell into a doze, even after the last of all reasonable hope had gone, he dreamed or imagined that he could hear Marius outside the door, and he started awake with a clutch at his heart. But nobody came.

CHAPTER NINE

AFTER THE STORM

IN FACT, there was nothing wrong with Marius. The Germans
had not made any new move, and everything was quiet in Furuflaten. What had stopped him coming to see Jan was simply
another storm. Just after his previous visit, it had started to blow
up from the south, and before the night when he had meant to
cross the fjord again there was such a sea running that the crossing
was quite impossible.

While Jan was lying groaning in the hut on the eastern side,
Marius was fretting impatiently on the west, and between them
four miles of furious sea made an impassable barrier. Nobody
could get to Revdal. Every day, Marius watched the grey
scudding water which was streaked with spindrift, and every
evening at dusk he went down to the beach at Furuflaten to make
sure that there was really no chance of going; but it was hopeless
even to try to launch a boat. At night he lay and listened for any
easing of the shrieks of wind.

But he was not really worried. There was no reason why he
should be. When he had left Jan, his health had been improving.
He had not been able to leave as much food as he would have
liked, but he reckoned that if Jan could spin it out, there was
enough to keep him from starving for some time yet. He knew
Jan would be disappointed and would be wondering what had
happened, but he was sure that he would guess it was the storm.
He did not realise that inside the log walls of the hut, with the
snow banked up all round them, Jan could not hear the howling
of the wind. Also, he still thought Jan was some kind of seaman
and would imagine for himself the fearsome effect of a southerly

gale in those narrow waters with a clear stretch of twenty miles
to windward.

So although Marius was naturally upset by the feeling that
he was letting Jan down, he had no immediate anxiety, and what
worried him most during the storm was the increasing menace
of the daylight. So far as his own help was still concerned, the
rescue of Jan was becoming a race against the midnight sun. It
was the beginning of the last week in April, and already it was
twilight all night. While the storm lasted, the nights were dark
enough, but when the sky cleared there would not be more than
a couple of hours in which he could sneak away from the Furuflaten beach without being seen by the sentry ; and if he left the
beach at the time when the twilight was deepest, he would have
to run the risk of landing again in broad daylight. In a fortnight's
time it would be so light all night that anyone with binoculars
would be able to watch him the whole way across the fjord, and
if the German motor-boat was still patrolling it would be able to
pick him up from miles away. Before then, whatever happened,
Jan would have to move on from Revdal.

It was exactly a week after Marius's second visit to the hut
when the storm began to show signs of ending. During that day,
when he and his family could see that the evening might bring a
chance of crossing, he collected everything he had to offer Jan
and packed it in his rucksack : food, and paraffin, and bottles of
milk, and a few cigarettes. At nightfall he put on his skis and
went down to the beach again. Two of his friends were there to
meet him. There was still some sea running, but not enough to
make the passage dangerous ; when the wind drops in that land-
locked water, the sea calms very quickly. They quietly launched
the boat, and began to row away. During the storm, nothing
had been seen of the motor-boat, but that made it seem all the
more likely that it would be out on patrol again that night.

However, the crossing was peaceful. Marius himself was
happy because he had some good news to bring to Jan. He had
just heard that Herr Legland had sent a message to the schoolmaster in Mandal, and that a favourable answer had come back.
There had evidently been some kind of a meeting in Mandal, and
there had been plenty of volunteers who would stand by to come

up to a rendezvous on top of the range between Mandal and Revdal where they would take delivery of Jan. Mandal was willing to take over the responsibility of looking after him, and the schoolmaster thought they would be able to escort him to the frontier. Marius imagined, in that brief moment of optimism while he crossed the fjord, that Jan might be in Sweden before a week had passed.

The shock when he got to Revdal was all the worse. Before he opened the door of the hut, he called " Hullo there ! " But there was no answer. He went in. It was pitch dark inside, and it stank of decay. In alarm, he called Jan by his name, and stooped over the bunk as the thought flashed through his mind that the Germans had been there and taken Jan away. But he felt the bundle of blankets and then, to his relief, he heard a faint sound as Jan turned his head.

" What's the matter ? " he said. " What's happened ? "

" There's the hell of a pain," Jan said.

Marius hastily shut the door and lit a lantern. The sight which he saw appalled him: Jan's face was as white as the face of a corpse beneath the dirt and the straggling beard. He slowly and wearily opened his eyes when the light fell on them, and made a feeble movement. The blankets round his legs were dark with blood.

Jan was too far gone to be pleased that Marius had arrived. It had happened to him so often before in dreams. For a few moments he was even unwilling to be dragged up out of his coma and forced to make the effort to live again. But when Marius boiled some water and made him take a hot drink he revived a little. He said that he had not had anything to eat or drink for several days. This puzzled Marius, who thought he had left enough ; but the fact was that three or four days before, what was left of the food had fallen off the table, and Jan had been too bemused to realise what had happened. Since then, he had lain there growing weak with hunger, while bread and dried fish was lying on the floor beside him, just out of his sight below the bunk board.

When Jan had come to himself enough to be able to talk coherently, Marius set himself to the unpleasant job of looking at his feet. Even before he saw them, he knew that it was gangrene. It was perfectly obvious that although Jan was alive, the toes of both of his feet had been dead for some time. Most of the blood on the blankets had come from cuts which Jan had made himself. Some days before, while he still had the strength to do it, he had started to operate on his feet with his pocket-knife. In the belief that it might be blood poisoning, he had reasoned that the only thing he could do was to draw off the blood, as people used to do with snake bites ; and so he had pulled up his legs in the bunk, one by one, and stabbed his feet with the knife and let them bleed.

Marius washed them as best he could and bound them up again. Both he and Jan knew, without having to say it, that Jan would never walk or ski to Sweden. Marius privately thought there was nothing to be done except to amputate both feet. He did not say so to Jan, for fear of depressing him ; but Jan had also come to the same conclusion.

Marius could not stay long that night because of the daylight, but before he left he promised Jan that he would either get a doctor, or else arrange somehow for him to be carried to Sweden, and that in any case he would come back in two or three days. Then he left him again to his solitude. But now that Jan knew that he still had active friends who were trying to help him, he felt he could face another few days in that abominable hut with equanimity. The mere sight of Marius had brought back his will to live. During the days that followed, between the bouts of pain, he began to come to terms with the idea of living as a cripple. At first he dwelt morbidly on all the active pursuits which he would lose, but by and by he began to look forward to the simple pleasures he would still be able to enjoy. The height of his ambition at that time was to get back to London and go into Kensington Gardens in a wheel-chair on a sunny day and watch the children playing.

Marius, rowing back across the fjord in the light of dawn, knew he had just made promises to Jan without any idea of how he could fulfil them ; but he had great faith in the idea that if you are ready to give up everything to the solution of any problem, you will always find an answer. He did not know of any doctor who he was sure would risk his life to go to Revdal, and he did not really believe that a doctor could do much without taking Jan to hospital, which Jan had refused to hear of. Still less did he know, at that moment, how Jan could be carried bodily across the mountains to the frontier. But one or other of those alternatives had got to be arranged, not only because he had promised it, but also because without either of them, Jan was obviously going to die.

As soon as he got home, he told all his friends in the organisation about the new and apparently insuperable difficulty that Jan was absolutely helpless. Herr Legland and the three Furuflaten men who had carried Jan over to Revdal all discussed it with him. Bit by bit they pieced together a not impossible plan. Messengers were sent to Tromsö and to Mandal and to a valley called Kaafjord even farther east. The news of the problem spread far and wide, whispered from one to another of the trusted people who might have help to offer. The dormant patriotic club went into action, inspired at last by a situation which was going to test its efficiency to the utmost. During the following evening, the messengers began to return, one by one, bringing criticisms and new suggestions and new offers of help back to the main conspirators. The plan took shape.

The man who had been to Tromsö brought back a message from Sverre Larsen simply promising financial support, without any qualifications. The one who had been to Mandal had a more complicated message, but it was almost equally welcome. A party of four of the Mandal men was ready to make the climb to the plateau at any moment and to take the responsibility of keeping Jan alive. If Marius and the Furuflaten men could get Jan up there and bring a sledge, they were also willing to try to haul it to the frontier. But this they regarded as a last resort. None of them had ever tried to haul a sledge across the plateau. It might take a long time, and if the weather broke again it might end in disaster. Furthermore, none of them knew the Swedish side of the mountains, and they had to point out that although the frontier was only twenty-five miles away, a man who did not know the country might easily have to go another hundred miles down into the forests towards the Baltic before he found any human habitation. If that happened, the journey would take so long that their absence could not possibly pass unnoticed, and that would mean that none of them could come back. They would have to go into exile, and this they were most unwilling to do because all of them had dependants. But they had a better proposal : to get the Lapps to make the journey.

The advantage of getting Lapps to go, rather than Norwegians, was obvious at once to Marius and Herr Legland, as it would be to anyone who knew the Lapps and the country. The only surprising thing was that anyone in Kaafjord or Mandal should know any Lapps well enough to have any hope of persuading them to make the journey. The Lapps are very peculiar people at any time, a small primitive race entirely distinct from anyone else in Europe ; and during the war they were more peculiar than usual. The kind of Lapps they had in mind are nomads who live by breeding reindeer, and since the beginning of history they have made the same migrations with their reindeer every year. The same families of Lapps come every spring with their herds to Kaafjord and Lyngseidet, always arriving within a day or two of the fifth of May. They spend the summer there, in Norway, and the winter in Finland or Sweden. National frontiers mean nothing to them, because they have been making their journeys since long before the frontiers existed. To stop them would mean that their race would die out, because the reindeer cannot survive without a seasonal change of feeding-ground, and the Lapps cannot survive without their reindeer. Probably the Germans would have liked to stop them, if only for the sake of tidiness, but they wisely never tried ; and all through the World War the Lapps wandered unconcerned between Finland, which was fighting on the side of Germany, and Norway, which was fighting as best it could on the Allied side, and Sweden, which was neutral.

One result of this unique situation was that the Lapps themselves naturally had no interest in the war at all. Probably none of them had any idea of what it was all about. It was no good appealing to them on any grounds of patriotism or idealogy. They were no more attached to one of the three countries than another, and they would never have heard of politics. Neither would the humanitarian grounds for helping Jan have meant very much to them, because they do not set a high value on human life. If a Lapp lost the use of his feet, like Jan, he would know he was useless and expect his family to leave him alone to die.

All the same, if any Lapps could be persuaded to take Jan to the frontier, they were much more likely to succeed than any Norwegian party could possibly be. For one thing, nobody could check their movements ; there was no limit to the time they could be away. Also, although they knew nothing about compasses or maps, they knew that uncharted country far better than anyone else. They were able to survive even the worst of winter weather in the open ; and finally, they had reindeer trained to draw sledges, and could cover much more ground in a day than a party of men drawing a sledge themselves. Therefore Marius, Herr Legland and the rest of the conspirators welcomed this suggestion. The first wave of the migration of reindeer was due to arrive within a week. They would already be somewhere on their way across the mountains. The message from Mandal had said that the best ski-runner in Kaafjord was ready to set off, along the migration tracks towards the Lapp settlement of Kautokeino, a hundred miles away, to try to locate the herds. A message was sent back, welcoming the idea and asking him to go at once.

Meanwhile, the main problem for Marius and the Furuflaten men was to get Jan up to the plateau. The place for meeting the party from Mandal had already been agreed. It was in a shallow depression on the plateau, half-way between Revdal and Mandal. To get there from the Revdal side was a steep climb for the first two thousand feet, and then a more gentle upward slope across about three miles of the open snowfield. The meeting place itself was at a height of about 2700 feet. Something of the nature of a stretcher which could be carried would be needed to get him up the first part of the climb, and a sledge would be easiest for the last part. They decided to try to combine both functions by building the lightest possible sledge.

All these discussions and the coming and going of messengers had been happening in the midst of the German garrison areas in Furuflaten and Lyngseidet. For building the sledge, the plot

was carried even farther into the German camp. The best joiner
anyone could think of was the caretaker of Herr Legland's school.
The school buildings had been requisitioned and the pupils turned
out to make room for the German district headquarters staff, but
the caretaker still worked there and still had access to what had
been the school workshop. He undertook to build the sledge;
and he did so, inside the German headquarters itself. The impertinence of this filled everyone who knew of it with a kind of
schoolboyish glee; and the only disadvantage of such an attractive
arrangement was that the joiner could not take the risk of putting
the sledge together, because the Germans who came in and out
while he was working would have been certain to ask what it
was for. However, he made each piece to careful measurements,
and was willing to guarantee that when the time came to assemble
it, everything would fit. It was built on a pair of ordinary skis,
and it had a slatted platform about a foot high, eighteen inches
wide and six feet long. Events proved that his workmanship was
good. The sledge not only fitted together, but stood up to week
after week of the hardest possible treatment.

It was ready on the third day after Marius had last been to
Revdal, and all the plans were completed on that day too, except
that the ski-runner from Kaafjord had not come back from his
search for the reindeer. Marius's three neighbours, Alvin Larsen,
Olaf Lanes and Amandus Lillevoll, were prepared to go over
with him to Revdal that night to make the attempt to haul Jan
up the mountain. Herr Legland telephoned to the schoolmaster
in Mandal to say in cautiously chosen words, in case the line was
tapped, that the parcel he was expecting was being sent at once.
Alvin Larsen was going that afternoon to fetch the sledge from
Lyngseidet; but that very morning an avalanche blocked the
road between Lyngseidet and Furuflaten.

Luckily, the avalanche did not delay him much, and on the
whole it was probably an advantage to their plans. It was also
the indirect cause of an incident which appealed to what might
be called the occupation sense of humour. The local people had
been expecting it to happen. The road just north of Furuflaten
runs along the shore of the fjord below a cliff a thousand feet
high, the same cliff which Jan had been trying to skirt when he

got lost in the mountains; and the snow from the gullies in the cliff always falls and blocks the road about the last week in April. It happens with such regularity that a jetty has been built at Furuflaten for a car ferry which provides a way through for traffic till the danger is past in May. Alvin Larsen had already arranged to go to Lyngseidet by boat if the avalanche started before the sledge was ready; but the Germans were not so well prepared for it, and the sudden blocking of the main road diverted their attention at that crucial moment from everything else that was happening.

Alvin got to Lyngseidet without any trouble, and tied up his boat at the pier. There was a German sentry on the pier who took no notice of him at all. He went up to the school and collected the bits of the sledge from the caretaker, together with a bag of bolts and screws, and minute instructions for putting it all together. The bundles of pieces of wood tied together with string and the pair of skis looked reasonably harmless. He carried them down through the village to the pier. But when he got there the tide was very low, and his boat was a long way down. He was afraid to throw the wood down into the boat in case it broke, and if he got down into the boat he could not reach up again to the level of the pier. So he called to the sentry to give him a hand. The sentry came over, and put down his rifle, and kindly handed the skis and the bundles down to Alvin one by one. Alvin thanked him gravely in Norwegian, and started his engine and steamed away.

CHAPTER TEN

THE ASCENT OF REVDAL

THAT EVENING, the sailing-boat which Marius used crossed over the fjord again, laden with the gear for the attempt to climb the mountain : the sledge, still in pieces, a sixty-foot rope, an old canvas sleeping-bag and two fresh blankets for Jan, two rucksacks full of spare clothing and food and a bottle of brandy, and the four pairs of skis of the men who were making the attempt.

The ascent of Revdal was the first of two feats of mountaineering during Jan's rescue which are possibly unique. It often happens after climbing accidents in peace time that an injured man has to be carried or lowered a long way down a mountain ; but there must rarely, if ever, have been any occasion before or since to carry an injured man up a mountain for three thousand feet in severe conditions of ice and snow. At the time, spurred on by the knowledge that Jan's life depended on it, the four men who attempted it never dreamed of failure ; but ever afterwards, when they looked up in cold blood at the mountain wall of Revdal, they wondered how they could possibly have done it.

When they got to the far shore of the fjord that evening, they walked up to the hut in some anxiety at what they would find inside, afraid of the effect which another three days of isolation might have had on Jan. But they found him more cheerful than he had been the time before. Physically, he was weaker, and those of the party who had not seen him since they had left him there twelve days earlier were shocked at the change in his appearance for he had lost a lot of weight and his eyes and cheeks were sunken. But he was much clearer in his head than he had been when Marius saw him, and he had even regained the vestige of a sense of humour. He told them his feet were no better and no worse. The toes, of course, could not get any worse, but the gangrene had not spread any farther, so far as he could tell. He said it was still just as painful; but they could see from his behaviour that he could stand up to the pain now that he knew he was not abandoned. All in all, he was a patient whom no hospital staff would have allowed out of bed for a moment, and looking down at him, all four men wondered whether it could be right to take him out into the snow and subject him to the treatment they intended. All of them thought it would very likely kill him. But they knew for certain that it was his only chance.

While two of them put the sledge together, the others wrapped him securely in two blankets, and then pushed and pulled him into the sleeping-bag. When the sledge was ready, they lifted him out of the bunk where he had lain for nearly a fortnight, and put him on the sledge and lashed him securely down with ropes, so that not much more than his eyes was showing and he could not move at all. They manoeuvred the sledge through the door and put it down in the snow outside. While they adjusted their individual loads of skis and ski-sticks, and ropes and rucksacks, Jan had a moment to glance for the last time, without any regret, at the hovel where he had expected to die. Then they took up the short hauling ropes they had tied to the sledge, and turned it towards the mountain. It was a little after midnight; but there was still the afterglow of the sun in the northern sky above the mouth of the fjord, and even beneath the mountain wall it was not very dark. There were roughly fifteen degrees of frost.

The first part of the climb straight up from the hut at Revdal is covered by the forest of birch scrub. It is not steep enough to be called more than a scramble in mountaineering terms, but in deep snow it is the most frustrating kind of scramble, even for a climber not carrying any burden. None of the miniature trees have trunks much thicker than an arm, but they have been growing and dying there unattended since primeval times, and the ground beneath them is covered with a thick matted tangle of rotten fallen logs which gives no foothold. The trees grow very close together, and they are interlaced with half-fallen branches bowed down or broken by the weight of snow. Some trees have died and are still standing, propped up by the others crowded round them, and these break and crumble away if some-one incautiously uses them for a handhold. When the deep springy mesh of fallen trees, lying piled on one another, is hidden by a smooth deceptive covering of snow, the forest is a place where a climber must go with care. It would be impossible to fall for more than a foot or two, but it would be very easy to break a leg in falling.

Getting Jan up through the forest was mostly a matter of brute strength and endless patience; but strength and patience, of course, were two of the qualities Marius had thought about when he chose his three companions. Alvin Larsen was slight and thin, and only about twenty-one years old, but he had just come back from the tough school of the Lofoten fishing and was in perfect training. Amandus Lillevoll was a little older, a small wiry man with a great reserve of strength, and an exceptional skier. Olaf Lanes was the only big man of them all. He had shoulders like an ox, and he hardly ever spoke unless he had to : the epitome of the strong silent man. As for patience, all four of them had the unending dogged patience which is typical of Arctic people.

Within the steep forest, they quickly discovered the technique which served them best. Two of them would hold the sledge, belayed to a tree to stop it from running backwards, while the others climbed on ahead with the rope, forcing their way through the frozen undergrowth. When the upper pair found a possible stance, they took a turn of the rope round a tree and hauled the sledge up towards them, the lower pair steering it, stopping it when it threatened to turn over, pushing as best they could, and lifting it bodily when it buried itself in drifts. Their progress was very slow. There was seldom a clear enough space to haul the sledge more than about a dozen feet at a time, and each change of stance meant a new belay and a new coiling and uncoiling of the icy rope. The leaders, treading a trail through the virgin snow, often fell through into holes in the rotten wood beneath, and it was difficult to climb out of these hidden traps. Before they had gained more than a few hundred feet, they began to be afraid that they had started something which it would be impossible to finish ; not so much because they thought their own stubbornness and strength would be unequal to the job, but because they were more and more afraid that Jan would not survive it. It was going to be a long time before they got to the top ; and they had found a new problem which had no answer, and which nobody had foreseen : the simple problem of whether to haul him feet first or head first. When they took him feet first, of course his head was always much lower than his feet, and sometimes in the steep drifts he was hanging almost vertically head downwards. He could not stand this for very long, certainly not for hour after hour ; but when they turned him round and took him up head first, the blood ran into his feet and burst out in new hæmorrhages, and his face showed them the pain he was trying to suffer in silence. But as the climb went on, he was more and more often unconscious when they looked at him. This was a mercy, but it made them all the more sure he would not last very long. This urgency, together with the blind faith which he seemed to have in them, made them press on with the strength of desperation. Every few feet of the forest brought them up against a new obstacle which had to be surmounted. They struggled with each one till they overcame it, and then turned to the next without daring to pause, hoping that Jan would last till they got to the top, and that then the Mandal men would be able to whisk him straight over to Sweden.

When they cleared the forest at last, at a height of about a thousand feet, they had to rest. They slewed the sledge round broadside to the hill and dug in one runner so that it stood level, and collapsed in the snow beside it. Jan was awake, and they gave him a nip of brandy, and sucked some ice themselves, and looked down at the way they had come. The climb had already taken nearly three hours, and it was day. The dawn light shone on the peaks above Furuflaten across the water, and Jaeggevarre glowed above them all on the western skyline. The fjord below was still, and there was no sign of life on it. In the shadow of the hill, the air was very cold.

Immediately above the treeline was a sheer face of rock, but to their right it was broken by a steep cleft with the frozen bed of a stream in the bottom of it. Each time they had crossed the fjord they had gazed up at the face as they approached it, and the cleft had seemed the most likely route to the summit. From closer at hand, it still looked possible. To get to the bottom of it they would have to traverse a steep snow slope about two hundred feet high and perhaps a hundred yards across. The slope was clear and smooth at the top, where they would have to cross it, but at the bottom it vanished in the forest. It had a firm crust on it, and there seemed to be no particular danger about it. When they had got their breath they gathered themselves together to attempt it.

This was the first time they had tried to traverse with the sledge; and crossing the slope turned out to be like a nightmare, like walking a tightrope in a dream. Three of them stood below the sledge and one above it. To keep it level and stop it rolling sideways down the hill, the three men below it had to carry the outer runner, letting the inner one slide in the snow. Very slowly they edged out across the slope, kicking steps and moving one man at a time till the whole slope yawned dizzily below them. It was impossible then to stop or go back. The sledge, resting on a single ski, moved all too easily. While they could keep it perfectly level, all was well, but they could feel that if they let it tilt the least bit either way, either down by the head or down by the foot, it would take charge and break away from them, and then in a split second the whole thing would be over. Kicking steps in a snow slope always demands a fair degree of balance because there is nothing whatever to hold on to. It is impossible to resist a sudden unexpected force. If the sledge had begun to slide they could have saved themselves by falling on their faces and digging their hands and toes into the snow ; but they could not have stopped the sledge, and when it crashed into the trees two hundred feet below it would have been travelling at a speed which it was horrifying to imagine. Perhaps it was just as well that Jan, lying on it on his back and lashed immovably in position, could only look up at the sky and the rock face above him, and not at the chasm down below. Before they reached the other side of that slope, the men were sweating and trembling with the effort and tension. At the foot of the cleft, where the gradient eased, they stopped again thankfully and anchored the sledge with ski-sticks driven into the snow, so that they could relax till their strength came back. From there, Jan could see the cleft soaring above them.

When they looked up at it, it seemed to be steeper than they had expected. The walls of it were sheer, and it was about thirty feet wide. The snow in the bed of it showed all the signs of being about to avalanche ; but it was safe enough on that western slope just after dawn. The cleft curved gently to the left, so that from the bottom they could not see very far up it ; but having seen it from the fjord they knew it had no pitch in it too steep for the snow to lie on, and that it led almost all the way to the easier slopes on the upper half of the mountain. It was certainly going to be difficult and it might be impossible, but now that they had come so far there was no alternative.

After a very short rest, two of them began to lead out the sixty-foot rope. They went up side by side, kicking two parallel sets of steps for the second pair to use. Within the cleft, they were able to use the full length of the rope for the first time, and the leaders did not pause till the whole of it was stretched up the snow above the sledge. Then they dug themselves as deep a stance as they could and braced themselves in it and took the strain of the weight of the sledge while the others down below them freed it from its anchors. So the first pitch of a long and heavy haul began.

In some ways, going straight up the slope was not so hard as trying to go across it. The balance of the sledge was not important : it hung at the end of the rope like a pendulum. But the physical effort was greater and more sustained. At each stance the two leaders hauled the sledge up towards them while the two men below followed it up the steps, pushing as best they could. At the end of each sixty feet it was anchored afresh ; but the ski-sticks could not be trusted to hold it alone, and even the effort of holding it was so exhausting that they could not afford to pause.

Beyond the bend, the cleft swept smoothly up to a skyline appallingly far above, and there was nothing in it which offered a chance of a rest : no boulder or chockstone, and no break in the vertical walls on either side.

Somewhere in the upper reaches of the cleft, Jan came as near a sudden death as he had been anywhere on his journey. All four of the climbers by then were in that extremely unpleasant dilemma which is experienced sooner or later by every mountaineer, when one knows one has outreached one's strength, and it is too late to go down by the way one has come, so that one must either win through to the top, or fall. It was at this stage, when they knew they could never manage to lower the sledge to the bottom, that what they had dreaded happened. Somebody slipped, somebody else was off balance ; in a fraction of a second the sledge shot backwards. But Amandus happened to be below it. It hit him hard in the chest and ran over him, and somehow he and the sledge became entangled together and his body acted as a brake and stopped it, and within the second the others had it under control again. The climb went on, and Jan did not know what had happened because he was unconscious. For the rest of the climb and long afterwards Amandus suffered from pain in his chest, and in retrospect it seems likely that some of his ribs were broken.

They got to the skyline ; but it was not the top. The cleft ended, and ahead of them they saw a frozen waterfall. The ice hung down it in smooth translucent curtains. There was no hope whatever of hauling the sledge up there. But at the bottom of it, more welcome than anything else in the world could have been, there was a boulder projecting through the snow, and with a final effort they heaved the sledge on top of it and wedged it there, and were able at last to rest.

They sat down in a group round the sledge, and looked up at the next pitch. It seemed as if it might be the last difficulty, but it looked the worst of all. The boulder was in the middle of a little *cirque* or bowl of rock and ice which enclosed it all round, except for the narrow gap where their own tracks plunged down out of sight into the cleft. This gap framed a distant view of the fjord waters, now gleaming far below, and the sunlit peaks beyond them. Almost all of the rim of the bowl was as steep and inaccessible as the waterfall itself. But just to the right of the waterfall there was one possible way of escape, up a narrow slope which had an ice cornice at the top. The acute angle of this slope suggested that the whole of it was ice, like the fall, and not snow ; but it was the only way out of the bowl which was even worth attempting.

As it turned out, this was the only part of the climb which was really rather easier than it looked. Hard ice would have stopped the party altogether, because none of them had ice-axes, and all they could use to cut steps was the toes of their boots and the tips of their ski-sticks. But when the leaders got on to the slope, they found it was made of hard ice crystals which could be dug away without very much trouble and compacted firmly under their weight. They went up it methodically, side by side as before, hacking out two sets of steps. The slope was too long for the sixty-foot rope, and they had to stop when they had taken out all they could, and dig themselves in again to haul the sledge up after them. This was the only dangerous moment. Again, the place was safe enough for the climbers themselves. If they had slipped out of their steps, they would certainly have gone down to the bottom of the bowl without being able to save themselves, but it would not have done very much harm. For Jan, trussed up on the sledge, it was a very different matter. If they had let him go, he would have gone down much faster, head first on his back, and certainly broken his neck at the bottom. But they took the risk and got away with it again. The second pair anchored the sledge about thirty feet below the cornice. The leaders set off once more, and standing below the cornice in their final steps, they hacked at it with their sticks till they brought a length of it crashing down. They hauled themselves through the gap which they had made, and got to their feet and looked around them. They were standing at last on the icy windswept edge of the plateau. Ahead, the slopes were gentle and the snow was firm.

As soon as the sledge was clear of the cornice, the men put on their skis and the climb took on a totally different aspect. On skis they felt far more at home than on their feet, and more able to cope with any new crisis which might face them. The dilemma of which way up was less painful for Jan was also solved at last, and with his usual resilience he soon began to recover from the rough handling they had given him. The main remaining worry on their minds was simply the matter of time : the climb had

taken hours longer than they had expected, and with a thousand
feet still to go they were late for the meeting with the Mandal
men already. Jan was spared from this worry, as he was from
so many others. As he had been unconscious on and off ever
since they started, he had no idea how long they had been on
the way.

The fear of missing the Mandal men made them press on
without another rest. All four of them made themselves fast to
the sledge with short ropes tied round their waists, and they
started at top speed inland across the plateau. They had no further
doubts about the route. To get to the rendezvous they had to go
through a shallow dip which leads up to a chain of small lakes
on the watershed between Revdal and Mandal. This dip can easily
be seen from across the fjord at Furuflaten, and though none of
the four men had ever been up there before, the distant view of
the place had been familiar to them all their lives. When they were
clear of the dangerous corniced edge, they struck off diagonally
to the right up the gently rising ground. The surface was ice,
covered here and there by ripples of powdery windblown snow.

Within half an hour the dip in the skyline was in sight. They
climbed up into it and entered a little valley among low hillocks
of snow. When this valley closed in about them, and cut off the
view of the fjord and the distant mountains behind them, they
began, each in his own way, to sense for the first time the threaten-
ing atmosphere of desolation which oppresses every one of the
few people who have ever ventured on to the plateau in winter.
The size and the barren loneliness of the plateau appals the least
sensitive of travellers. From Lyngenfjord it stretches away into
Sweden and Finland, far to the eastward towards the border of
Soviet Russia, and then on again beyond the narrow lowlands of
Petsamo, to the White Sea and the vastness of Siberia. The valley
which they entered that early morning is only on the very verge
of it, and yet it is unlikely that any human being will set eyes on
that place from one decade's end to the next. Whoever does so,
especially when the plateau is under snow, becomes bitterly aware
of the hundreds of miles of featureless wilderness beyond him,
the endless horizons one after another, and every one the same ;
the unimaginable numbers of silent ice-bound valleys and sterile,

gaunt, deserted hills. Mankind has no business there. It is a
dead world, where the affairs of the human race are of no account
whatever. In war or peace, it is always the same, and always so
fiercely inimical to life that one has to think of it, when one is
enclosed within it, as an active malignant enemy. One knows
that the human body is too frail a thing to defend itself against
that kind of enemy, which attacks with hunger and frostbite and
storm-blindness. One knows all too well that the plateau can kill
a man easily and quickly and impartially, whether he is English
or German or Norwegian, or patriot or traitor. Into these dreadful surroundings the little group of men crept silently, dragging
the passive, half-conscious body of Jan behind them.

It had not been very easy to decide on a place for the meeting,
because hardly any spot on the plateau can be distinguished from
any other, and because there was no map which showed anything
more than its outline. But from Furuflaten a single steep bluff
could be seen in profile on the far horizon, and for want of anywhere better they had told the Mandal men to meet them at the
foot of it.

They came on the place almost unexpectedly, as they breasted
a little rise in the valley floor. Before them was a level area, a
hundred yards or so across, which was probably a lake or a bog
in summer. Beyond it the valley rose again to the watershed,
which was still out of sight. On the right was the bluff. It was
quite unmistakable, the only piece of black, naked vertical rock
in sight. On top of it there was a thick snow cornice like the
icing on a cake of festive richness, which they had seen with a
telescope from the other side. But down below, at its foot, in
the valley, nobody was waiting.

They stood there aghast for a moment at this failure of their
hopes. Their first thought, of course, when they saw the empty
valley, was that in spite of all their efforts they had arrived too
late and the Mandal men had gone. But it only needed a minute
or two of search to show that there were no ski tracks anywhere
in the valley bottom. Nobody had been there at all, certainly
since the last storm had abated, and probably for years.

They all jumped to the conclusion then that something had
gone wrong with their instructions about the meeting-place, and

that the Mandal men were waiting somewhere else. They had a hurried discussion, grouped round the sledge in the valley below the bluff. It seemed extremely queer that the others should have missed the landmark, which had turned out to be even more conspicuous than they expected. A forlorn hope struck them that the men might be somewhere quite close at hand, hidden perhaps in one of the shallow deceptive hollows in the valley. Someone suggested they should raise a shout. They were strangely reluctant to do so. It seemed rash to break the deathly silence of the plateau. They had been so secretive for so long that they all felt the same absurd fear : that if they shouted, they might be heard by someone who could not be trusted. Yet of course they knew it was inconceivable that anyone could be within earshot except people on the same business as themselves. After a moment's superstitious hesitation, they all shouted in unison. But the sound fell dead, muffled by the blanket of the snow ; and nobody answered.

After this, each of them set off in a different direction to search for the Mandal men, leaving Jan lying where he was. To hunt for a party of men on the plateau was not such a hopeless project as it might seem. It was not a matter of finding the men themselves, but of looking for their tracks. If the men had been standing still, it would have been perfectly futile, but a party on the move would leave tracks which could be seen from hundreds of yards away ; and in fact a search parallel to the Mandal valley could not miss them if they were there at all.

While Jan was left lying there alone, lashed to the sledge and staring at the sky, he had time to get over whatever disappointment he may have felt at the failure of the meeting, and to make up his mind to the worst that could possibly happen. As he had taken no part in the arrangements, perhaps he was not so surprised as the others that something had gone so obviously wrong. He felt it had been too much to hope for all along that there would really be men waiting for him up there, ready to take him at once to Sweden. He had never seriously pictured himself safely across the border within the next day or two. Besides, after the agony he had suffered while he was being pulled up the mountain, to be allowed to lie still was such an acute relief that nothing else seemed to matter. To lie still and rest, and perhaps to doze a little, was all he really wanted. He even felt rather glad that there was going to be some delay, and that he had not got to set off again at once. And one thing was perfectly clear to him ; whatever happened, even to save his life, he simply could not face being taken down again.

When they came back, one by one, he could see from the face of each of them before he spoke that there was no sign of the Mandal party. Amandus was the last one to return. He had been right up across the watershed, and down to the head of the tributary valley running up out of Mandal, which was the route they expected the Mandal men to take. There were no tracks leading out of it. To make doubly sure, he had skirted right round the head of it and gone out on to a sheer bastion of rock which divides the side valley from Mandal itself. From there, leaning out over a vertical drop of nearly three thousand feet, he had looked down the whole length of Mandal. He had seen the houses scattered in the bed of the valley. There was no sign of life among them.

Jan knew that the four men had stayed with him already far longer than was safe. They had to get home, quickly, or their absence was perfectly certain to be discovered, and that would be the end of them, and of him as well. Marius and the others, for their part, also knew what Jan had already made up his mind to tell them ; that it was out of the question to take him down again. It would take an impossibly long time ; they had not enough strength left to do it : and finally, they were quite certain, as he himself was, that he would not get to the bottom alive.

Thus the decision to abandon him on the plateau did not need very much discussion. There was nothing else whatever to be done. It was a bitter decision for them all, especially for Marius, who blamed himself because the meeting had been a failure. He promised Jan he would get a message through to Mandal the moment he got home, and do everything he could to make sure that the Mandal men would come up and find him the next night. But he made this promise with a heavy heart, because he did not really believe that under the open sky Jan would last through to another day. He thought all the efforts he had made were going to end in failure, and that his hopes of redeeming his own inactive part in Norway's war were never to be fulfilled.

They searched for a place to put Jan where he would have a little shelter, and they found a boulder where the wind had scooped out a hole in the snow. The hole was four feet deep, and exactly the size of a grave. They took off their skis, and lowered him down into it, sledge and all, and then untied the lashings which held him down. They gave him what little food they had, and the remains of the bottle of brandy.

After the last of them had climbed out of the hole, they stood grouped round it, looking down at the haggard, bearded, emaciated face which grinned up at them. Jan said he would be all right, and thanked them as best as he could. They hated what they were doing, and illogically hated themselves for doing it. But neither Jan nor Marius nor any of the others felt like being histrionic about it. One by one they said good-bye, and turned away to put on their skis again. Amandus, as it happened, was the last of them to go, and he always remembered the last words that were spoken, because they were so absurd.

"There's nothing else we can give you?" he asked Jan.

"No thanks," Jan said. "I've got everything. Except hot and cold water."

They began the descent, feeling sure they had left him to die.

CHAPTER ELEVEN

THE PLATEAU

THE WAR had not had very much effect upon Mandal before Herr Legland's urgent message was delivered. The place had had no interest for the Germans and they had left it alone, so that its placid and rather primitive and impoverished life went on much the same as usual. It is quite difficult for a stranger to see how the Mandal people can manage to make a living and feed and bring up families in such a forlorn and isolated home. There are millions of people, of course, even in Europe, who live happily enough without any road to connect them with civilisation, and a good many of them even prefer it. But the situation of Mandal seems to have nothing in its favour. The men go fishing, but their jetty is far away from either the fishing grounds or the open sea or the markets. They also farm, but their land is snow-covered and frozen for eight months of the year and the valley faces north : on every other side it is so steeply hemmed in by hills that the sun only shines into it when it is high. Only a little distance to the west, the Lyngen Alps attract tourists who provide a rich annual harvest ; but Mandal has no spectacular allurements to offer to visitors, and so any stranger who comes there is a nine-days' wonder.

But in spite of all this, between six and seven hundred people do live there, and they do not want to live anywhere else. They are far from rich, but their houses and farms are neat and tidy, and they themselves are not by any means lacking in self-respect. Their houses are scattered all up the valley for a distance of about ten miles from the jetty and shop at the seaward end. There is a road which connects them, and at least one motor truck which runs up and down it in summer but can never go farther afield.

A mile and a half up from the jetty is the school; and it was this
school which became the headquarters of Mandal's efforts in
rescuing Jan.

The schoolmaster, Herr Nordnes, was a local man himself
and he had lived there all his life. He was another disciple in
learning of Herr Legland, which no doubt was the reason why
Legland chose him to organise the rescue. He knew everybody
who lived in the valley, and almost everything that went on there,
and practically all the young men in the place had received the
whole of their education from him and regarded him still as their
teacher. He himself was in middle age, but there could not have
been a better choice for a job which called for the mobilisation
of the valley's youth.

When he got Legland's message and had given himself time
to think it over, he went to call on a few of his recent pupils and
told them what he had heard and what was needed. They
responded eagerly. In spite of the isolation of Mandal, and the
fact that most Mandal people had not seen a German soldier or a
German ship or even an aircraft, and had heard no authentic news
of the world outside for years, there was much of the same feeling
as on the west side of Lyngenfjord: the reason being that nobody
had had a chance so far to show what he could do to help the war.
Nordnes had no lack of volunteers. His only embarrassment was
to prevent the news spreading too quickly, and to avoid having
too many people who wanted to take some part of this novel
adventure. Yet their enthusiasm was surprising, because the
appeal for help, as it reached them, was quite impersonal. They
did not have the incentive of having seen Jan, and had no idea
what kind of person he was. The whole story was third or fourth
hand. Not even Legland had seen him, and nor had the messenger.
The only reason for thinking that he deserved their help at all
was that Legland had said so, and had told Nordnes that the man
who was in trouble had come all the way from England.

The Mandal men would have been more than human, in these
circumstances, if they had not pointed out, as their first reaction,
that to take an injured man to Sweden was not so easy as it looked.
The people in Tromsö and Lyngseidet, they thought, probably
had no real idea of the difficulties of what they were asking Mandal

to do. They might have looked at a map and seen the frontier on it, twenty-five miles away, and imagined some kind of fence with Swedish frontier guards who would take care of Jan on the spot. They probably did not realise that there was nothing there whatever, except cairns at intervals of miles, so that you could cross the border without ever knowing you had done it, and plunge down into endless forests on the Swedish side where you might be lost for weeks without seeing a house or a road. There were no defences on the frontier simply because it was so difficult to cross that no defences were needed.

Having registered their protest, and suggested quite rightly that Lapps were better qualified to make the actual journey, they were perfectly willing to try it themselves if it was really necessary; and they were willing in any case to meet the Furuflaten men at the rendezvous they suggested, and to look after the injured man when he was handed over. They almost certainly felt some satisfaction at being asked to pull chestnuts out of the fire on behalf of a place like Furuflaten, which had always affected to despise Mandal because it was not on the road.

During the week which elapsed after the first message from Legland, while the gale was blowing which imprisoned Jan in Revdal, the Mandal people heard nothing more about what was happening. They went on with the ordinary chores of early spring, and probably their first enthusiasm faded. The whole story only existed for them in the form of a single sudden visit by a messenger. It began to seem likely that the organisation had found some other way of moving their man, or that he had died or been captured, and that they were not going to be asked to do anything after all. It was disappointing, and made them feel a little foolish.

This was the situation when the second urgent message arrived by telephone. It was very obscure : the parcel Herr Nordnes was expecting was being sent at once. It told them nothing of what was happening in Furuflaten, whether the Germans were hot on the trail, or whether the man they were expected to look after was seriously ill or not. They understood, of course, that it was impossible to say more on the telephone, but it did leave them entirely in the dark. The only shade of meaning it conveyed was one of urgency; and urgency, in that context, suggested that the Germans were suspicious.

However, what it asked them to do was clear enough, and Herr Nordnes rounded up his first party of volunteers and told them the job was on again. They were all men in their early twenties, whom he had chosen because they had been intelligent and resourceful at school, and because they were fit and strong. There had never been any question of him climbing up to the plateau himself, partly because he was a generation older than the climbers he had chosen and would only have held them back, and more especially because he was one of the very few people in Mandal who had to be at work exactly on time in the morning. But his volunteers were still willing, and all said they could make the climb that night. There was still no news of the Lapps from the ski-runner who had set off from Kaafjord to find them; but at least they could take charge of Furuflaten's stranger till they heard if the Lapps were coming. Each of them went off to make his preparations: to change his clothes and wax his skis and pack a rucksack, and perhaps to get a little sleep before he started.

It was at this precise moment that a strange boat was sighted approaching Mandal. This was a very rare event, and plenty of people watched the boat, some with telescopes and binoculars, from the houses near the bottom of the valley. As it approached the jetty, they saw something which was to put the whole valley in a state of turmoil and apprehension: there was a party of German soldiers on board it. The boat reached the jetty, and the Germans came ashore; and a number of people who were in the know put on their skis and pelted up to the schoolhouse to warn Herr Nordnes. As the news spread up the valley, all the people he had consulted began to converge on the school to talk about this sinister development.

They all took it for granted that it had something to do with the plot which was afoot. It seemed certain that the organisation in Furuflaten had been broken up, and that the Germans knew that Mandal was involved in it; or else that somebody higher in the organisation, in Tromsö perhaps, had been arrested and that the Germans were planning a simultaneous raid both sides of the mountain. At all events, it would have been crazy to make

the climb that night, before the Germans had shown some sign
of what they meant to do. Herr Nordnes himself knew that his
own name was the only one in Mandal so far which anyone
outside could connect with the affair, and he did the only thing
he could do : he told all the others to stay at home and say
nothing ; and for himself, he resolved that if he was arrested he
would try not to give them away whatever was done to him.

That evening, the people of Mandal watched every move
which the Germans made ; but they seemed to be in no hurry
to do anything at all. The second wave of news which spread
up the valley reported that there were only six soldiers and an
n.c.o. This seemed to suggest that they had come to arrest one
single individual. But later rumour said that they were taking
over a house as a billet, down by the jetty. Nobody knew whether
it was for one night or for good, but obviously if there was going
to be an arrest, it was not going to happen before nightfall. That
night while Marius and his party were hauling the sledge up
Revdal and searching the plateau, nobody was sleeping soundly
in Mandal, except perhaps the Germans. When Amandus looked
down from the top of the buttress in the early morning, the silent
houses he saw far down below him were kept silent by anxiety
and fear.

But during the night nothing happened at all. The Germans
stayed in their billet, and in the morning they sallied forth and
began a house-to-house check of all the inhabitants of Mandal.
On the whole this relieved the tension. It pointed to a general
vague suspicion of Mandal as a whole, rather than something
definite against a particular person. But it meant that nobody
could go away from home until the check of his own house had
been completed, and to judge by the desultory way that the
Germans went to work, this would put a stop to any journey to
the frontier for several days. It also made it impossible for the
present for anyone to go over to Lyngseidet by boat to find out
what had happened ; and even to ring up Herr Legland would
be asking for trouble, in case he had been arrested.

The whole thing remained a mystery all that day. Whatever
way Nordnes and the other conspirators looked at it, it was hard
to believe that after years without a garrison, the sudden arrival

of even a section of Germans on the very evening when the ascent of the plateau was planned could be simply a coincidence. Yet nothing the Germans did, once they had landed, seemed to have any bearing on the plot, or to suggest in any way that they knew what was going on.

This particular mystery, as it happened, was never solved. To this day it still seems incredible that the Germans arrived there by chance ; yet there is no reason to think they had any suspicion, at that particular moment, that Jan had been taken across to the east side of Lyngenfjord. The last time they had seen him was when he was ski-ing through Lyngseidet, and that was nearly three weeks earlier. But perhaps the fact that he had slipped through their grasp and disappeared had brought it home to somebody in the local command that the routes to the frontier were not very well controlled. Perhaps somebody else had had a rap on the knuckles. The somewhat pathetic little garrison sent to Mandal, as well as the motor-boats which suddenly appeared on Lyngenfjord, may have been part of a general tightening of the grip on the frontier, an indirect result of Jan's journey rather than a deliberate search for him. If anyone knows the answer to this, it can only be some German officer.

However, the immediate mystery for Herr Nordnes was cleared up to some extent by an urgent message which arrived that night. It had come by a devious route, but it had originated from Marius, and it told Nordnes that Jan had been left at the meeting-place on the plateau and begged him to have him collected without delay. It also told him, by the mere fact that it had been sent, that there was nothing wrong in the rest of the organisation and that they did not even know that the Germans had come to Mandal. He went out to round up his team again, and to see whether they thought it was safe to start at once. But before the point was decided, it began to snow.

Standing outside the schoolhouse in Mandal, one can see almost the whole of the route to the plateau which they intended to use. As Marius and Amandus had expected, it lies up the side valley which leads out of Mandal on its southern side. This lesser valley is called Kjerringdal, the word *kjerring* meaning an old woman or hag, to correspond with the man of Mandal. Kjerringdal rises steeply, in a series of gleaming curved terraces of snow, and in spring almost the whole of it is swept by avalanches ; but there is one route up it clear of the avalanche tracks which is known to the local men. It ends in a wide couloir. From Mandal the rim of the couloir stands against the sky, three thousand feet above ; and two miles beyond the rim is the place where Jan was lying.

That night, the snow clouds gathered first above the head of Mandal, and then, even as Nordnes and his men were watching them and debating the weather, they swept up from the south across the plateau, and poured over the edge of the couloir and down into Kjerringdal. Minute by minute they grew thicker and nearer, blotting out the high terraces one by one, till the clouds from Kjerringdal joined with the ones from Mandal and swirled round the vertical crag which divides the two valleys. A few moments later they were overhead, and the snow began to fall, softly and thickly, on the floor of the valley where the men were standing. Soon there was nothing but snowflakes to be seen.

None of them liked to think of a man lying ill and unprotected and helpless up there in the heart of the clouds ; but falling snow put an end to whatever hopes they had had of reaching him for the present. The German garrison might have been avoided, and even in snow the ascent of Kjerringdal might not have been impossible ; but to find the meeting-place would have been out of the question. Nobody in Mandal knew exactly where it was. They would have to depend on seeing the steep bluff which the Furuflaten message had described, and to begin to search for it when they could not see more than a few yards in front of them would be futile and suicidal. There was nothing for it but to wait till the snowstorm ended.

It went on snowing all night, and all the morning. Going about their business in the valley the following day none of them had much hope for the man on the top of the mountain. Perhaps they regretted then they had not gone up on the night that the Germans came. As it turned out, they could have done it without being caught ; but nobody could have known that at the time. Now, everything depended on the snow. They were ready to go the moment it showed the first sign of easing. It was simply a question of whether the man would survive till then.

The chance came on the third night after Marius had left Jan up there. There were breaks in the cloud that evening, and the local men, with their knowledge of Mandal weather, believed it would be clear before the morning. The party of four volunteers assembled. The Germans had been watched and counted to make sure they were all out of sight in the billet at the foot of the valley. Everything seemed auspicious.

The ascent of Kjerringdal went off without any serious trouble, though under the best of conditions it is not a safe or easy climb at that time of year. From time to time Nordnes caught sight of the men toiling on up the valley, picking their course to avoid the avalanche tracks. After four hours, on skis all the way, they got to the rim of the plateau. The snow had stopped by then, as they had hoped, and they struck off right-handed to make the level trek across the watershed and then down towards Revdal.

They saw the steep bluff well ahead of them. A series of gentle gullies and frozen lakes led down to the foot of it, and they ran down into the shallow valley which Marius and his party had reached three nights before. The fresh snow which had fallen lay thick over everything. The valley seemed just as deserted and still as the rest of the plateau. There were no tracks and no sign whatever that anyone had ever been there. They searched the foot of the bluff, and the whole of the valley bed above it and below, but they could not find anything at all. They scoured the plateau round about, shouting, but there was no answer. For two hours they hunted far and wide ; but then they had to give it up and make back for the head of Kjerringdal again, in order to be at home before the Germans began their day's work of checking the houses. The ski-run down Kjerringdal was very fast, and they were back in Mandal by the time the place was stirring.

When they all talked over this night's expedition with Nordnes, the only conclusion they could come to was that the man who had been left up there had gone off somewhere by himself. They still knew very little about him. They had heard he was crippled, but for all they could tell, he might still have been able to drag himself along. It seemed most likely that when the snow had started, he had tried to get down again on the Revdal side to look for shelter. It had also crossed their minds, of course, that he might have died and been buried by the snow. In fact, they thought anyone who had stayed on the plateau for the past three days would almost certainly be dead; but they dismissed the idea that he had died anywhere near the rendezvous, because they thought they would have found his body. There had not been any avalanche up there, and there was very little drifting, and they would have expected a dead man's body to show as a visible mound on the snowfield. Even if he had dug himself in and then been buried, there should have been something to show where he had done it. But there was nothing at all. He had simply disappeared.

For all practical purposes, Mandal just then was entirely cut off from the outside world. The Germans had been making strict inquiries about anyone they found was not at home, and they expected an explanation of where every man was and what he was doing. Until they had finished their slow and laborious progress from house to house up the whole of the valley, it was obvious that they would not let anyone leave it; and Nordnes could not send a messenger over the fjord to tell Herr Legland what had happened. He could not use the telephone, either. It had always been tapped on and off, and it was sure to be tapped, or simply cut off, while the German search was going on; and the whole mystery was too complicated to discuss in disguised language without any pre-arranged code. If Nordnes had been able to have five minutes' conversation with Marius, everything would have been easy, but they might as well have been on different continents; and besides, at that time neither of them knew who was the organiser of the other village's part in the affair. The only way of communication between them was through Legland, and for the present that way was blocked.

Without any help or advice from outside, the only thing the Mandal men could do was to try again. A second party therefore made the long climb on the following night, the fourth since Jan had been abandoned on the plateau. They regarded it as almost a hopeless effort; but Mandal, in the person of Herr Nordnes, had promised it would do its best, and besides, while there was any chance at all that there was a man alive up there, none of them could have slept easily in their beds.

This time, when they got to the valley below the bluff, it was still covered with the ski-tracks from the night before. They extended the search farther down towards the edge of the drop into Revdal, and inland across the plateau. Every few yards they broke the oppressive silence of the plateau with a shout, and listened while it died again to silence.

Somebody had decided on a password which had been given both to Jan and the Mandal men. Presumably as a tribute to Jan's English training, the Mandal men were to identify themselves to him by saying, " Hallo, gentleman." People in Norway often suppose that the word gentleman can be used as a form of address in the singular, as indeed it could if there were any logic in the English language. That night the plateau rang with this repeated cry; but nobody in either Mandal or Furuflaten spoke any English at all, and so there was nobody there who would have thought it odd or ludicrous; except Jan, and he could not hear it. Towards morning, the party retreated again by way of Kjerringdal without finding anything. As they went down, the weather was worsening.

This second sortie had made it clear that it was no use to search any more without some kind of consultation with Furuflaten. To put a final end to any thought of another expedition, the snow began again, and during the day the wind got up and increased to a blizzard. This was far worse than the calm snowfall of two days before. In the sheltered valley, the temperature fell abruptly and visibility was restricted, and any outside work became impossible. On the plateau, as the Mandal people knew from generations of experience, no search party would have a hope of finding anything; it would be all they could do to move at all against the wind, or in fact, after a very short time, even to keep themselves alive.

But the blizzard did have one helpful consequence, in that it hampered the German troops as much as anyone. They could not keep their eye any longer on the whole of the foot of the valley, even if they did venture out into the blinding snow; and under the unexpected cover of this storm, a skier slipped out of the valley and brought the news of Mandal's plight to friends in Kaafjord. From there, after a day's delay in which a boat was found which could cross the fjord in such wild weather, the news reached Herr Legland, and he sent a message at once to Marius.

This message undoubtedly was a terrible shock to Marius. It reached him in Furuflaten when the blizzard was still at its height and had already been blowing for days. It meant only one thing to him: that after all Jan had suffered, and all that had been risked for him, he was dead. It was exactly a week since Marius had said good-bye to him when he put him in the snow-grave on the plateau. All that time, as he had not heard any more, he had taken it for granted that the Mandal men had found him, and he had even thought of him safe already in a Swedish hospital. It was dreadful for Marius to think that nobody had ever come to take him out of that hole again. His own knowledge of the Arctic mountains, and the wisdom he had learned from older people, all made him certain that nobody had ever survived, or ever could survive, a week of snow and storm on the plateau, under the open sky. He could have wept to think of the pitifully inadequate protection Jan had had: two blankets, and a canvas bag which was not even waterproof, and not more than a day's supply of food. He hated to think what Jan must have thought of him when he knew his end was coming.

Marius's imagination would not let him rest on the day when he got the message. He took the news round to all the people he could tell, those who had helped in different ways. They were all of the same opinion: that it was a pity it had to end that way, but after all, everyone had done his best. Nobody even suggested that Jan might still be alive. Yet Marius knew all the time, in the back of his mind, that he would have to go up to the plateau again that night, whatever the weather, and whatever the risk of being seen and arrested by the Germans when it was really too late to matter. Of course he had not forgotten the solemn promise he had made to Jan; and assuming that Jan was dead, the promise had been broken. He had to go, if only to see for himself. He disliked the idea of leaving Jan's body up there where it lay, till the spring thaw exposed the last remains of it. He wondered if Jan would have left him a message, written on paper perhaps, which the thaw would destroy. Perhaps he had some idea, as people do when the death of a friend leaves them remorseful, of making his peace with Jan by going to look at his body. At any rate, whether it was rational or not, and whether it was suicidally dangerous or not, he knew he was going.

It was a question who would come with him. To go alone would have added a lot to the danger : two people on a mountain in a blizzard are always more than twice as safe as one. But of the three men who had been with him before, Alvin Larsen and Olaf Lanes were away again fishing, and probably storm-stayed somewhere down the coast, and Amandus Lillevoll was having such pain with his broken ribs that it was foolish to think of him making the climb again. There were no other men in the village in the know, only women : his own sisters and mother, and the families of the men who had come with him.

Olaf Lanes had several sisters, and one of them was called Agnethe. Agnethe knew Marius well, and she was fond of him, and so was he of her. When she heard that he was determined to go that night, she knew quite well that if nobody else would go with him, he would go alone ; and rather than let him do that, she went and told him firmly that she was coming too. Probably if any other girl had said the same thing, he would have refused her offer without a second thought. It was certainly not an expedition for a girl. But Agnethe was as good as any man on skis, and she was strong as well as pretty ; and, perhaps even more important, she was the only person that day who really understood the whole depth of what he was feeling, and agreed with him that it was right to go. He possibly needed sympathy just then even more than physical help. She offered him both, and he was grateful ; and because there was really no sensible alternative, he agreed to let her come.

At dusk, which was all that was left by then of the vanishing nights, these two embarked on what was to be the last crossing of Lyngenfjord to Revdal. Amandus had come with them to help them to handle the boat and to look after it at Revdal. The crossing was wet and wild, and the small boat under sail was beaten down by heavy squalls from the mountains. But at least it was hidden from German eyes as long as the snow went on falling. They reached the other shore drenched and cold but safe, and beached the boat about half a mile south of Revdal. Agnethe and Marius landed.

They took a new route up the mountain. It looked easier for unladen climbers than the one which Marius had taken with the sledge, but it included some pitches of simple rock climbing, in narrow chimneys, on which the sledge would have been a hopeless hindrance. Marius looked after Agnethe with affection and admiration, but she needed no help from him. On rock she was more agile than he was, and perhaps she was even more anxious to reach the plateau and see the worst, so that his mind would be set at rest.

They climbed the first steep two thousand feet very quickly. But on the steep face they were more or less in shelter. When they had almost got up to the rim of the plateau, they began to hear a new note in the wind above them, and when they looked up through the murk they could see the snow blowing over the edge. It looked like hard grey pellets, and it shot over in jets with a power and speed which warned them that the dangerous part of the climb was only beginning.

When they crossed the rim and stood up on the level surface beyond it, the wind snatched at their clothes and threw them off their balance and drowned their voices. The air was so full of whirling particles of snow that it took their breath away and they felt as if they were suffocating. Both of them, of course, were properly dressed, in windproof trousers and anaraks with hoods; but the snow lashed the exposed parts of their faces with such violent pain that they could not bear to turn unprotected into the wind. Marius shouted to Agnethe, half-persuaded himself that what they were doing was madness; but she was already untying her skis, which had been bound together for carrying. She dropped them on the shifting surface, and bent down to buckle on the bindings.

The way for the last three miles from there to the rendezvous was against the wind. If it had not been so, it certainly would have been more than foolish to go on, because of the danger of over-reaching themselves and being unable to return. They pulled their hoods down as far as they would go, and covered their mouths with their hands to ward off the snow and make breathing possible. Marius set off in the lead, because he knew the way, and marched on with his head bent low, snatching a painful glance ahead of him now and then. Agnethe followed close after him in his tracks. Neither of them could see normally or hear anything but the howling of the wind, and their sense of touch was numbed by cold. When the senses are numbed, a mental numbness cannot be avoided. In this state they went on and on, yard by yard into the wilderness, thinking no farther ahead than the next step and the one after that. They climbed with that thoughtless stubbornness, against all reason, which is often the mainspring of great deeds : Marius driven on by his own compelling conscience, and Agnethe by her sympathy and love.

When they came to the bluff they could see the loom of it above them through the snow-mist ; but even Marius had to hesitate before he could find the boulder where Jan had been laid. Everything was changed. The fresh snowfall and the high wind had made new drifts, exposed new rocks and hidden others. The boulder which had stood conspicuously clear of the surface was almost buried, and in the lee of it, where the open hole had been, there was now a smooth windswept surface. The puzzle of why the Mandal men had found nothing there was solved : there was nothing whatever to be seen. Yet Marius felt certain of his bearings. He was sure he had found the right boulder, and that Jan could not have moved, and that therefore, his body was buried far down below that virgin surface. He took off his skis and went down on his knees in the soft snow and began to dig. He scratched the snow away with his hands. Agnethe crouched beside him in an agony of cold. She was exhausted.

When Marius had dug away three feet of snow, the rest collapsed into a cavity underneath, and he knew he was right. He cleared it away, and saw Jan's ghastly waxen face below him. The eyes were shut, and the head was covered with rime.

" Don't look," he said to Agnethe. " He's dead."

At the sound of his voice, Jan stirred.

"I'm not dead, damn you," he said, in a feeble voice but with every sign of indignation.

Then he opened his eyes, and saw the astounded face of Marius peering down at him, and he grinned.

"You can't kill an old fox," he said.

CHAPTER TWELVE

BURIED ALIVE

NOBODY CAN give an exact account of what happened to Jan during all the weeks he spent lying alone on the plateau. By the time he had leisure to look back on it, his memory was confused. He had the same difficulty that one has in trying to bring back to mind the events and one's feelings during a serious illness; and in fact, of course, he was seriously ill all the time. Some incidents and impressions were perfectly clear to him, but as he remembered them they had no context; they were isolated, like distant memories of childhood, and he had only a hazy idea of what had led up to them, or what followed after. But most of the episodes he remembered were confirmed in one way or another by the people who visited him up there from time to time. In general, oddly enough, he had no impression of being bored. Once when somebody asked him how he had passed the time, he said he had never been so busy in his life. And one thing, at least, which is perfectly certain is the length of time his extraordinary ordeal lasted. He lay in the sleeping-bag in the snow for no less than 27 consecutive days, from the night of the 25th of April, when Marius took him up to the plateau, till the night of the 22nd of May, when they were to carry him down again in despair.

That first week, in the snow grave, was the worst in some respects, partly because he was not so used to that way of living as he became towards the end, and partly because he was forced to believe, for the second time, that his friends had abandoned him, or lost him, or all been killed themselves. He did not think he would ever get out of the grave again.

At first, he had been so relieved to be allowed to lie still that he said good-bye to Marius and the other three men without any fear of another spell of solitude. He settled down in the sleeping-bag on the sledge, with the wall of snow on one side of him and the rock on the other, and the small segment of sky up above, and he thought he would go to sleep. But only too soon this mood of contentment was driven away by the cold. It was much too cold to sleep. During the climb the sleeping-bag and the blankets had got wet, and in the hole in the snow the moisture froze them stiff. They were to remain either wet or frozen for the whole of the time he was there, and he discovered one thing at once which was to plague him through all those weeks : he could never sleep, because the cold always woke him and he had to keep moving inside the blankets to ward off another attack of frostbite. At the best, he could only fall into an uneasy doze.

Apart from the cold, the sledge made a very uncomfortable bed. It had been a mistake to make the top out of narrow slats with spaces in between them. There were only two layers of blankets and one of canvas, besides his clothes, between him and the wooden slats ; and because he had to keep moving he soon got sores all over his back and sides which made the discomfort infinitely worse.

During the first two days and night, before it began to snow, he kept imagining that among the occasional whispering sounds of the plateau he heard the hiss of skis. Sometimes he shouted to the people he thought were there. But this was not the kind of hallucination he had had after the avalanche. On the plateau, his brain was quite clear. Perhaps the sounds were made by little snowballs rolling down the snow-covered scree at the foot of the bluff above him.

As soon as it started to snow, on the second night he lay in the hole, he knew that his chance of being found was very small, at least till the snow stopped falling ; and there was an extra worry added to this, because at about the same time he finished the few bits of food they had left him, and he was beginning to get very hungry.

By that time his movements and the heat of his body had made a cavity in the snow, and the sledge had sunk deeper than it had been. The fresh snowfall soon covered his body. He could brush it off his face and his head, but in the narrow hole he could not throw it off the rest of him. Slowly it sifted over his trunk and legs till they were encased in a kind of tunnel, bridged over by a thickening layer of snow which he could not move. For some hours he kept a hole clear to the surface above his head, so that he could still see the open air above him. But the snow grew deeper and deeper till he could not reach up to the surface any more even with his arm stretched out above him. Then the snow closed over the opening, and buried him alive.

He was buried for either four or five days. What kept him alive is a mystery. It was not hope, because he had none, and it was not any of the physical conditions which are usually supposed to be essential to human life. Perhaps it is nearest to the truth to put his survival down to a stubborn distaste for dying in such gruesome circumstances.

He lay on his back in a little vault in the snow. At the sides and above his body there were a few inches of space, and above his head there was over a foot, but there was not enough room for him to draw up his knees or reach down to touch his feet. A dim light filtered down from above, like the light below the surface of the sea. He had no trouble in breathing, because the snow above him was fresh and porous, but he lay all the time in fear that the roof would fall in and pin his arms down and cover his mouth and choke him.

He could imagine quite well the change that had taken place on the surface of the plateau in such a heavy snowfall, and he knew that even if the Mandal men did come to look for him, it was very unlikely that they would find him before the summer thaw exposed his body. Of course, he knew he could not live till then, because in the first stages of the thaw the snow would become compacted and impervious and he would be very, very slowly suffocated.

The only vestige of physical comfort he had in all this time was his dregs of the bottle of brandy. There was not very much in it when he was left there, but as he was weak and starving, less than a mouthful of it was enough to make him slightly drunk. He made it last out for some time after the food was gone. When everything became intolerable he had the bottle to think about.

He would put off taking a sip for hours, so that he could enjoy
the anticipation of the warmth going down his throat ; and when
at last he grasped the precious bottle, and wrestled weakly with
the cork, and struggled in the confines of the grave to tilt it to
his mouth, the spoonful of raw spirit dulled his pains and made
the next hour or two slip past more easily. At times he was even
struck by the humour of lying buried in one's grave and swig-
ging a bottle of brandy. But of course the moment came when
there was only one more spoonful in the bottle. This he kept as
if it were his only link with life, and it was still there when Marius
relieved him.

There was one benefit of being buried. Certainly it prevented
the Mandal men from finding him, and thereby was nearly the
end of him ; but to compensate for this, it protected him from
everything that happened on the surface. If he had been exposed,
the blizzard after the snowfall would have killed him ; but in his
grave he was no more aware of the howling wind than he was
of the shouts of the Mandal party. The blizzard blew over him,
but down in the vault in the snow it was always perfectly silent
and perfectly calm, and the temperature was always steady, a few
degrees below zero.

So he lay while the days and nights passed over. He had no
inclination by then to indulge himself with daydreams, or to
philosophise as he had in the hut at Revdal. His mind was
occupied with the minute details of physical existence : to keep
moving, to be on the watch for frostbite, to try to ease the pain
of his feet and the sores on his back ; to try the impossible task
of keeping his body in some state of sanitation ; to stop the snow
roof falling down, to prevent the bottle of brandy falling over.
Each of these tasks became an absorbing activity which occupied
him for hours on end, and each one of them was an important
part of his conscious effort not to die. He added to them, typically,
the task of cleaning the revolver which he still wore in its holster.
When any of the tasks were accomplished for the moment, he felt
he had warded off death for a few more minutes. He sometimes
visualised death as a physical being who prowled about him. He
parried the lunges this creature made at him, and he was proud
of himself when he thrust off another of its attacks. It did not

occur to him then that he might have welcomed death's more
compassionate advances.

When Marius broke through the snow above him he was
dozing, and he heard his voice in a dream, as he often had before.
In the dream he was annoyed that the voice said he was dead.
It seemed too bad of Marius to suggest that he had lost the
battle with death, when he had been trying so hard to win it,
so he denied it hotly. Then he opened his eyes and it was real :
and Marius looked so surprised that he laughed and, half-
conscious, he said out loud the Norwegian proverb which had
been running in his head. " You can't kill an old fox, you know.
You can't kill an old fox."

This voice from the dead did in fact almost paralyse Marius
for a moment while he reorganised his thoughts. A surge of relief
made his heart beat faster ; but immediately after it came the fore-
knowledge of the problems which had come to life again with
Jan. Jan himself was beyond being surprised by then by anything
that happened : it did not strike him as particularly strange,
though it was pleasant, to see a hooded and yet unmistakably
feminine and attractive face looking down at him by the side of
Marius. Marius and Agnethe scraped away more snow till Marius
could climb down into the hole and clear a space round Jan so
that he had a little more freedom to move about. He had brought
food with him, more as an offering to fate than with any hope of
using it. He fed Jan with bread and bits of fish, while he was
explaining how the Mandal men had tried to find him. He had
also brought more brandy and some tobacco. Jan could not eat
much, but he had a craving for a cigarette, and Marius rolled him
one and crouched over him to shelter him while he lit it.

Puffing at this cigarette, while the snow drifted into the hole
and the wind shrieked overhead in the grey half-darkness, Jan
began to feel almost himself again. It was the belief that he was
forgotten that always brought him down to his lowest depths.
Now his own hardships faded, and he noticed that Agnethe was
in terrible distress. By then, in fact, she was so cold that she could
hardly speak. As soon as Jan realised what she was suffering,
and all on his behalf, he insisted that they should leave him and

get down to the fjord again while they were still able to do it.

Marius himself knew he could not do any good by staying. The only useful thing he could do was to go down and make perfectly certain, as quickly as possible of getting a large enough party up from one side of the mountain or the other to move Jan away from where he was. The message from Mandal had said they would make the climb again as soon as the weather allowed it. Marius told Jan of this, and to help them to find him if they did come he made a flag by tying a piece of cloth to a ski-stick which he stuck in the snow by the side of the hole. So, after staying with Jan for only half an hour, they left him again with this forlorn signal flapping wildly in the storm above him.

As ever, Marius's unrelenting conscience asked him whether he had done all that was humanly possible, and this time he had to admit to himself that he had not. There was still the slight chance that the Mandal men might be on their way up at that very minute. It was true that the weather had not improved at all, but he felt that he ought to be there, just in case they had chosen to come that night, to make sure that they found the flag. He could not afford to waste time by waiting. The only way to make sure of it quickly was to go on towards Mandal and see if they were coming. Accordingly, instead of turning back down the wind and downhill towards Revdal and home, he and Agnethe faced up into the wind again and climbed on towards the watershed.

In those awful conditions, this was a very brave thing to do, and like many brave and admirable deeds it was also foolhardy. Agnethe agreed with it willingly when Marius proposed it, but she very nearly died as a result. They reached the watershed, fighting against the wind for every step. Up there, they lost their way, but were saved by a sudden momentary clearance. They pressed on and got right across to the rim of the couloir at the head of Kjerringdal. Here there is a small isolated rock from which one can see in clear weather right down to the bottom of Mandal. Marius clung to the lee of this rock and peered down into the depths below. This was the point at which the Mandal men would come up out of Kjerringdal on to the plateau. But that night, although it was light by then, he could only see a few yards down the valley through the scudding snow. There was nobody in sight. While he was searching over the edge, Agnethe collapsed by the side of the rock behind him. When he saw her and turned back to her in alarm, he found she was unconscious.

Both their lives depended then on whether he could revive her, because of course he would never have left her. He set about it in the most drastic way. He shook her limp body, and hit her and slapped her face. He believed, he said afterwards, that apart from anything else this would make her angry, and that anger would improve her circulation. Whether this was the way it worked or not, it did bring her back to consciousness, and as soon as she gave any sign of life he dragged her to her feet and started off, half-carrying her, determined, whatever happened, to keep her on the move.

Luckily, going down-wind was infinitely easier than going against it, and once they had got back the first mile across the watershed the rest of the way was downhill. Luckily also, although the climb and the cold had used up the last of Agnethe's physical strength, she had an unlimited strength of will. Many people who are exhausted by exposure lose even the will to help those who try to rescue them. If Agnethe had resisted the rough treatment Marius gave her as he hauled her and bullied her along, or if she had ever succumbed to the insidious temptation to give up, neither of them would ever have been seen alive again. But there was a tough arctic quality in the girl which kept her going, and between them they won through to the head of Revdal and staggered down to the shore where Amandus was keeping the boat.

The climb did her no permanent physical harm, but the memory of the sight of Jan lying in the hole was to haunt her for years. It had been such a terrible sight that she thought when she saw him that he had nothing left to live for and would have been better dead.

CHAPTER THIRTEEN

ATTEMPT ON THE FRONTIER

WHEN A message reached Mandal to say that Jan was still up on
the plateau and still alive, they began to make final preparations
for an all-out attempt on the frontier as soon as the blizzard died
down. For the last few days, they had not been expecting to have
to try it, because when they looked up towards the loom of the
mountains through the wildly driving snow, it was incredible
that up there, away beyond the very top of Kjerringdal, there
could be a man still living. But the fact that he had survived so
far made it seem all the more worth while to try to save him.
The preparations were rather grim. They knew they were
running a big risk of never coming back, either because of some
disaster on the plateau or through getting lost or interned in
Sweden. But if a sick man could exist on the plateau, it would
have been a disgrace to admit that four fit men could not try to
move him across it to safety.

The plan for getting the Lapps to help had fallen through, at
least for the time being. The ski-runner who had gone out from
Kaafjord to look for them had come back, just missing the worst
of the blizzard, but the news he had brought was discouraging.
The reindeer were still much farther away than they usually were
at that time of year. He had followed their migration track back
across the plateau to the south-east for over fifty miles before he
sighted the vast herds, halted and digging for the moss beneath
the snow. The Lapps he was looking for were camped among
them in their deerskin tents.

He was criticised afterwards for not having made allowance
for the queer psychology of Lapps. He had broached the subject
of Jan and the journey to the frontier while he was sitting with

the Lapps in a tent which was full of women and children ; and the Lapps had simply refused to say yes or no. They were friendly, as Lapps always are, but they would not give the least sign of whether they might be willing, or even whether they really understood what they were being asked to do. People who knew the Lapps well, being wise after the event, said they would never commit themselves to any decision while their families were listening.

Certainly the mental processes of Lapps are very strange. They do not seem to grasp the idea of expressing an opinion. On a matter of fact which is within their own experience they will be quite dogmatic and clear-headed ; but their minds do not work in terms of probabilities, and if they are asked whether something is likely to happen, they are genuinely puzzled and think the question is foolish. People tell the story of a Norwegian tourist who wanted to fish for salmon and asked a Lapp if he thought he would be able to get one in a particular local river ; and the Lapp, who knew him well, shook his head with a sigh, and answered : " Really, I sometimes think you Norwegians are crazy. How could I answer a question like that ? Of course there are plenty of salmon in the river, but why should you think I can tell you if you can catch them ? "

This curious limitation naturally makes it difficult for a Lapp to make up his mind what he is going to do. When there is a question of immediate action, provided it is something to do with reindeer or the technique of wresting a living from the Arctic, he may be a shrewder man than anyone ; and he can think ahead in terms of the unalterable cycles of nature, the rising and setting of the sun, the seasons and the movements of the deer. But in other matters, he is no good at all at planning things far ahead.

So the question which was put to the Kaafjord Lapps was one which they were probably incapable of answering. The ski-runner did not ask them to come at once, because he knew they could not leave their reindeer, and the herds could not be hurried. The question was whether they would help Jan when they arrived with the herds at Kaafjord, and this was too far ahead for them to contemplate. It probably bogged their minds in impossible speculations. Endless imponderable ideas would have upset them and confused them : their reindeer might be sick, the weather might be bad, they might be sick themselves : anything might happen. Nobody, in fact, could have promised more at that moment than that he would do his best when the time came, and a Lapp either cannot think in such vague terms or cannot express them in language. His answer must be precise and literal. A Lapp could only say, quite definitely : " When I get to Kaafjord, I will take a man to Sweden"; and to say a thing like that would be absurd. After all, a Lapp would reason, by that time the man might be dead ; and then, if he had said he was going to take him to Sweden, he would look ridiculous.

So for the present this scheme was at a standstill. The people in Kaafjord still hoped that when the first Lapps actually arrived there, they would be able to persuade them to do the job. But the migration was late already, and the blizzard would hold it up still further. None of the herds would get there for three or four days, at least, after the weather improved. The Mandal people thought this was too long to wait, especially on the mere chance that any Lapps would agree.

The blizzard, in fact, began to moderate on the day after Marius and Agnethe made their expedition, and on the following night a third party of volunteers made the ascent of Kjerringdal. They took with them everything they could muster for a long journey, but nobody in Mandal possessed the proper equipment for a winter encampment on the plateau. The Lapps, primitive though they are, would have been far more suitably fitted out, with tents of hide, and clothes of reindeer skin with the hair left on, and with centuries of experience of going to ground when the Arctic weather was at its worst. In fact, the most elaborate civilised camping outfit would be less suited to those Arctic uplands than the Lapps' equipment, which is entirely home-made of various parts of reindeer ; and the best which could be found in Mandal was far from elaborate. Nobody even had a tent, or a stove which would burn in a wind, because nobody in living memory had ever needed to make such a winter journey. But in a place like Mandal, people never waste time in wishing for things which they have not got ; they make do with what comes to hand. They could only hope the weather would not be bad.

As soon as they got within sight of the meeting-place that night, they saw the flag. They hurried down towards it on their skis, shouting the password, " Hallo, gentleman ! " For the first time, Jan heard this joyful and comic greeting, and he shouted " Hallo, there ! " in reply ; and in a minute his solitary grave was surrounded by helpful strangers who hacked away its walls and dragged him bodily out on the sledge to the world which he had not seen for a week and had not expected ever to see again.

Those of the men who had been there on either of the earlier climbs were amazed that they had not found him. They thought they had actually skied over the top of him while he was buried there ; and this is not impossible, even though he never heard them, because four feet of snow absorbs a lot of sound, and his senses were probably not so acute as he may have thought they were.

Without wasting more time than it took to explain to him what they were doing, they lashed him to the sledge again and started off on their desperate bid to cross the plateau on the way to the Swedish border. When they climbed out of the valley, their hopes were high, because they had found him without the delay of searching. Even Jan, who had learnt not to hope for much, was cautiously happy to be on the move again, and could not help thinking how few were the miles between himself and Sweden.

But from the beginning, their progress was very slow. The plateau is much more difficult ground for man-hauling a sledge than the flat ice-fields of the Arctic and Antarctic. None of the plateau is flat. It is covered all over with miniature hills and valleys. Hardly any of the hills are more than one or two hundred feet above the valleys, but one is always going either uphill or down. This is no obstacle to a skier, because the time which he loses in climbing is made up on the free runs down. But the sledge could never be allowed to run. Hauling it up the hills was slow, and going down again it always had to be checked so that it did not get out of control. Both were equally tiring. Once, the sledge did get away on a downward slope, and Jan careered madly down the hill, feet first, lashed down and helpless. But luckily the slope was smooth and the sledge did not overturn, but came to rest on a level snowfield at the bottom, with the breathless skiers chasing close behind it.

The maze of little hills, jumbled together without any form or pattern, also destroy any sense of direction. It is impossible to keep a straight compass course. Probably the best way to steer is by the sun, but when the sky is heavily overcast, as it was on that day, one has to stop every few minutes to take bearings. In normally open country, one can take a bearing of a landmark two or three miles away, and then make towards it. But on the plateau, one can seldom see far ahead and there are seldom any recognisable landmarks. If one happens from one hilltop to sight a conspicuous rock on a distant skyline, one loses it again in the valleys, and before one has reached it it seems to have disappeared. There is only one way to avoid making useless deviations, and that is to stop at the top of each tiny hill or ridge and take a bearing of some stone or fold in the snow on the next, which may be only a hundred yards away. It takes time, and a lot of patience.

As the four men, with Jan's helpless body dragging through the snow, crept farther and farther into this wilderness, steering south towards Sweden, the endless hills which were still ahead of them, with their endless petty checks and obstacles, began to seem like an impenetrable web. In forcing a way through them, they were not limited by the mountaineer's usual worry of being benighted. There was still a fortnight before the sun would actually be above the horizon night and day, but it was quite light enough for the party to keep moving through the night. The only limit to the journey was their own endurance. A time would come when they would have to try to sleep, and they were so poorly equipped that they could not expect to sleep soundly enough to restore their strength to normal. After a sleep, the second stage would be slower and shorter than the first ; and the first was being so desperately slow that a new danger began to loom ahead : the danger of reaching the point of exhaustion before they came to Sweden, and after they had gone too far to be able to get home again.

So as they went on, their hopeful spirit faded, and gave way to a growing fear that they were trying something entirely beyond their powers. None of them wanted to be the first to admit defeat, and they went on a long way after it was hopeless. What finally turned the doubt into despair was the weather. During the morning the wind had sprung up again, and the snowclouds began to pile up and darken the southern sky. It looked as if the improvement in the night had only been a lull, and as if the blizzard was going to start again, as furiously as ever. They halted on top of a hill. They had been hauling the sledge for six hours then, apart from the four hours' climb up Kjerringdal. None of them knew how far they had come, but there was certainly a long way still to go. It was the sort of unwelcome decision which nobody needs to discuss. With hardly a word between them, they turned the sledge round and started back towards Mandal.

During the long weary hopeless journey back, the blizzard did come on again in earnest, and proved the decision was right. Going back, the wind was almost behind them; they could never have made any progress going south against it.

When at last they got back to the steep edge of Mandal, they found they were some distance farther up the valley than the point they had started from. This was simply due to the difficulty of setting a course on the plateau, but it had some advantages. To climb straight down into the valley from where they were would avoid Kjerringdal, which was certain to avalanche at any minute. There was no point in going all the way back to the place where Jan had been lying when they found him.

The question arose again of what to do with Jan. Remembering the experience of being hauled up the mountain, he was still very reluctant to go down again. Apart from the pain of it, it would have been such a depressing step in the wrong direction. Besides, he could see that the Mandal men were dog-tired. They had been at full stretch for something like sixteen hours, and for tired men to try to lower him down to the valley in the blizzard had obvious risks for them all. They themselves thought that if he could face another few days on the plateau, he would really be safer there. He decided to stay.

They found him another rock which would serve as a landmark, and dragged him to the foot of it. They untied him from the sledge, and stowed their spare food beside him, and then they built a low wall of snow to shelter him from the wind. This was all they could do for him, and in fact it was all he wanted. When it was finished, and they had promised to come up again, they turned downhill for home, and all vanished into the mist of snow, and left him alone again. For all the day's journeying, he was about two miles nearer Sweden than when he started.

CHAPTER FOURTEEN

THE LAST DUTY

HE LAY between the snow wall and the rock for nearly three weeks. In some ways it was better than the grave : he could see rather more of the sky, although he could not see round him beyond the wall ; and there was enough room to move about so far as he was able. But in other ways it was worse : it was more exposed to the wind and weather, and it was much more affected by the change in temperature between night and day. In the grave, it had always been a bit below freezing point. In the open, whenever the sun broke through the clouds it melted his sleeping-bag and the snow around him till he was soaked ; and when the sun dipped down at night towards the north horizon, his blankets and clothes froze solid. But although this was extremely uncomfortable it never made him ill. In conditions which were more than enough to give a man pneumonia, he never even caught a cold, because there are no germs of such human diseases on the plateau.

He was well stocked with food when they left him there, and different parties of men came up from the valley every three or four days to keep him supplied. None of it struck him as very nice to eat, especially after it had been thawed and frozen several times, and he had nothing to cook with. But still, one can live without such refinements as cookery and he was very grateful for it. There was dried fish, and cod liver oil, and bread. It was a question whether the bread was worse to eat when it was wet or when it was frozen. There was also some powdered milk which had to be mixed with water. It occupied him for long hours to melt the snow between his hands so that it dripped into the cup he had been given, and then to stir the powder into it. Later on, when the thaw began in earnest, an icicle on the rock beside him began to drip. At the full stretch of his arm, he could just reach out to put the cup under the drip, and then he would lie and watch it, counting the slow drops as they fell, and waiting in suspense as each one trembled glistening on the tip. Sometimes when the cup had a little water in the bottom, the drops splashed out and half of each one was lost. When he was feeling weak, this seemed a disaster, and he would swear feebly to himself in vexation. But in the end he invented the idea of putting a lump of snow on top of the cup, so that the drops fell through it without splashing. It took hours to fill the cup. The end result, with the milk powder mixed in it cold, was a horrible drink, but it helped to keep his strength up, and he drank it as a duty.

Sometimes in those solitary days, between the chores which always kept him busy, he still had the strength of mind to laugh at the contrast between himself as he used to be and his present state of elementary existence. Looking back, his life before the war, and even in the army, seemed prim and over-fastidious. There was a certain kind of humour in the thought that he had once taken some pride in his appearance, chosen ties as if they were important, pressed his trousers, kept his hair cut, and even manicured his nails. Grubbing about in the snow for a crust of bread reminded him of a time he had had to complain in an Oslo restaurant because there was a coffee stain on the tablecloth, and of how apologetic the waiter had been when he changed it for a clean one. It had seemed important; in fact, it had been important to him as he was in those days. If the man he had then been could have seen the man he was now, the sight would have made him sick. He had not washed or shaved or combed his hair for weeks, or taken off his clothes. He had reached that stage of filth when one's clothes seem to be part of one's body, and he smelt. But, luckily, what had happened to him in the last few weeks had changed him, and he did not mind his dirt. It had changed him more fundamentally than merely by making him dirty and ill and emaciated and crippling his legs. It had changed him so that it was quite difficult for him to recognise the spark of life which still lingered inside that feeble disgusting body as himself. He knew already that if he lived through it all he would never be the same person again. He would have lost his feet, he supposed, but he would have grown in experience. He felt he would never dare to be impatient again, that he would always be placid and tolerant, and that none of the irritations of civilised life would have the power to annoy him any more. Travel broadens the mind, he thought, and laughed out loud because the plateau was so oppressively silent.

When he fell into a doze during those days, he often dreamed of wolves. This was a fear he had been spared during the first week on the plateau, because nobody had told him there were wolves up there; but there are. They sometimes attack the reindeer herds, and the Lapps on skis fight running battles with them. They seldom, if ever, attack a man, even if he is alone; but nobody could say for certain whether they would attack a helpless man if they were hungry, as they often are in the time of the early spring. The Mandal men had taken the danger seriously enough to warn Jan about it and give him a stick to defend himself. Later, when they realised that a stick was no good because he had not enough strength to beat off a rabbit with it, they brought up brushwood and paraffin so that he could fire it if the wolves closed in on him. Of course he had a pistol; but it only had three rounds left in it, and he said he wanted to keep them for bigger game than wolves. Jan felt it was silly to be afraid of an animal, or even a pack of them, which had never actually been known to kill a man, so far as anyone could tell him. Yet the thought of it worked on his nerves. Until he was told of the wolves, he had only the inanimate forces of the plateau to contend with. He had relied on his solitude, feeling as safe from a sudden intrusion as he would in a house with the doors and windows locked. With all the dangers that surrounded him, at least he had not had to keep alert for any sudden crisis. But now, as he lay behind his wall of snow, unable to see what was happening on the snowfield around him, helplessly wrapped in his sleeping-bag, he knew he might see the sharp teeth and the pointed muzzle at any moment within a yard of him, or feel the hot breath on his face when he was sleeping, or hear the baying and know they were watching him and waiting. This, more than anything, made him feel his loneliness.

In the comparatively roomy space behind the snow wall, he could wriggle one leg at a time out of the sleeping-bag and look carefully at his feet, which he had never been able to do inside the grave. They were a very disgusting sight. His toes were still worse than anything else, but the whole of each foot was so bad that it was frost-bitten right through from one side to the other between the Achilles' tendon and the bone. All the way up to his knees there were patches of black and grey. He had quite given up thinking of ever being able to walk on them again. As soon as he got to a hospital, he supposed, somebody would put him straight on an operating table and cut off his feet without thinking twice about it. He was resigned to that, but he still very much wanted not to lose his legs. Apart from the problems of keeping himself alive, he had thought more about his legs than anything else, wondering whether there was anything he could do to help to save them. He had made up his mind some time before about one drastic course of action, but in the grave there had not been enough room to put it into effect. He was still under the impression, rightly or wrongly, that gangrene would go on spreading, unless one got rid of it, like dry rot in a house. The source of it all was his toes. They were not part of him any more, although they were still attached to him, and it seemed only common sense that he would be better without them. There was nobody he could expect to help him ; but now the time and the chance had come, and he made his preparations to cut off his toes himself.

He still had his pocket-knife, and he still had some brandy. With the brandy as anæsthetic, and the knife as a scalpel, lying curled up on his side in the snow with his leg drawn up so that he could reach it, he cut off nine of his toes.

When he had finished, he felt very much better in his mind. Of course, there was no immediate improvement in his legs, but it gave him some satisfaction to have done something which he hoped would help to save them ; it was better to know that the rotten revolting things were gone and could not poison him any more. It made him feel cleaner.

After it was all done, he went back with relief to the simple routine of his daily life : feeding himself, collecting ice-water, mixing milk, trying to clean his pistol; once in a while, as seldom as he could, rolling a cigarette with infinite care and finding the box of matches which he kept inside his underclothes next to his skin; trying to put ointment on the sores on his back without getting too cold; sometimes treating himself to a sip of brandy; and always keeping on the watch for new attacks of frostbite. It was terribly difficult not to lie there listening, imagining the sound of skis or the distant snarl of wolves. Sometimes he stopped up his ears to keep out the ghastly silence, and sometimes he talked to himself so that there was something to listen to. When people did come from Mandal, shouting "Hallo, gentleman" from far off, the sudden disturbance of the silence was a shock, and often it took him some time to find his voice to answer.

They paid him faithful visits all those weeks, toiling up the long climb every third or fourth night. When they came, they always brought fresh food, and usually some dry wood to make a fire to heat a drink for him; but lighting fires always made them uneasy in case the smoke or the light was seen. Whenever he heard them coming, he pulled himself together and tried to look as alive as he could, because he had a fear at the back of his mind that they might get depressed and give him up as a bad job and stop coming any more. On their side, they felt they had to cheer him up, so that the meetings were usually happy, although the happiness was forced. Sometimes there was even something to laugh at, like the time when one man forgot the password. The story of how Jan had shot the Gestapo officer had got around, and he had the reputation in Mandal of being trigger-conscious and a deadly shot. So when this man found that the words "Hallo, gentleman" had quite escaped his mind at the critical moment, he hurriedly dropped on his hands and knees and crawled up to Jan on his stomach, keeping well under cover till he was close enough to talk to him and make perfectly certain that there would not be any unfortunate misunderstanding.

On one of their visits, Jan asked them for something to read. What he really wanted was an English thriller or a French one, because during the last couple of years he had got more used to reading foreign languages than his own. But nobody knew of anything like that in Mandal, and the man he happened to ask could only offer him religious works in Norwegian. He declined that offer, but afterwards the man remembered an annual edition of a weekly magazine which he could borrow. Jan thanked him, and the heavy volume was carried up the mountain. But as a matter of fact, Jan did not read very much of it. He never seemed to have time.

Somebody had the brilliant idea, when Jan had been up there for some time, of bringing up a roll of the kind of thick paper which is used for insulating buildings. They bent this over Jan in an arch, like a miniature Nissen hut, and covered it over with snow, and blocked up one end with a snow wall. It was just big enough for Jan to lie in, and it protected him quite well. In fact, it sometimes seemed warm inside. But it had its drawbacks; whenever it seemed to be going to get tolerably warm, the snow on top of it melted and dripped through on him mercilessly, and made him even wetter than before.

Sometimes his visitors came with high hopes, but more often the news they brought him from the valley was disappointing. On one night soon after they left him there, two men came up full of excitement to say that a Lapp had arrived in Kaafjord and promised to take him to the frontier straight away. They expected him either that night or the next, and they waited all night to help Jan when he came. But the morning came without any sign of him. For the next three successive nights men came from the valley to wait with Jan for the Lapp's arrival, and to make sure he did not miss the place. They kept watch for him hour by hour; but no movement broke the skylines of the plateau. On the fourth day they heard that the Lapp had changed his mind because of a rumour that the Germans had sent out ski patrols on the frontier.

During the next few days this rumour was confirmed from a good many different sources. Recently, everyone had been so completely absorbed by the problems of Jan's health, and the weather, and the journey across the plateau, that they were well on the way to forgetting about the Germans. It was a long time since the garrison had come to Mandal, and that had been the last German move, so far as anyone knew, which had seemed at the time to be part of a deliberate search. The Mandal men had got used to the garrison and begun to despise it. But now it began to look as if the Germans were still on the hunt for Jan and even had a rough idea of where he was. When Jan was told about it, he reflected that the Germans had got a jump ahead of him for the first time in his flight. In the early days, when he was on the move, they had never done more than bark at his heels; but now, it seemed, they had thrown out a patrol line right on the part of the frontier which one day he would have to cross; and unless he crossed it within a few days, he would have to do it in daylight. If only he had been fit, both he and the Mandal men would have treated the patrol as a joke, because like all Norwegians they had a profound contempt, which may not have been justified, for the Germans' skill on skis. Even as things were, nobody except the Lapp was deterred by this extra danger. If they could only get to the frontier, they were sure they would get across somehow.

But soon after this rumour started, there was an extraordinary event on the plateau which really did make them take the danger of Germans more seriously. The most remarkable thing about life on the plateau had always been that nothing happened whatever. Day after day could pass without any event, even of the most trivial kind; and Jan discovered that most of the events which he seemed to remember were really things he had dreamed or imagined. His commonest dream or hallucination was that he heard someone coming. One day, when he was dozing, he heard voices approaching. It had often happened before; but this time, as they came near him, he realised that they were speaking German. He could not understand what they were saying, and they soon faded away again; and when he was fully awake, he thought no more of what seemed a slight variation of his old familiar dream. But the next night, when a party from Mandal came up to see him, they arrived in consternation, because there were two sets of ski tracks which passed thirty yards from the place where Jan was lying, and none of the Mandal men had made them.

It was one of those utterly mysterious things which start endless speculation. Up till then, they had always regarded the plateau as a sanctuary from the Germans, partly because they had never thought the Germans would venture to go up there, and partly because the job of looking for one man in all those hundreds of miles of snow was so hopeless that they had been sure the Germans would not waste time in trying it. Nobody could imagine where the small party of men who had made the tracks could have come from, or where they had been going, or what they had meant to do. They were not from the Mandal garrison, because that was always kept under observation, and the place was more than a day's journey from any other German post. They could not have been part of a frontier patrol, because it was much too far from the frontier. Yet if they were searching for Jan, it seemed an incredible coincidence that they should have passed so near him, unless there were hundreds of patrols all over the plateau, or unless they had a very good idea of where he was. Besides, to search in that secretive way was un-German. If they did know where he was, they would know he could not be living up there unless Mandal was looking after him, and their reaction to that would certainly be to use threats and arrests in Mandal in the hope of finding someone who would give him away and save them losing face by having to scour the mountains.

They argued round and round the mystery for a long time on the plateau that night, with a new feeling of insecurity and apprehension. It had been pure luck that the Germans, whatever they were doing, had not seen Jan when they passed him. There had been a snowfall earlier in the day which had covered the trampled snow around his lair and all the old ski tracks which led up to it from Mandal. But if they came back again, they would find the new tracks and follow them straight to the spot. Altogether, it was alarming, and the only comforting suggestion that anybody thought of was that the tracks might possibly have been made by German deserters trying to get to Sweden. Nobody ever found out the truth of it. Those voices in the night remained a vague menace in the background ever after.

When the Lapp lost courage and changed his mind, it was only the first of a series of disappointments. Hopeful stories of reindeer sledges expected at any moment kept coming in from Kaafjord and other valleys in the district; but every time the hope was doomed to die. After a fortnight in which all their plans were frustrated and came to nothing, the Mandal men got desperate. Every time they went up to look at Jan they found him a little weaker. He seemed to be dying by very slow degrees. Besides that, the spring thaw was beginning in earnest, and with every day the crossing of the plateau and even the climb out of the valley was getting more difficult. The snow was rotten and sticky already on the southern slopes, and the next week or two would see the last chance of a sledge journey before the following winter. During the thaw every year the plateau becomes a bog, criss-crossed by swollen streams, and nobody can cross it; and after the thaw, when the snow is all gone, the only way to move a helpless man would be to carry him, which would be even slower and more laborious than dragging him on a sledge.

So they decided to make a final attempt to man-haul the sledge to Sweden while there was still time, using a larger party which could work in relays. Accordingly, six men went up on the night of the ninth of May, and dragged Jan out of the paper tent and started off again to the southward. But this attempt achieved nothing except to raise false hopes once more. They had only covered a mile or two when clouds came down so thickly that they could only see a few feet ahead of them. They could not steer a course in those conditions, so they turned round and followed their own tracks back to where they had started, and put Jan into the paper tent again.

After this failure, Jan really began to get despondent. He never lost faith in the Mandal men, and still believed they would get him to Sweden somehow if they went on trying long enough; but he began to doubt if it was worth it. Nobody had told him much about what was going on, but he could see for himself what an enormous effort Mandal and the surrounding district was making on his behalf. So many different men had come up from the valley by then that he had lost count of them, and he had some vague idea of the organisation which must lie behind such frequent visits. As time went on, it seemed more and more fantastic that the German garrison could go on living down there in the valley, in the midst of all this hectic activity, and remain in happy ignorance of what was happening. Every new man who came up to help him meant a new family more or less involved in his affairs, so that the longer Mandal had to go on looking

after him the more awful would be the disaster in the valley if the
Germans did find out about it. Jan knew, and so did the Mandal
men, the results of the uncontrolled anger of Germans when they
found out that a whole community had deceived them. It had
happened on the west coast, and villages had been systematically
burnt, all the men in them shipped to Germany and the women
and children herded into concentration camps in Norway. There
was no doubt this might happen to Mandal, now that so many
people were involved, and Jan had to ask himself what the reward
of running this risk would be. To save his life was the only
objective. When he looked at it coolly, it seemed a very bad
bargain. There was no patriotic motive in it any more, no idea
of saving a trained soldier to fight again ; looking at his legs, and
the wasted remains of what had once been such a healthy body,
he did not think he would be any use as a soldier any more. If
he died, he thought, it would be no more loss to the army : he
was a dead loss anyway. And it was not as if he were married,
or even engaged. Nobody depended entirely on him for their
happiness or livelihood. His father had another son and daughter:
his brother Nils would be quite grown up by now : and even
Bitten, his young sister whom he had loved so much, must have
learned, he supposed, to get on without him, and perhaps would
never depend on him again as much as he had always imagined.
He wondered whether they had all given him up for dead already,
and whether he would ever see them again even if he did live on.
As for his war-time friends of the last two years in England, he
knew they would all have assumed he was dead if they knew
where he was at all.

This idea only came to him slowly, in the course of about ten
lonely days after the last abortive journey. It took him a long
time to come to a firm conclusion, because by nature he had such
a very strong instinct to live. But inevitably the time came, in
the end, when he unwillingly saw one duty left before him. His
own life was not of any overriding value to anyone but himself ;
and to himself, life only meant a few more weeks of suffering and
a hideous death, or at best, he believed, a future as a more or less
useless cripple. The life of any one of his many helpers, healthy
and perhaps the focus and support of a family, outweighed it in

the balance. He saw quite clearly that he ought not to let them run any more risks for him, and he knew there was only one way he could possibly stop them. His last duty was to die.

To decide to commit suicide when one's instinct is utterly against it argues great strength of mind. Jan's mind was still active and clear, but his decision had come too late. By the time he reached it, his body was too weak to carry it out. He still had his loaded pistol. Lying alone in his sleeping-bag among the wastes of snow, he dragged it out of its holster and held it in his hands. He had used it to save his life already, and he meant to use it again to end it. Until the last week he had always looked after it with the love he had always had for fine mechanism, but lately he had begun to neglect it, and it grieved him to find it was rusty. He held it in the old familiar grip, to cock it for a final shot, but it was stiff and his fingers were very weak. He struggled feebly with the simple action he had been trained to do in a fraction of a second, but it was not the slightest use. He no longer had the strength in his hands to pull back against the spring. He felt a friend had failed him.

It was absurd really. He felt he had made a fool of himself. He had struggled so long to preserve his own life that now he had not enough strength in his fingers to kill himself. If he had not felt ashamed, he would have laughed.

CHAPTER FIFTEEN

THE SANDS RUN OUT

When Jan came to this mental crisis, the men who came up to see him noticed the difference. Up to then, he had always seemed cheerful, and none of them knew what this appearance had sometimes cost him. But now there was no humour left in him, and he would hardly speak to them. In fact, up to then the occasional visits of strangers had been all he had had to look forward to, but now he was almost resentful when he heard " Hallo, gentlemen," because it meant that he had to make an effort when he wanted to lie in peace. He did not tell them till later about the conclusion he had come to. It simply seemed to them that he had lost heart. They went down and told Herr Nordnes that he was dying at last.

It had never occurred to them, as it had to Jan, that what they were doing might not be worth the risk, and if he had died up there on the plateau, after all the effort they had put into trying to save him, they would have been very much disappointed and almost angry with him. But they were certainly right in their fears. The weeks of exposure had really worn him down to the point when his life might quietly end without any further warning. Only one course was left to them, since they never considered just letting him die in peace. They would have to carry him down to the valley again, and try to fatten him up and build up his strength till he was fit for another attempt on Sweden.

There were the Germans to think of. No house in the place was free of the risk of a sudden search. At night, by that time, there was no darkness left at all, and it would have been taking too much of a chance to have carried him all the way down to the inhabited part of the valley in broad daylight. But the valley extends for ten miles beyond the last of the houses, and all of it is more sheltered than the open plateau, and a few degrees warmer. Somebody remembered a cave right up at the head of the valley. There was a meeting in the schoolhouse, and it was agreed that the only hope of spinning out his life was to cut their losses, bring him down and install him in the cave, and begin all over again.

This was a hard decision for them all, and especially for Jan when they told him what they thought. It meant going back to the stage of the journey he had reached when he was first carried into the hut at Revdal nearly six weeks before. It meant that everything he had suffered since then had been wasted. And it also meant, above all, that before he could ever hope to reach Sweden he would have to go through the ordeal of being hauled up the mountain again.

However, he was too far gone to care, and the Mandal men assured him there was nothing else for it ; so he let himself be pulled out of the paper tent and lashed yet again to the sledge. Six men lowered him laboriously down to the bed of the valley, throwing away the height and the distance which the past weeks had so painfully won.

While this party was bringing him down, another was preparing the cave, by laying a bed of birch branches and grass inside it. When they got him there and pushed him inside and finally left him, he was in a state of luxury which he had not enjoyed since Marius's barn. They had taken him off the sledge, and after its wooden slats the birch bed was wonderfully soft. He slowly got dry, for the first time in a month ; and when his clothes had dried out he even began to get warm, a sensation which seemed an entirely novel experience ; and when he was warm he fell at long last into a dreamless sleep.

He lay in the cave for four days, sleeping most of the time. When he did wake he lay staring at the roof which was only a couple of feet above his head, enjoying the gloom after the snow-glare of the plateau. The roof was damp, and there were some-times drips on it. He found them fascinating to watch and study. When one of them was just about to fall, he would draw a trail with his finger on the slimy rock so that the drop slid down it and fell clear of his body. When he rolled a cigarette he prepared for it by laying trails for all the ripening drops which he could see, so that he could be sure to have his smoke in peace. During those days, he discovered anew the pleasures of the very simplest things; the delight of sleep, the joy of anticipating eating, the unutterable luxury of yawning.

The mouth of the cave was often darkened as a visitor crawled in beside him, to feed him with the best that Mandal could afford and to attend so far as he could to any wish that he expressed. The visitors sat and gossiped when he was awake, and left him alone when he was sleepy. One day, they brought him the news that one of the German soldiers in their garrison had run away to Sweden, which gave them all a quite disproportionate happiness. Every day, whoever had come to him talked about the Lapps, who were now arriving in greater numbers in Kaafjord and the other neighbouring valleys and were being coaxed and offered rewards by the local members of the organisation in the hope that sooner or later one of them would make up his mind to help. But Jan had stopped pinning much faith in Lapps. The only plan he had was to sleep till he really felt he had slept enough. By then, he thought, he would be stronger, and that would be soon enough to think about the future. Then he would decide whether to go on leaning on the kindness of the Mandal folk still longer, right through the summer perhaps, or whether to put an end to it all as soon as his fingers could cock the pistol.

But suddenly, on his fourth or fifth day in the cave, a whole deputation arrived in excitement, to say that at last a Lapp had made a firm promise. He had demanded brandy, blankets, coffee and tobacco, which were all the most difficult and expensive things to get, but the organisation was sure to be able to find enough to satisfy him, and people who knew him said he was a reliable character who would not change his mind. But his reindeer were still up on the plateau, and he did not want to bring them down and then have to take them up again. So to make sure of not missing the chance, Jan would have to be moved straight away and hauled up to the plateau to meet the Lapp and his herd.

Jan was not really ready to leave the comfortable cave. A little more rest would have made him fitter to start the struggle again. But he could not refuse to fall in with a plan which had raised the hopes of the Mandal men so high ; and although he had been disappointed too often, it did seem that this might be the opportunity they had all been waiting for. He tried to show more enthusiasm than he felt, and they pulled him out into the glaring daylight and tied him down to the familiar slats of the sledge again.

A large party of men assembled for the climb out of the valley. Eight actually took part in it. In many ways this ascent was less arduous, at least for Jan, than the earlier one from Revdal. There were twice as many men to handle the sledge; and by then Jan was much less of a load to carry. His weight ultimately fell to 78 pounds, which was less than half what he weighed when he left the Shetland Islands.

The eight men were therefore able to carry him bodily for a lot of the way, and he was not so often left hanging feet downwards or upside down. But the ascent lasted no less than thirteen hours, and by the time they got him to the top Jan was exhausted, and the good effect of his rest in the cave had been undone. After these hours of rough handling, he got angry for the first time in all those weeks, and in his weakness he forgot that he owed absolutely everything to the men who were carrying him. One of them had promised to bring tobacco for him, and in the excitement it had been forgotten. When Jan heard of this, it seemed for some reason the last straw. The prospect of even a day or two on the plateau without a cigarette was too much for him, and he snapped irritably: "You would go and forget the most important thing of the lot." It was an absurdly ungrateful thing to say, especially when tobacco was so rare and expensive that almost everyone in Mandal had had to give up smoking. But none of them took any notice, because they could see he had been pushed almost beyond endurance and was not really aware any more of what he was saying.

As a matter of fact, the organisation in Mandal and Kaafjord was being remarkably thoughtful and efficient, as it had been throughout the operation. When the climbing party got Jan to the new rendezvous on the plateau where he was to meet the Lapp, two men from Kaafjord had already arrived there. They had been detailed to relieve the climbers by taking over Jan and looking after him until the Lapp arrived, and they had been chosen as Lapp interpreters. The Lappish language is said to have no relation to any other language in the world except Hungarian, and there are very few people except the Lapps who understand it. Most of the Lapps themselves can also speak one or another of the languages of the countries they live in, either Swedish, Norwegian or Finnish, but the man who was expected that night was a Finnish Lapp, and so he and Jan would not have a single word in common.

The men who had brought him up were tired out when they got to the meeting-place, so they handed Jan over to the Kaafjord men and retreated to the valley without any further delay. These two stayed with him to keep him company all through the following night. But events began to take a course which was terribly familiar. Jan lay passively on the sledge while the chill of the night froze the dampness of the day in his clothes. The men who were guarding him watched the snow-bound horizon patiently hour by hour. But no sign of the Lapp was seen, and nothing stirred. In the early morning, the men had to go down to their daily work, and Jan was abandoned again to his solitude.

The vigil began again with all its rigour and discomfort and the same hopeless dreariness. He was in a different place on the plateau, but it looked almost exactly the same. There was no rock with icicles to fill his cup, and there was no snow wall or paper tent. The snow immediately round him was clean and fresh, and not stained and fouled by weeks of improvised existence. But the low hills and the dead shallow valleys within his vision could hardly be distinguished from any others, and the familiar numbing cold, the snow-glare and the silence made the days in the cave appear like a half-remembered dream which had done nothing but give a fleeting glimpse of comfort and so emphasise the misery of the plateau. He lay dazed, floating into and out of coma, and he began to listen again. The thin wind sighed on a distant hill, and stirred the loose snow in feeble eddies with an infinitesimal rustle, and died to silence again. In his moments of clarity he knew these soft sibilant sounds threatened another blizzard. When his mind lost its grip on reality, he heard the wolves again padding secretively round him. He began once more to start into wakefulness when he imagined voices or the hiss of skis.

The next night two more interpreters came to stand by him. One speaks of night and day, but by then the midnight sun was up. It was broad daylight all the time, and night only meant that the shadows on the plateau were longer and that when they lengthened the air became more chill. Throughout this brilliant, glaring, frosty night the men watched over him. But nobody came. Jan had made up his mind that the Lapp would never come. The sun passed across the north horizon and climbed again into the east. The men had to give up waiting, and went away, and left him to face another glaring day.

Four days and nights dragged by before they broke it to him that this Lapp had also changed his mind and made the excuse that he was ill. It was no surprise. Jan knew it before they told him. This time, nobody could think of any alternative. To take Jan down to the valley again in the quickly melting snow was a final admission of defeat, because they could never get him up again over naked rock. Down in the valley, there was nothing they could do except feed him till the Germans found him and took them all. To leave him where he was only condemned him to a quicker, kinder death. It seemed to them all, and to Jan too, that they had reached the end. For the first time, they had no plans whatever for the future, no hopes to offer him, nothing to say which would encourage him. The only thing they could have done in mercy would have been to deny him the food which had served to spin out his existence, and to let him fade out as quickly as possible and in peace. Whatever they did, they knew it would not be long. It was useless even to promise to come to see him again. When they left him they gave him food, but they made him no promise. They expected to come again, twice; once to find his body and protect it from the birds and wolves, and again, when the snow was gone and the earth was thawed, to bury him.

When their voices had faded and the last of them had gone, Jan lay quite still. The doleful wind ruffled his hair and sifted a little snow across his face. His mind was at rest in the peace which sometimes follows the final acceptance of death.

CHAPTER SIXTEEN

REINDEER

WHEN HE opened his eyes, there was a man standing looking at him.

Jan had never seen a Lapp before, except in pictures. The man stood there on skis, silent and perfectly motionless, leaning on his ski-sticks. He was very small. He had a lean swarthy face and narrow eyes with a slant. He was wearing a long tunic of dark blue embroidered with red and yellow, and leather leggings, and embroidered boots of hairy reindeer skin with turned-up pointed toes. He had a wide leather belt with two sheath-knives hanging from it. He was wearing it loosely round his hips, not round his waist, so that he looked all body and no legs, like a gnome. Jan had not heard him coming. He was simply there.

They stared at each other for a long time before Jan could speak. His brain was slow to readjust itself, and his memory was muddled. Had someone told him this man was coming ? Had he dreamed it was all over ? Was this a dream ? At last, with supreme inadequacy, he said : " Good morning." The Lapp did not move or answer, but he gave a grunt, and Jan dimly remembered then that he probably could not understand a word he said. He shut his eyes again because he was too tired to make any effort to think what to say or do.

He had an uneasy feeling that he ought to know who the man was and where he had come from. There had been a lot of talk about Lapps coming to help him, he could remember that ; but it had all been a long time ago, and it had all come to nothing in the end. They had given it up as a bad job. He could not think of any sense or reason in a Lapp being there on the plateau all alone. He looked again to make sure if he had seen what he thought he had seen, and the man was still standing there just the same, with his ski-sticks tucked under his armpits and no expression whatever on his face.

Jan could not rest with the feeling whenever he shut his eyes that someone was silently staring at him. He could not even tell if the stare was friendly or hostile, if the extraordinary creature he had seen was wanting to help him or fingering the long knives at the belt. He wished he would go away. It seemed to him that the man stood there for hours and did not move or speak or change his curious stooped position. But then, without any sound, the man had gone. Jan was relieved, and sank back into the daze which this sudden apparition had disturbed.

In fact, this man was one of the Lapps whom the ski-runner from Kaafjord had gone to see on his journey a month before. He had just arrived with his herds and his tents and family in the mountains at the head of Kaafjord, and he must have been thinking over the message all that time. When he had first been asked, the whole matter was in the vague imponderable future. Now it was in the present, and the first thing he had done when he got to Kaafjord had been to find out where Jan was lying, and then to go himself to see whether the story was true. He did stand looking at Jan for three or four hours. He was making up his mind. As soon as he had done so, he went down into the valley and announced that he was going to the frontier. Immediately the gifts which had been prepared for the Lapps who had defaulted were pressed upon him; the blankets, coffee, brandy, and tobacco which had been bought here and there at enormous prices and carefully hoarded for this purpose.

The next thing that brought Jan to his senses was a sound of snorting and shuffling unlike anything he had ever heard before, hoarse shouts, the clanging of bells and a peculiar acrid animal smell, and when he opened his eyes the barren snowfield round him which had been empty for weeks was teeming with hundred upon hundred of reindeer milling round him in an unending horde, and he was lying flat on the ground among all their trampling feet. Then two Lapps were standing over him talking their strange incomprehensible tongue. They both bent down and picked him bodily up, talking all the time, but not to him.

For a moment he could not imagine what they were going to do ; but then he understood he was being moved from his own sledge to a larger one. They muffled him up to his eyes in blankets and skins, and stowed packages and bundles on top of him and around him and lashed him and everything down with thongs of reindeer hide and sinew. There was a jerk, and the sledge began to move.

This had all happened so fast that Jan was bewildered. A few minutes before he had been lying torpid and alone ; now he was being dragged feet first at increasing speed in the middle of a wild tumult, and nobody had given him a word of explanation. He squinted along his body, and saw the hindquarters of a deer which was harnessed to the sledge. A Lapp on skis was leading it. It was one of the bell deer of the herd, and as it snorted and pawed the snow and the sledge got under way and the bell on its neck began a rhythmic clang, the herd fell in behind it, five hundred strong, anxiously padding along in its wake. From the corner of his eye he could see a few dozen of the leaders, jostling for position. The mass of deer flowed on behind ; it streamed out in a hurrying narrow column when the sledge flew fast on the level snow, and when the sledge was checked the herd surged round it and also halted. Sometimes in these involuntary halts Jan found himself looking up from where he lay on his back a foot above the ground at the ungainly heads and large mournful eyes and snuffling nostrils immediately above him. But when this happened, one or the other of the two Lapps appeared, urging on the draught deer which pulled the sledge, and sometimes giving the sledge a heave himself till the obstacle was passed and the rumble of hoofs began again, and the snow-hiss beneath the runners.

All day the enormous mass of beasts swept on across the plateau, cutting a wide swath of trampled snow which hid the tracks of the sledge which carried Jan : the most strange and majestic escort ever offered to a fugitive in war. Jan lay on the sledge feeling that events had got beyond him ; but he was content to let them take their course, because he had seen the position of the sun and knew that at last, whatever happened next, he was on his way towards the south and towards the border.

Sometime in the evening they halted. The two Lapps gave him some dried reindeer meat and some reindeer milk to drink, and then he saw them pitching a little tent made of skins. The reindeer were wandering aimlessly round and digging in the snow with their forelegs to look for the moss on the rocks far down below. Jan was left lying on the sledge. On the whole he was glad of this, because the tent was certainly only made for two ; but when he was left alone among the deer he still found them alarming. They came and sniffed at him, most obviously wondering whether he was fit to eat, and Jan, who knew very little about the tastes of reindeer, was not sure if he was or not. If ever he shut his eyes, hot breath and wet hairy muzzles woke him.

After the Lapps had disappeared inside the tent, a most peculiar noise began to come out of it : a monotonous kind of chant which rose to howls and died away to moaning. When the first eerie shrieks rolled out across the plateau Jan thought they must be fighting, and when one of them burst out of the tent after a little while and staggered through the snow towards him with the knives dangling at his belt, he thought an entirely unexpected death was in store for him. But the Lapp stooped over him and a waft of his breath explained the whole fearsome interlude. The Lapps were drunk, and they were singing. They had been getting to work on the brandy which had been given to them as a reward, and one had come reeling forth on his short bow legs with no more evil intention than to offer Jan a swig at the bottle. It came back to Jan then that years before he had either read or been told about Lappish singing. It is called yoicking. It is said to be a kind of ballad which tells stories of heroic Lappish deeds, but it is not in the least like the usual conception of music, and to people who have not been instructed in its arts it is apt to seem no more than a mournful wail, like a dog's howling at the moon, but somewhat sadder.

The day's sudden journey had revived Jan's interest in life, and when the Lapp thrust the brandy bottle at him he laughed : for a moment, with the wry humour which never left him except on the verge of death, he had had a glimpse of the ludicrous indignity, after all that had happened before, of being slaughtered by a drunken Lapp on the very last stage of the way to the frontier. He took a small sip from the bottle and was glad of it, but the Lapp began to talk. Not a single word that he said conveyed anything to Jan, but the general meaning was clear enough. He was pressing Jan to drink more, with the embarrassing hospitality of drunk people of any nation, and he was going to be offended if Jan refused. But Jan knew from the experience of the last few weeks that one sip was enough to make him feel better, and that two might make him a great deal worse. So he smiled and shut his eyes and shammed unconsciousness, and after a while the Lapp finished the bottle himself and wandered back to the tent to start yoicking again.

It was a good thing to be relieved of the expectation of being murdered, but the situation was alarming still. As the lugubrious sounds of revelry rolled out again, Jan thought of the German voices he had heard in the night, and of the ski patrols which were said to be out on the frontier. He had no idea how far he was from the frontier, but the dreadful noise in the quiet frosty air sounded as if a patrol might hear it miles away. It made him nervous, and there was no possible way he could hope to persuade them to stop it.

From time to time the Lapps made further sorties to offer him drinks or merely to look at him. Sometimes the bottles they brought were full, and sometimes nearly empty. He wondered how many bottles the organisation had bought, and how long it would be before the two men got over this rare and splendid orgy and were fit to go on with the journey again. He was so helplessly in their hands. He felt as a passenger in an aeroplane might feel if he discovered the pilot and crew were very far from sober. All in all, he spent an anxious night.

But during the night the singing slowly flagged and gave place to a blessed silence, and some time in the morning the tent shook and the Lapps emerged, apparently none the worse, and immediately set about striking the tent and harnessing the reindeer. They seemed as brisk as ever. He thought they must have remarkable constitutions. Soon the herd was rounded up, the sledge started, and the headlong rush of hoofs began again.

On this second day Jan lost the last of his sense of position and direction. He did not know where he was being taken, and he could not ask what plans the Lapps had made, or try to change them whatever they might be. But simply because there was something happening, some positive action going on at last, he had roused himself out of his mental apathy, and even felt physically better than he had when all hope had seemed to have come to an end. The lurching and swaying of the sledge and its sudden stops and starts were sickening and tiring, but he summoned up every bit of strength which he still possessed, inspired if not by hope, at least by curiosity. He wanted to see what was going to happen next. This wish in itself must have helped him to keep alive.

Everything happened, very quickly. The sledge lurched to a halt, perhaps for the hundredth time. The herd, swept on by its own momentum, came milling all round him again. Then he found that both the Lapps were trying to tell him something. They were pointing with their ski-sticks. He tried to look in the direction they showed him but he could not see very much between the hundreds of legs of deer. He listened to what they were saying, but it meant nothing to him at all. And then he caught a single word, the first word they had ever said which he understood. It was " Kilpisjarvi," and he remembered it. It is the name of a lake. He looked again, with a sudden uncontrollable excitement, and caught a glimpse of a steep slope which fell away from where the herd was standing, and down below, at the foot of the slope, an enormous expanse of smooth unsullied snow. It was the frozen lake, in sight ; and he had remembered that the frontier runs across the middle of it. The low banks of snow on the other side were Sweden. Slowly there dawned the wild incredible hope that he was going to win.

The Lapps were still talking. He shut his mind to that blinding blaze of hope, and tried to attend to them. They picked up handfuls of sodden snow and squeezed it so that the water ran down, pointed again to the lake and shook their heads. That was it : they were trying to tell him that the thaw had gone too far and the ice of the lake was rotten and unsafe. He looked down at the lake again, and then he saw here and there the greenish translucent patches which showed where the ice was melting.

He remembered Kilpisjarvi on the map. It was miles long, seven or eight miles at least, and the head of it was near the summer road, where there was sure to be a guard post. At the other end there must be a river. It came back to him : there was a river, and the frontier ran down it. But if the lake was melting, the river ice would surely be broken up and the river in spate and uncrossable. They must cross the lake : they must chance it : he had to make them try. Stop the herd, let him try it alone on the sledge : one man on skis, one deer and the sledge. But he could not explain it. He started to say it in Norwegian but their faces were blank and he stopped in an agony of frustration, and began again to try to control his impatience and to think of a way to make it all clear to them by dumb show. If only he had a pencil and paper to draw maps and pictures—

There was a crack, the unmistakable lash of a bullet overhead and then the report of a rifle. The deer froze where they stood and raised their heads, scenting danger. The Lapps froze, silent and staring. Jan struggled to raise his head. There were six skiers on the crest of another hill. One of them was kneeling with a rifle, and in the split second while Jan glanced at them another shot went over and he saw three of the men turn down off the crest and come fast towards the herd.

After seconds of stunned silence the Lapps started talking in shrill excited voices. Jan found he was shouting, " Get on, get on ! Across the lake ! " The deer moved nervously, running together in groups, stopping to sniff the wind. The Lapps glanced at him and back at the patrol, the picture of indecision. The patrol was down off the hill, racing across the flats. In an access of frenzied strength Jan half raised his head and shoulders from the sledge, forgetting that words were useless, shouting, " They're out of range ! For God's sake move ! Move ! " One of the Lapps shouted back a quick meaningless answer. The other waved both hands towards the rifleman as if he was begging him not to shoot. In an inspiration Jan fumbled in his jacket and drew his useless automatic and brandished it at the Lapps. They stared at it aghast : heaven knows what they thought, whether Jan was meaning to threaten them or defend them. With a final glance at the skiers approaching, one jumped to the head of the deer which pulled the sledge. The other shouted and suddenly, like a flood released, the herd poured over the edge of the hill and down the steep slope towards the lake, the sledge rocking and careering down among them, snow flying from the pounding hoofs, rifle shots whining past and over, across the frozen beach, out in a mad stampede on to the slushy groaning ice and away full tilt towards the Swedish shore.

EPILOGUE

ESCAPE STORIES end when freedom and safety are reached, but this story can hardly be ended without telling what happened to the people in it after it was all over.

Jan and Marius and the Mandal men had dreamed so long of the Swedish frontier that they had never thought much about what would happen on the other side of it. Of course they all knew it was a very long way from the border to a town or hospital, but to travel in a country where there were no Germans seemed so absurdly easy that none of them worried about the distance.

But as it turned out it was quite a long time after the hectic dash across the lake before Jan was put to bed in a Swedish hospital. Once the tension was over, his memory went to pieces. He remembers a day which he spent in a hut with a lot of Lapps, and another day in a canoe going down a fast river of which one bank was Finland and therefore controlled by the Germans, and the other Sweden. Eventually the river led to a telegraph station, where the operator sent an urgent message to the Swedish Red Cross.

That excellent organisation sent an ambulance seaplane, which made a perilous landing on a stretch of the river where the ice was still breaking up. Before the plane could take off again, a squad of men had to break more of the ice to give it a longer run. That take-off was the last of the experiences which Jan recollects as having scared him out of his wits. After it, he had a complete blank in his memory until a doctor told him he had been in hospital for a week.

In hospital, he had the very unusual satisfaction of being asked what surgeon had amputated his toes, and of saying with a casual air that he had done it himself; and later he had a satisfaction which was even greater, when he was told that his operation had saved his feet. The decision about his feet remained in the balance for a long time. He very nearly lost them when the doctors first unwrapped them; but they called in a specialist who decided to try to redeem them, and after three months' treatment they were declared to be safe.

As soon as he woke up in hospital, he began to try to get a confidential report of what had happened through to London. It was not very easy. As Sweden was neutral, there were naturally Germans and German agents around, and if his report had got into the wrong hands, of course it would have been a death warrant for the people in Norway who had helped him. He was worried too by the recollection that the Swedes had only let him out of prison three years before on condition that he left the country, so that they had every right to put him in again. But some of his story had filtered across the border, and no doubt the Swedes who heard rumours of it felt he had earned the best treatment they could give him. They let him get into touch with a secretary in the Norwegian embassy, and to her he dictated all that he could remember of the story.

In England, we already knew, of course, that the expedition had come to grief, and vague reports had come through of what had happened to the *Brattholm*. There had been a long, sarcastic and gloating story in the *Deutsche Zeitung* about the brave and ever-vigilant defenders who had won the battle of Toftefjord, and this German view of the affair had even been quoted in brief in the London papers in early June, while Jan was still lying unconscious. But Jan's report gave the first news of the unlucky chance which had betrayed the landing, and it was also the first indication we had that one of the twelve men who had sailed from Shetland had survived.

Jan himself flew back to England in the autumn, after being away from his unit for seven months. In some ways, his return to war-time London must have been a disappointment to him after he had dreamed of it for so long. When the welcoming drinks and the official compliments were over, there was hardly anyone he wanted to talk to about what had happened to him. The Linge Company in which he had been trained was a company of adventurers, and nobody in it talked much about personal experience : for one thing, everybody in it was waiting his own call to go to Norway and knew it was best not to be burdened with other people's secrets. The few staff officers to whom Jan could talk freely had already seen his report and were busy with other plans, and anyhow were sated with stories of desperate adventure. There was nobody who could share the pictures which were still so vivid in his own mind : pictures of the endless snow, the cold, the glaring nights, the procession of faces of people who had offered their lives for his and whose names he had never known, the sound and smells of the northern waste-lands, the solitude and hopelessness and pain. In the busy, grey autumnal streets of London, these things began to seem like a private dream ; a dream which was overcast and darkened by anxiety, because he did not know what had happened in those desolate valleys after he got away, so that he was haunted, for the whole of the rest of the war, by the thought that his own life might have been bought at the cost of appalling reprisals. To help himself to live with this burden of worry, he threw all his energy into the routine of army life, and into training himself to walk and run without losing his balance, and getting himself fit again in the hope that he would be allowed to go back to Norway.

But if nobody in England could share in Jan's anxiety, it had its counterpart in Arctic Norway. For month after month, in Furuflaten and Lyngseidet and Mandal, Kaafjord and Tromsö and the islands, all the people who had helped to save him went about their daily business in the constant fear that something would still be found out which would give them away to the Germans. But time passed and nothing disastrous happened, and the fear very slowly faded ; and in fact the Germans never discovered anything, and nobody was ever punished for Jan's escape. Furuflaten and Lyngseidet survived the war intact, but Mandal, on the other side of the fjord, was the very last of the places which the Germans destroyed in a futile "scorched earth" policy when their retreat began. The people were driven out and every house was burnt to the ground. For a long time the valley was deserted. But now, it has spacious new houses and its people have returned. The valley is still as remote as ever : it still has no road : but its placid life has begun again, and Herr Nordnes has a new generation of pupils in a new school, the sons and daughters of the men who went up to the plateau.

As I write, the midwife of Ringvassöy is still at work ; the same people live in the cottage in Toftefjord ; and old Bernhard Sörensen, who rowed Jan across the sound among the searchlights, still thinks nothing of getting his feet wet at 82. But his son Einar died some years ago, and the two grandsons who made Jan tell them a story are grown up and have gone to work in town, so that Bjorneskar is a lonely place for the old man and his wife.

The village of Furuflaten is very prosperous. Marius has formed a partnership with three other local men, one of whom is Alvin Larsen, who was with him that awful night when they dragged the sledge up Revdal. They are building contractors, and they have also put up a factory in the village, just by the place where they hauled Jan across the road below the schoolhouse. In the factory they make concrete blocks, and a special kind of Arctic prefabricated house, and, most unexpectedly, ready-made trousers. The business is growing : they are starting on jackets to match the trousers, and there is no end to their plans.

Marius, I am glad to say, married Agnethe Lanes, whom he treated so roughly on the night they climbed up to the plateau. They are bringing up a family in a new house they have built beside the log cabin where Jan stumbled in at the door. Marius is beginning to worry about his figure, but he still has his quite irresistible chuckle, and I think he always will have.

As for Jan, he got his own way in the end and was sent over again to Norway as an agent, sailing once more from the base in the Shetland Islands. So it happened that he was on active service there when the capitulation came. In the midst of the national rejoicing and the hectic work of accepting the surrender of the Germans, he picked up the telephone and asked for his father's number, and heard at last that his family were safe and well. When he was free to go to Oslo to meet them, his schoolgirl sister, Bitten, for whom he had worried so long, astonished him by being twenty and having grown up very well, as he saw at a glance, without the benefit of his brotherly hand to guide her.

Jan is a married man now. His wife Evie is American. Jan and his father work together again, importing mathematical and surveying instruments from abroad. To meet Jan, absorbed in theodolites and his family affairs, in his house in the pinewoods in the outskirts of Oslo, you would never guess the story which he remembers. But you would see for yourself that it has a happy ending.

ARCTIC OCEAN

Toftefjord
Hersöy
Ribbenesöy
Ringvassöy
Grötsund
Snarby
TROMSO
Balsfjord
LYNGEN ALPS
Kjosen
Lyngenfjord
Revdal
Furuflaten
Mandal
THE PLATEAU
SWEDEN
FINLAND

+ *Brattholm sunk by Germans*
1 *The Midwife's House*
2 *Bjorneskar*
3 *Lyngseidet*
4 *Kjerringdal*

English Miles
0 5 10   20

0 5 10   20 Kilometres

9° East of Oslo

JAN BAALSRUD'S ROUTE FROM TOFTEFJORD
TO SWEDEN

APPENDIX I

CHRONOLOGICAL TABLE

March 24 *Brattholm* sailed from Shetland.
    29 Landfall off Senja.
    30 The fight in Toftefjord.
    31 Jan in Ringvassöy at the midwife's house.
April 3 Reached Bjorneskar.
    4 Rowed across sound.
    5 To Kjosen by motor boat: through Lyngseidet at dawn.
    5 to 8. Lost in Lyngen Alps.
    8 Found Marius's farm at Furuflaten.
    12 Across Lyngenfjord to Revdal.
    12 to 25. In the hut at Revdal.
    25 Ascent of Revdal.
    25 to May 2. In the snow grave.
May   1 Marius and Agnethe climb the plateau.
    2 Mandal men arrive: first attempt on frontier.
    9 Second attempt on frontier.
    22 Carried down to cave in Mandal.
    26 Carried up to plateau again.
June   1 Crossed the Swedish border.

APPENDIX II

*A German newspaper account of the ' Brattholm ' incident
taken from Deutsche Zeitung, 8th June, 1943*

FISHING BOAT WITH STRANGE CARGO

British sabotage group rendered harmless on Norwegian Coast

IN THE twilight of a spring evening a large seaworthy fishing-boat
steams slowly out of a little harbour in the Shetland Islands. In the
light breeze which blows in from the sea, flutters the Norwegian
military flag—it has only been hoisted as the ship left port. No
security measures were to be neglected. Even before sailing, everything had been done to prevent unwanted people approaching the
boat or her crew. After all, even in England it is not every day that
a fishing-boat is made ready for a trip to Norway. No wonder the
greatest pains were taken to get the enterprise off to a good start.

Twelve men comprise the crew of this boat as it sails towards
the east. Anyone who overheard them would soon be able to establish
that all the men were talking Norwegian. A certain Sigurd Eskesund
is leader of the expedition. He was born on a mountain range in
Norway, but his parents died prematurely when he was young, and
so he left his native country and made his way, as so many did at
that time, to the United States. For years in America he fought
starvation, tried his luck here and there, until at last he found food
and shelter and the necessities of life on a farm. When war broke
out, unemployment threatened again. Then one day he was urged
to go to England to join the Norwegian legion. For two days he
thought the matter over. But time had helped him to make a decision.
The spectre of being without food hung over him again, and more-
over he was being accused again of being a foreigner. And so he
reported himself to the recruiting centre. A little later, he arrived in
England. There he underwent his military training, and also attended

a sabotage school and was taught to be a paratrooper. Months passed, months that were used in London and in Scotland to forge plans—not for the daring invasion that was always being talked about, but merely plans to decide where and how and when the Norwegian sabotage troops could be utilised. And now at last such an enterprise was under way.

Four days passed. Three men stand on the upper deck of the Norwegian boat and look eastwards. To-day they are wearing —according to orders—civilian clothing. They are the three men of the sabotage party. The real crew are no longer allowed to show themselves. Once again, to the best of their knowledge, all precautionary measures have been taken. I hope, said one of the men, Harald, that behind this fog bank there lies our coast. For it was about time. Engine trouble yesterday had forced them to slow down.

They sail on to a small outlying island which is only inhabited by a few fisher folk. This really ought to be an ideal hide-out. They hope it will be, for none of them feel happy on their lame vessel any longer—especially since a German reconnaissance plane continually swoops over the boat. In the faces of these twelve men on the fishing-boat *Bariholm* there is consternation : have we been recognised? It is true the Norwegian battle flag has now been hauled down, but there is still the danger that the German is not quite satisfied.

For all three members of the sabotage party one thing is certain : as soon as they get ashore they will set up their radio and send this report to London—that the German air reconnaissance and coastal guard are very strong indeed. There is no way of slipping in unobserved. Not even a chance for a cleverly disguised fishing-boat— though God knows there are plenty of herring barrels on board to disguise her. All one has to do is to take them to bits, without any fear that salt water will pour over one's sea-boots, or that twitching fish will wriggle and slither away. No, all that has to be done is to open these barrels and there are wonderful well-oiled machine-guns. And it is the same with the fish boxes, only they contain hand grenades.

Now the coast looms up out of the fog. A small bay is selected as it has high rocks to protect it. Here the boat will probably be well concealed. Somewhat reassured by this, but none the less anxious and nervous, the sabotage party paddles ashore in a dinghy. It is a fair distance they have to cover. So they are glad when at last they

touch land and jump out on to the beach. After long years they have
Norwegian soil under their feet again!

They set off in a direction where they can see smoke. An old
woman comes towards them—the first Norwegian in their own homeland! What greeting and reception will they get on this far-flung
islet? They begin to ask her questions. They ask for someone who
understands engines and can help them to repair the engine of their
boat. But the woman will not help them. Next they meet a boy.
Yes, he says, he will fetch his father who is a fisherman. They seldom
see foreigners there, he says. Harald looks at Sigurd. But Sigurd
behaves as if he has not heard what the boy said. He tries to do
business with the fisherman. No, says he, he can give them no
advice. In their short talk he has already summed up these intruders.
What is the meaning of it all, Sigurd wonders.

They go on and on, like spurned beggars in a foreign land. Again
and again they are told with a shrug that no help can be given. So
the three offer first money, and then food which had been specially
issued to them for bribery. But even that is useless.

Their task unaccomplished, they can only go back, grumbling and
tired, to the hideout of their boat. Damn it, what is to be done now?
Over here the boat is no further use to them. They must bury its
valuable cargo. A thousand kilograms of dynamite are stowed
in the hold. Where to put it? First of all let's get back, says Sigurd,
to look at the maps on board and think it over! Little do they
imagine what surprise awaits them.

Downcast by their cool reception in their one-time homeland, by
the unsuccessful pleading and attempts at bribery, they push off again
in their dinghy. Hardly have they come in sight of their boat when
close by they see a German warship. They turn towards land again,
there is yet one more chance—escape! But they hear the shout of
"Halt!" The three of them row with all their might. A burst
of machine-gun fire from the warship sweeps over the water.
Onward! shouts Sigurd. A fresh wave of machine-gun bullets
smashes the side of the boat. The water begins to rise in it. There
is nothing for it but to swim for shore. And now they see that two
boats have cast off from the German warship. They are trying to
cut off their escape. It is a matter of life and death! The water is
cold, it grips the heart.

When finally they get to land, a party of German soldiers and sailors is waiting to receive them. The long swim in the cold water, the strong current, and perhaps also their experience ashore, have taken more toll of their strength than they realised. Helpless, shivering with cold, with no will-power left, they drag themselves up the stone quay—and give themselves up as prisoners. Sabotage operation " M " is broken up. Norwegians, who once believed they were helping to free their country, have once again been cynically and uselessly sacrificed by England. When their countrymen who had taken part in the capture heard the Wehrmacht communiqué, they expressed their verdict in a single word : " Misled."

Return Ticket

by

ANTHONY
DEANE-DRUMMOND

Contents

To

SHIRLEY

born January 13th, 1945

CHAPTER ONE

The Plan

"RISE AND SHINE, Pommy, breakfast's up and Portugal is on the horizon."

For a moment I could not remember where I was. It gradually dawned on me that a penetrating Australian voice was shouting that breakfast was ready, and that we had just made landfall near the northern tip of Portugal. I was on the way to Malta in a Royal Australian Air Force Sunderland flying boat, on an enterprise the like of which had never before been attempted by the British Army.

As I lay in my bunk, still only half awake, with the muffled roaring of the Sunderland's four engines pervading everything, I started to think over the last eight months. Certainly it had been the most strenuous period of my life. As athletes are trained for a race so we had been trained for battle. Four weeks' intensive physical training had been followed by real parachuting. In those days when relatively little was known about the tricks of this particular trade, we had to learn by trial and error and on the basis of our own experience. There were surprisingly few fatal accidents and there was every incentive not to repeat a mistake. All of us were volunteers coming from every conceivable unit in the British Army and nothing appeared to dampen the men's enthusiasm. So long as they thought it would bring the day nearer when they would go into action, they did not mind how dangerous or exhausting their training might be.

After parachuting we went up to Scotland to train as

7

infantry and to be toughened up. At the end of a month of extreme physical activity which included shooting, marching, climbing and so on, a miscellaneous collection of enthusiastic individuals had been transformed into a team, fit, efficient and above all, terribly keen to exhibit its prowess.

The next five months were, in consequence, rather an anticlimax. We relapsed into routine training because there was nothing more useful for us to do. To us it seemed that no one knew how, or when, or where we were going to be used—and no one appeared to care. We had joined for adventure and action. After you have done it a few times the excitement of parachuting wears pretty thin, so that now all we wanted was to go anywhere and do anything to prove ourselves in battle.

Around Christmas Day 1940, six of us had our answer. We had been chosen, together with about thirty men, for an operation which was due to come off in about a month. Our excitement can be imagined, and we all congratulated ourselves on our good fortune in having been chosen for the job from the whole commando. Major T. A. G. Pritchard, M.B.E., Royal Welch Fusiliers, was to command us. " Tag " Pritchard was a regular soldier; he had got out of running a transit camp (hotel keeping he always used to call it) in order to go on active service by volunteering to parachute. In fact he was rather heavy for a parachutist, having been a good heavy-weight boxer in his younger days. In spite of a rather gruff and inarticulate manner, there could not have been a more likeable or a more loyal commanding officer. Of the remaining five officers two were demolition experts from the Royal Engineers, Captain G. F. K. Daly and 2/Lt. G. R. Patterson, a young and tireless Canadian. The protection party consisted of Captain C. G. Lea, myself, a lieutenant in Royal Signals, and 2/Lt. A. G. Jowett, our second Canadian, who prided himself on being more Scottish than the Scots, and more bloodthirsty than anyone else. At this stage we were only told enough to allow us to train efficiently—namely that we were to blow up a bridge somewhere in enemy territory.

Early in January we were joined by two Italian interpreters,

Flight-Lt. Lucky of the R.A.F. and Sgt. Pichi. Both were about forty-five which is a healthy age to start parachuting. Sgt. Pichi was perhaps the most surprising member of our party—and certainly not the least courageous. In civilian life he had been banqueting manager at the Savoy Hotel. He had been interned as an alien at the beginning of the war; but, with a lot like him, he had volunteered for any job that the British Government might give him. He was fanatical, both in his hatred of the Fascists and his love of Italy. Uniform did not change him much. He was still the suave and polite little man, with a bald top to his head and a slight middle-age spread, who might be expected to be in charge of banquets at the Savoy, and no one would have recognised him as the hero he proved to be.

We all trained hard in that cold month of January, 1941. We had left our comfortable billets in Knutsford, Cheshire, and had been concentrated on Ringway Airfield for the final rehearsals.

At Ringway we lived hard. Before breakfast each morning we went for a three mile run, followed by thirty minutes' P.T. After breakfast we normally had a 12-15 mile " parachute march." This meant covering at least eleven miles every two hours and it took some doing while carrying full equipment. The afternoon was spent rehearsing on the mock up of the bridge that had been built of wood in Tatton Park, about five miles from Ringway. It was in this park that we had done all our early parachute jumps and it was here that we carried out a complete rehearsal, including parachuting from the aircraft which we were to use on the actual operation.

Previously we had been using two or three old Mk. I Whitleys, which were all the Air Ministry could spare for Churchill's newly formed airborne forces. The Whitley was not a very suitable aircraft from which to parachute. It was originally designed to carry a gunner half-way down the fuselage in a kind of dustbin, and when this was removed, it left a hole about four feet across through which it was possible to jump one at a time. The fuselage was about four feet high and not much wider than the hole itself, so a drill was evolved with half the parachutists sitting aft of the hole and half forward. When the pilot gave us warning over the intercom that it was fifteen minutes to the target, a scene of frenzied activity used to take place. Equipment was checked over, parachute static lines clipped to a bar above the hole, and the parachute exit doors loosened, but not opened. The doors were normally only opened five minutes before dropping, to stop the men getting frozen stiff. When the red light came on, indicating five seconds to drop, the two nearest to the hole sat on its edge facing each other, and the remaining six edged up as close as they could get. As soon as the green light came on, we dropped alternately from front and rear of the hole and it took about fifteen seconds to clear the whole " stick " of eight parachutists. The great idea was to jump as quickly as possible one on top of the other so as to land close together on the ground. One of the difficulties of " hole jumping " was to make a completely clean exit without touching the sides. If you pushed off too hard, your face encountered the far edge as you went out. If you slid out too gently, the parachute on your back bounced you off your side of the hole so that your face again met the far side! Nor did the slip-stream help, for as it acted first on the legs of the parachutist as he emerged from the aircraft, it tended to topple him over unless he went out perfectly straight. As may be imagined, there were quite a few bruised and bleeding faces walking about Knutsford and Ringway in those days, disfigured by what came to be called a " Whitley kiss." The parachute we used was of the self-opening type that required no action on the part of the parachutist. A static line was fastened between the plane and the bag containing the parachute on the man's back. Only when the parachute was pulled completely out of the bag did a weak link of thin nylon cord break and sever the parachute from the aeroplane.

As we trained, so our efficiency improved and eventually we found we could place the half ton or so of explosive in position in just over half an hour. Our N.C.O.s and men could not have been better. We planned to put six parachutists, together with their arms and explosives, into each of six aircraft, leaving two aircraft spare which could be used for diversionary bombing if they proved to be serviceable on the day. In each aircraft was one officer, one sergeant or corporal, and four other ranks, whilst in containers suspended in the bomb bays, were the arms and explosives. We actually released the containers with their coloured parachutes in the middle of the " stick " of parachutists, to reduce the chances of losing all the arms and explosives. In case some failed to arrive we carried double the amount of explosive that it was estimated we would require.

I need hardly say that in spite of every precaution our final rehearsal did not go according to plan. A cloudy night and a strong wind combined to make the dropping inaccurate and in consequence it proved difficult and in some cases impossible for the men to collect together on the ground. About half the aircraft dropped their loads in the wrong place, so that the wretched parachutists landed in the trees along one side of Tatton Park. Those that did land correctly were dragged by their parachutes on landing, or, worse still, had to chase their arms and explosive containers which were bowling along at a brisk ten or fifteen m.p.h. over the ground. The men that had landed in the trees were unhurt, but continued to dangle in their harness unable to get down or climb up without the help of the local fire brigade, which was perhaps rather humiliating. From this minor fiasco we deduced that the operation was not feasible in a strong wind, and that though landing in a tree rarely did anyone any material harm, it was often quite impossible to get down without outside help.

At the end of the month I was told that I was going ahead to our advanced base at Malta by Sunderland flying boat and would leave immediately. I was also to act as liaison officer carrying the operation orders to the Army, Navy and Air Force chiefs at Malta, and would have to answer any questions they might want to put to me. I was then let into the secret for the first time. We were to blow up an aqueduct in the heart of Southern Italy, and then be taken off by submarine from the west coast. The aqueduct fed the naval ports of Bari, Brindisi

and Taranto which were being used to supply Mussolini's inglorious war in Albania and Greece. The operation had been
rather cynically given the code name of "Colossus."

As I went over each point in turn with our planning staff, I
soon realised that our chances of blowing up the bridge were
excellent, but our chances of getting away depended on whether
or not we could march the sixty miles through mountainous
enemy country to the coast.

I took the train to Plymouth where the Sunderlands were
based, and for the next seven days hung about waiting for
suitable weather. At last the met. predicted a clear patch at
about 4 a.m., and we took off from a crowded Plymouth harbour
between two air raids. I then fell asleep on my bunk and, as I
have already related, was awakened by a cheerful Australian
dishing up one of the best breakfasts I have ever eaten. On the
port side the sun was just rising behind the Portuguese mountains and to starboard was the endless Atlantic.

All that day we flew down the Portuguese coast and about
tea-time we made a beautiful landing in Gibraltar harbour.
That night we spent merrily in a brightly-lit Gibraltar which
was a strange contrast to the gloomy blackout of England.

We took off at dawn the following day on the thousand mile
hop to Malta. The weather was glorious with the bright
Mediterranean sun shining down on the calm and glistening sea.
It made me pity all those in England which, at that time, was
shrouded in fog and snow storms. As each hour droned idly by,
I could think of little except how the adventure was going to
turn out.

When at last we sighted Malta, I remember being astounded
by its brownness, and by the countless tiny little fields into which
it was divided. Even the houses appeared to be brown and to
merge into the brown-looking land. We landed at the seaplane
base of Kalafrana towards dusk, and I was immediately whisked
away to deliver up my documents and to meet the Governor,
General Dobbie.

When I met General Dobbie I was struck by his piercing

gaze, and the calm and hospitable atmosphere which surrounded him and those about him. He very kindly put me up for the night at his house.

On the next day there followed a frantic rush round all the various Naval, Military and Air Force H.Q.s in Malta, fixing up accommodation for the party which was due to arrive any day. The aircraft carrier *Illustrious* had been dive-bombed in Valletta harbour only about a month before and a suitable barracks which satisfied all the security requirements was exceedingly difficult to find. At length I found that the old quarantine hospital of Lazaretto, on Manuel Island, would fill the bill. It had just been taken over as a naval base and included the submarine *Triumph* which had been detailed to take us off from Italy.

When the men arrived they were highly amused by suddenly talking about mess decks and hammocks instead of mess rooms and beds. They were not so amused when they found that they had actually to sleep in them. In addition to the accommodation, which was the main worry, all the explosives and other stores that we wanted had to be drawn up, and arrangements made to transport them to the airfield. I was in Malta about forty-eight hours before the main party arrived, but those forty-eight hours seemed to pass in a flash. While I was there we had about five or six air raids, generally by single Italian aircraft which did no damage. The gun-fire sounded good and I think it was mistaken by the Maltese for bombs.

At dawn on the 9th February, 1941, all eight Whitleys arrived, much to the surprise of the R.A.F. in Malta who had expected one or two to fall by the wayside, as had always happened on previous flights to the island. They had flown the 1,400 miles from Mildenhall in Suffolk, with a following wind, and they arrived in record time. The officers and men were soon seated at breakfast and then the rush started. We had just thirty-six hours to get the planes and troops prepared for the trip. The explosive had to be loaded up into the containers and the containers into the planes. Arms and ammunition had to be checked over and all rations for the operation to be dealt out. In addition the men had to be rested.

By 4 p.m. on the 10th, all was ready and then for the first time " Tag " Pritchard briefed all ranks on the actual object and the hoped-for result of our operation. Up till this point everybody had thought we were going to go to Abyssinia. Maps of East Africa had been left in offices and pictures of railway bridges near Addis Ababa examined. All the troops cheered when they heard that it was going to be Italy itself. Maps were issued and the whole plan gone over again and again.

I may say that although the blowing up of the bridge had been practised and rehearsed to the minutest detail, the actual orders for getting to the coast were necessarily vague. We were told that we would split up into several parties and rendezvous at the same spot on the coast five days later. Light signals were arranged for bringing the submarine in, but routes were left to the individual parties to work out for themselves. I don't think any of us worried too much about this, for all we thought of was how to blow up the bridge, and we relied on luck to get us out of the country.

All we needed now was a favourable weather report and we would be off. So far so good, and we all prayed that our luck would hold.

CHAPTER TWO

The Operation

THE WEATHER report was satisfactory and at about 5 p.m. we gulped down some hot tea and hard boiled eggs. I did not feel at all hungry and as one of the men put it, "These Maltese eggs seem coated with glue." We were dressed in all our paraphernalia—over the webbing pouches we wore a loose garment called a jumping jacket and on top of that went the parachutes. Feeling very over-dressed and clumsy, we took a truck to the waiting aeroplane and squeezed laboriously down the rather narrow tunnel of the Whitley. While the men settled down in unaccustomed silence, all the lights and bomb-release switches were tested. Then we heard crackling through the intercom, "N for nuts now ready to take off—over." Back came the reply, "Hallo N for nuts, O.K. Good luck. Off." We had started on our great adventure.

Our eardrums tightened as the aeroplane climbed through the sky and soon the pilot told us that we were flying at ten thousand feet over Sicily. Just over the northern coast the aeroplane started to rock and bump and we could hear the engines speed up and then slow down. This was the flak about which we had been warned, but it did not seem very alarming from the inside of a Whitley.

By now most of the men had settled down comfortably and were nicely asleep, but it seemed quite soon when we heard the cry, "Fifteen minutes to target." Everybody was immediately electrified into action. Equipment was checked over, parachute static lines sorted out and the parachute exit doors loosened.

After what seemed like a very long fifteen minutes, we were astounded to see the rear gunner come through from his perch in the tail and shout out, " You are due to drop in under a minute. Get cracking." The intercom had failed at the last minute, and for about ten seconds there was a pandemonium while we wrestled with the doors.

Suddenly I saw the light of a village flash by underneath, not a hundred feet below. I now knew that we might expect our red light in a few seconds, as the run-up to the target went straight over the middle of the village of Calitri. Sure enough, on came the red light and we all braced ourselves for the jump. We knew we had five more seconds in the plane before we started on our adventure. It seemed unreal. Why on earth was I sitting at the edge of a gaping hole looking down on Italy? Those five seconds were interminably long. I seemed to have time to think about everything. I glanced at the rest of my section, wondering what was passing through their minds. They looked cheerful but pale, and they too, were looking around at their companions. Through the hole at my feet some houses and then a river flashed by in the moonlight. It could not be long now.

" Green light!" A sudden jolt into reality. I was number five. Number six, the last one out, started counting " No. 1." " No. 2." " No. 3." " Containers." (The containers release switch was pressed and out dropped all the containers.) The men had gone out superbly so far—and after a slight interval for the containers No. 4 opposite me dropped out and I followed.

The first thing I noticed was the silence after the incessant drone of the engines. There was a slight jerk and I found myself swinging gently a few hundred feet above the ground. I looked round to see where the rest of my " stick " were. The containers were bunched together, oscillating rhythmically under their coloured parachutes a very few yards away, and beyond them were the first four parachutes swinging like myself in the light of the full moon.

We had been dropped rather low, from not more than five hundred feet, which gave us about fifteen seconds before we touched down. I could only be about two hundred feet up at the most, and I started to take a more intelligent interest in the few square yards of Italy that I was going to land on. It seemed that I was going to drop on to a small bridge with a few cottages about a hundred and fifty yards away from it. This was our bridge. It stood out clearly, looking just as it did in the air photograph. The cottages were those that my section had to clear of all inhabitants to prevent them giving the alarm. The aqueduct was exactly as it had been described to us except that the surrounding country was far wilder and tilted at far sharper angles than we had expected. I was drifting towards the hillside just above the bridge. The ground was rushing upwards at me now and I braced myself for the landing. Just as my toes touched, I pulled on my rigging lines with all my might. Over I went on one side and the canopy of the parachute slowly lost its shape and flopped its yards of silk and rigging lines all over me. It was the best landing I had ever made.

I had come down in a ploughed field on the side of a hill about a hundred yards above the aqueduct. As I lay on the ground, I fumbled feverishly with my quick-release box, and eventually disentangled myself from the parachute and its rigging lines which seemed determined to prevent me moving off. The arms and explosive containers were only a few yards away, and these were quickly opened with the help of one or two of my section who had already joined me. I moved down to the bridge and ordered the rest of my men to divide into two parties. One was to clear some shacks just above where we had landed, and the other to clear the cottages just below the bridge which we had to destroy. I myself would be at the aqueduct and all inhabitants were to be brought to me there.

I could hardly believe that I was really in enemy Italy. The Italian countryside in the hard, clear light of the full moon looked utterly peaceful and curiously like a Scottish glen. The hills were of course much higher, some being five or six thousand feet. The chief difference was that instead of grass and heather as in Scotland, the whole country was ploughed, even up the steepest and most inaccessible slopes.

The aqueduct turned out to be much the same as the one we had practised on, with one important difference. It was made of reinforced concrete. We had expected a masonry bridge and as reinforced concrete is a far harder substance to destroy, our supplies of explosives might well prove insufficient. That, however, was a problem for the sappers to solve. While all this was going on, the buzzing of aeroplanes grew more frequent and by the flare of an occasional green Very light, we knew that further droppings were about to begin.

I was wide awake, and kept straining my eyes through the night for any signs of the rest of our party. In the original plan my plane was due to drop third at 9.42 p.m. We dropped on the tick of 9.42 but it was not until about 10.15 that there was any sign of anybody else. I remember having a rather funny feeling somewhere inside me when it occurred to me that perhaps all the other planes had lost their way and ours was the only one to arrive. I think we all had the same thought. Then we saw the parachutes idly floating down in the silent night.

There was a loud crashing through the bushes and thorn ash in the valley bottom. My men took the cue and prepared to fire, only waiting my signal in case it should be one of our own sections. But when the trees parted out came old Tag by himself, a little out of breath, as his plane load had been landed about a mile away down by the river. Carrying up all the explosives was clearly going to be hell and we decided then and there to use all the tame Italians we could find to help us. It was a funny business. We had all been prepared to kill Italians and when we arrived at the spot there were only a few peasants and they were only too willing to work for us.

By now a lot of our men were arriving at the bridge. Some were preparing to defend it, and the remainder were helping to set the charges beneath it as the Italians arrived with the boxes of explosive. The peasants told us that it would give them enough to talk about for the rest of their lives! It would be interesting to know what account of the raid is being passed from mouth to mouth at the present time.

My section was just below the bridge. Near it were the cottages into which we had put the women and children; Christopher Lea's was on either side of the bridge and Geoff Jowett was opposite to me on the north side of the stream. Our orders were to give warning of anybody coming up the valley and, if necessary, to prevent interference with the parties carrying the explosive. There was to be no firing unless it was unavoidable. As it happened the only man in uniform who appeared was the local station-master from Calitri railway station. He was duly impressed into the labour gang and made quite a good porter, as was only proper. His biggest worry was that he would be late taking over from his relief and might get the sack. If he was sacked he would be put in the army and sent to the front, which he pointed out was far too terrible a punishment for kind people like us to inflict on him. We told him that his skilled labour was required, but that if he liked we would give him a certificate to say that he had been detained against his will. This cheered him up tremendously and from then on nobody could stop him talking. He said he might even get a medal for his heroic labours. We heard later that most of these civilians were awarded medals for their brave conduct in face of the enemy.

All the time gangs of men had been passing up the track through our position, loaded with 50 lb. boxes of gun cotton. Muffled swear words streamed from their lips as they sweated. This was the only noise to be heard apart from the occasional yapping of dogs and the tinkling of a stream close by. As soon as enough explosive had been carried up to the bridge I stopped the last of the porters, who was carrying two boxes on his shoulders. It seemed such a pity to waste it so I put it under one end of a small bridge carrying the track which led to the main aqueduct. This would delay the repair work. Cpl. Watson, R.E. placed the charges and I sent a message to Tag to explain what was happening and that the small bridge would be blown up as soon as I heard the big bang. The explosion of a single slab of gun cotton was the signal that the aqueduct was about to be blown up. This was to act as a warning for all the defence sections, and when they heard it everybody had to move to a safe position about two hundred yards to the west.

The sound of the warning explosion in that still air echoed and re-echoed among the hills. There was a small pause, and then we immediately started to move quickly. Cpl. Watson and I stayed behind to deal with the little bridge while I ordered the rest of my section to go to the rendezvous.

Cpl. Watson lit the fuse and we withdrew just behind the cottages waiting for the two explosions, the one of the aqueduct and the other from our own little bridge.

"Whoomf!" Our bridge went up in a cloud of flying concrete, iron rails and bits of masonry. I had never expected so much debris, and we were showered with blocks of concrete and bits of iron. The wretched people in the cottages set up a wail and a woman ran out of the house with a baby in her arms when the bits started thudding down on the roof. Not thirty seconds later up went the main bridge with a tremendous roar. About a third of a ton of gun cotton had been carefully slung into place against one of the piers under George Patterson's orders. The aqueduct was constructed in three piers and we had planned to blow up all three. The senior Royal Engineer officer, Captain Gerry Daly, had not arrived by the time the bridge was due to go up and we had to assume that his plane had either been lost or had failed to take off. Pat took over his duties and he decided to concentrate all the explosive on one pier. Even then, the chance that it would break was small, but it was the only hope of success, and all depended on the quality of the Italian concrete.

Cpl. Watson and I went up to inspect the damage we had done to the little bridge before joining the rest of the party, who by now were all assembled about two hundred yards to the west of the aqueduct. Our bridge had been neatly cut and one end lay in the bed of the stream. We then slowly clambered up to where the rest were standing and eagerly asked for the news of the aqueduct. Tag and Pat had gone back to look at the damage and had left the rest of the men at the assembly position. Impatiently we awaited their return, all wondering what on earth we should do if there was no damage. We had been keyed up for this moment for the past six weeks and failure would have been unbearable.

Tag and Pat came back without a smile on their faces. Was it a fiasco? Tag put up his hand and everybody stopped talking. All he said was, "Listen." We all strained our ears and sure enough we heard the sound of a great waterfall. It was a success. How we cheered and cheered! We could hardly imagine that we were in enemy country. Those British cheers must have been heard a good mile or two away.

All our inward hopes and fears about the success of the venture were now soothed and the reaction made us all feel very tired. What was more tiring still was the thought of having to walk some sixty or seventy miles across the mountains to the coast.

Tag had decided before we started that we would have the best chance of getting to our coastal rendezvous if we split up into small parties and made our own way to the sea, and accordingly he divided us into three, each with about ten men and two officers. Tag and myself were with the first party, Christopher Lea and George Patterson the second and Flight-Lt. Lucky and Geoff Jowett the third.

The barks of a dog pierced the night. It seemed impossible that we would not have all Italy on our heels by the morning. We bent our backs and laboured slowly through the mud up the hills.

CHAPTER THREE

Man Hunt

A MAN HUNT is an unpleasant thing. If you are the man it is worse still. The bridge was blown up and we had achieved all we had set out to do. Now came the anti-climax; we had to get to the coast as quickly and as secretly as possible. Tag gave orders to lighten our loads and so all our heavier weapons, which included Bren and tommy-guns, were taken to bits and pushed into the mud soon after leaving the bridge. This still left each man with a 30 lb. pack containing five days' rations, together with his mess tin, waterbottle and a miniature primus stove. For arms, we only retained our Colt automatic pistols, because we relied on getting to our rendezvous on the coast unseen and unheard.

Our plan was to climb the mountain behind the aqueduct and then follow the ridge until we reached the Sele watershed. From there we would make our way down the north side of the Sele valley towards the Mediterranean. Right from the start we met difficulties. Fields knee-deep in mud, impassable little ravines, innumerable farmhouses all with noisy dogs, were only a few of our obstacles. We soon learnt to disregard the dogs, as does everybody else in Italy. Their function in life was to yap for twenty-four hours on end if need be. Any excuse would do, from the farmyard cat to a sudden gust of wind rattling the kennel roof.

Every three quarters of an hour Tag stopped and we sat down, munching chocolate or sipping a little water till we were sufficiently recovered to continue. On and on we tramped, pulling ourselves up the sides of steep little gorges on our hands and then slithering down the other side on our seats. All the jagged prominences and rocks were exaggerated by the moonlight and appeared twice their real distance away. Occasionally we had a glimpse from the tops of some of the ridges and the countryside seemed endless in its variety of obstacles, all supremely difficult for marching troops. How we cursed all Italy, the Italians and everything Italian that night!

We had left the bridge at 1.30 a.m. and we halted about 7 a.m. By that time we must have covered at least fifteen miles over the ground, but had only done six out of the sixty we had to do before reaching the coast. This meant that on future nights we would have to double our mileage if we were to get there in time.

We found a nice, sheltered little ravine in which to lie up during the day. There was a stream nearby and plenty of cover. Off came our equipment and some of us attempted to sleep before cold made it impossible. A few tried to cook some food before lying down. I had always found it best to sleep first while still warm and, when the cold wakes me, to start thinking about a meal. After a wonderful three hours' rest we were woken at 10 a.m. by the noise of a low-flying aeroplane. It was obviously looking for us and was only about five hundred feet above where we were hiding, but after ten minutes, during which we all kept our faces well down, it flew away and we did not see it again.

Miniature primus stoves were pulled out of our rucksacks, and after some splutters and abortive hissing, we soon had mess tins of boiling water in which we brewed sweet tea or made a greasy porridge of pemmican and biscuits. Pemmican, which is the old polar explorers' standby, is made of meat extract, with added fat, and tastes like concentrated greasy Bovril. Personally I found it quite nauseating although it may well be ideal for Arctic expeditions.

From our hiding place in the bushes we could see the Italian peasants at their work in the fields and, over on the other side of the valley, our old friend the village of Calitri perched on a small knoll half-way up the mountain. The brilliant sun and the scent of wild thyme and olive trees were all wonderful, but our hunted feeling rather prevented us from appreciating fully the countryside around us.

I shall always remember the boulders. The little ravine in which we were sheltering was filled completely with enormous boulders of all shapes and sizes. Some seemed strung together like a necklace whilst others were perched on top of one another in defiance of all the laws of gravity. Straight in front of us, not more than a quarter of a mile away, rose a sheer cliff which we would have to scale that evening. More hell to come!

Night came at last and on went our packs, with our pistols at our belts. Tag had noticed a shepherd with a flock of goats come down a path in the cliff during the day, and he said he thought he could find it. Before climbing we had to cross a small stream, not more than ten yards wide, but most unpleasant to fall into as it had deep pools and a swift current flowing between round slippery boulders. Eventually we found a crossing place which provided stepping stones most of the way over except for a gap in the middle. Nearly all jumped it successfully, but I saw one man slip and tumble in. He had to travel the rest of that night in soaked clothes.

Tag led the way and we started to approach our cliff. When we reached its foot, we discovered that it was not so steep as had appeared from our hiding place and with a bit of difficulty we could pull ourselves up. Every bit of scrub and long grass came in handy now, and we sweated and heaved our way up the three hundred feet of mud and shingle which formed most of the surface. As we arrived at the top each man threw himself panting on the ground. It had taken every ounce of our energy to climb that hill and we felt it later on.

I was leading now and slowly we crept on in single file with ears strained for the slightest sound. We could see a few cottages against the skyline and we assumed that they must be the outskirts of Pescopegano. Dogs could be heard barking all over the village and farther up the valley. Perhaps it was one of the other parties that was causing the disturbance. I kept wondering how they were getting on.

The country looked wilder and more impossible than ever. The moonlight distorted every natural hummock and glade into grotesque and weird shapes. Before us stretched mile upon mile of the roughest country we had ever seen. Few landmarks could be picked out and so we decided to march by compass to a large crossroad near the source of the Sele river. During this night's march we had to cover some twenty miles and then to find hideouts for the following day somewhere along the north side of the Sele valley. We crossed countless small streams and stumbled through wild junipers and stunted oak thickets. We were always walking either up or down or along the side of a hill. Compass marching in this sort of country is not easy, but we managed to strike a small road which we were expecting to find.

At this stage we decided it was too risky to walk along the road, but preferred to use it as a guide, keeping it about a quarter of a mile below us. Gradually we worked our way forward, trying to avoid the scattered little farmhouses, which were becoming more numerous. At each brook we came to we first threw ourselves flat on our faces and sucked up some clear ice-cold water. Our mouths were dry with exhaustion and some of the men were completely worn out. We skirted several villages and eventually Tag decided to stop and make some sweet tea to keep us going. Soon the primus was spurting and hissing, and a welcome steam was coming off the mess tin. It was the best dixie of tea I've ever had. New energy seemed to pour into our veins as we sipped the hot sugary liquid, and when we got up a new briskness was obvious in all our party.

It was about one o'clock in the morning and as we had not seen anything on the road for some time past, Tag very wisely decided to march straight along it and damn the risk. The change of walking along that road after trudging through the mud revived us both mentally and physically. A soldier can march for miles along a road. He gets into a swing and it is only when he has to falter and stumble across country that his real weariness comes to the surface.

For five or six miles we tramped along the road and eventually we reached the big crossroad which was the highest point on our route to the coast. From now on the way ran downhill and our only task before dawn was to find a hiding place for the following day. As we scurried over the crossroad, we looked down the valley. We could see it stretching for miles in the moonlight, with rugged cultivated sides. The country looked forbidding and we could hardly believe that things would continue to go as well.

A light clopping of hooves on the road ahead startled us out of our contemplation. We were too tired and there was too little cover near the road to make a run for it and so Tag formed us into file and made Private Nastri call the step in Italian. A pony cart laden with vegetables came into view, with its big hood pulled down over a peasant woman driver. She was fast asleep and was probably taking her wares to the local village market.

The road led over the hill and away from the line of the valley, so we left it and, keeping about the same height, made our way down the side of the valley. Our route closely followed the line of the subterranean aqueduct, which at this point had been tunnelled through the hill to tap the waters on the far side. The tunnel, which is blasted through some eight miles of solid rock, is a remarkable feat of engineering.

My feet ached as they had never ached before, and my whole body was limp with exhaustion. Immediately we left the road we had to pay attention to avoid stumbling. This added to our general weariness. We continued to search for a hiding place, but nowhere suitable was to be seen. Some of us were near the end of our tether and either a hiding place had to be found soon or we would have men falling out, which was unthinkable. Our maps showed trees covering the top of a nearby hill and Tag decided to try and lie up there. We were still among ploughed fields with occasional farmhouses nestling in a fold of the valley side. As we plodded on, more and more will-power and mental energy were needed to keep us on our feet. We were drawn forward only by the fear of being discovered in those naked fields when dawn came. Thirst was again upon us, and there were no welcome streamlets in which to soak our weary faces and draw some of the cool, clear water down our dry sore throats. We had filled our waterbottles of course, but these would be needed next day and we always kept them in reserve for real emergencies.

We climbed gradually now, hoping to strike the trees, but none could be found. Eventually we even came up to cloud level which was here below the tops of the hills. At last some trees loomed up through the mist, but when we approached we discovered to our chagrin that they sheltered a farmhouse. To have our hopes raised so high and then dashed mercilessly to the ground a moment later was no medicine for men in our condition, and we collapsed on the ground as one man. Our sweat-soaked clothes quickly became ice-cold and in the raw mist we were soon shivering from cold and exhaustion. Tag and I decided to climb up a little higher, to try to find a hiding place. We knew we could not go much farther and the men were in the same state, so it seemed the only course to take. Less than fifty yards higher up cultivation ceased, and we came upon boulders and small juniper bushes which we thought might serve as temporary hiding places. Tag went back and brought up the men and soon we had found cover of some sort to hide in. Two or three men found a tiny cave which just concealed them. It was not good, but we were unable to move another step from sheer exhaustion. We had passed the caring stage and I suppose were a little over-confident of our powers of avoiding detection.

The time was about 5.30 a.m. We had been on the move about ten hours and had covered twenty miles as the crow flies, across enemy country which had truly lived up to its name. Our feet must have travelled a good forty miles through the mud and so it was hardly surprising that we had not much energy left.

The men soon curled themselves up and fell asleep. I was not long following suit and did not wake up till dawn came an hour later. Every bone in my body ached and shivered, my clothes were still soured with sweat and my teeth would not stop chattering.

At first I could not believe my eyes but it was unfortunately too true. A peasant was standing not a hundred yards away looking intently in our direction. He had obviously spotted us and started to walk away. Tag made a quick decision and sent Pichi after him to try and convince him of our honest intentions. I knew in my heart that the game was up, but I could not believe that this was the end. We were fools to think so, but failure when we had travelled so far was unbelievable after the success that had attended our venture up till then.

Pichi came back and said he thought he had satisfied the farmer, but that there were a lot of women and children who had seen us. Some of these had gone off hot foot while he had been at the farm, to warn the local carabinieri police. He did not hold out much hope that we would get away with it. Tag decided that it was useless to try to move off as it would only attract even more attention and so we sat where we were, feeling apprehensive about what was going to happen next.

Some half naked and filthy Italian children with a few mongrel dogs were our first spectators. They sat down about a hundred yards away from us, sucking their dirty thumbs and gazing at us as if we were men from the moon. A minute or two later a peasant appeared with two pointers and a shotgun from over the hill just above our position. He seemed very frightened as he pointed his shotgun straight at Tag and kept up a running commentary, which of course was unintelligible to us. By this time quite a ring of spectators had collected, including a few peasant women who seemed to be the children's mothers. They were typical Italian peasants with nut-brown wrinkled faces, and long dirty black dresses which looked most unsuitable garments for the manual labour to which they are accustomed. Pichi was now asking the man with the shotgun what it was all about. The man then gabbled something and ended by waving his gun around to emphasise his sentences. Eventually we discovered that he wanted us to lay down our arms. As these consisted only of .32 automatics, it seemed a lot of fuss to make about singularly ineffective weapons.

The crowd surrounding our position had now become quite large and we were rather uncertain what to do. One easy way out would have been to chuck two or three hand grenades about and then make a bolt for it. On the other hand the whole countryside seemed to be on the move towards where we were and we would not have lasted long. In addition the grenades would have killed some of the women and children, who had in the meantime been joined by more men.

I remember telling Tag that I did not agree with him when he gave the order to lay down arms.

" All right, Tony," he said, " you throw a grenade at those people on the right and I will throw mine over there."

At that moment I realised I could not do it. Women, children and unarmed peasants were everywhere and we would not be able to avoid casualties among them. All we could achieve were a few extra hours of freedom at the price of a particularly odious and inglorious action.

Disconsolately I agreed with Tag and he told the men. There was dead silence for a moment and then one man asked in an incredulous voice:

" Aren't we going to make a fight for it, sir?"

I had never seen such a look of anguish on anybody's face as on Tag's at that moment. He just looked at the women and then at the man who had asked the question, and said that he was sorry but that they would have to give in. Our hearts ached as we put down our pistols and told Pichi to tell the Italian that we were giving in because of the women and children. As soon as the peasants saw that we had dropped our pistols they came surging up to us and took all our equipment from us, much to our chagrin and disgust. I have never felt so ashamed before or since, that we should have surrendered to a lot of practically un-armed Italian peasants. This was the morning of February 13th, 1941.

Our farmer captors were now grinning from ear to ear with

self-congratulation. Now they could truly be called the Duce's
"Eroici Truppe," whom they had heard so much about in the
newspapers when describing some of the more inglorious
moments of the Italian army in Libya. In addition to the farmers,
there were a number of creatures in army uniform who tried
ineffectually to take charge and slowly we were led off to the
local police, or carabinieri as they are called in Italy.

Carabinieri is a word which will recur in this story. They are
a regiment in the Italian army and combine the duties of civil
and military police. The local bobby in Italy is a carabinieri as
well as being the military policeman in the army. They are supposed to be specially selected and seem to be of a slightly better
stamp than the average Italian soldier.

We had our first experience of these warriors just as we had
breasted the rise, not more than three hundred yards from our
position on the hill. A fat little "sargente di Carabinieri" led
about half a dozen others. All wore navy-blue serge jackets and
knickerbockers of the same colour, which had a thin red stripe
down the outside. They were mostly armed with an inferior
type of automatic pistol which was suspended from one of the
lower pockets of their jackets. Worn bandolier fashion over
one shoulder was a white belt which had a small rectangular
box riveted to it containing handcuffs. Their hats were of the
ordinary round military type and bore the carabinieri badge of a
large flaming grenade. A few carried rifles in addition to the
automatic. The bayonets were hinged and folded back into the
fore-end, which gave the rifle a double-barrelled appearance
from any distance. The rest of the rifle was absurdly small and
light. Some British officers whom we met later, who had used
some captured Italian rifles, said the accuracy was fair up to a
hundred yards. Above a hundred yards even first-class shots
considered it lucky to hit a four-foot target! This was the
standard rifle in use by the Italian army, and could hardly have
inspired confidence in the troops who used it.

As they came up to us we could see that they were dripping
in sweat. When they saw us they immediately cocked their rifles

and automatics as though we were about to attack them. Little had these people thought that war would come to those quiet Italian villages; a "cushy" job is the aim of nearly every Italian, and the carabinieri were rightly annoyed that we should have been so presumptuous as to disturb their peaceful life which up till that time had seemed to them to be a hundred-per-cent safe.

Breathing their foul, garlicky breath into our faces they searched us for arms, and tied us together in parties of three or four. The Italian handcuff is made of chain and can be tightened so that the links dig into one's flesh. Some of us had them put on so tight that no feeling remained in our fingers and our guards refused to loosen them. Only Tag was spared this ignominy. Just before we started to move again he noticed that one of our grenades had a broken split pin. He told Nastri to tell the carabinieri this, and also to tell them that he should throw it away—without pulling the pin—as it was dangerous in its present condition. The flap was wonderful! The sargente began talking and shouting and waving his arms around like a side-show at a circus. He eventually drew out his revolver and, cocking it, held its muzzle right against Tag's head. His finger was on the trigger and he was trembling so violently with rage that I expected to see it go off any minute. Tag lobbed the grenade into the mud where it stuck, and may be still sitting there to this day for all I know. The commotion over, the poor little sargente, who was pouring in sweat down his unshaven face, collapsed like a pricked balloon. He looked a bit sheepish as if ashamed of his own impetuosity.

A narrow winding track led us down into the nearby village of Teora where a small crowd was out to meet us. A few shouts went up, "Viva carabinieri!" "Viva Duce!" as if the carabinieri had had any part at all in our inglorious capture. We were led into the local carabinieri police station which struck damp and cold after the warm sunshine outside. The room in which they locked us up had bare whitewashed walls, and a cold red-tiled floor. Its window looked out through heavy one-inch bars on to the green hillside down which we had just come

CHAPTER FOUR

Jail Birds

AFTER BEING thoroughly searched again we began to feel the reaction to all our adventures. Food and water were asked for and eventually appeared with hunks of bread and a few tins of Italian bully beef. These we greedily devoured and immediately felt a new energy and hope surge through our veins.

That evening we were all pushed into a lorry and driven to the railway station. Guards sat on all sides of us and the men were kept chained together. We felt like a travelling circus moving its animals from one town to the next. But we were the animals. Hungrily we gazed at the free world outside the lorries, with a deep, hopeless feeling inside which increased with every minute as we sped along. The Italians were obviously taking no chances with us, and we never had a hope of making a dash for it.

After about half an hour we arrived at the station and were immediately hustled into an evil-smelling waiting-room which we were told would house us for the night. The stench of our guards who reeked of garlic and spat every three or four minutes on the sawdust covered floor, when combined with our own rank, sour smell, would have been nauseating if we had not been so tired. Gradually we all dozed off where we were sitting from sheer exhaustion, and all that could be heard was a continuous heavy snoring interspersed by the usual Italian throat-clearing followed by a spit, a habit to which I never accustomed myself during the whole of my stay in Italy.

Morning came at last and brought with it the other two parties which had been captured not very far from where we had been taken. One of Geoff Jowett's party had fired a tommy-gun that he had kept, and killed an Italian officer and two peasants. When they were captured soon after, due to lack of ammunition, their clothes were ripped from them and they were rather roughly handled until they arrived at the station.

It was not until about 10 a.m. the next morning that our train came in. The men were put all together in a carriage like a dining saloon with a carabinieri in every seat near a window. The officers were split into pairs and put into ordinary six-seater compartments with four carabinieri who sat in each corner. They certainly did not mean to lose us, and we had so many guards that it was laughable. It rather flattered us that the Italians thought us such desperate characters.

We sat in the same seats all that day and eventually arrived at Naples about an hour after sunset. At the beginning of our journey our guards kept up such a monotonous series of spittings that it ceased to be a joke and Pat became so annoyed that he swore at the guards in as loud and offensive a tone as possible and pointed to the *non sputare* notice in the compartment. This terrified the poor little guards so much that a miracle happened, and the rate of spitting dropped to about one an hour. They even went out of the compartment and did it in the corridor, just to humour the mad Englishmen.

Vesuvius glowed red against the stars and we knew we had arrived at Naples. Lorries were waiting to take us to the local military detention barracks, but before the men were allowed to leave the train they were all chained together once again and taken across the station to the waiting trucks. They were outwardly very cheerful and many were the jokes dropped about the Italians and such remarks as " They say you get to like a ball and chain after the first ten years."

After a lot of talking the carabinieri eventually had us stacked in the lorries with guards on the outside all round us and ten minutes later we were herded into Naples Military Prison. The Italian version of the " glass house " is not so comfortable as in England. A high wall surrounded the prison into which a sentry box was built at each corner. The sentries were able to walk along the top of it and look down into the passage which surrounded the main prison building itself. My cell was about ten feet long and five feet broad. Along one side there was a large concrete block about two feet off the ground and about six feet long. On this was scattered a little straw, which had obviously been used before and had become damp from condensation in the cell. A very small square pane of glass high up in the end of the cell gave the only light. The door was heavily barred and bolted with a small peep hole for the sentry stationed in the corridor.

Our depression was at its lowest when we were pushed into those cells. All that night we slept by fits and starts, turning over from one hip to the other and back again. Morning came at last and with it a sentry who banged open the door and planked down a bowl of ersatz coffee with a small piece of dried fig. We heard that we were soon going to be interrogated and I think we rather looked forward to it. We were all quite confident that nothing would be got out of us, but we had heard so much about the questioning of prisoners of war that we were all curious to see what it was really like.

When the interrogator arrived he was given a room and we were all herded together in the passage outside our cells. I saw Pichi looking very depressed and tried to cheer him up. All he would say was that he was going to make a clean breast of it. " I know nobody likes the Fascists," he said. " They will soon see that I am a true lover of Italy, but at the same time a hater of the Fascist regime." It alarmed me when I heard him talking like that and I told him to keep quiet and stick to his story—that he was a Free Frenchman. I am sure he did not take my advice when he went in to be questioned and I can well imagine him telling the Fascists what he thought of them till he was led off. We never saw him again.

Eventually it came to my turn, and wondering what was going to come next I went into the room. A well-dressed man in civilian clothes was seated at a desk in one corner and immediately behind him were stationed two obvious Fascists. They did not ask any questions themselves, but just stood and watched and listened. At each of the interrogations that I had in the next fifteen months in Italy there were always two black crows standing behind the questioner.

"I am the Commandant of the camp you are going to," he said, "and all I want are a few details for the Red Cross." This was a lie, of course, but it was designed to put me at ease. I then butted in on his suavity and said, "My number is 71076, my rank is lieutenant, and my name is Deane-Drummond and you can expect nothing else." He then followed up with a few innocent questions like the address of next-of-kin, mother's name, etc., and suddenly put a real question. To all of these I told him, "I can't say." Eventually he gave it up and I was sent out. Heaving a sigh of relief at having finished something unpleasant, I went out and rejoined Tag and Christopher who had already been through. They told much the same story, but the questioner had used the line that all he wanted to do was establish who was guilty of shooting the three men. This was absurd as they already knew the answer, and anyhow we were quite within our rights to shoot anybody who attempted to interfere with us, while we were getting to the coast.

Back we went to our cells and found a tolerably good lunch waiting for us, and afterwards a shave by a barber who had come in from the town. We felt immeasurably better now and ready to face anything. Lucky was taken off to another part of Naples and we heard no more till the evening. Suddenly, just after dusk we were surprised and relieved to hear we were going to be moved to the aerodrome, where Lucky had gone already and where there was much better accommodation and food. Up till the time we had been questioned, the Italians believed we must be semi-lunatics or at least criminals who had been reprieved on the scaffold provided we jumped out of an aeroplane. This always seemed the attitude of the average Italian. They could never understand that we enjoyed our job. The word *paracadutisti* always raised awe in the Italian when

mentioned and we found it a disadvantage later when it came
to escaping from prison camps.

On arrival at the aerodrome we were immediately hustled
up the stairs of a four-storey building, and discovered that we
had been allotted bedrooms on the top floor. Here were clean
sheets and comfortable beds, with a wash room not far off down
the corridor. I was put in a room with Geoff Jowett and we
were soon fast asleep.

I woke up at about 9 a.m. to find sun streaming in through
the windows, which looked straight out over the aerodrome, with
Vesuvius in the distance. By looking half right from our window
we could see the whole of the Bay of Naples, with Capri on the
skyline. It really was a heavenly room and we would have enjoyed it but for the shame of being prisoners of war.

Lunch and dinner we had together, in Tag's room. The food
was sent up from the officers' mess and was plentiful and good.
We were still hungry and polished off enormous plates of
minestrone soup, followed by equally large dishes of macaroni,
meat and vegetables. Fruit and wine were put on the table as a
matter of course. During the fortnight that we were in Naples,
we ate solidly and took practically no exercise, with the result
that we all became very fat and spotty.

After great difficulty we succeeded in convincing the authorities that a little exercise was necessary for our health and we
would be led around the aerodrome at a slow stroll by an equal
number of guards. Most Italians have short legs and immediately
we began to walk out to stretch our house-cramped limbs, plaintive bleats went up from the guards. We were eventually told that
unless we walked slower we would have no more walks. As a
makeshift we asked to go up on to the flat roof of our building,
where we paced up and down as fast as we could, trying to keep
fit. The guards were all for this kind of exercise because they
just sat and watched.

One day we were suddenly told to get into one room as the
civil *Questura* or Gestapo had come to take our fingerprints and
get our photographs. Tag made a vigorous protest through

Lucky and said that they had no right to do this as we were not civil prisoners, but prisoners of war. After a lot of arguing they started to take photographs, Tag scowling like a real criminal. In the middle of the proceedings the C.O. of the aerodrome arrived, and flew into a passionate rage when he discovered what was happening. The *Questura* had apparently come to our rooms direct, before seeing him and without his knowledge. He was livid. In so many words he told them that we were his prisoners and not theirs, that we were officers and what miserable worms they were. He ended up by smashing all the photographic plates that the wretched men had brought, including the unexposed ones. I have never seen anybody go away looking quite so sheepish as they did. We burst out laughing as soon as they had left and all voted the aerodrome C.O. to be several shades better than any Italian we had met up to that time.

About four days after we had arrived on the aerodrome, Gerry Daly turned up. He had stayed out five days, after being dropped about two miles north of the correct bridge. His plane had lost the way and his drop took place two hours late. He had not been on the ground more than forty minutes when he heard the two explosions from the bridges, and he had then walked to within fifteen miles of the coast and had been caught trying to get a truck. He thought that we must have all reached the beach and his only hope to get there on time was to obtain transport. Eventually he was taken to Naples jail, from which he escaped the first night. He had noticed that the lock to his door was rotten, and sure enough it broke open to quite a small push when he tried it at about 11 p.m. With his rubber-soled boots he slipped past three sentries and wandered around Naples all that night. Eventually he found the railway with the intention of hopping on to a goods train to try and reach the submarine rendezvous. It was not until about eleven the next morning that a slow enough train came along and when he made a jump for it he somehow missed his hold and went sprawling on to the footpath. He was knocked out, and when he came to he found a soldier pointing a rifle at his head and jabbering Italian. The

Naples carabinieri were the laughing-stock of all Naples when the news of Gerry's escape spread around.

Lucky was allowed to go down into Naples, under escort, to buy clothes for us, which at that time were very plentiful. I don't think Lucky realised that he was getting more freedom then than at any time afterwards when he was a prisoner. He brought back wondrous tales about the outside world, some true and some untrue. Lucky rather annoyed us at times. We had a greasy, half-shaved carabinieri officer who was in charge of our guard, and who occasionally visited us. Lucky used to kow-tow to this creature in order to get more privileges, and it sent cold shivers down our spines whenever we saw it going on. However it did have the great advantage that we obtained a lot of concessions and generally more considerate treatment through it. By the time we were moved on to our proper camp we had accumulated quite a respectable wardrobe of washing kit and shirts, underclothes, pyjamas, etc. These we found invaluable later, and we were much better off than most of the other prisoners.

Just before we were moved, we were given a thorough search and the Italians discovered nearly everything which we had obtained before we left England. Every officer had equipped himself with some money, maps, and a compass needle. The search was quite good, but very stupidly they left a little on everybody, and when we arrived at the camp we were able to muster just about one complete set of escaping equipment, which was a great help to us later on.

We moved on the last day of February. We were told that we were going the night before and to have everything ready by 4 a.m. We packed our few clothes into some suitcases that we had bought and at 4 a.m. we were ushered into a string of ambulances. The carabinieri were all dressed in their best blue and the guard consisted of 1 colonel, 1 captain, 1 subaltern and 35 carabinieri, for the 35 of us. We were always considered desperadoes by the average Italian.

The train slowly puffed its way out of Naples, after a lot of talking and gesticulating by every railway official in the station. We thought we were being given a special send-off, but Lucky told us that the same sort of thing preceded every train departure in Italy. We did not believe him at the time but later on I was to discover how right he was.

The track wound its way through the mountains to Sulmona all that day. At times we were perched on the side of precipices and at others we clattered through evil-smelling tunnels. The scenery grew wilder and more desolate as we neared Sulmona, the birthplace of Ovid.

About four o'clock in the afternoon we burst out of a tunnel and found ourselves rattling along a hillside high above a green and beautiful valley, sparkling in the sunshine with little streams and red-roofed whitewashed farmhouses. After the desolate country we had come through it was like looking down into a real promised land. Before many months were out we were to hate that little valley, surrounded as it was on all sides by five-thousand-foot mountains.

By the time we had all been bundled out of the train by the carabinieri, it was obvious that all hopes of escape on the way to the prison camp were very nearly ruled out. An Italian officer from the camp who could speak English met our party. He was dressed in the olive green field service uniform of an Italian 2nd/lt. and wore an enormous pair of heavily-studded alpine boots. I wondered whether our camp was up one of the hillsides but was soon to learn that the Italian dresses more for effect than utility. He told us we had five miles to walk which cheered us up as we had not had any real exercise for the past fortnight. The carabinieri did not seem at all pleased when they heard this news and as it was starting to spit with rain they looked far more depressed than their prisoners. The Italian is accustomed to sunshine and siestas. When they discovered that our road was about six inches deep in mud, nothing could conceal their disgust. The poor old carabinieri colonel was stepping gingerly along holding his coat tails under each arm to keep them out of the mud, until about half-way when he could stand it no longer and called out to ask the Italian subaltern who led the party whether this was really necessary. The Italian, whom we soon nicknamed "Fish-eyes" because his eyes were set very wide apart, merely grinned and said it was just as far forward as back and they might as well complete the journey. We were enjoying it hugely. It was our first exercise for the last week or two and there were some very successful efforts on the part of some of us to splash mud all over our guard.

In a way we had rather looked forward to getting to the camp. We had visions of Red Cross parcels and plenty of company from the others. We were soon to realise what a mistaken idea we all had of prison camps. On arrival we were led in through tall barbed-wire gates, and then through a door in a brick wall about ten feet high, and up a narrow passage between more high walls to a long low hut devoid of any furniture whatsoever. One end was partitioned off and one by one we were searched. Nothing was found on us and soon we were led off through a maze of walls and passages and shown our homes for the next two months. The Italians had gone to the trouble of making a small walled-off compound in the middle of the camp especially for our benefit. The officers were put in this, and the men were led off by themselves and locked up in another one which again had been specially constructed in their honour.

All the view we could see from outside the hut was the sky and a sheer mountainside. Half-way up, an old hermit's house had been built into the side of the rock, and it was the only sign of habitation that was visible from our prison. Our depression was not eased when we heard that we were not to be allowed out of our compound for any reason whatsoever. We had to feed, sleep, and exercise ourselves all in a little courtyard thirty yards long by three yards broad. It was not two days before I was down with a mild attack of jaundice, which did not help to cheer me up.

The next two months were hell. It hurt us more than most because we were used to an active life with plenty of exercise. The only saving grace was the food. At this stage of the war

Italy had not yet introduced rationing, and we were able to gorge ourselves on as many eggs and as much meat as we wanted. Later on we were to know the meaning of starvation rations, but at this period we had far more than was good for us. Tag became larger every day and was reaching a colossal size when he suddenly realised it and starting cutting down on his food. We soon saw that with a guard on a tower just above our yard, and also one inside all night, escape was hopeless for the time being. At first they even tried to make us keep our windows closed, but this was too much for us. As fast as the sentry tried to shut our windows from outside our hut, we opened them up again and a terrific hullabaloo started. Fish-eyes was eventually summoned and forgot all his English in his rage. Then another Italian officer arrived who was a little more phlegmatic and reasonable and we were allowed to leave them open.

Petty annoyances of this sort continued for the whole of our stay in Italy and had the net result of making us hate and despise the Italians. This helped us in some ways when it came to trying out any particularly hare-brained scheme to escape. Anything would be better than the continual humiliation of being kept a prisoner by the Italians.

Two weary months passed before we were promoted to the top compound where all the other officers were eking out their existence. After a week or so in our first compound the atmosphere had become very strained and unnatural. We were studiously polite to each other but lack of any occupation and with not even a glimpse of the outside world except the sky above and the four walls around us, was rapidly pushing us round the bend of reason. Geoff Jowett, our Canadian backwoodsman, became more and more mopey. Gerry Daly retreated within himself and set himself mathematical problems to solve. Christopher Lea and I had pipe dreams about mad schemes to escape, but the sage old Tag ever counselled patience till we were sent to the top compound where we would at least have contact with the outside of the camp. He was right, of course, but it was irksome to us at the time.

The American military attaché from Rome, a Colonel Fiske, visited us towards the end of our first month, and we were vociferous in our complaints of unfair and prejudicial treatment, just because we were parachutists. "You sure got the Wops scared," he said, "but I will plug the Geneva Convention at them, and I reckon I will get you outa here pretty soon." He cheered us up tremendously, but the Italians could never quite rid themselves of the idea that no one could possibly want to parachute and would only do so to avoid service in Russia or a long term of imprisonment!

CHAPTER FIVE

Prisoners of War

AT LAST the great day arrived and we were led up to the top compound. I remember we were held up for about twenty minutes before being let in. We grouped together and sang " God Save the King." It sounds odd now, long after the event, but it shows how tense and worked up we must have been. Then we all trooped in through the gate feeling very self-conscious and awkward. After having seen nothing except each other for so long it really was quite extraordinary to be once more in contact with the outside world, or so it seemed to us at that time. Soon we were to tire of the company of even the hundred or so officers of our new compound and once again became more and more introspective.

While we had been down in the bottom compound the Italians had been strengthening the wire obstacles. They had erected three barbed-wire fences, each ten feet high, round the complete perimeter of the camp. The fences had been well constructed with taut strands of barbed wire six inches apart, the bottom strand running along ground level. Each fence was spaced four or five feet from the next, and just outside the outer one lights had been put up on the top of twelve-foot poles. These lights were ten yards apart and were kept on all night. In addition every third pole had a powerful double floodlight pointing each way along the wire. These could be switched on from the nearest sentry boxes, which were dispersed every twenty yards between the first two rows of wire. As the camp formed a rectangle about 300 yards long by 150 yards broad a guard of forty-five was required to man the sentry boxes alone.

A track for carts ran round the whole camp between the wire fences and the compound walls which were ten feet high with broken glass set in the cement along the top. Inside each compound were two carabinieri who patrolled by day and night. Still not content with what were by now most formidable defences, the Italians had erected two towers thirty or forty feet high in the middle of the camp. By day two sentries could look down on all our activities and by night they could continue with the aid of a moveable searchlight.

Such was the problem set to every would-be escaper. The over-liberal use of wire obstacles and walls, and a standing guard of fifty to sixty men on duty at any one time, made the whole camp an extremely difficult one from which to escape. Most officers said it was impossible. A few said that perhaps it was possible to get out, but only through a tunnel. Nearly everybody said that having got out, the chances of reaching a neutral country were a million to one against.

Our new compound was 150 yards long by 20 yards broad, which felt almost spacious after our previous quarters. Down each long side were four low brick bungalows with tiled roofs, which were to house us for the rest of the time we spent in Sulmona. A wide gravel path ran down the middle, and we were to find out that six round trips to each end and back again would give us a mile's worth of exercise.

We were allotted to bungalows according to our rank. Subalterns were housed in a dormitory, captains shared small rooms, whilst field officers had cubicles to themselves. Geoff Jowett, George Patterson and I shambled off to our dormitory carrying our suitcases which were eyed with envy and surprise by the other officers. Our room held twenty, and I was given a bed by the door. In the middle stood a red earthenware stove with the pipe going out of the wall. The floor had the usual chequered red and white tiles, which in winter were horribly dank and cold.

By each bed there was a small cupboard and one or two chests of drawers were scattered round the room. On some beds

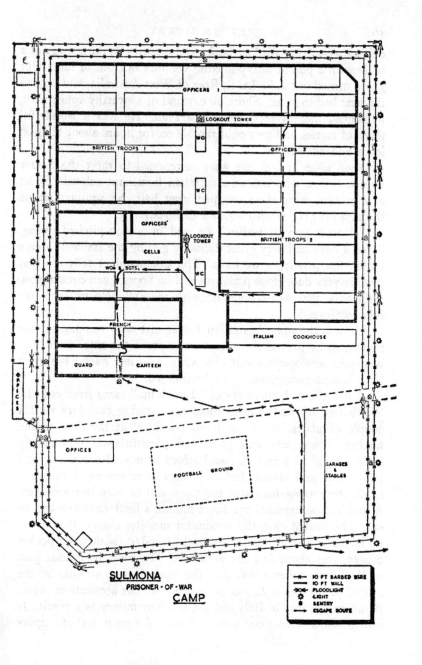

SULMONA
PRISONER · OF · WAR
CAMP

┼┼┼┼	10 FT BARBED WIRE
────	10 FT WALL
✕	FLOODLIGHT
✿	LIGHT
🏛	SENTRY
→	ESCAPE ROUTE

Labels within map: OFFICERS 1, LOOKOUT TOWER, WC, BRITISH TROOPS 1, OFFICERS 2, OFFICERS' CELLS, LOOKOUT TOWER, BRITISH TROOPS 2, WOs & SGTS., FRENCH, ITALIAN COOKHOUSE, GUARD, CANTEEN, OFFICES, OFFICES, FOOTBALL GROUND, GARAGES & STABLES officers were lying reading books and one was working away at a table with a pile of heavy-looking volumes in front of him. Our guide turned out to be Lt. R. Ross of West Australia, and he had the next bed to mine. Short, stocky and of a swarthy appearance, he looked more Greek than Australian. He was a wonderful teller of stories and he would ramble on for hours about his past loves and adventures.

Soon after arrival, we were summoned to meet the Senior British Officer who was an Australian lieutenant-colonel. Short and grizzly, with close cropped grey hair, he squinted at us through his glasses with obvious disfavour.

" I want you to realise," he said in a high-pitched twang, " that I have had very great difficulty getting the Italians to give us the few privileges we have. The Commandant tells me that you are very dangerous prisoners and he hopes I can control you. I do hope you will co-operate with me and help us keep our few comforts."

He was the only Australian I ever met who was not an ace fighter, so he proved the exception to prove the rule. Bob Ross was quite apologetic about him when we came back. We must have looked very gloomy and bewildered.

A bell clanged, and a cry of " Lunch up " came from outside. We drifted off to the mess room and, arming ourselves with a couple of plates, were doled out our meal at the door to the kitchen. Food was still good and plentiful and was chiefly limited to what a 2nd/lt. could afford to pay. No rations were issued free and several Italian officers were employed full time to do our buying for us in the town and to keep our accounts. A 2nd/lt. was credited 750 lire a month, a lieutenant 950 and so on. This meant that the maximum messing charge that could be levied and still leave the wretched 2nd/lt. with some pocket money, was about 600 lire a month. The most iniquitous part of the whole scheme was that the equivalent in sterling at the rate of 72 lire to the £, was deducted from our accounts at home. A junior prisoner in Italy did not save any money as a result. It also meant that the more senior officer had a great deal of surplus cash, with which he could buy extra food and clothing. At this early date we had so much that it did not matter. Later on, in September 1941, when Italy suddenly enforced very strict rationing, it was to cause many bitter feelings. All non-rationed foods became fantastically expensive and the senior officers were the only ones able to afford the prices.

The number of officers who really wanted to escape from Sulmona was very small indeed. A minority said quite openly they did not want to escape, they saw no point in it and if ever a tunnel was built and if they were ordered to get out through it, they would start building another one now, through which to get back inside the camp again. One great oaf over six feet tall, with size fourteen shoes and who continually boasted about his pre-war membership of Lloyds, said this, and that he could not see any point in exerting himself or endangering his body, and was quite content to while away the time until the end of the war. He was honest enough to admit it and there were many who felt exactly the same, but did not talk so openly.

The average officer would make an attempt to escape if given a really safe way out through a tunnel or some other means, but did not have the imagination or the guts to get on with it by himself. Secretly in his own heart his mind had been numbed by being taken prisoner, and he no longer had the power to make himself take risks against what he liked to regard as his better judgment. Some were married and uttered the age-old cry of, " But I have to think of my wife and children "; others said they were engaged; others had neither the brains nor the imagination, both of which are essential to a successful escape, to do anything except follow in somebody else's lead. If you really wanted to be openly disliked by about twenty-five per cent of the officers and secretly disliked by another fifty per cent, it was to announce that you were actually making plans to escape. " Oh, but think of all the privileges we shall lose when they discover your escape," they would say. " And anyhow once you have got out of this place, which is obviously impossible, it is equally ridiculous to expect anybody not talking good Italian and dressed in perfect civilian clothes, to reach the Swiss frontier, which is over six hundred miles away by road."

Those of us that were keen to get away set the pace for the rest. Lt. Michael Pope, R.N., had been caught after the submarine *Oswald* was rammed in the Messina strait, and a nicer chap was difficult to imagine. He and Flight-Lt. Garrard-Cole had escaped from Sulmona about three months before we arrived, and had walked over the mountains through deep snow to the coast hoping to get a boat to Jugoslavia. A coastguard patrol had picked them up just when a likely boat was being looked over, and that ended the first real escape from Sulmona. After this the sentries were doubled and all the outside wire was put up, the lighting improved and in the end the impregnability or rather the inescapability of Sulmona became a byword in Italy.

Shortly after arriving in the top compound, all six of us feverishly looked round to find a way out, causing not a little amusement to the rest of the camp and not a little chagrin to some. A tunnel was projected and was soon under way. A piece of cracked concrete served as the opening and the entrance and cover were prepared. The big mistake with this attempt was the number of officers employed on it. Some twenty were digging and scattering the soil and at least another twenty were in positions round about watching for the approach of any of the carabinieri guard.

After my brief experience of tunnelling in an eighteen inch square hole, I will vote the maximum increase to any miner that cares to strike for more wages. The entrance gave on to a fifteen-foot shaft lined and revetted with firewood to stop the loose sand crumbling and filling in the tunnel. From the initial shaft a tunnel went straight under the wire, a good forty yards away, and would then have to continue at least another thirty yards before it would be safe to strike upwards. Six weeks of hard work went into it with the usual tunnellers' method of scattering earth everywhere in thin streams from pockets. If one saw a collection of officers shambling around, hands in pockets, one knew that a steady stream of sandy earth was coming out of sacks held inside their trousers like hour glasses running out. The level of ground in the officers' compound must have been appreciably raised over the years that would-be tunnellers steadily scattered literally tons of earth evenly over the whole area. But tunnels in this camp were doomed to failure, especially when large numbers were employed on making them. Somehow the news always leaked out and sooner or later the other ranks compound heard of it. As soon as this happened the Italians seemed to know. There was at least one informer among the other ranks and I don't believe he was ever caught out. One day a party of carabinieri came in and walked straight to the tunnel entrance and dug it up. All our labours of the last six to eight weeks had been in vain, and one more tunnel proved to be an abortive effort.

Ever since this occasion I decided that if ever I should escape it would be a solo or at most, a dual effort, and then there would be no chance of anybody else getting to hear of it. Many said that it was not feasible to go many hundreds of miles in enemy territory alone. I always felt that alone I would only have myself to worry about and, given self-confidence and a lot of luck, that there were good chances of success. My later experiences proved to me that I was right. Since then I have talked to several other successful escapers and they have all agreed with me that very few complete parties were ever successful, and nearly all those that got away arrived in a neutral country by themselves. This perhaps does not apply to the evading type of escape so common during the Second World War, when pilots who had never been made prisoners of war walked through occupied countries in large groups. In these cases they were aided by a complete underground organisation and it was probably more convenient to move evaders in batches; but this would never have worked in Italy before the Italian Armistice in September, 1943, or in Germany.

CHAPTER SIX

Planning for Freedom

THE SUMMER passed and still we had made no serious attempt to get out. Prison routine was beginning to numb our senses and like the older inhabitants we had half convinced ourselves that it was impossible to escape from Sulmona.

It was Christopher Lea who broke the spell. One morning, when we were striding up and down the compound, he said:

"You know, Tony, it is high time we made some effort to get out. It is all very well to say it is wellnigh impossible, but there must be a way out somewhere."

"I only wish I could see one."

"Well, what about putting a ladder against the wire in the corner and just running across."

"You have two sentries within a few yards and they would have plenty of time to shoot at you."

"They might miss."

"Not at ten yards. No, Christopher, we must do better than that. We must have at least a fifty per cent chance of getting out undetected."

"We just must do something."

"All right. Let us do it methodically. We must examine every inch of the whole perimeter wire and see if there is anywhere which is less well covered by sentries or where the wire is not continuous."

"That's right. And having found the weak spot we must then work out a way of getting there from our compound. Come on, let's draw a plan from the outside wire and check it off as we get a chance of looking at it."

The best opportunity we had of inspecting the outside wire was when we were taken for walks. We were then led out of our compound and round the outside walls till we reached the sentries by the main entrance gate. Four or five weeks elapsed before either one or other of us saw the place we were to use some six weeks later. It was right down at the bottom end of the camp where the ground level changed at a wall. The three rows of wire ended there and then were started again at the top, but about ten feet higher up. The end poles of the top three fences were spaced back from the edge of the wall by about eight inches to allow the poles to be stayed by wires running at an angle. Apart from these stay wires, the ledge was free of obstruction and led to freedom.

We had found a gap in the wire which had seemed so impregnable, but there were many snags. In the first place a sentry box was placed about fifteen yards away on the lower level. Secondly a light shone continuously on the gap from the wall of the stable and kept the whole ledge lit up. Thirdly the gap we had found was at the diametrically opposite end of the camp to where we were. To any but us poor caged birds the problems would have seemed insurmountable, but we had now been prisoners nine months in the hands of our despised Italian captors, and we were willing to take any reasonable risks. It took us a month to work out a plan between the two of us. First I would have a bright idea and then Christopher would have a better one, and each of us spent all day and every day with our minds concentrated on this one problem.

We first of all decided that, provided the night was dark enough, we could get along the ledge if the light was put out. This was the crucial point on which the success or failure of the whole plan turned. A really wet night with no moon behind the clouds would have suited us admirably. One of the first problems we came up against was how to turn out the light. We thought of everything. We could fuse the whole camp supply, but turned this down because it would alert all the guards and the fuse might be repaired before we could get to the right

place. Anyhow it turned out that the perimeter lights were on
a separate circuit from our own.

Our next idea was to bribe the Italian electrician. However,
at this time our guards appeared to be singularly incorruptible
and we thought we might easily be doublecrossed. Only a few
weeks before, one of the officers had tried to bribe a guard who
immediately told his officer about it. He was allowed to keep the
bribe and was promoted lance-corporal! It turned out that this
was a standard rule in Italy at this time and was instigated by
Mussolini in an attempt to eliminate corruption among his
Italians.

Our next idea was to wait for a thunderstorm and hope that
the lights would go out. Power systems in Italy did not seem
as efficient as in Britain and nearly always broke down in heavy
rain. We rejected this scheme because it gave the initiative to
the weather, a most unreliable factor.

Eventually I had a brainwave. We would carry a ladder to
the light and, pretending we were Italian electricians, would
climb up the ladder and unscrew the bulb. It all seemed so
simple once we had thought of it. So often it is the obvious
that eludes one.

There were difficulties of course, not the least being the
manufacture of the ladder and getting out over the compound
walls to start our walk to the light. Italian uniforms would have
to be made and worn over our escaping clothes, which we were
busy collecting together in the meanwhile. Tag gave me a
civilian-looking raincoat, which he had persuaded the Italians
to buy for him while we were in Naples. The biggest problems
were the hat, trousers and shoes. To get the material for the
trousers, I induced the Italian lieutenant, who did some shopping
for us, that some really strong cloth was required for a home-
made deck chair that I had constructed. He came back with
two yards of dark green corduroy which was ideal for my purpose and I set to work with needle and thread to sew them into
some semblance of trousers. They were shaped on the model
of battledress trousers but unfortunately I made them far too

tight across the seat which was to have repercussions, or rather rendings, later on.

Our last serious hurdle was how to transport ourselves and our ladder, once made, outside the compound walls without exciting suspicion. This problem alone might have floored us, but we had so nearly found the solution that there would have to be an answer to this one. The top three sides of the camp had sentries facing the outer walls and only a few paces from it. We could never have dropped over that wall with a twelve-foot ladder and got away with it. The only place where the sentries were away from the outer wall was in the bottom end of the camp and next to the French compound.

Yet another difficulty cropped up: could we trust the French not to raise the alarm if they saw us passing through? Eventually a reliable Frenchman called Pierre was vouched for by Sgt. Clements who was one of our own N.C.Os. We, of course, would not tell Pierre a word of our plans, but on the chosen night Clements would get hold of him and he would keep the rest quiet while we went through. At the bottom of the French compound was a narrow passage between their boundary wall and the guard room. There was no sentry in this passage and a corridor led through the guard room from the one side to the other and connected the passage to the outside. All we had to do was to drop over the wall at the bottom end of the French compound into the passage, and then to march boldly through the corridor and out the other side. There was a sentry outside the door, but he would be looking outwards and he certainly would not expect prisoners to come out of his own guard room carrying ladders! We would then walk with our ladder straight to the lamp-post and proceed as before.

All we had to do now was to make a twelve-foot ladder and transport it down to our starting point in the N.C.O.s' compound. Ladders do not grow on trees in prison camps, but compared with our other problems this required but little thought. A loose plank was soon split down the middle, to make the two shafts and pieces of firewood and chairs made the rungs. We decided it would be easiest to take the ladder down in pieces to the N.C.O.s' compound two nights before the attempt, and for our N.C.O.s to assemble it down there. They had an excellent hiding place under some rafters and were confident that they could conceal the sound of hammering with a lot of table beating and singing. Those two excellent N.C.O.s of ours Sgts. Lawley and Clements offered to do the whole transportation and assembly and we let them carry on. They came up to our compound, fetched the bits and pieces, and took them down to their compound over two of the intervening walls and practically under the very eyes of the " Crows " patrolling in the compounds. They would wait until they were looking the other way or round one corner of a building to rush the pieces of wood another fifty yards on their way. As the searchlight's beam from the tower swung round, it would find them and their load motionless in some shadow. Sgts. Lawley and Clements completed this operation with a hundred per cent success, and the ladder was assembled in the next few days in the N.C.O.s' compound without any suspicions being aroused on the part of the Italians.

We were ready for our big adventure. It was December 4th, 1941 and we had been in the bag for nearly ten months. We were tremendously excited at the prospect of being able to do something at long last. It had been full moon on December 2nd, so that by about the 7th or 8th we would have the first half of the night with no moon at all. The year was getting late but the weather was still tolerably fine. Soon we would come up against the bad weather, likely in January, and we decided, rightly or wrongly, not to wait for a wet night but to make our first attempt on the night of December 7th.

Christopher and I disagreed violently on the best method to use once out of camp. Mine was to walk the fifty odd miles to Pescara and buy a ticket on a train from there. His plan was to hop goods trains all the way up Italy. Mine was certainly the quickest and more spectacular, but Christopher thought that it had little chance of success. He did not think that an English-

man with fair hair could go into a southern Italian railway
station and buy a ticket hardly knowing a word of Italian and
get away with it. It was too fantastic for both Christopher and
the members of the committee to whom we related our detailed
plans to get away. But I insisted that booking-office clerks have
a difficult time, and all they wanted to hear was " Third single
London " or " Milan " to push over a ticket automatically. I
learnt and relearnt the phrase asking for a ticket to Milan.
" *Terzo Milano* " became my sleeping song and my pronuncia-
tion was said to be perfect by our tame linguist, old Lucky. My
idea was always to make for large towns, and to mingle with
people and queues where possible. Safety in numbers would be
my motto. I also relied on walking to Pescara in three nights.
The first night I would go straight up the Majella Mountains at
our back and get over the top. During the next two nights I
would drop down on to the main Rome-Pescara road and walk
along it for some twenty miles on each subsequent night. The
first day I planned to stay up in the mountains and the next one
in a culvert under the main road. I estimated that I should
arrive at Pescara on the third morning and buy my ticket on the
8 a.m. to Milan. Our official railway timetable told me exactly
when to arrive at the station for the train. This, although a
small point, was essential to avoid a long wait before the train
came in. From Milan I planned to buy another ticket to Como
and from there to get over the Swiss frontier, only about two
miles away, at Chiasso. Such was the plan I told to the
committee and although they encouraged me, they did not think
I had much hope of success. I, for my part, was supremely
confident that, given a reasonable degree of luck, I would pull it
off and the pessimists made me even more determined that I
should succeed.

December 7th was a lovely fine day, and slowly the evening
came on. A glorious feeling of tenseness rose up within us like
before a race or a parachute jump. My nerves and brain were
working at a speed they had nearly forgotten in the previous

dulling months. Maps, money and a tiny compass were all concealed in an oilskin package and stuck with sticky plaster between my legs.

I pulled on my corduroy trousers and made a bundle of the raincoat and sham Italian uniform. We would put these on at the last moment before going over the wall of the French compound. A battledress jacket covered up my coloured shirt so that in the dark my clothes would pass as reasonable uniform. No badges of rank were worn because we were going to be in both the private soldiers' and the N.C.O.s' compound and might well be seen by one of the more alert carabinieri patrols. Christopher was dressed likewise, and on the evening of the 7th as soon as darkness had fallen, we ate a good meal and went down to the N.C.O.s' compound arriving there about 9 p.m. We had two hours before the moon rose and we planned to start out about 10 p.m. Hurriedly and nervously we dressed in a hut, watched over by the faithful Clements and Lawley. In the meantime an excellent C.S.M. was watching the wall into the French compound and to our chagrin the carabinieri patrol stood under the wall talking to each other from ten minutes to ten until nearly half-past. Already light was beginning to come from the rising moon still below the horizon, and we decided we would have to go back to our compound and try again the next night. We left our escape clothes in bundles in the N.C.O.s' compound, and at about 10.50 p.m. we started back. Christopher got over the wall all right and I was just about to follow, and was actually hanging by my hands from the top when I heard shouting behind and carabinieri came running up. I would not be able to pull myself up and drop over the other side in time, so I dropped back into the N.C.O.s' compound and decided to make a run for it. I had not taken a dozen paces before I tripped up and went flat on my face. The two "crows" pounced on me from behind. In a true Italian way I was led off with the muzzle of a rifle drilling the small of my back with its owner screaming at me in high-pitched Italian, saying I would get twenty-eight days on bread and water. I thought I would, too.

As I was wearing no badges of rank I was mistaken for an other rank and I for my part was in no hurry to advise them differently until after I had been searched.

We arrived at the guard room and I was then searched fairly well, all seams being felt through, but my package remained concealed and eventually I was led off and dumped in an other ranks' cell. My name soon trickled through to the Italian officers and I was yanked out and taken back to the officers' compound because all the officers' cells were full. I was in real luck this time because I would be able to have another try next night unless they made room for me the following day in the cells.

Fish-eyes, the interpreter, had great pleasure in calling me out at the Roll Call the next morning and telling me that I would have twenty-one days' solitary confinement as soon as there was room. " Just to make sure you have a happy Christmas," he said as an afterthought. I was furious with the horrible little man, but outwardly I hope I showed a blank face and went away to discuss with Christopher the plans for the night's work. We decided to go through with the same timings because it would give us an extra hour as the moon rises one hour later each night.

All went well. We arrived down at the N.C.O.s' compound after a big send-off from Tag and Gerry Daly.

By this time many knew that we were up to something, but very few knew what we proposed to do. I remember Gerry Daly and Nigel Strutt gave us a wonderful meal of Canadian Red Cross biscuits and cheese and butter, followed by some soused herrings. Not exactly a Lord Mayor's banquet, but it was a feast for us and we were to need every ounce of energy in the days to come. Because of our method of getting out, which involved sidling along an eight-inch wide ledge with a wire fence on one side, we both decided that we could not afford to bulge ourselves out with supplies of food. I took only two packets of biscuits and a pound of chocolate. Later on I discovered that thirst and not hunger was to be my principal enemy. On my timetable it would be five days before I crossed

into Switzerland and anybody can go without food for five days
and feel none the worse for it.

Soon we had dressed with our mock Italian overcoats and
hats covering our semi-civilian get up. An N.C.O. stood by with
the ladder waiting for the moment when the carabinieri were at
the farthermost point from where we were to cross into the
French compound. We were both a bit nervous at this stage, but
I at any rate had complete confidence in the successful outcome
of our scheme. It was like walking round the paddock before
riding in a point-to-point. My heart was beating a bit faster and
nerves were taut whilst waiting for the signal to move off to
the start. Only here our stakes were sky high. We both knew
that if we failed we would be in solitary confinement for at least
twenty-eight days, and it would be a minimum of six months
before we would be able to think up another way out.

A hushed whisper of " it's O.K." started us moving. We
used the ladder to help us over the wall and dropped down into
the French compound. We quickly walked across accompanied
by Pierre, and put our ladder against the bottom wall, the other
side of which was the passage in front of the Italian guard room
and canteen. A quick glance over the top to make sure there
was no sentry, and we both dropped silently over. However, in
so doing, we had not allowed for the broken glass on top of the
walls, and we both cut our hands quite badly. We lay down in
the shadow and bandaged them before taking on the next
hurdle.

We then stood up and, carrying our ladder with coils of
flex and electric light bulbs held prominently in front of us, we
went straight for the open door which led into the corridor
which separated the guard room from the canteen. The doors
leading into the canteen and guard room were both ajar, but
without looking into either we walked straight through and past
the sentry outside who made no effort to challenge us. So far so
good, and it gave us encouragement for what we knew were
going to be the far harder tasks ahead. Everything was so normal
that it was almost uncanny. Sentries were in their boxes, peri-

meter lights outlined the edge of the camp and a faint noise of
some concert came from one of the compounds. The sky was
starlit, and this it was which gave us the most worry. We had
counted on a clouded night in our planning, but we had taken
the decision for better or for worse and now we were on our
way. There was certainly no going back and we walked grimly
on, each of us wondering what the next few seconds would have
in store. We came level with the end of the half-completed
football field and turned down towards the fateful lamp. I
could see the sentry quite clearly outlined against his box and a
moment later we were standing underneath the light. Christopher put the ladder against the wall and I climbed up. As I was
climbing up the sentry shouted something to us and my heart
missed a beat. However, we had thought of this and I shouted
back "*Lampa*" in as confident a voice as I could muster for
the occasion. We counted on the dumbness of the average Italian
soldier not to start questioning us but to accept the extraordinary
fact that in the middle of the night we were about to change a
bulb that was already burning perfectly. I was always confident
on this point in our plans, but many to whom I have told this
story can hardly believe it to be true. The reactions of the enemy
sentry is as important a subject to study as any other.

By this time I was at the top of the ladder and soon un-
screwed the bulb. I made pretence of changing them and
screwed the same one back, but only half-way. Now came the
crucial test. We had to move sideways along ten yards of ledge,
between the bottom of the wall where our ladder was and the
outside wire, without arousing the sentry's suspicions. We then
made our only mistake. We had decided that, on a really dark
night, we could carry the ladder along this ledge and drop it
down outside without the sentry seeing anything. We were so
obsessed with this plan that we did not make any allowance for
the starlit sky and we tried to go through with our original
scheme. I climbed half-way down the ladder and side-stepped
on to the ledge and moved about a yard along it at the same
time signalling to Christopher to come up the ladder on to the

ledge too. Then came the tricky business that we had rehearsed mentally, of Christopher reaching down with one hand, catching hold of the ladder at the point of balance and passing it to me to hold. We started to move slowly along the ledge. Our coats seemed to catch in the barbed wire and seconds, which seemed like hours, elapsed before we could free each other. We had just arrived level with the first row of barbed wire when the sentry came running up from his box and started screaming at us. Christopher realised the game was up a fraction of a second before I did and shouted at me to throw the damn' thing away. If it hadn't been for the ladder we could both have dropped down outside by the time this happened. I tossed the ladder away and it landed across three rows of wire which were now beneath us. It came down with a crash and the wires set up a twanging noise that must have been heard all over the camp. The sentry must then have realised that it was up to him to stop us, and he fired a shot. Something flicked past my cheek and I could feel the sting and blood started to run. By this time I was hanging by my hands to the parapet on the outside of the camp and had dropped into the road outside. The sentry had only managed to get off one round and as this had apparently grazed me, I assumed Christopher was all right and walked straight off. Our plans were to divide immediately on dropping outside the camp and so confuse any pursuers.

I heard later that Christopher had been hit in the thigh by the same shot that had grazed my cheek. The Italians, unknown to us, had issued their sentries with a type of bullet that disintegrated on its way down the barrel and came out in fragments about the size of buckshot. One of the fragments had grazed me, but most had gone into Christopher's leg. He did not even utter a murmur or make any sign to me when we both dropped down outside. He knew that I should have stayed with him for at least a few seconds if I had known and he waited till I was out of sight before calling for help. An artery was punctured and he was ill from loss of blood for a week or two, but luckily he was fully recovered a month later.

As I walked rapidly away it gradually dawned on me that I had actually succeeded in getting out and I was now on the high road to freedom. I now had to prove that I could get to Switzerland. A determination seized me to make it or bust in the attempt. What a thrill it was, and I chuckled to myself when I thought of old Fish-eyes' face when he realised that the man to whom he had just given twenty-one days' solitary confinement, had got out of his camp on the following night.

My plan was to circle the camp round to the left so that any who saw me whilst I was still nearby would not know in which direction I had gone. Soon I was striking up the mountain at the back with fearful looks over my shoulder in case any guards were already on my trail. My imagination kept telling me that those flashes of light on the hillside below were coming up after me and this spurred me on to ever greater speed. With my breath all gone I eventually decided that I was safe and sat down on the mountainside. The camp stood out like a rectangular Blackpool with all its searchlights blazing and I could imagine checks going on all night to see who had got away, with everybody doing their best to annoy and hinder, and the Italians getting more and more infuriated.

On and on up the mountain I went, steering due north by the pole star, and the outline of the valley below. The moon was just rising and soon the whole hillside was lit as clear as daylight. The snow on the hills just above me stood out in startling whiteness and I could see the snowy peaks of the Gran Sasso range thirty miles away to the north. The hillside up which I was labouring was covered with small black thorn bushes and some of these caught in my mackintosh and coat, causing triangular rents that would not help my appearance later on. I sat down for another rest just short of the snowline and ate some chocolate, washing it down with a lump of snow, a most unsatisfying sort of drink but certainly better than nothing. My seat felt very cold and I suddenly realised that my beautiful home-made corduroy trousers had split all the way up the back seam. I had no cotton to mend it and so it looked as though I would have to go through Italy with an enormous hole in my trousers and this would not help when it came to bluffing on to the train. I tried without much success to wash the blood off my face with melted snow, so that at least I should look reasonably presentable if I had to walk through a village.

At first I tried walking up through the snow, but mental and physical reactions were beginning to tell and I decided to skirt the mountain just beneath the snow line and to drop down on to the Sulmona-Pescara road just beyond Popoli, which was a tiny village at the head of the gorge leading out of the Sulmona valley towards Pescara. At last I climbed over a spur of the main ridge and could see round the corner down the Pescara valley. The country changed a little here and became steeper and more rugged with great jagged outcrops of rock, which did not help a poor footsore traveller like myself.

Eventually, at about 5 o'clock in the morning, I decided it was time to find a place in which to lie up during the following day. The pinewoods were attractive, but the newly cut trees suggested that woodcutters were at work, and I might be discovered by them in daylight. The undergrowth in the pinewoods was anyhow very sparse and it would have been difficult to find a good hiding place. I decided that the best spot would be in one of the scattered clumps of juniper bushes that grew here and there over the whole hillside. Nobody would be likely to stumble on my hiding place as there were so many bushes from which to choose. It would also seem an unlikely place to hide if they tried to follow me up the mountain. Eventually I found a good-sized bush and crept in underneath. After a little scraping with my hands I had my legs covered with dead foliage and with my green Italian overcoat over my head, I must have been nearly invisible. I then settled down to a little sleep and did not wake up until about 11 a.m. when I felt rather cold and cramped. The rhythmic tapping of the woodcutter's axe and an occasional splintering sound as another pine tree crashed to the ground, were the only noises to disturb the peace. I stretched my legs and tried to make myself more comfortable, at the same time looking out from my perch on the hillside to get a wonderful view over the sunny valley. The snow was only a few hundred feet above me and out of the sun it was bitterly cold. I attempted to eat some chocolate and biscuits but my mouth was so dry that I could not get them down and I wished that I had a waterbottle with me even at the expense of some of the chocolate.

CHAPTER SEVEN

By Road and Rail

LITTLE BY LITTLE the tapping in the woods petered out and eventually all was silent as dusk fell. There were no houses at that height and all the peasants who worked up there probably lived in one or other of the villages down in the valley. When it was quite dark, I got up and stretched myself and massaged my stiff muscles back to life. I was looking forward to some exercise to warm my cold hands and feet and also to a drink from a stream. I started off and stumbled my way along a track that I had seen being used by the old goat-herd when he went down the hill. I was now as high as I need be and would be able to drop down on to the main road running through the gorge. First of all I tried going across the grain of the hillside, but it became more and more broken and I was using up so much energy clambering over the rocks that, when I hit a well-worn track leading straight down the mountain, I decided to take it. The general direction seemed about right although it might bring me nearer to Popoli than I intended. As it turned out it led straight to Popoli, through a series of crevices and ravines with vertical rock faces on either side that gave me no choice but to follow the track and hope for the best. After three hours' walking I crossed a brow and there was Popoli, not a couple of hundred feet below me. It was obvious that I would have to go right through the village to get to the main road on the other side. The time was 9 p.m. and so there should be plenty of people in the streets, through which I hoped to pass unnoticed. My only worry was if they put a check on the outskirts of the village to stop all travellers. I decided to risk this as it was a main road and therefore should have many like myself walking along it. In Italy there are a lot more law-abiding citizens that rely on Shanks' Pony than in England, and it is not uncommon to see men and women walking from village to village by night. The dangerous time was of course between about 11 p.m. and 4.30 a.m., and I decided that I would not walk between those hours when I might well be the only one on the road. However I still had two hours of exercise ahead of me before 11 p.m., and that would be plenty.

My track led straight into the village and soon I was on a main road which was full of people, and I continued to walk with as much confidence as I could muster through the town. I did not appear to excite any abnormal interest and I was soon clear of the houses and walking along the main road which ran through a steep-sided ravine alongside the Pescara River. My walk that night was uneventful and on several occasions I passed two or three Italian soldiers on the road without exciting any attention. Many a long drink I had from watering troughs which are on the side of every main road, and I felt I could not absorb enough water to satisfy my needs. I wanted to get to within 25km. of Pescara that evening, which would leave quite a short walk for the following night, and I just did it by 11.45 p.m. Almost on the 25km. stone there was a large dry culvert running under the main road, which was about six inches deep in dead leaves. It was the ideal hiding place and right on my route for the next night's walk. Footsore and weary I dragged myself inside, and covering myself as best I could with leaves went into the deep sleep of the mentally and physically exhausted.

Numbness and cold woke me just as it was getting light at about 6.30 a.m., and I tried to do some P.T. and massage my stiff muscles back into life again. My only worry was school children. They might start playing around my hiding place and discover me, but again my luck was in and I was bothered by nobody. By nightfall, after a very cold and boring day, I was still safe and undiscovered in my culvert. My plan was to walk to within 5 or 6km. of Pescara and then rest near there till about 6 a.m. the following morning. I would then have two hours to walk in and catch the 8 a.m. to Milan with the minimum time to wait about the platform.

My feet were hurting quite a lot now and, with a steady limp, I trudged along the main road resting every half hour or so and taking a drink when I could. That 20km. seemed never ending, but now I was in the coastal plain and there were many more houses flanking the road. The nearer I came to Pescara the more populated it became and I was getting quite worried about finding a resting place near enough to the town. Fortunately the country opened up a little and soon after the 6km. stone I found a ploughed field at least four hundred yards from any house and lay flat on my back in a furrow in the centre of the field. It would be a very unlikely place to be stumbled on by accident in the middle of the night and it would do till the following morning as I would be on my way by daybreak. I remember the cold very vividly, but otherwise the night was uneventful.

By 4 a.m. I was getting myself ready. A dry scrape with a razor to remove the worst of my beard—nobody is very fussy in Italy—and my Italian overcoat was pushed into a ditch after it had been used to rub most of the mud off my boots and trousers. The mackintosh was a little bedraggled with its small triangular rents caused by the thorn bushes in the mountains, and streaks of blood from my cheek. By rubbing the material between the palms of my hands I managed to remove most of the bloodstains and my corduroy trousers were similarly treated. The sticking plaster holding my maps and money was unstuck from between my legs and some money carefully folded into the breast pocket of my coat where I would not have to fumble for it when buying my ticket. My Swastika badge was clipped into my buttonhole, and I had my faked German passport in my pocket. This latter document was a product of the imagination of Sandy Clayton, and I don't suppose bore any relation to the real thing. However it looked good and had plenty of rubber stamps and German and Italian signatures authorising nearly everything.

By 5.45 a.m. I was as ready as I could be and started slowly along my last lap to Pescara, which I reached at 7 a.m. I stopped the first woman I saw and asked her the way to the station in halting Italian, introducing my question by *io sono tedesco* (I am a German). The station was right at the north end of the town and on the other side of the Pescara River. To walk right through an enemy town in daylight was quite amusing, and gave me confidence in my dress. Nobody took the slightest notice and there were plenty of other people carrying a little black bag on their way to work somewhere. Whenever I went anywhere in Italy I always contrived to carry something in my hands. It gave me a *raison d'être* and anybody looking at me obviously thought that my bag was my excuse for going somewhere. Nobody walks anywhere or travels long distances without at least a small bag. Mine was actually a British army officer's satchel made of canvas webbing, dyed in blue-black ink, and looked good enough.

At twenty minutes to eight by the station clock I walked into the main entrance of Pescara station past two carabinieri on duty by the door, and joined a queue at the ticket office. Nobody seemed to take much notice of me, but I saw two more carabinieri standing behind the ticket inspector at the gate leading on to the platforms. A five hundred lire note was in the palm of my hand and I was now only two places away from the ticket office window. Silently I mouthed my oft-repeated phrase for getting a ticket and my pulse seemed to hammer away in my forehead at a terrific rate. I felt everybody's eyes upon me as I took my turn and uttered a barely audible " *terzo Milano* " at the same time pushing my five hundred lire note over the counter. Before I knew where I was, a ticket and change were pushed at me and the man behind me was asking for his destination. The blood rushed back into my cheeks, and with renewed confidence I quickly followed the man in front on to the platform, brandishing my ticket in front of me as my passport. The ticket inspector punched my ticket and said *terzo*-something or other in my ear, which I took to mean Platform 3, and after walking over the railway lines I joined a few others also waiting for the same train. A bookstall was selling papers and I bought a copy of *Signal* which was a German propaganda illustrated paper and published in each language all over Europe. This would act as a further outward and visible passport in addition to my fair hair and Swastika badge. I felt I was now the complete Hun and kept a little aloof from the rest of the passengers to heighten the illusion. The time was now 7.55 a.m. and the train was due in five minutes. My timing could not have been better and so far everything had gone completely according to plan.

The train came in five minutes late and I had soon found a corner seat which I was fated to sit in for the next fourteen hours, all the way to Milan. To my horror a couple of cara-binieri came into the same compartment and sat down one next to me and one opposite. Questions went racing through my head. " Had I been spotted and were these two following me?" " Were they going to arrest me then and there?" My confidence came back when one of them cleared his throat in the true Italian style and spat on the floor, rubbing the spittle in with the toe of his boot. He was obviously settling down and apparently I was not under suspicion yet. Three other civilians were in the same compartment and they all added to the quota of spitting that was to continue all the way to Milan at a regular spit per man per ten minutes.

One of the occupants in my carriage leant out of the window at one of the stations and bought a " cistina." This is a card-board box containing a roll, a leg of chicken, an orange and a bit of cheese. The smell nearly drove me mad with a reawakened hunger, and I decided to risk buying one at our next station, which was to be Bologna. Sure enough a trolley was pushed along the train and I bought a cistina for nine lire. I have hardly ever enjoyed a meal so much and I could barely restrain myself from eating even the orange peel. This was to be my one and only meal on the whole journey, and I could have eaten half a dozen with ease except for the suspicion it might have caused.

My confidence was increasing with every mile and when at last, at about 9.45 p.m., we started to go through Milan suburbs, my morale could not have been higher. I could only hope for a train on to Como without much delay. A sudden doubt crossed my mind that they might have a more thorough check at a big terminus like Milan, but I tried to reassure myself that where there was a crowd I should be safe. Eventually the train pulled in to a platform in Milan Central Station at 10 p.m. and everybody got out on to the platform. The ticket collector by the barrier had two or three carabinieri standing by him, but there was such a crowd that they would not have much chance and were probably only looking for people without tickets trying to give them the slip.

In some ways Milan Central is rather like a small Waterloo, and the same system was employed to indicate arrivals and departures of trains. I discovered that the last train for Como had left ten minutes previously and I was in a complete quandary what to do till 7 a.m. the following morning when the next one was due to leave. An awful reaction set in as a result of the anti-climax to my plans and in a fit of over-confidence I decided to spend the night in an hotel in Milan. I told myself that if I could get away with it on a train journey, I could surely do the same in an hotel. I suppose this idiotic decision was partly due to my tired mental and physical state, and partly to an overpowering over-confidence that seems to grip escapers as they get close to freedom. Switzerland is only twenty miles from Milan. However, be that as it may, I walked down the long flight of steps from the platform level to the main booking hall and went straight up to a porter and asked him for the name of an hotel where I could stay the night, introducing my halting Italian by telling him I was German. He immediately gave me a name and a little urchin was buttonholed and told to lead me there. I remember how we stumbled across the blacked-out square outside the station and then went down a small street to the right to find the entrance about two hundred yards farther on. The name of the hotel was " Vittoria."

The receptionist was standing behind his desk, and once more my halting Italian came out, asking for a room and some coffee to be sent up. To my horror he answered me in German! He was obviously an Austrian or Tyrolean and that was why I had been sent to this hotel. I mumbled back something in the schoolboy German I had learnt while in prison, and his only answer was, "You are no German"—in German. My pulse beat a bit faster but I determined to have my say and told him, " *Ich bin ein Sudetener — Heil Hitler.*" This seemed to satisfy him and he pushed across a card for me to fill in, which I did giving the details of my bogus identity card, which to my horror he asked to look at. He shook his head and said he had never seen one like that before, but I hurriedly interjected that it was for Sudeteners of course. He then led me upstairs to a comfortable room with a bath next door. Five minutes later a cup of coffee came up on a tray and as the door closed I wolfed it down. I decided to have a rough wash down before going to bed and never have I enjoyed a cold bath more. There was no spare fuel for unnecessary luxuries like hot baths in Italy at this time. After I had dried myself and had another scrape with the razor, I began to look almost respectable. Then I collapsed on the bed in a state of semi-exhaustion.

In spite of being tired in every limb, I began to reflect on what the receptionist had said. My brain at last started to work, and I suddenly realised what an absolute idiot I had been. The man had obviously realised I was not who I said I was, and was probably even now telephoning to Police Headquarters for someone to come round and look me over. I decided to dress and leave the hotel straight away and my clothes flew on to my body as quick as lightning. I went downstairs; it was only a small pension hotel; and the same man was sitting at his desk, and not unnaturally, seemed a little surprised to see me. I mumbled something about making a mistake in my train timings and put down thirty lire for my bed. He got slowly up from his seat and said quite softly in German, "You are not a Sudetener, you are an Englishman." I drew myself up as best I could and asked for my change, and told him he was not only making a fool of himself but was being very impertinent. This seemed to take him aback, but he still looked very suspicious and asked me where I was going. I told him "Torino" which was the direction diametrically opposite to Como and also quite likely to have a train in the middle of the night. He slowly pushed the change across, and trying hard not to hurry, I put it in my pocket and walked out of the door. It was a narrow squeak, and I am sure he had asked for the police to come and investigate. I could feel it in the tone of his voice. With shaking knees I walked straight back to the station and decided to spend the rest of the night in the waiting-room. This was big and half-full already with sleeping bodies. It was the ideal place to hide away until morning.

At 6 a.m. I went down to the main booking-hall for my ticket to Como and was cheered up when out it came as easily as before. Back upstairs and into the 3rd Class Buffet for three cups of steaming hot *caffe al latte*. It was synthetic coffee, but it was hot and wet, and tasted wonderful.

I stepped aboard the 7 a.m. electric train for Como and was soon rattling out of Milan towards the frontier. My only worry was that there might be a check on all trains going towards Switzerland, but I was in luck. My spirits were rising with every minute and in a few minutes we were passing through country-side that was looking hillier and more alpine in texture every minute. We stopped at every station and anxiously I looked out to see any signs of police boarding the train to check papers, but there were none in sight. At last we pulled into Como station and the lake was just visible over the houses to the north. The ticket collector took the ticket and I walked straight past the scrutinising glare of some more carabinieri. I was now on the last lap, but unfortunately I had the whole day to spend before starting towards the frontier at nightfall.

This was my second mistake. I should have remained in

Milan all that day and come on to Como at dusk. As it was, I had been so keen to get out of Milan after the hotel incident that I took the first train in the morning. Como and its area was suburban and it was going to be very difficult to find a hiding place for the day. I was soon walking through the streets towards the north and realised I should have to go some way before finding a path off the main road into the country. A little farther along I could see my road climbing a small hill, half-way up which there appeared to be a possible turning-off. When about three hundred yards from the road junction, I saw two frontier guards coming in the opposite direction dressed in their Alpine uniform. I don't know why it was, but I had a feeling that all was not going to be well before I came up to them, but on the other hand I thought it would look even more suspicious if I turned round and retraced my steps. I thought I might just make the turn-off before reaching the two soldiers, in which case they would hardly have a chance to stop me. How I afterwards cursed that decision! I could easily have turned about when they were still two or three hundred yards away and they would never have been any the wiser.

To cut a long story short, they stopped me and asked me where I was going. Having blustered a bit, I showed them my papers, but very politely I was told that I would have to come along to their H.Q. which was only a few hundred yards away. This I did, and was given a drink of wine while I waited. Eventually I was told that I would have to be taken to the frontier post because there was somebody there who could talk German. My heart felt suddenly very heavy. I might perhaps give them the slip on the way, but my foot hurt quite a lot now and I would not have a chance against two fit Alpinis. If only it had been dark it might have been easy to make a dash for freedom, but it was broad daylight and about 12 o'clock on a glorious sunny and cloudless day.

We boarded a trolley-bus which took us down to the frontier post at Chiasso, a village half in Switzerland and half in Italy. The main road had a huge barricade on the frontier, with the frontier post just beside it. I half-knew the game was up, but determined to put up a show till the last. As I was ushered into a room where a dirty little weed of an official, wearing an outsize chauffeur's cap and horn-rimmed spectacles, was sitting behind a desk, I gave him a heel click and " Heil Hitler." It was still just faintly possible that his German would have been worse than mine, but hardly likely. It wasn't!

Almost at once he had sized me up and told me I was English and asked me who I was—in English. I told him my name and, on looking down a list, he discovered mine amongst some others. Quite surprising efficiency for Italians, and all the frontier posts must have had the warning. I was then searched and nothing was discovered except some money, as I had chucked my maps away when walking with the two Alpinis.

The little comic-opera official seemed highly delighted at his capture, and became quite affable. " There will be promotion all round for this," he said, and asked me if I would like anything to eat. I told him I could eat a horse. I also asked him if the two soldiers who stopped me knew why they had done so. The two men seemed rather at a loss to know why, but one said that it was my general appearance, above all my dirty boots! Another lesson learnt and not to be forgotten in future attempts.

I was put into another room, with two guards watching me, and a meal was soon brought in from a local restaurant. I remember its savour to this day, but my enjoyment was tempered by the thought that I had got so near and yet so far. Even then I was within twenty yards of Swiss soil and this might be my last chance in the war to be so close, and it would certainly be six months before I should be able to have another try.

I have never been so depressed, before or since. My world, which had been getting brighter and brighter, was now inky black. Although I can usually make the best of most things, I found my present plight difficult to stomach. While I sat moping, I dropped off to sleep in fits and starts and hoping the guards would follow suit; but it had no effect and they remained as watchful as ever.

After about two hours, three plain-clothes policemen came in and I was hustled into a waiting car and driven off very fast down the main road to Milan. I had a good look at the frontier wire before going and also the scenery. My luck might hold and I might be back in the area trying to cross the frontier again one day.

Driving through Milan was interesting and I could see no signs of bomb damage. The town looked like a rather dirty version of one of our own midland towns, but with the usual continental touch of cafés on the pavements and paper kiosks at street corners.

The car stopped outside an impressive building which proved to be Police H.Q., and I was hustled into a small room with two fat carabinieri looking on. They had a paper and started to bait me with its news. Japan, they said, was now fighting us, and already she had sunk the whole American Navy at Pearl Harbour and two British battleships. England was in a hopeless position, they chorused and ended by a "*Viva Duce. Duce e forte.*" All this was news to me, but I pretended I knew all about it and told them it was all propaganda and lies. "*Tutte mensogne,*" I told them. "Look," I said, "how your papers lied about the Eritrean and Libyan fighting, and see where we are now. The British always win the last battle, as your own Garibaldi used to say."

This seemed to surprise them as I had not obviously taken their propaganda as had been intended, and instead of being depressed had actually had the impertinence to say the British would win in the end. However, with an angry "*Duce e forte, Duce e forte,*" they stopped trying to tease me and sat glumly looking down the barrels of their rifles. Just occasionally the fatter of the two would draw himself up and shout his "*Duce e forte*" chorus again to reassure himself that his Duce really was strong and all-powerful. At last I was shown into a cell and told I would be questioned in the morning. There was a pile of straw in one corner, which I soon spread out and, with two blankets round me, slept the sleep of the truly weary both in body and spirit. What a day it had been, so full of hope and confidence, only to be dashed to the ground and broken into a thousand pieces. My life seemed to have crumbled about me but my weary bones at last overcame my spirit. All this happened on December 13th, 1941.

CHAPTER EIGHT

Solitary Confinement

MY INTERROGATION started next morning and went on more or less continuously for over twenty-four hours. I was put on a hard seat with a powerful floodlamp shining in my face. A little, suave man was sitting behind a desk and first he started pleading and coaxing. "All I want to know," he said, "is the name of the Italian who helped you to get to the frontier." They just could not believe that anybody could have reached the frontier without help; but in order to mystify him and prevent any tightening up in the railway regulations, I told him, "I can't say." This answer became mechanical and I must have repeated myself thousands of times during the questionings. After four hours his relief came in and started off with the brilliant idea that I could be bribed into telling. "If only you will give me the name of the Italian," he said, "you can choose the camp you go to, be it by the sea or up in the mountains or in the south."

So it went on all the morning until midday when I said:

"I am sick of all this nonsense. I want some lunch."

"You can have some lunch when you answer my questions like a gentleman should."

"You know perfectly well that I will not answer your damn' silly questions. If you won't give me anything to eat, which I may remind you is contrary to the Geneva Convention, then please allow me to use the lavatory."

"All right and I will look forward to seeing you this afternoon after I have had my own lunch."

76

After relieving myself, I was put back in the cell for an hour or so, and then the whole performance started over again, and went on continuously till the evening when one of them lost his temper.

"You filthy Englishman sitting there so smiling. Roma has telephoned to say that any methods can now be used. If necessary you will be shot as a spy, and for wearing the uniform of our Army."

"That won't help me answer your questions."

"Oh, you think yourself funny, do you. So. You will now stand up and answer, do you hear me, *answer* my questions."

He ended in a high-pitched scream and told the soldier behind me to take away my chair and keep the muzzle of his rifle in my back.

All night long the same old questions were put to me. Sometimes he used a quiet voice pleading to my better judgment and what he called my "instincts as a gentleman." More often he was angry and insulting and shouted at me across his desk. If I tried to move at all, the rifle in my back gave me a hard jab, and by morning had made it very tender. It was several weeks before the soreness wore off.

About dawn the following morning, a burst of firing suddenly came to my ears and it was announced dramatically that yet another British spy had been shot. "Now will you tell us? Surely it is not worth dying to save one of your enemies?"

I told them I was bored, tired and not amused. This of course enraged them and a torrent of invectives came out in rapid Italian before the once suave interrogator could be calmed down. Then he told the guard to take me away and give me a meal. As I went out of the door, he said with malice that he would see that I would get very special treatment for the next month or two, just to make sure that I did not try to do the same thing again. The grilling had not been enjoyable but it had been an interesting experience of the Fascist police machine at work.

Next morning I went by car to the Central Station between

two burly carabinieri and by 9 a.m. was on a train for Piacenza, a small town in the Po valley about seventy miles from Milan. We climbed out at a little station between Alessandria and Piacenza, and had to walk about three miles to my new home by name of Montalbo. It was here that I was to undergo my thirty days' solitary confinement for escaping and I actually never went into the main camp itself.

Montalbo was an old castle built on the top of a little hill overlooking the Po plain. An officers' punishment cell had just been built adjoining one wing of the castle, which was surrounded by a narrow perimeter of barbed wire only a few feet away from the walls. At that time Montalbo had only been opened a few months and was for the exclusive use of about eighty officer prisoners of war. Immediately on arrival I was put straight into the cell, accompanied by the usual Italian shouting and screaming whenever things were not quite right.

Life was very uncomfortable, except for the food which was comparatively good and plentiful and came from the officers' kitchen in the main camp. No books were allowed, nor were writing materials or even pencils. I only had half an hour's exercise each day and that in a kind of bird-cage outside the door to my cell. This was about twenty yards long by two yards wide, and was hardly big enough even to stretch my arms let alone swing the proverbial cat. The most exercise that I ever got was to walk to the lavatory in the castle, so that three times a day (the maximum allowed) I had a lovely hundred yards' walk, which was at least a change from my cell.

Whilst eating my lunch on the second day, I discovered under the cabbage a stub of pencil and a note. It told me to write my needs on a piece of lavatory paper the next time I went there and to leave it on top of the cistern. This I did, asking for books. At the same time I said who I was and why I was in a cell. Next time I went to the lavatory I collected a book and hid it under my coat on the way back. The pencil was invaluable and I was soon making up new crossword puzzles complete with clues on pieces of lavatory paper.

The books lasted till Boxing Day, when the Italians discovered the trick and stopped me using the castle lavatory. A bucket was given me as a substitute. The Italian Commandant occasionally visited me, and when I complained that he was breaking the Geneva Convention by not giving me books, by not allowing me writing material and by failing to take sanitary precautions which rendered my cell unfit to house pigs, he just laughed and went away.

After I lost the books I took to making up bigger and better crosswords on bits of lavatory paper. I came to the conclusion that making up crosswords was far harder than solving them, and it gave me a mental occupation which stopped me getting too depressed. In between making up crosswords I tried to remember all the poetry I had ever learnt at school and recited it to myself. I found that by concentration I could remember a surprising amount. My only other brain occupation was multiplying two numbers together in my head. Eventually I found I could multiply two six figure numbers together and then write down the answer and check it on paper. A childish occupation, perhaps, but it helped to pass many a long, weary hour.

My thirty days were up on the 14th January, but still the Italians refused to release me. It was not until the 19th January that I was told that I was being taken back to Sulmona, and was to leave straight away. A captain, a lieutenant and two private soldiers had come up specially to escort the " very dangerous " prisoner back to camp. It was really rather ludicrous, but it gave me satisfaction to realise how troublesome my escape had been to the Italians. They took escapes seriously and made every effort to stop them, which was one of the biggest reasons why we must go on trying and was the only way we had left to help in the war effort.

My guards became quite friendly on the way back, and told me that the Sulmona Commandant had been sent to the Russian front as a result of our escape from the camp. It was surely a very heavy sentence for so mild an offence, they thought. I laughed aloud and they thought it in extremely bad taste. They also told me that Christopher had been wounded, but was now all right. As this was the first news that I had had of it, I could scarcely believe their words, though I was glad to hear that he had recovered.

Evidently my guards thought that I had hopped on to a goods train in the Sulmona valley; they even said that railway guards had seen me doing it! So much the better, I thought to myself, as this would enable me to repeat the same method of getting a ticket the next time I got out.

A car met us at Sulmona station, and I was driven back to the camp from which I had escaped six weeks before. It was almost like coming back home, and great was my welcome by all my friends. In some ways my recapture was a good thing because it provided a whole lot of new information which might be useful to future escapers. It also dispelled the bogey once and for all that it was impossible for anybody to escape and also have a reasonable chance of getting to a neutral country. There could no longer be any excuse for not having a try on that score, and I think it gave confidence to some who had sat on the fence not quite knowing whether to take the plunge or not.

I was so ashamed of my stupidity in the Milan hotel incident that I never breathed a word about it. It is funny how sensitive one can become in a prison camp, and I somehow felt that I might be branded as an idiot who threw away good chances of success, and therefore should not be allowed to try again.

I had not been back in Sulmona more than a few days when the Italians announced that a special camp for dangerous prisoners was being started near Pisa. Seven officers were to go to it straight away and included both Commander Brown, R.N. and Tag Pritchard. Both these officers were suspected of having organised escapes. They had not escaped themselves but on this occasion the Italians were not far short of the truth. I was not included but was told by the camp officials not to worry as I was certain to follow as soon as Roma realised that I was back at Sulmona and therefore capable of being moved up to the new camp. I rather looked forward to going, because not only was the new camp another three hundred miles nearer Switzerland than Sulmona, but Sulmona was really getting a very hard camp from which to get out, except by tunnelling. My marching orders came exactly one month after getting back to Sulmona and nobody was more pleased than I.

CHAPTER NINE

Monastery Life

A CAPTAIN and a lieutenant acted as escort to take me to Campo 27 between Pisa and Florence, and an Italian private soldier came to carry my kit. By this time I had accumulated quite a lot of luggage. I took with me two suitcases, an army pack, a roll of blankets and a wooden crate full of books. It never seemed to worry the Italians how much kit we took, since they regarded it as quite normal for officers. Their own took about thirty large trunks, mostly full of different uniforms, wherever they moved, even on active service. A paltry suitcase or two was very small beer by comparison.

We climbed aboard the train for Rome, and apparently orders had been issued that one of the two escorting officers would have a drawn revolver in his hand at all times. It was repeatedly explained to me that if I budged an inch off my seat I should be shot. This was explained in the usual Latin way, with much flourishing of the loaded revolver, and always repeated whenever anybody was within earshot. Having harangued me, my escort would then turn to the audience and tell them that I was a most dangerous prisoner who had escaped over twenty times before, so they must keep well clear. The crowd never believed the story for they were Italians and had themselves told similar stories. They then edged closer to have a good look. The compartment in which I sat was like a booth at a fair, and relays of passengers came in and sat down for a few minutes, while the bravery of the escort in taking such a dangerous criminal on a public train was implied a dozen times to the admiration and disbelief of the onlookers.

Eventually we arrived at Rome at 7 p.m. and my brave Captain announced that we had a three-hour wait before catching the train to Pisa. I told him that the Geneva Convention insisted that all prisoners of war must be reasonably fed, and suggested going to have dinner in an hotel. I had hoped that their attention might be relaxed after a good dinner with plenty of vino and might give me a chance to give them the slip. After a lot of argument, during which I threatened to report him both to the Protecting Power and to the Papal Emissary, the next time they visited our camp, he eventually gave in, and all three of us trooped into the station restaurant. We sat down at a table in the middle and soon the loud voices of my escorts informed all present who I was, while I was ordering the biggest meal I could get out of a fawning English-speaking Italian waiter, who said he had worked in London before the war.

At last we got up from the table feeling much better, and I was led off to a waiting-room until the train came in, an hour late, at 11 p.m. After another three-hour wait at Pisa for a slow train to take us along the line to Florence, we alighted at 6 a.m. at a little station only about half a mile from our new camp and about a third of the distance between Pisa and Florence.

My new home proved to be part of an old monastery. From outside it looked like a prison, and this impression was heightened by the massive iron and oak door leading into the cloisters, whence a bare stone staircase led to the monk cells, each of which now housed two prisoners of war. In one I found Tag still lying down half asleep and I heard the story of Campo 27 whilst he shaved and dressed.

There were eight British officers including myself, and about thirty Greeks. All the British had come from Sulmona and had either made an escape or had been suspected by the Italians of organising one. The Greek officers were an odd-looking lot. Most had deserted during the war in Albania and were active Italian sympathisers. A few were excellent types, who had been made prisoner after being wounded, and warned us about their brother officers.

"If it weren't for these Greeks, we would be out of this camp by now, so easy are the obstacles compared with Sulmona. Every scheme we have thought of so far has had to be turned down because the Greeks would give the show away. It is obvious why the Wops sent us here. The defences are within the camp rather than all round it. But never mind. We have some other ideas, which we hope will bear fruit in a month or two. Let's go and have some breakfast."

We went downstairs to the old monks' refectory hall and sat down to a breakfast consisting of a large cup of ersatz coffee and two small slices of dry bread. George Patterson came in at the same time and after a cheery greeting said:

"You know, Tony, that bread has to last you all day and weights exactly 150 grammes to the nearest crumb."

"Don't pull my leg."

"For once I mean it. We are damned hungry, but we don't seem to be much the worse for it yet. The Greeks do all the cooking and as there is only one kitchen and we are in the minority, we have to lump it."

"Do they pinch the rations then?"

"No, I don't think so, but they have no idea how to make the food go a long way, and some of their dishes make us squirm a bit. We haven't had any Red Cross parcels since we arrived here in spite of repeated letters to the Protecting Power and even the Pope."

"It all sounds rather grim."

"Well it is not too bad really. It is a wonderful change after Sulmona and we are much nearer Switzerland."

George finished his coffee and we went out into the Monastery garden to look around. Half the building was still occupied by monks, but brick walls had been built to shut us off completely and all round were the usual sentries, barbed wire and lights. Wherever we went there were Greeks and it was obvious that any scheme to get out would have to include some plan to divert their attention.

Lunch came round and consisted of a plate of vegetable

soup and any bread left over from breakfast. Supper was much the same except that the soup usually had about half an inch of rice at the bottom of the plate. On Sundays enough macaroni had accumulated from the daily ration allowance to have a soup plate full each and this was the only comparatively solid meal of the week. Our canteen allowed us half a litre of vino a day and also fruit, if one could afford the high prices charged.

To our great surprise our diet at first seemed to make no appreciable difference to our health, except for an almost continuous hunger pain at the pit of our stomachs. We went out for walks twice a week, and the country was lovely in the spring. Sheltered little farms and vineyards dotted the landscape as if the white houses and red roofs had been shaken out of a giant pepper pot and had landed haphazardly on hill and dale. Young corn gave a bright green sheen to the picture which was only occasionally broken by regular rows of vines or olives. Higher up the hills to the north, were nearly continuous olive groves, with the little town of Lucca, of olive oil fame, only about thirty miles away.

After about six weeks, the effect of the starvation rations began to be noticed. Although we felt quite fit, we no longer had the desire for walks that we had on our arrival, and getting up in the morning began to be more and more of an effort. At Sulmona, Tag had swollen to the most enormous size, in spite of his forty minutes' P.T. every day. At Campo 27 he visibly shrank and in the end was unable to do his P.T., which was an astounding break in his routine. After three months we just wandered listlessly around the garden, praying and hoping for Red Cross parcels. To our delight these turned up unexpectedly soon after. Solid bully beef and biscuits, scrumptious cheese, packets of raisins, chocolate, tea, milk, and even sugar. How we blessed the Red Cross and their parcels! Every mouthful was chewed and chewed and almost regretfully swallowed. We could each of us have polished off a Red Cross box on the spot, but very wisely limited ourselves to one a week, both to spare our digestions, long unused to such fare, and eke out the supply of food. After the arrival of the Red Cross boxes we all had a smile on our faces and once more felt hopeful for our future, redoubling our efforts to find a way out which the Greeks would not spot.

One of the Greeks could speak a little English; we called him Peter, and he was an excellent little chap who told us many tales of his country and his home in Athens. One Greek major had fought in the 1914 war against us while acting as an interpreter between the Turks and Germans. Apparently he had had a very cosmopolitan education and could speak Turkish and German like his native tongue. Tag and I used to practise our German on him, and in the end we became quite good, thanks to his help.

In spite of repeated demands by us for visits from outside officials, the Italians did not allow them near our camp. They were a little alarmed at the prospects of an investigation, and from the Commandant downwards were scared stiff that any of us should escape because then they might be punished for negligence by being sent abroad to fight.

It was towards the end of our second month that we gradually formulated a plan to get us all out. During those eight weeks Lucky had been piecing together the geography of the other side of the wall, by pretending he was a Roman Catholic and asking for confessions with one of the monks next door. He was taken round regularly each week, and contrived to be taken back a different way each time. Eventually we had a very clear idea of the layout. The corridors, off which led our bedroom cells, had once upon a time communicated with the rest of the monastery, and we discovered that the wall of an end cell led into a deserted passage on the monks' side. Unfortunately all the cells in this corridor, except for the end one, were occupied by Greek officers and it would have been impossible to tunnel through the wall without the whole passage knowing about it.

The big problem was how to distract the Greeks, while we made the hole. We had a clue to the solution a fortnight later, when the Greeks all celebrated a feast day, and invited us to attend as guests. The party started at about 6 p.m. and went on for thirty-six hours. They had all saved up their vino for a whole month past and drank on and off continuously. After about twenty-four hours they were decidedly merry and nearly hoarse from singing weird Greek songs and shanties; by 6 a.m. next morning they were all sleeping the sleep of the drunk. What a party! They were quite offended when we tried to go about midnight on the first night. At last we managed to creep out about 2 a.m., when we suddenly realised, to our great surprise, that it was going to go on all through the next day and night. They looked terrible for about a week afterwards.

We decided that we would save up all our wine for the next two months. That should keep them going for at least twelve hours, which would be sufficient for our purpose. Lt. Sullivan, a Naval Swordfish pilot, revealed himself an expert forger and produced the most wonderful identity cards. All the usual paraphernalia of escaping, such as clothes and money, were sorted out, and standard phrases learnt. Our equipment was really first-class, and the plan was to take a train to Florence and from there to Milan and the Swiss frontier. Our chances were excellent once we were clear of the camp.

We drew lots who should make the hole in the wall, and it fell to Commander Brown and me. The chosen day arrived and we started to ply the Greeks with drink as rapidly as possible starting after lunch at about 2 p.m. We reckoned they would be nicely merry by about 9 p.m., when we planned to start work, and we thought we would be through the hole and away by 11 p.m. Although the wall was only of one brick thickness and of fairly soft texture, it was no easy matter to make a hole without any noise. Our instruments were a sharp bit of iron and a carving knife, and we soon realised that the job was not going to be as easy as we thought. As a result we probably made more noise than we had intended.

We had just pushed the point of our instrument through the bricks, when a light was shone on the hole from the other side and somebody was shouting in Italian and banging on the wall. We had obviously been discovered and so ran quickly back to our rooms and gave the alarm. Our kit, maps, food and clothes were quickly hidden, and in a few seconds we had undressed and were lying in bed. Just as we pulled the sheets up the Italians arrived, having taken about five minutes to gather together. We all pretended to turn over sleepily in our beds, but this did not impress the Italians, who were livid. They all talked at once as they went through our rooms with a fine tooth comb. They only found incriminating articles on Tag and George Patterson. The next day poor old Tag and Pat were both doing twenty-eight days' solitary, and I am afraid Commander Brown and I both smiled a little when we realised that it really should have been us behind the bars. If the Italians had been clever and had come round to us silently without flashing torches and banging on the wall, they would have caught both of us red-handed.

Unfortunately we had chosen the one night in the week when a monk cleaned out the chapel. Normally he would have come from the chapel and, crossing a small courtyard, gone back to his cell without coming upstairs near our wall. On this particular night it had been raining and to avoid getting wet he had decided to take the disused corridor. We were all greatly disappointed as we had great confidence in our scheme and with a little more luck it would almost certainly have succeeded.

CHAPTER TEN

Malingering

I T W A S about a month later, at the end of April, that we first
heard a rumour that headquarters in Rome had decided that our
camp was not good enough for desperate characters like us, and
were opening a really escape-proof prison somewhere in the
south of Italy. It turned out later on that this camp was to be
the notorious Number 5, which was located even farther north
than Campo 27.

Realising that our next camp was going to be no sinecure, I
decided that I must make an attempt before the move. But
when we were warned on May 7th that we would leave on the
15th, no time remained to plan a new way out of our camp. My
only chance seemed to be to get to a hospital whilst still in the
north of Italy. I had been operated on for mastoids behind my
left ear when I was a boy, and so it was not difficult to pretend
extreme pain and deafness. The local doctor said I must see a
specialist at once, so the next day I was taken to Florence
Military Hospital.

The big snag of the hospital idea was the question of the
clothes that I was going to wear when I got out. I would
almost certainly be searched on entering the hospital, and any
but the simplest of disguises would be impossible to take in with
me. As a result of my experiences on the Italian railways six
months before, I finally decided that clothes did not really matter
as long as they were not obviously uniform. Eventually I took
with me to hospital a navy blue roll neck pullover which my
mother had just sent me, battledress trousers with the outside

pockets removed, and brown shoes. As a hat I had one which
had been issued to me by the Italians and was in the form of one
of their own field service hats dyed a dark chocolate brown
colour; the peak could be pulled down and the straps going
over the top of the cap cut off, to make quite a presentable
peasant's cap as worn all over northern Italy. My money and
maps were in the usual place between my legs and stuck to me
with sticking plaster.

The train journey to Florence and the cab ride out to the
hospital were uneventful, but I tried to remember the way,
especially the direction of the station. The hospital was a large
building facing the main Florence-Bologna road, and stood about
two miles from the centre of the town. I was hustled up to the
top storey and was searched quite thoroughly by a carabinieri
who signed for me from my escort. I was then shown into my
room, which was not unlike that in many English hospitals and
contained three beds.

The wing where I was had rooms all about the same size,
two on each side of the corridor. In addition there was a
sitting-room and a balcony where I was allowed to sit in the
morning. The balcony looked on to the main road outside the
hospital, and this bird's-eye view of life outside was a constant
attraction to me. The room next door was occupied by a
Blackshirt lieutenant who had been wounded in Russia, and
whom I rarely saw. On the other side of the corridor one room
was empty and the second occupied by two Jugoslav generals
who had been captured when their country was overrun. One
had had an operation on his eye and the other on his ear, and
both were at least sixty years old. We used to meet on the
balcony every morning and they were cheery souls who disliked
the Italians intensely. We got on quite well speaking German,
and their tales were the usual hard-luck stories which every
prisoner of war has and which can always be produced on
demand. While I was in hospital, one of them had a letter to
say that his whole family, wife and three children had been shot
by the Germans because there had been sabotage on the railway

FLORENCE MILITARY HOSPITAL
PART OF FOURTH FLOOR.

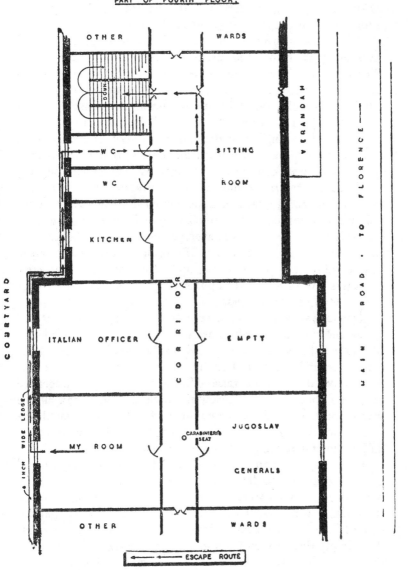

OTHER WARDS

DOWN

WC

WC

SITTING ROOM

KITCHEN

VERANDAH

MAIN ROAD · TO FLORENCE

COURTYARD

6 INCH WIDE LEDGE

CORRIDOR

ITALIAN OFFICER

EMPTY

JUGOSLAV

CARABINIERE'S SEAT

MY ROOM

GENERALS

OTHER WARDS

ESCAPE ROUTE

near the village where they lived. Poor old soul, he grew ten years older overnight; everything that he had been living for had suddenly been cut away from under his feet.

When I was in my room a carabinieri guard was on watch outside my door continuously, being relieved every eight hours. The door was kept locked. Every time I wanted to go to the lavatory I had to bang on it, when it was unlocked, and the carabinieri would walk with me to the lavatory just down the passage. When I sat on the verandah he came too, and the prospects of getting away did not seem very bright. Luckily the prison camp had not warned the hospital that I had escaped before and was considered "dangerous" or otherwise they would have taken rather more stringent precautions. Six months later in England I heard that the wretched commandant of the prison camp was sent to the Russian Front for not having warned the hospital! The dread the average Italian has for fighting for his country always amused me. He would be prepared to go to any lengths for a job at home, and being posted to an active front was always regarded as punishment. No wonder they were never much use as soldiers.

Outside my window was a seventy-foot drop to the courtyard below and no handy drain pipes to slide down. The old device of knotted sheets for a rope could not be used because of their rottenness and the fact that the number I would require was many more than I could raise. However there was a decorative moulding about four feet below my building, which ran all the way round the outside of the building. The top of the moulding was in the form of a slightly sloping ledge about five inches wide, and I thought it might be just wide enough to use.

Gradually my plan evolved. I would get out of my window and move along the ledge, past the Italian officer's bedroom window, round the corner of the building and then in at one of the lavatory windows. I could easily make sure it was open by going to the lavatory about midnight. I would then go through the lavatory door, which I would also leave open, and then down the stairs which were in a well of their own and separated by doors from all landings. The snag was that I could not very well open the door leading down the stairs when I went to the lavatory, but I hoped that over a course of days I would be lucky one night and find that it had been left open. The carabiniere always sat in his chair facing my door and he would be most unlikely to hear me flit in stockinged feet between the already-opened lavatory and the stairway doors. Having reached the ground floor I would jump out through a window into the courtyard, and circling round the building to the right I could quite easily get on the main road leading down into Florence.

I had been in the hospital a fortnight when my plan had crystallised. About then a Flight-Sergeant Cox came into my room for three days with tonsilitis. He was working as a batman at the Generals' Prison Camp at Fiesole, just outside Florence, having been captured when Air Vice-Marshal Boyd was landed by mistake in Sicily instead of Malta. He gave me all their news. He told me how Air Marshal Boyd spent his whole time doing carpentry, how General Gambier-Parry was a very able sketcher and artist, and how General Younghusband was a most successful gardener within the limited area which was available. General Carton de Wiart was the only one he could not understand, but " he has only one arm, one eye, and a V.C., so that must explain a lot." I agreed.

At the time I thought it was just possible that he was a stooge and so I did not tell him of my intentions. It was a welcome respite, however, to be able to talk in English again.

As soon as Cox had gone back to Campo 12 at Fiesole, I started my midnight visits to the lavatory, but it wasn't until ten days later, on the evening of June 13th, 1942, that the door leading down the stairway was left open. June 13th was St. Anthony's Day, which I felt was a good omen for my adventure.

I decided to start about 3 a.m. and aimed at being on the main road by 4 a.m. This would give me two hours to walk into Florence and get an early train to Milan. In planning for our escape from Campo 27 I had remembered that an express train for Milan was due to leave at 6 a.m., and that was the one I hoped to catch.

I dressed as silently as possible putting one shoe in each trouser pocket where they would not be in my way, and at 3 a.m., in my stockinged feet, I swung my legs over into the darkness and found the ledge with my toes. Holding on to the shutter outside the window with one hand I started to move sideways to the left, flattening myself against the wall as much as possible. I had not gone more than a few steps when an attack of giddiness seized me, and I quickly went back just managing to clutch on to my shutter again. My knees were shaking and teeth chattering with excitement as I climbed back into my bedroom.

Ten minutes went by while I recovered my breath and my nerve. An occasional grunt came through the door from the carabiniere or a squeak from his chair as he shifted his seat, but otherwise the night was silent. My imagination kept telling me that I might slip off the ledge, or it might crumble under my weight. But I knew I must do it. This was my chance; I might never get another one.

Once again I tiptoed to the window and without looking downwards, levered myself out and slowly slithered my feet down the wall on to the ledge. This time I was not going to get back into the room and to make sure of it, I swung the outside shutters across the window, and I heard a click from the latch on the inside.

I had always meant to do this to keep the Italians guessing how I had got out, but on my first try I had forgotten all about it in my excitement. I had bought some particularly obnoxious and sticky hair oil whilst in the hospital, and I had used this to lubricate all the hinges and catches on the shutters and on the lavatory door, to stop any squeaks.

There was no going back now. I held on to the closed shutter with my right hand and slid as far as I could along the ledge. My left hand could not reach the shutter over the next window but I forced myself on and inch by inch moved along the ledge.

I wanted to press against the rough wall as tightly as possible, but if I did this it made a scraping noise which might alarm some wakeful patient.

After six feet with nothing to hang on to, I reached the next lot of shutters and using them as hand holds, quickly passed under the window. I then came to the worst part of the ledge, where it went round the corner of the building out of reach of all shutters. Again I had to leave go with my right hand and move spreadeagled to the corner. Here the fingertips of my left hand were able to follow the wall around and give slightly more security. At the same moment the ledge under my left foot suddenly felt loose, and I had visions of the whole corner of the building breaking away. All at once my giddiness returned and I felt sweat slowly trickling down the side of my nose. My knees shook, but I held them still by pressing against the wall, while I gingerly transferred my weight to my other foot and felt around with my left toe to see what was loose. Something was very wobbly right on the corner and looking down I could just see that the cement surface was quite free and if dislodged, a three-foot length would crash into the courtyard below. The moulding underneath the surface felt solid enough. It made a gritting noise as it wobbled and felt very insecure, but I slowly worked my way round the corner and then along a short length of wall to another corner, which was an inside one and much easier. A few more yards and I was under the lavatory window.

I heaved myself up and dropped on to the lavatory floor where I stood for a minute or two to get my breath. Never have I felt so relieved as I did when I had finished that awful traverse along the face of the building in pitch darkness. Never do I want to do anything like it again. It might have been child's play to an expert mountaineer, but I was not one.

Cautiously peering round the corner of the lavatory door I saw the carabiniere awake and looking disconsolately at the ground in front of his chair. I saw that, if I crossed the passage to the other side before moving along opposite the doorway to the stairs, he could not see me if he looked up. All went well and soon I was standing opposite to the doorway leading down the stairs. There was not enough room for me to get through and I prayed and hoped that it would not squeak when I opened it a further few inches. The door opened without a murmur and, like a flash, I passed down the stairs without the carabiniere knowing what was happening. I would have a clear five hours' start till about 8 a.m. when I was called, and by that time I hoped to be well on the way to Milan. In case the carabiniere put his head inside my room during the remainder of the night, I had rolled up a greatcoat to look like me in bed, and I was confident it would pass all right for any casual look.

Creeping down the stairs I arrived at the bottom, and dropped into the courtyard through an open window on the ground floor. I rather misjudged the height because I landed on the paving stones on all fours and severely strained my wrist in the process. I crept round the outside of the hospital and then through an allotment and so came to the wall bordering the main road where I put on my shoes. I also pulled out a brown paper parcel from my trouser seat, which I planned to carry instead of a bag to give me the necessary *raison d'être*. It was five minutes to four, and at four o'clock precisely I swung over the wall and started to walk down the main road towards Florence.

CHAPTER ELEVEN

German Seaman

THIS TIME I had decided to wear no outer insignia to suggest that I was a German. I did not in fact have any papers with me as it would have been too risky to bring them into hospital. Only if I was challenged would I say I was a German, and then only if I had to say more than a word or two in Italian. By 5 a.m. I had reached the centre of Florence and had to ask my way to the station which I reached about twenty minutes later. To my relief I found that there was a 6 a.m. to Milan, but decided to wander round the station till about ten minutes to six before buying my ticket. By that time there would be a good-sized queue and this would give the booking-clerk less time to look at me closely.

Florence station is modern, and puts ours to shame by its cleanliness and neat layout. I looked round for a bench where I feigned sleep to avoid complications in talking. When the time came I pulled out my money and rose to join the queue for tickets. Unfortunately my 500 lire note was slightly mutilated because it had been hidden up the tubular leg of an iron bedstead at Campo 27 and little holes had been torn in it. Eventually my turn came and I said my usual " *Terzo Milano*," at the same time pushing over the note. To my horror the official started turning the note over and over, examining it against the light, and, after what seemed hours, asked me if I had another. I replied with a shake of the head and a monosyllabic mumbled "˻no." However with a shrug of his shoulders he pushed the ticket and change towards me. Cold sweat had started on my brow and the palms of my hands were decidedly damp as I walked away.

The express from Rome came in ten minutes late, and was very full. As soon as it came to a halt the crowd surged forward, myself included, and we fought for places on the steps leading up to the carriages. Putting my head down I got aboard after giving a kick on the shins to a man on my left who had tried to pull me back to get in himself. At last we all crammed into the corridor where I stood in the corner near the lavatory, chin on chest, pretending to doze. I kept my ticket in my hand and whenever the collector passed up and down the train, which happened frequently, he just took the ticket out of my hand, punched it and put it back without apparently waking me up.

A lot of people got out at Bologna and I was glad to find a seat to myself in a compartment, as I would need all my energy when I reached the frontier. Unfortunately no " cistina " lunches were being sold on the stations, rations in Italy being much shorter now than when I had travelled to Milan six months earlier.

On one occasion when the ticket collector came round he had two railway police behind him, and they took a good look at me when punching the ticket. He took the ticket out into the corridor and started examining it closely with his back to me. After a minute or two he returned it and passed on to the next person. Scare over! Apparently they had a special key which fitted the ticket exactly for detecting forgeries. In all my travels on the railway I always saw hundreds of carabinieri, railway policemen and ordinary railway officials but they were always more concerned with the traveller who had no ticket. As long as you had a bona-fide ticket they did not seem to worry.

I managed to avoid all conversation by pretending to sleep in my corner, and at 11 a.m. we pulled into Milan Central station. My plan was to hang about the station till about 4.30 p.m. and then take a train to Varese, as I thought Como might be watched by now. The frontier was only thirteen kilometres from Varese at Porto Cerisio on the edge of Lake Lugano. If I arrived at Varese about dusk I would then walk to within two kilometres of Porto Cerisio and then strike up the hill and with a bit of luck might be in Switzerland within twenty-four hours of getting away from Florence.

The waiting-room was much emptier this time and I killed time by wandering round the station. I bought my ticket, just in case anybody asked me what I was doing and got a return this time to make my travelling to a frontier town more plausible, " *Terzo Vareze andate e ritorno*," accompanied by a 50 lire note produced my ticket without any questions being asked. I was always a little self-conscious about my dress, but it never seemed to excite any suspicions. Luckily it was fairly cool at that date and the roll-neck pullover did not look too out of place.

I had a cup of *caffe al latte* for my lunch, and buying a few papers took them to the waiting-room for a four-hour wait till my train, which left at 4.37. I saw in the paper that a German ship had been sunk in the Mediterranean and the survivors landed at Genoa. This might be a useful story if ever I was stopped, and my navy blue sweater would help. I could always pretend I was taking a short holiday before going on to Germany.

The journey to Varese by electric train was without incident and I arrived at about 6.15 p.m., just when it was beginning to get dark. My half ticket was taken without any questions being asked, and I went out into the town. My plan was to strike off along the road which led roughly in the right direction and hope it brought me to a signpost which would put me on my way. I walked right through the centre of the town and past groups of men and women gossiping on the pavements and sitting at open air cafés; but they seemed to be far more interested in their own conversations than in me, so I passed through unmolested.

A crossroad on the north side of the town put me on the right road and told me I had twelve kilometres to Porto Cerisio. By this time it was dark and the sky was overcast, but a moon shone behind the clouds for the first half of the night. The road twisted and turned in all directions but always seemed to be flanked by small fields, high walls or precipitous mountainsides. It was no country to choose one's own route until much closer to the frontier. The road seemed to be interminable. My month in hospital without exercise had not helped and my muscles were very soft. I passed through one or two tiny villages and eventually came to the three kilometre stone from Porto Cerisio, where I could see Lago Lugano with its search-lights playing on the water. By this time it was 10 p.m. and I struck up the hillside through a wood which flanked the road at this point. Thorn bushes seemed to reach out and grab me with every step I took and made progress very slow and painful. It was dark in the wood and I was forced to move so slowly that, having gone about two hundred yards, I decided to wait until morning when I would be able to avoid some of the worst hazards. Feeling thirsty, tired and cold, I curled myself up in some dead leaves and went to sleep. The cold woke me up about an hour before dawn, and after rubbing my stiff muscles back to life I crawled up the hill trying to avoid the demon thorn bushes. After half an hour, I saw I was coming to the top of the ridge. Suddenly, outlined against the morning sky, I saw a sentry box with a tall row of barbed wire behind it. I immediately dropped to the ground and saw that the sentry boxes were spaced about fifty yards apart all along the top of the hill. Just round the corner, and lower down, I could see what looked like a cemetery. This was really too much! My map did not show the frontier in any great detail but I had never expected to find it so close to the main road and so well guarded. In a minor panic I slithered back down the hill up which I had just crawled, and wondered what to do next. I was really flabbergasted, having hoped that this piece of frontier would not have been more difficult than the part near Chiasso that I had seen six months before. Rightly or wrongly I decided to lie up where I was for the rest of that day, and then to walk back to Varese and on to Como that night. I would then try to get over a piece of frontier that I knew.

Later on, in Switzerland, I found a large-scale map of where I had been, and the frontier could not have been there at all and was at least another two kilometres farther on. To this day I do not know what I had stumbled into, and can only suppose that it was some kind of military dump that was being extra well guarded. I had not bargained for that sort of bad luck. To make matters worse it rained cats and dogs all that day, and I was soaked to the skin. I had to remain perfectly still so as not to attract attention and I don't think I have ever been so cold, in all my life. My teeth kept up a permanent chatter and the feeling went out of my hands and feet after an hour or two. Slowly the time went by and at last it was dark enough to allow me to walk down to the main road and get my circulation going once more. It was about twenty miles to Como and I thought I could arrive in its vicinity by midnight.

It was lovely to be warm again and my clothes soon dried out, but I was certainly not out of the wood yet. I passed through Varese for the second time about 9 p.m., and found the Como road without difficulty. I began to feel extraordinarily tired and my brown Italian shoes were working up beautiful blisters on my heels which did not help progress. To my left I could see the outline of hills and over them I knew lay Switzerland, my dream country for over a year past. The road seemed never ending and I began to curse myself for having decided to walk all the way round to Como before trying again. If I had had a more accurate map of the frontier I would have gone across country but it was too risky on my own and would have been more guesswork than map reading.

I don't know what possessed me but I went on walking after midnight, always a dangerous thing to do. At about 1 a.m., while passing through the little village of Ogliate, I was challenged. My spirits fell as I went up to the man who proved to be a Maresciallo of Bersaglieri (equivalent of R.S.M.). He asked me for my papers. I went into a long explanation of who I was and brought out my newspaper to prove it, but all I could get out of him was that I would have to go in " *dentro* " (inside) for the night. The last card I had to play was to knock him on the head, seize his bicycle and make a run for it, but before this I tried my last piece of bluff. I told him that if the German Consular authorities in Como did not see me by 8 a.m. in the morning, there would be trouble for anyone who had held me. I said this with much gusto and repeated myself several times. With much head-shaking and more muttering of "*dentro*" he said I could go on this time, but it was most irregular and I must not do it again. My luck was holding out, but that scare had brought me to my senses and I did not make such a stupid mistake again. I went on through the village and slept in a ditch about one kilometre along the road till about 4.30, when I started to walk again. I passed through another village and had a dirty look from a carabiniere on duty, but soon after this I discovered a little wood near the road that would do as shelter for the day. Creeping in under some undergrowth, I curled up and went to sleep, mentally and physically exhausted but thankful that I was still a free man.

I woke up at 11 a.m. to the sound of woodcutting and children playing about a hundred and fifty yards away in my wood. Children and dogs were my worst enemies that day, but luckily none came near enough to find me, though it had the effect of keeping me mentally alert and awake all the time. I was now getting very hungry and thirsty and my blistered feet did not help my physical condition. However I knew that I was now within a few miles of freedom and that, given a bit of luck and provided I did not make a fool of myself, I would have a good chance of succeeding. It was my gamble against at least another six months in prison, if not for the whole war. I was playing for uncomfortably high stakes. I suppose the chances of getting out of a prison camp are at least a hundred-to-one against. In Italy at this time, one's chances of getting to the frontier area having got out of camp were about twenty-to-one against—provided one did not do anything too stupid. Having got to within five miles of the frontier the chances of getting over would be about evens, I had now, for the second time in six months, arrived within five miles of the frontier, so I considered my chances were really good but did not mean to take any risks.

That day, thank goodness, was dry; for I don't think I could have stood another soaking. When dusk came I started on what I hoped would be my last lap. The road began to climb and, in a series of gentle turns, I went on upwards for the first three hours. The country was getting very hilly and the mountains to the north seemed to tower to endless heights above me. An occasional car swept by and I would shield my face from the lights and try to keep in the shadows on the sides of the road. Houses were built on either side and became more frequent. They were obviously summer villas for rich business men from Milan, and must have been delightful with an endless view stretching out over the Lombardy plain.

A few men passed me going the other way and once two or three soldiers went by, but they had no eyes for me and I certainly had none for them. At last my road started to wend its way down the hillside and, far below, I could see some lights with a lake beyond. At the time I assumed they must be Como, but I discovered later that it was the goods yard at Chiasso, on the frontier, at which I was now looking.

Eventually at about 11 p.m. I came to a road junction and turned left towards the lights thinking that it would lead me to Como through which I should have to pass before reaching the frontier area at Chiasso. In fact, of course, my road had by-passed Como, and I had just joined the Como-Chiasso road where I had been caught before. I suppose I should have recognised it, but it looked very different by night and distances were deceptive.

I walked on down the hill to Chiasso and did not realise my mistake until suddenly I saw the frontier barrier right across the road and not two hundred yards away from me. I nearly had a fit on the spot. Trying not to hurry myself, I retraced my steps to the outskirts of Chiasso, and, not wishing to be caught on the roads again after hours, I decided to sleep in a culvert under the road until about 4.30 a.m., when I would go back towards Como for about a mile and then strike up the hill. My culvert could not have been more than a few hundred yards from the frontier, but it was a case of safety first at this stage. Unfortunately it was not entirely dry and an evil-smelling stream of dirty black water trickled down the middle. I had an uncomfortable, worrying five hours perched on some flat stones which remained dry at one side of the stream.

At last 4.30 a.m. crept round on my watch and, making sure that nobody saw me coming out of the culvert, I started walking back down the road. In ten minutes I found a convenient turning-off and soon I was following a small footpath that led up the hillside and in approximately the right general direction. I would be much too early for any woodcutters going to work, and my only worry was the possibility of frontier guards coming back from duty along my track. However I reasoned to myself that the relief guard would surely have to use my track to go out, and I could not imagine a changeover much before 6.30 a.m. With any luck my path would be all right for at least an hour, and after that I must keep well clear of all tracks. My progress along the path was five times as quick as it would have been across country, as by now I was climbing nearly vertical slopes with thick thorny undergrowth on either side.

At 6 a.m. I decided to leave the track and started climbing straight up the hill. I was now about 2,000 feet above the valley. I could see Chiasso quite plainly with its long goods sidings, and an obvious fence at right angles through the middle which was the frontier.

I decided to climb for about another hour and then to start moving very slowly along the hillside till I sighted the frontier. I would then lie up all day watching the sentries, and try to get over that night.

I thrust my way up the mountainside and swept aside the bushes that tried to hold me back; what did a few scratches matter now? Soon I came to a belt of pine trees, and walking through them was a great relief after the thorn scrub lower down. I came out of the pine trees and went on upwards through hazel plantations and every sort of mountain shrub, which all grew in profusion everywhere. At last I thought I was high enough and I started to move cautiously along the hillside in the direction where I knew the frontier to be. I had not been going more than half an hour, when, just across a little valley and not more than four hundred yards away, I saw a sentry box amongst the trees. I dropped down on one knee and could pick out one or two more and the line of fence poles behind. The little valley between me and the frontier was quite bare and open and the fence and sentry boxes were a few yards inside the wood beyond. I found a comfortable hole full of dead leaves in which I could sleep and from which I could watch the frontier. I had a very welcome meal of blueberries, which grew all around, and after watching the frontier for an hour or two fell asleep.

About half a mile up on my left hand, and just about where the frontier ought to be, I could see a red roof. I assumed this to be one of the posts which housed the relief sentries, and occasionally I could see one wandering along the wire. They changed over every even hour. The sentry boxes were about two hundred yards apart, which was not too bad, and I carefully marked down the route I should take that night in order to bring me out exactly between two boxes.

At last darkness fell and, although I felt like going bald-headed at it, I had decided to play safe and try to cross at 11 p.m. I would allow an hour to crawl the four hundred yards and that would give me at least another hour before there was any more large movement of sentries to and fro. The sentries on that frontier were not over keen on wandering about by day, so with any luck they would be even less alert at night. A light rain started to fall about 10 p.m. and I cheered inwardly to myself. No Italian sentry would wander about in the rain unless given a direct order by an officer!

I crawled slowly through the undergrowth and across the open patch at the bottom of the valley. I did not make much noise, but to my ears I sounded like a bull charging around. The rain pattering on the leaves made all the difference as it blanketed my sounds from the sentries. I could just hear one singing away to himself in his box, little suspecting that a British officer was at that very moment within a hundred yards of his post.

By 11 p.m. I had reached the path used by the sentries and just over the other side the frontier wire was stretched. I saw that it was a fairly formidable obstacle. It was made of diamond mesh wire of fairly heavy gauge and was constructed all in one piece and at least twelve feet high. Poles in the form of an inverted V suspended the wire from its apex, and all along the top bells were hung. The slightest touch on the wire would start them clanging. The problem was how to get over, through or under. No branches overhung the wire anywhere near and as I had no pliers my only alternative was to try to burrow a way underneath. I could have risked the bells and climbed over the top but it might have gone wrong and was not worth it if I could find another way.

The bottom of the fence was pegged every six inches with eighteen inch wooden stakes, but luckily the soil in the wood was mostly leaf mould, and the stakes pulled up easily without shaking the fence. I had soon freed about a three foot length, pausing between each stake to listen for any footsteps on the path.

All was quiet. The sentry on my left was still crooning away to himself about his " Mama mia," but still I could hear nothing from the one on my right. The rain came down a little harder now, and a damp moist smell came up from the disturbed earth when I started to scrape it away with my hands. It remided me of sheltering from the rain in an English wood in autumn after a dry summer. It was a musty clean smell quite different from the usual pungent Italian aromas.

I slowly scraped away, using one of the stakes to loosen the earth, and then removing it with my hands.

After I had been going about ten minutes there was quite a respectable hole and I tried to squeeze underneath the wire but there was too small a gap and I became stuck with one shoulder and one arm in Switzerland and the rest of me in Italy.

Several things then happened at once. The bell above me

gave a very small tinkle, a branch crashed down nearby, the
sentry stopped singing and the noise of shunting goods wagons
in Chiasso suddenly became very loud due to a change in the
wind.

I prayed that the sentries would stay where they were, whilst
I slowly pushed myself back into Italy. The hole would have to
be bigger.

After a few very long seconds I was clear and I crawled back
over the track and lay in a bush for a few minutes. If the
sentry had heard anything he would surely come along and
inspect the wire at once.

My luck was in and after five minutes' complete silence
except for the rain on the leaves, and the noise of the shunting,
I crawled back across the track once more. On this occasion I
was not going to be stuck under the wire, and worked away for
ten minutes before the gap was big enough. My hands reached
through to Switzerland, this time much farther, and I was able
to grasp a tree root and draw myself through without shaking the
fence above me.

CHAPTER TWELVE

Switzerland, June 1942

I WAS NOW in Switzerland and free! My hunger, tiredness and sore feet were all forgotten in my elation and satisfaction Walking erect, and no longer afraid of making a noise, I went a few hundred yards away from the line of the wire and then started down the hill with the lights of Chiasso to guide me. I then struck the most enormous patch of thorn bushes and only after about half an hour of struggling did I manage to free myself. As a result I decided to sleep the rest of the night on the hillside and to walk down in the morning when I could see where I was going.

I curled up under a large tree that kept off most of the rain, and slept till about 4 a.m. when I woke to see the eastern sky just starting to lighten. Overhead the clouds had gone, making visibility much better, and gradually I began to see where I was. By 5 a.m. I was on my way and I soon struck a path which I followed till it eventually brought me on to a road that led down into Chiasso. The atmosphere was altogether different, the people just stirring at the backs of their houses looked clean and hospitable and the occasional Swiss sign reassured me that the almost unbelievable had come true, and that I had actually arrived in a neutral country.

I was soon walking through the outskirts of the town and, on reaching the main square, I sat down on a bench while deciding what to do next. I knew that in theory all I had to do was to present myself to the first Swiss policeman, and that he would take care of the rest and see that I was taken to the nearest

Consulate. We had heard in the prison camp that it was still possible to get back from Switzerland to England, in spite of Vichy France and Spain being in the way. My reasoning had become ultra-cautious by now and I said to myself that if I could get to the British Embassy in Berne without the Swiss knowing, I might be in an even stronger position to be sent back to England. After all, if I could travel through Italy without being spotted, I ought to be able to do so easily enough in peaceful Switzerland. Anyway, I would go to the station and see if I could change my Italian money for Swiss. Without Swiss money I could do nothing. I would then try to buy a ticket to Berne and then if there was time I would go out and have a shave and some breakfast.

I found the station and the bureau de change, and received twenty-five Swiss francs in exchange for about four hundred lire. So far so good. I next bought a ticket, speaking German this time, and to my surprise out came my third class ticket to Berne. It was almost too good to be true and could not last. It didn't!

I had an hour to spare before the next train went and was just walking out of the station when a Swiss policeman politely asked me who I was. The game was up, and so I told him in German that I was a British officer escaped from Italy and I was just going out to have a shave before taking the 7.15 a.m. train to Berne. This took his breath away a bit, and all he could mutter was, " It is most irregular." I agreed with him and said that I did not suppose it happened every day, but then I was lucky and would he mind telling me the way to the nearest barber?

By this time he had come to his senses and told me he did not believe a word that I had said and that I was probably a German spy. Anyway, I would have to come down to the frontier post for interrogation by his boss. Frontier posts in Chiasso seemed to have a fatal attraction for me, but I hoped this one would be a little more hospitable. I went with the policeman to the post and there, not twenty yards away, was the Italian equivalent which housed me only six months before.

I was searched and questioned and after a little telephoning I was told that the H.Q. at Bellinzona wanted to check up on me and that I should be going there in a few hours. All the officials were most polite and after I had told them that I had not washed, eaten or slept for three days, immediately sent for some breakfast and a barber.

A huge bowl of coffee soon slipped down, accompanied by several crisp, warm rolls spread with delicious butter and jam. My morale was picking up with every mouthful and after a wash and a shave I felt like a million dollars. Everything was wonderful, the countryside clean and well-cared-for, with happy smiling people who looked so different from their neighbours across the frontier. I wore rose-tinted spectacles that day.

After breakfast we walked to the station and I was soon on my way to Bellinzona, accompanied by a policeman. A sudden weariness overcame me on the train and I slept all the way until I was nudged to get out when we walked through the town to the Police H.Q.

I was led in front of the Chief of Police, and the first question he asked me was why I had not given myself up instead of going to Berne direct. I told him that I was frightened of the delay and red tape that might prevent me getting to Berne quickly. I reminded him that I had been with the Italians for a year and a half where " *Domani* " or " to-morrow " was the watchword and everything could wait. This riled him a little, and he sharply reminded me that I was now in Switzerland and not Italy. Anyhow it had the desired effect because I was in Berne by 7 p.m. that night. Having rebuked me, he asked me if I would like anything to eat and I told him I would like a really large steak with fried potatoes and half a litre of beer. Before the meal I went to wash my hands and had the shock of my life when I saw my face in the glass. I looked quite frightful with a thin, pinched face and weary eyes sunk into the cheek bones. I weighed myself the next day in Berne and found that I was forty pounds under my normal weight.

That meal was one of the best and most satisfying I have ever eaten, and I don't think the old Chief of Police had ever seen anyone eat so hungrily. His eyes nearly popped out of his head as he saw it all disappearing down my throat, and we parted on the best of terms when the time came to catch the train to Berne. I dozed on and off all the way, but we passed through the most lovely scenery imaginable, and I was so enthralled with the view that only occasionally did my eyelids take control and close over my eyes for half an hour or so. It was evening when we drew into Berne station.

We took a taxi to a military H.Q. and the things that struck me most were the lighted shop windows and the enormous variety of goods for sale everywhere. It was quite a revelation and helped me to become a little more normal and a little less affected by my period in prison. We arrived at a big stone building and I was interviewed by a charming young officer who said I would be questioned in the morning, but that I would have to spend to-night in the refugees' hostel. He took me there and I found a babel of voices speaking every tongue from all over Europe. Little Switzerland was a haven for oppressed peoples and the Swiss were in the embarrassing situation of entertaining thousands of penniless refugees without a country, and who for humanitarian reasons alone could not be turned back.

The little Swiss officer left me after I had found a bed, and rather disconsolately I lay on my back wondering what to do next. Visions of a bath and food at the best restaurant in Berne faded before the rather hospital-like rugged simplicity of the refugees' hostel. Outside, guards patrolled all round the building and I began to feel a little depressed.

I was reprieved more quickly than I expected because two hours later the same officer came back, and said that I could stay in an hotel for the night if I promised not to try and communicate with my embassy. I readily agreed and we walked round to it by way of his flat, where I picked up some clothes which he lent me till I could get some others, as he thought I would be a little uncomfortable in my battledress trousers and now dirty roll-neck pullover in a big Berne hotel. This was very kind of him and most thoughtful. I was shown my room by the hotel manager, who became most effusive as soon as he knew who I was. In the luxury of a steaming hot bath, I lay back and forgot all my worries. It was my first for fifteen months and a wonderful relaxation after my long journey.

The next day I was questioned and apparently I satisfied them that my story was bona fide. The following fortnight in Switzerland was almost like a fairy tale. Cocktail parties, dinners, dances, sailing and swimming. I had my first real holiday of the war and I don't think I let the grass grow under my feet. The feeling of freedom was so pleasant and the kindly, hospitable people and the cleanliness of the streets contrasted vividly with wartime Italy.

I then moved down to Geneva, which was the start of my next lap. Now, of course, it was a very different matter because instead of having to work out my own route, provide myself with clothes, money, etc., it was all done for me.

My grey suit was chosen for its continental style and cut and had wide trousers, padded shoulders and patch pockets. A little dark-blue beret and an attaché case completed my outfit for my new role of a Czechoslovak refugee.

I joined up with two R.A.F. sergeant-pilots who had walked all the way to Switzerland from northern France, and we three were to travel together to Marseilles. We all lived in an unobtrusive hotel in Geneva, waiting for the word to start us once more on our adventures. I went for long walks round the city each day, including seeing over that expensive white elephant, the Palace of the League of Nations. Then I used to bathe and go out for sails on the lake. In the evening my still insatiable hunger would get the better of me and I would go to the open-air lakeside restaurants for an exquisite meal, which of course was to prove far better than any I was able to get in London a few weeks later. Meals at restaurants were rationed and no more than three meal coupons could be expended at any one restaurant for a single meal. As I had been given a whole month's coupons, and I knew I was only going to be there about another week, I used to have hors d'œuvres and fish at one restaurant, and then move along to the next and finish off my meal. I was still about two stone under weight and my appetite always appeared to demand more.

At last our moment came and about an hour before dawn one morning a car picked us up at our hotel and drove us rapidly to the place where we were going to cross the frontier. A guide led the way through a churchyard and along the edge of a wood which had a small stream running through it. An occasional Swiss soldier could be seen on frontier duty, but a mumbled pass word from our guide was sufficient to make the sentry turn away and carry on along his beat. I am sure we were not the only ones to use that crossing-point, and it was clear that the Swiss authorities did not know what was going on.

Our guide pointed out our route and with a " Good luck " and a handshake he left us alone. After we had taken off our shoes we stepped gingerly across the stream, which was only about nine inches deep, and climbed up the farther bank. We then had to cross a small field and go through a gate on to a road. I knew we had to move about a hundred yards along this road when Simon, our next guide, would come out from behind a hedge with a bicycle on his left side. I saw the bit of hedge that had been described to me, but to my dismay no Simon appeared. The two R.A.F. sergeants, who had not been given the instructions, wanted to know if I had remembered the right way and couldn't it have been in the opposite direction. Just when we were looking a bit sheepish at one another, Simon came bicycling up the road and said he was sorry he was late in a very casual tone.

We then walked to his house where Madame Simon produced the biggest and best omelet I have ever seen or tasted. It must have been made with a dozen eggs and about half a pound of butter. Not much starvation here, but no doubt it was all purchased on the black market.

After breakfast we cleaned ourselves up and awaited our

next guide who took us to the other side of the town and nearer to the railway station from which we were to catch the night train to Marseilles. Henri appeared at nine o'clock and he led us round by a carefully chosen route to his house. He knew exactly when all the patrols went by, and by which route. A little palm-greasing here and there and our route seemed as safe as walking through Hyde Park.

We had another excellent meal with Henri and passed the rest of the day in his house. We were rather bored but heard many tales of the difficulties and dangers of a patriot in France at this time. German Gestapo men in plain clothes were everywhere and nobody knew who was friend or foe. Suddenly someone would disappear and never be heard of again, except six months or perhaps a year later a small box containing ashes arrived by post for his relations.

With our tickets already in our hands, we walked a few hundred yards to the station and went straight into the buffet to await the arrival of the train. The Gestapo were wandering around on the platform and occasionally checked up on papers. Apparently they never came into the buffet. As soon as the train came in, Georges, our new guide, called us on to the platform and we ran for a carriage door. Soon we were on board and sitting in opposite corners of the same compartment pretending not to recognise each other. Dumbness was the order of the day and we spoke not a word all that night on our way down the Rhone valley to Marseilles, which we reached next morning at 7 a.m.

Marseilles was meant to have about 30,000 police of one sort or another in it but it was such a large town that any crook might well have hidden away in it for years without discovery, which was a fact well known to every wanted man in France. Georges led the way down the main street from the station, past the hotel where the German-Italian Commission was housed, and into a little café which had opened early for the sale of ersatz coffee and rolls, which were very welcome to us. Jean, our next guide, came in a few minutes later and after thanking

Georges profusely we were led off for quite a distance through the streets.

No praise can be too high for these guides of the French Resistance. They asked for no reward and they looked embarrassed when thanked; all they wanted was to do something towards the day when France would be liberated. Each had his sector to work and did not know where the next guide went. Only one master brain knew all the links in the chain.

We walked through a very poor quarter and up the winding stairs of a dirty apartment house. This was not our final goal and we collected our next guide, a young girl of about twenty, who took us to a modern block of flats overlooking the old harbour. A gendarme was standing outside the door, but without faltering we went straight in and up in the lift to Madame Nouveau's flat, a luxurious apartment through which many an escaper like me passed during the course of the war. I believe I was number 123 to go through the flat and nothing could have been more hospitable than Madame during the ten days I spent there from July 2nd to 12th, 1942.

Her husband was up north on a job for the Resistance and Madame was carrying on in his absence. Six months later he was caught and put in Buchenwald Concentration Camp for the rest of the war. He had only been arrested on suspicion or otherwise he would have been executed. Luckily Madame Nouveau heard of her husband's arrest in time to go underground, and she remained undetected for two years until at last her hideaway in Haute Savoi was overrun by the U.S. 7th Army. Before fleeing she had stripped her flat of everything from books to carpets and from ornaments to heavy oak chests-of-drawers. All her friends took what they could and promised to keep it for her till that glorious day, the day of Liberation.

When it did come and Madame returned, her friends brought everything back and she says she lost not a single tiny ornament or even a book. I revisited her flat in 1945 when my plane taking me to the Middle East broke down at Istres. This gave me an extra twenty-four hours, and I took the chance to hook a lift into

Marseilles and found the flat I had known so well in 1942. With trepidation I knocked on the door, and to my enormous surprise and relief saw Monsieur and Madame together in their flat, which looked exactly as I had remembered it in 1942. I soon had their news and I was told that I was the first of those whom they had helped during the war who had revisited them. Right royally did they welcome me once more, and once more all I could do was to thank them again and again for all they had done for poor wretches like me.

The resistance cell of which Monsieur Nouveau was, I believe, the leader, was highly organised and very efficient. They had direct wireless communication with England and all our instructions came that way. Apparently the Spanish route that had been used successfully for some time was very hot at the moment and they did not think it feasible. We were going out by a special method that had not been used for prisoners before, but had been employed for Polish refugees.

At last the day came for our departure and, in two parties, we made our way to the station and boarded a train for the west. We changed trains once at a small station, then at about 4 p.m. arrived at our destination about fifty miles from Marseilles and quite close to the sea. Our guides took us along different routes, but eventually we all met at our rendezvous in a small wood a few hundred yards from the Mediterranean. In addition to those of us that had come from Marseilles, two more parties of R.A.F. arrived at our wood before nightfall, to make the total of eight British with half a dozen French guides. We munched some sandwiches and drank coffee from Thermoses and dozed off for a few hours' sleep before our next move which was not to be before eleven o'clock that night. We were all in the highest spirits and all talked excitedly about what we would do when we arrived home, and we wondered how long it would take.

At 11 p.m. we all moved off in single file. The night was dark with no moon, and scudding clouds that alternately gave inky blackness or a feeble light that enabled us to see about a hundred yards. We wound our way in and out of enormous boulders going parallel to the sea-shore and a few hundred yards from it, and after about two miles' stumbling along this rocky labyrinth, we made our way down to the beach and walked along it for about another mile. The white, foamy edge of surf stood out in the darkness on our left and gave us a guide to walk by, while an occasional seaside villa on our right made us realise that the coast was inhabited and there might be many a slip twixt cup and lip. Lighthouses were flashing ahead and behind us and must have been about five miles apart on small promontories that protruded from either end of our beach.

When our guide judged us to be about half-way between the two lights he stopped, and pulled out a torch which had a special blue filter over the glass. The time was now midnight and the ship which was coming to take us off, due at 1 a.m. on July 13th, would flash two long dashes of blue light which would be answered by three flashes from our torch. A rowing-boat would then come in and take us off.

Patiently we sat down and tried to keep warm while the hour went slowly by. A fine rain started that did not help and I think we were all wondering what on earth would happen if the boat failed to find us. We could not have hung around that beach until the next night, and there would have been an awful anti-climax and no little risk while we found hiding places for the day somewhere in the neighbourhood.

Our doubts and fear were laid at rest when at 1 a.m. precisely two faint blue flashes came out of the darkness in the bay and were answered by our signal. All we had to do now was to wait for the rowing-boat which might be twenty minutes coming in. Half an hour went by and still no sign of the boat. We gave some more flashes on our lamp, but these were not answered by the ship. What could have happened? Had we dreamt those blue flashes? However we decided to give it another twenty minutes before we did anything more.

The twenty minutes went by and another twenty minutes as well. It was now ten past two and still no sign of any rowing-boats. We just went on flashing while hoping for the best and giving our lamp as wide an arc as possible in case the ship had drifted down-wind.

At half-past two there was still no sign and our guides began to look worried. We were by now a very big party and would have been no easy problem for them. They would have to get us away by 3 a.m. if they were going to have a reasonable chance of finding somewhere for us to hide by daylight.

Suddenly a blue flash came from the sea and not more than a few hundred yards out. Soon we heard the padded noise made by muffled rowlocks, and at 2.45 a.m. the rowing-boat beached. A midshipman in naval uniform was in the stern and a couple of husky A.B.s were at the oars. Apparently the off-shore wind and current had been very strong and, after making one abortive effort to row ashore, they had returned to the ship for another hand.

We piled aboard and pulled off after saying good-bye with many " *au revoirs* " to our brave guides. Two of us lent a hand at the oars and in ten minutes we sighted the outline of a small ship against the night sky, and had soon climbed up a scaling net helped by many willing hands on deck. We were then taken into the fo'castle and had enormous mugs of Navy cocoa, bread and jam and cheese thrust into our hands. It was wonderful to hear the cheery naval slang going on all round and English being talked again. Even while we sipped the boiling cocoa, the ship's engines started to murmur and we were heading out to sea away from our bay.

The captain of the ship came in to speak to us and see who we were. He told us it was so nice to pick up Englishmen, as usually he had nothing but Poles. We asked him how on earth he managed to sail so close to an enemy shore with so small a ship, and he told us we would see how in the morning when we took a look round. A twinkle came into his eye, as he said, " You see, we look just like a peaceable fishing trawler. And by the way," he said as an afterthought, " if any planes come out and have a look at us in the morning, I want you all below decks. All my crew have the right clothes to keep the make-believe going, and I don't want any plane to become suspicious at the numbers we are carrying aboard." He bade us a cheery good night and we turned in to some spare bunks. We were soon sleeping the sleep of the just and thankful.

Morning came with a bright blue sky, and I was on deck to see what sort of ship she was. Outwardly she looked a dirty, brown trawler, with bits of rope strewn everywhere and nothing at all shipshape. Some of the crew were working in old reefers, and the captain was on the bridge in a garb not much better. It was on a closer inspection that the little trawler became interesting. The big steam winch was a 3.7 in. gun. Another gun was fixed aft under the guise of an engine-room hatch and machine-guns galore all over the ship could be swung into place in a jiffy. It must have been something like World War I's Q ships and looked quite effective.

We were going to be taken to Gibraltar, and we were at sea two days in a really bad storm, which made our little trawler stand on its head and tail alternately, with great seas sweeping over us from stem to stern. At times the bridge was the only part of us above the waves, and for the first time in my life I was seasick. So, too, were most of the crew for it was one of the worst summer storms that they had experienced in the Mediterranean.

When there were only about thirty-six hours sailing yet to do before we arrived at Gibraltar, our Captain announced that to-night would be " painting night." It was the thirteenth complete coat of paint that he had given his ship in four months, and by morning we had to be a nice grey H.M. Trawler in all its glory with White Ensign flying, guns oiled, decks scrubbed and ropes neatly coiled everywhere. Everybody was dished out a pot of grey paint and a brush, and all night we painted, till by 4 a.m. the transformation had been completed and our little ship had had its face lifted again.

I don't think even we who had lived on the ship for close on six days had realised that there were so many guns aboard her. They seemed to sprout from every corner, and we would have given any attacker something to think about if he had poked his nose too close.

All the following day we sailed on westwards in the lovely Mediterranean sunshine, and now we began to feel we were really getting somewhere. We were due in at Gibraltar that night but would have to wait till dawn next morning before we were allowed in through the boom.

The authorities in Gibraltar were most surprised to find a party of escapers on board, because nobody had warned them that we were coming. Everybody was very helpful however and somehow we were squeezed into a troopship that was sailing for Britain the next morning.

We dropped anchor off Gourock in the Clyde after ten days of zig-zagging in convoy across the Atlantic. On this occasion I was singled out by the Movements Officer who came aboard. He had been told to get me to London as quickly as possible. An hour later I was seated in a fast train going south and had been the first passenger to leave the ship. I eagerly looked forward to a few days of enjoyment and renewal of old friendships and memories.

As I dozed, a feeling of deep satisfaction spread over me, a feeling of successful achievement, which in my conceit I thought I had justified. The sight of some W.V.S. doling out tea on a platform brought me to my senses. They were doing things for others. I realised then what I owed to all my friends still in prison in Italy and to the dozens of brave Frenchmen and their wonderful organisation. If it had not been for them I would still be languishing behind barbed wire with all its mental anguish and petty horrors, which become magnified and distorted in so unnatural a life.

As I fell asleep I thanked God for my good fortune and prayed that others besides myself would have some of my luck.

CHAPTER THIRTEEN

Arnhem, Switzerland 1944

I WOKE up cramped, thirsty, and hungry. Was it yesterday that I had escaped from Italy, only to find myself to-day hiding in a tiny wall cupboard in Holland? My memory took me back the two years with a sudden vividness, and once more the horrors of life in a prison camp were hanging over me unless I could find a way out.

After ten days' leave I had been sent down to Bulford to serve as Signal Officer to the newly-formed 2nd Parachute Brigade. And in March 1943 we sailed for North Africa. Six months later when Italy surrendered unconditionally the 1st Airborne Division were the only Allied troops in the " heel " of Italy. But at the beginning of December we received word that the Division was returning home before Christmas. 1st Airborne Division was to take part in the cross-Channel invasion, and we were all glad to be returning for what was obviously going to be the climax of the war.

We had to be ready for operations by the end of April barely four months hence. There was no time to lose and we entered a period of extremely intensive training, culminating in divisional exercises in Yorkshire and in the Cotswolds. By the beginning of May every man was convinced that he belonged to the best division in the British Army. This was reflected in their efficiency and enthusiasm both on exercises in the field and in their country house barracks in Lincolnshire. Our new commander, Major-General R. E. Urquhart, was well liked by all ranks, although he had not commanded airborne troops before. A large man with an imposing figure, he was too heavy to parachute, but everywhere he went he radiated self-confidence. He himself planned to land by glider with about half his H.Q. The other half would go to war by parachute.

The Division consisted of two Parachute Brigades, one Airlanding Brigade (gliders) and one attached Polish Parachute Brigade. 1st Parachute Brigade consisted of veterans from the N. Africa and Sicily campaigns. 4th Parachute Brigade had been formed from British units in the Middle East and India, and although not so experienced as 1st Parachute Brigade had an *esprit de corps* all of its own. 1st Airlanding Brigade was made up of ordinary infantry battalions who were carried to battle in gliders. The air-landing battalions were also very efficient and experienced and had been used in the initial glider assault into Sicily. In addition there was the usual complement of gunners, sappers, signals and service troops. All these were on a much reduced scale when compared with a normal division, due to weight restrictions. I was second-in-command of the Divisional Signals and we had to make do with small wireless sets of much reduced power compared with those used in a normal division. We hoped that a higher standard of training would make up for some of the deficiencies of the equipment, and we were repeatedly assured that the Airborne Division would never be employed on a wide front, but would be landed and would fight within a small perimeter " perhaps as much as three miles in diameter."

D-day came on June 6th and with it the eternal question, " When is the Division going to be used, sir?" We read of great doings in France and felt sure we should be there too. We had worked the men up to a pitch of training that only action against the enemy would satisfy.

We soon had our answer. We had to prepare to land on the hills to the south of Caen in Normandy and help capture this important point in conjunction with 7th Armoured Division. We loaded up our transports and gliders, but on June 13th the operation was cancelled. Altogether seventeen operations were planned for 1st Airborne Division in the fourteen weeks between D-day and Arnhem, but of these only four came to the ears of the troops. Four times the aircraft were loaded up and four times unloaded again within a few hours.

On September 12th yet another airborne operation was planned, this time to take place in Holland between Eindhoven and Arnhem. Three Airborne Divisions were going to be used and an Airborne Corps H.Q. Once again we loaded our aircraft and gliders; a task which had by now become a very well known drill and did not take long. The same old procedure of briefing the men took place and all the time we expected a cancellation to come through.

It was not till September 16th that I heard details of the whole operation. In general the task was to seize a fifty mile long corridor spanning eight major water obstacles including the Meuse, the Waal and the Lower Rhine at Arnhem. If this could be done, Field Marshal Montgomery would be able to sweep forward into Holland and thence towards the vital Ruhr, thus turning the flank of the Siegfried Line, which ended at Aachen.

The planning had been done by 1st British Airborne Corps H.Q. under command of Lt.-General F. A. M. Browning, and there were many difficulties to be overcome.

In the first place, and by far the most important, there were only sufficient aircraft to lift about half the force. It was decided to allocate about a third to each division, and this would mean that the landing would be spread over at least two days.

The task given to 1st Airborne Division was to seize the bridge over the Lower Rhine at Arnhem. Corps H.Q. had sent air photographs of the area and had suggested some dropping zones which were eight miles to the west of Arnhem on some open heathland.

Sunday, September 17th, 1944, dawned fine and to our great surprise we had not yet received any cancellations. A lorry duly arrived at our Lincolnshire country house with our parachutes. An hour later more lorries arrived and we climbed

aboard to go to an airfield near Grantham. Everything seemed
so unreal. We had never got as far as this on any of our previous
abortive operations.

All down one side of the airfield were some fifty C.47s, or
Dakotas, lined up in staggered rows. We drove to our allotted
aircraft and rechecked the loading which had been done on the
previous day. Everything was all right and our American crews
came over and helped us. They were a grand lot and mutual
respect for each other had grown up in the preceding months.
We could not have been served better, and but for them there
would not have been any large-scale airborne operations.

The word came to put on parachutes and get into the aircraft.
A few minutes later we were roaring down the runway at thirty-
second intervals, and then flew in a wide circle, low over
the villages we knew so well, while the rest took off and joined
the armada. Now we were in tight formation, all fifty of us,
flying south-east over the sunlit fen country. Looking out of
the pilots' window I saw that my aircraft was the leader of our
V formation and that half a mile ahead were another fifty
Dakotas, flying steadily on, all bunched together. Behind us was
a similar lot making one hundred and fifty in all, carrying 1st
Parachute Brigade complete, together with the parachuting part
of the Divisional Signals, and the Reconnaissance Squadron.
The next day the same aircraft would bring the 4th Parachute
Brigade, and the day after the Polish Parachute Brigade, if they
were required.

The glider element was taking off simultaneously from eleven
airfields in Wiltshire and Hampshire, carrying two-thirds of the
1st Airlanding Brigade and the remainder of Divisional Headquarters and the Reconnaissance Squadron, in three hundred
gliders. The towing aircraft were all found from No. 38 and No.
46 Groups R.A.F., and would return for a second lift of another
three hundred gliders on the following day.

The flight plan phased in all the aircraft into one continuous
stream and from the ground must have looked an impressive
sight. From the air we could see the streets of the villages we

passed over thronged with people looking upwards and an occasional handkerchief could be seen waving a farewell. It was midday when we crossed the coast and flew out across the North Sea, which for once was like a millpond with scarcely a ripple to disturb its brown-looking water.

The men in my plane were nearly all asleep by now as is the custom of the British private soldier. He had no worries, he placed supreme confidence in his officers and he often lacked all imagination. Little did he care that he was taking part in the biggest airborne operation ever launched; all that mattered was that he did his own job to the best of his ability. Therein lay his strength as a fighting soldier in adversity, and as events were to prove he was not found wanting.

Thirty-five minutes after leaving the Suffolk coastline there was a bustling amongst the crew in the cockpit up forward, and I could see them strapping on steel helmets. The Dutch coast was in sight and a few minutes later we flew in low over the island of Schonwen just south of Rotterdam. A moment later I saw several fighters with United States markings come up level with us for a second or two and then turn off and fly away out of sight. It was a comforting thought to remember that at least 1,200 fighters were on patrol to protect us during our flight. The Luftwaffe missed a golden opportunity on that Sunday morning.

A little later on we crossed the Dutch coast proper, and were surprised to see some Horsa gliders already landed in the fields below us. We heard later that about ten per cent had broken their tow ropes and had come down short of the correct landing zone.

The Dutch farms looked peaceful enough from above and there was no sign of any enemy. As in England, civilians looked upwards at us and an occasional handkerchief could be seen waving. I heard afterwards from a Dutch patriot who watched us from below, that it was the most thrilling spectacle of his whole life, and surpassed even the day of his final liberation by the Canadians some eight months later.

There were now only twenty minutes left to the time we were

due to drop and so far we had not suffered a scratch. No enemy fighters had come near, nor had any flak guns seen fit to fire in our direction. It was almost too good to be true, and I was just congratulating myself when a noise like a sledge hammer beating the outside of our fuselage woke up everybody, including my batman, Lance-Corporal Turner, who was an inveterate sleeper when in aeroplanes. Through our open doorway we could see a light flak gun shooting straight at us. Little yellow tongues of flame spat in our direction and a few seconds later some more hammer blows could be heard. There appeared to be no casualties so perhaps the shells were just grazing the fuselage, and this seemed to be confirmed when I saw about a foot of a wingtip suddenly disappear from the aircraft flying just opposite the open doorway, and only twenty or thirty feet away. We had just time to see six fighters diving down on the flak gun, all cannons blazing, and the German crew running for their slit trenches.

Still we droned on, and after a signal from the pilot, I gave the order, "Stand up, hook up and check equipment." The whole plane load leapt into activity. Parachutes were adjusted, static lines hooked on to the wire running down the side of the fuselage, and steel helmets given a further tighten up. After hooking myself up, I took up position at the open door with the rest of the men as close as they could get behind me. I could hear the engines change their note as the pilot throttled down to jumping speed, and as a large river flashed by underneath, the red light came on. That must be the Rhine and we were nearly there. I could see some parachutes lying at the end of a field. An enormous T had been laid out on the ground by the pathfinder company. "Green Light." I was out of the aircraft and a moment later was gently swinging beneath my parachute.

All round me were parachutists as all fifty aircraft ejected their loads. For those privileged to be there, it was a most inspiring sight and one which I shall never forget.

I touched down in some heather and rolled over backwards, banging my head on a steel container in the process. For a few seconds I could not think what I was doing, but by now the next group of fifty aircraft were roaring overhead, and as if by magic another thousand parachutes came out of their bodies and floated earthwards on top of us.

I had soon gathered my plane load and we were off towards the pre-arranged collecting point for Divisional H.Q. An occasional rifle shot could be heard, but apart from this the whole landing operation could have taken place in England. There was hardly any wind and the sun streamed down on us. We had come down on a large open heath covered with heather and ringed by pine forests which gave out a singularly attractive scent, which contrasted with the tang of aviation petrol that hangs around military transport aircraft.

We arrived at the side of the heath in amongst a great clutter of crashed gliders. In one corner we met up with the rest of my men who had come by glider and a little farther on I could see the General and Lt.-Colonel C. Mackenzie, the G.S.O. I of the Division. I reported all present and we were soon at work setting up the nucleus of a Divisional H.Q., based on the two or three jeeps that had already arrived, after being extracted from the tails of the gliders. Communications were established to 1st Parachute Brigade who were ready to move off within an hour of landing. It had been planned to send off the Recce Squadron under Major C. H. F. Gough to seize the Arnhem bridge by *coup de main*. The Squadron was equipped with heavily-armed jeeps specially mounted with machine-guns pointing forwards and backwards. Unfortunately most of the gliders carrying his jeeps had failed to arrive due to broken tow ropes, and that part of the plan was discarded. For the time being Divisional H.Q. would remain where it was, and we saw 1st Parachute Brigade moving off by companies through the trees towards Arnhem.

The two battalions of the 1st Airlanding Brigade to come in by glider, the 7th Battalion King's Own Scottish Borderers and 1st Battalion the Border Regiment, took up their defensive positions round the perimeter of the dropping zone. So far everything had gone to plan except for the Recce Squadron's jeeps.

Reports began to come in that 1st Parachute Brigade were meeting with considerable opposition on their way to the bridge. Three roughly parallel roads were being used for the advance, one for each battalion, and the southern one alone was found to be moderately clear of the enemy. Along this route Lt.-Colonel J. D. Frost and 2nd Parachute Battalion pushed as fast as they could, and by 8 p.m. that evening had established Battalion H.Q. and one company at the north end of the bridge. A little later a second company arrived and a large part of Brigade H.Q., the Signals section and some sappers.

In the meantime the other two battalions in the brigade had become heavily engaged in the woods when about half-way between the dropping zone and Arnhem.

The Division was now in three bits. Brigade H.Q., together with most of one battalion, were on the bridge, while the remainder of the brigade were about two miles away on the edge of the town. The rest of the division including Divisional H.Q. was back near the dropping zone. This was a military nightmare, which would lead to disaster if the Germans attacked in strength. Luckily they attacked piece meal, although precious little was to be saved out of the mess.

Back at Divisional H.Q. on the first afternoon I was worried. Our communications back to the base in England were weak and erratic, and being constantly interfered with by a strong German station. We had no communication direct to Corps H.Q., although messages could be sent via England. We had lost touch with 1st Parachute Brigade H.Q., when they were only about five miles away from our H.Q. in spite of every effort on our part to improve the position of our Divisional H.Q. sets. My Colonel asked me to go forward as early as possible next morning and see what the trouble was. He also ordered a change in frequency for our main Divisional Command wireless set. This change would not be known to 1st Parachute Brigade unless they were informed, and he asked me to do this and clear up the trouble.

We had no idea at the time where they had reached, or what the enemy was doing.

At first light on the 18th there was still no improvement and I set off with my batman, Lance-Corporal Turner, who was an excellent man to have around in a tricky situation. In peacetime he had been a valet-chauffeur and nothing worried him. His dry sense of humour was an asset anywhere and I have never before or since had such fine and faithful service from anybody. By keeping our eyes open we were able to avoid trouble, and scouted round many pockets of Germans who were keeping up an irregular sniping action on the Brigade's route of advance.

Eventually we arrived at H.Q. 1st Parachute Battalion, commanded by Lt.-Colonel D. Dobie, which had just reached the outskirts of Arnhem proper, next to the St. Elizabeth Hospital. The battalion was preparing to attack with the aim of reaching the bridge through two miles of enemy-held streets. Lt.-Colonel Dobie had received his orders by wireless from Brigade H.Q. on the bridge, where Lt.-Colonel Frost was now acting as Brigade Commander.

1st Battalion was now under concentrated fire from mortars and snipers. It was clear that the enemy had quickly appreciated our real purpose and was resisting with a surprising energy. Little did we realise that Field Marshal Model, who commanded the German Army Group B, had his tactical H.Q. at Oosterbeek, not a mile from where we were, and had witnessed the drop on the previous day. He had immediately ordered armoured reinforcements from the 9th S.S. Panzer Division, who as the Dutch had reported on the 15th, were re-equipping with the latest Panther tanks just north of Arnhem.

Nobody of course knew of this at the time, and preparations for the attack went through with confidence. I managed to speak on the wireless to the Brigade Major, Major Hibbert, at Brigade H.Q., and tell him of the change in frequency, but as they were still out of touch with Divisional H.Q. and I wanted to see how their communications were functioning I decided to attach myself to the Battalion and go through to the bridge with them. Like everybody else I completely failed to appreciate the strength of the opposition we were up against.

From the start the going was tough. I found myself in the position of encouraging some of the slower men in the battalion, who were cluttering up Battalion H.Q. One of the companies, which had the job of clearing the river banks along the Rhine, was running into difficulties and Lance-Corporal Turner and I went forward to see what the trouble was. The company commander, who had been leading his men with great dash and energy, had just been killed. To take over seemed to be the only thing to do.

Street-fighting is always a pretty nasty business, and this was no exception.

About four hundred yards farther along our side of the river, just level with the pontoon bridge, the bank was broken by a thirty-feet wide channel leading to a small harbour in the middle of the town. A group of houses stood just short of the channel and I gave orders to capture and hold them while the rest of the battalion caught up with us on our left.

While we advanced under cover of the river bank, we were under constant small-arms fire, and at one point the Germans were able to toss stick grenades in our midst. These did little damage, and they soon stopped when we threw back our Mills bombs. Eventually we arrived at the group of houses, but only about twenty men were left out of the whole company. A little reconnaissance soon showed that we had left the rest of the battalion far to the rear and our position was quite untenable for any length of time. A check up on our ammunition revealed that we only had about a hundred rounds between us, which was very little. The time was about 4 p.m. and I gave orders to take up defensive positions in the area. We distributed ourselves between three houses which gave us a commanding all-round view. Our big difficulty was that we had no way of telling Battalion H.Q. where we were or how successful our attack had been. I reckoned that the enemy would attack our position the following dawn, and unless we were relieved by then we would be in a sorry plight.

We kept up a sniping action to keep the Germans from getting too close, but by nightfall nearly all our ammunition had gone. From what little I could see, the battalion was still fighting in the area of the St. Elizabeth Hospital over eight hundred yards farther back. I decided that it was a hopeless position, and that our best course would be to try and get back to Battalion H.Q. by night, even if we had to swim the Rhine to avoid the town, where most of the Germans seemed to be placed. To give the best chance to everybody the remains of the company were split into three groups, Lance-Corporal Turner and three other men coming with me. It would have been impossible to get twenty men back through the lines without being discovered. A lieutenant and a sergeant, whose names I do not know to this day, commanded the two other parties, and we all agreed it was the only practical solution. I decided to move to a house near the water as a jumping-off point, and broke in through a ground-floor window. We were just looking out of the window on the other side of the house when I heard somebody, obviously a German, trying to get into the front door of the house. I thought it most unlikely that we had been seen, and so we all dived into the lavatory and locked the door on the inside.

Eventually he broke in through the door, and to our dismay a section of about ten German soldiers followed him in and on upstairs. From the sounds of tile removing and furniture shifting, the house was being converted into a strong point in the German defensive position.

We sat in turns on that lavatory seat for the following three nights and three days until September 21st. During this time we could hear the almost incessant firing at the Bridge just up the river, and the sounds of more distant fighting from the rest of the Division about three miles away. By night the sky was red with flames from burning houses, and occasionally lit up by a brilliant white light from a star shell or Very pistol. We were in an extraordinary position; a German machine-gun post above us and two more dug into the pavement outside the ground-floor windows. We would need luck to avoid capture in this predicament.

Eventually I could stand it no longer and I said we would make the attempt on the fourth night. Often during those three days, Germans would come and try the door, but on finding it engaged politely went away and tried elsewhere. By the fourth night firing had died down considerably and apparently most of the Germans in the area had pulled out, although the post in our roof could be heard letting off a burst or two occasionally. My plan was to swim the river and, because of the current and our different swimming powers, we would rendezvous together on the far side at the blown railway bridge about a mile downstream.

We all took off our boots and heavier clothing and tied them inside our semi-waterproof smocks which could then be floated across the river without impeding our swimming. Our plan was to open the front door as quietly as possible and, using the shadows, walk down to the river not twenty yards away. The light from burning buildings in the bridge area was still annoying, but not half as bad as it had been on previous nights.

About 1 a.m. on September 22nd we crept out of the lavatory and opened the front door an inch or two. The machine-gun posts were no longer manned although the equipment was still in position. The Germans must have been asleep nearby. Waiting for another phase of continuous firing, which I hoped would blanket the noise we would make, we quickly dodged from shadow to shadow and down to the river bank. A second later we were all swimming reasonably noiselessly. Occasionally a burst of firing would break out, and the reflections of burning buildings in the water made me feel that we could not help being seen. As we came out into the current, I was rapidly swept downstream and lost touch with the rest of the men. The Rhine at this point was about four hundred yards across and due to the distance I swam as slowly as possible to avoid getting overtired or out of breath. Eventually the chimneys of a brick factory loomed above me and I was clambering up the slippery bank. I had hoped that the Second Army might have reached that bank by now for if they had not done so they would be three days behind schedule. However, I was not going to take any risks, and would move as though the enemy were in possession.

Having untied my bundle and put on my clothes, which were surprisingly dry, I started to move slowly down the river bank to the railway bridge, where I had planned to meet the rest of the men. It would have been better to have chosen a closer rendezvous, but this was the only unmistakable one, and seemed the easiest for them to find. The time was now 2.30 a.m. and we only had three hours left before dawn. Slowly I walked or crawled along the bank, straining my eyes and ears for any sounds of the enemy. A burning haystack on one side showed that the area was still active and now and again I could hear firing coming from my front. After about an hour and a half I began to see the outlines of the old railway bridge about four hundred yards away which was occasionally brilliantly lit up by a star shell. During all this time I saw nothing of the men, which was surprising because we all should have been moving down the same way.

I was getting quite close to the bridge when I had to leave the river bank to skirt round a dyke which flowed into the Rhine. I was just getting over a wide ditch when I heard a shrill whistle blown about thirty yards away. It was still about one hour to dawn. I suddenly realised what had happened. The Germans were manning the railway embankment leading to the bridge and were " standing to " an hour before dawn, as is the custom in the British Army. This is to ensure that all defences are manned in case of a dawn attack and is almost standard front-line procedure in any army.

What accursed luck I had! I was now in the German front line with only a few yards to go, and I had arrived in time for the German " stand to." I quickly ran forward; with any luck

I might still beat them to it and was just climbing up the embankment when I fell into a slit trench on top of a German who was bending down at that moment. He started shouting and one of his pals came over from his trench about two yards away, to find me struggling with a rather sleepy German in a wet trench some four feet long and about four feet deep.

CHAPTER FOURTEEN

Cupboard Love

THE GAME was up and I was a prisoner again. Once more I went through the indignity of being searched by the enemy, but on this occasion I at least had no weapons to surrender. I had to let go my sten gun and pistol whilst swimming across the Rhine.

No longer was I a free man and the anti-climax suddenly made me remember my hunger, and how every bone and muscle in my body ached for rest. Wearily, so wearily, I was marched down the road to the Company H.Q., watched by sleepy-eyed Germans from slit trenches dug into the verge.

We stopped at a farmhouse and I was shown into a room, after pushing aside a blackout blanket which had been nailed over the doorway. Inside, a hot aroma of unwashed bodies, the acrid stench of stale German tobacco smoke and seasoned sausage combined to stifle my nostrils. A hurricane lamp turned low gave the only light, and in the gloom my smarting eyes could now see gently-heaving bodies wrapped up in greatcoats lying all over the floor, with mounds of equipment taking up every vacant space. The only sounds were wheezes and snores except for the faint noise of a conversation in German coming from a next-door room.

One of my escort of three pushed by, and after mumbling what I took to be swear words, woke up one of the prostrate Germans. He turned out to be an N.C.O. and was soon kicking other bodies to life, who grunted in a dialect I did not understand, and then stood up and stretched. A piece of paper passed hands and I was off again out of the house with three new guards to Battalion H.Q. which was about a mile away.

This time everything was much more orderly, and after a German sentry had examined the piece of paper carried by my escort, we went down some steps into a cellar whose roof had been chocked up with large baulks of timber. A clean-shaven, middle-aged, German subaltern sat at a table with a lamp on one corner. He motioned to me to sit down and said in broken English:

"I must to you questions ask. You will answer."

"Oh."

"Your name, please?"

I told him.

"What day you jumped?"

"I can't say."

"How many more are you?"

"I can't say."

His eyes seemed to bulge a bit behind his glasses, and an angry flush spread up his neck.

"O.K. You no speak. We will see."

He ended with some instructions in German and I was shown outside into the back of an open Volkswagen car, in which I was driven along the road towards Arnhem.

We crossed the Rhine using the main bridge for which so many lives had been sacrificed. I could see many marks of the fighting which had taken place as we threaded our way in and out of shell holes and burnt-out German tanks. Smoke was still coming from the ruins of the buildings on the north side of the river.

We sped on through deserted streets to the outskirts of the town and stopped outside a newly-built church which had sentries posted all round it. I was told to get out and wait inside. There I found the church full of newly-captured prisoners of war standing in little groups everywhere. In one corner I could see a few officers, none of whom I knew, and I learnt from them that the Division was now fighting inside a small perimeter round Oosterbeek, a suburb about three miles from the centre of Arnhem.

In another corner I saw Lance-Corporal Turner and the three others who had shared the lavatory with me. They too had been captured that morning in various places not far from where I had been taken. All touch had been lost while swimming across, and Turner had been caught whilst trying to find a hiding place in a farmhouse. Daylight had come before he had reached a point anywhere near the railway bridge.

We all looked pretty scruffy in that church. I had a five days' growth of beard, not having had a chance to shave, and many were like me. All had the slightly haggard and drawn look of soldiers who have been without sleep, and seen their best friends die, not knowing when their own turn might come. Some were rummaging in their pockets or haversacks for any crumbs left over from the once despised forty-eight-hour concentrated ration that we all carried. Many were lying down full length on the pews fast asleep, snoring away with mouths slightly open and heads twisted at any angle.

As the morning drew on, the air in the church became warmer, and more and more of us lay down where we were on the hard tiles and went fast asleep. I followed suit after checking that all doors were guarded and there was no way of getting out.

The Germans still gave us nothing to eat and by midday we were all getting very hungry and thirsty. Some men I spoke to asked me if I could get the Germans to do something about it.

After some argument I managed to get hold of an officer who could speak some English and in a mixture of the two languages I told him that we expected to be given food within an hour, or else I would see that his name was remembered after the war when the time came to deal with the war criminals who disobeyed the Geneva Convention.

He became quite angry and spluttered:

" You can all think yourselves lucky to be alive and you will get food when it pleases us. Anyhow what do you know about Geneva Conventions?"

"You would be surprised," I replied, "but food we must have, and it is your responsibility to provide."

"Let me tell you, Herr Major, I have just received orders to march you all to a prison near here run by the S.S. I am sure they will feed you."

With a glint in his eye, he turned on his heel, and five minutes later we were on the march with guards on all sides. For two miles we went through the suburbs and saw very few civilians, one or two of whom were brave enough to wave and smile as we went by.

Eventually we arrived at a house on the outskirts of Arnhem in another suburb called Velp. This was used as a prisoner of war cage and was guarded by an under-strength company of fifty-five men. It was a typical large suburban house, about twenty yards back from the main road and with exactly similar ones on either side. Two monkey-puzzle trees stood on the front lawn.

Inside the house were about five hundred all ranks of the Division, whose spirits were high except for the ignominy of being prisoners. The Germans fed us on tins of lard and coarse brown bread, but we were not fussy and I wolfed my share down. I had not had a really square meal since leaving England, my last being breakfast on the 17th, and to-day was the 22nd. What months it all seemed and yet it was only five days.

I heard that the bridge had been captured by the Germans soon after dawn on the 21st, when nearly all the original defenders were killed or wounded, and all ammunition had been expended. For three days and nights this gallant force had held out against overwhelming odds, including tanks, which came up and gradually knocked down or set on fire every house that was being used for the defence. Some of these tanks had been stalked on foot and blown up with grenades. Fighting patrols had gone out every night to drive the Germans out of houses which over-looked the bridge. The Division had been ordered to hold the bridge for forty-eight hours until the arrival of the Second Army.

It had been held for seventy-two hours by six hundred men, but unfortunately to no avail.

We now realised what a failure the whole operation had been but we still hoped that the Division could hold on where it was and provide Second Army with a bridgehead through which the advance could continue.

All this time I was looking for ways out of the house or garden. I was determined to escape and not be a prisoner longer than I could help. Now would be the time and it would be infinitely easier than later on.

Some of the officers were already saying that they would leave trying to escape till they arrived at the German prison camp. It would all be " laid on " there. It is so easy to put off action till to-morrow and all this sort of talk was so reminiscent of my experiences in Italy. I told everybody I saw that their one and only chance of getting away would be before they left Holland. The farther they went back along the evacuation channels, the more difficult would escape become. I think they believed me, but most of them could not see any possible way out with any hope of success. When I started looking over the whole house and garden, there were many smiles cast in my direction. It was not possible to get away they said, they had already been over the place with a fine tooth comb. The trouble was that most of them were numbed by the anti-climax of being prisoners, and they did not realise that small though the chances of getting away were at the moment, they would be better now than at any future date.

I reasoned that the cage would only be temporary and would last as long as the Division did. From all accounts this would not be long, so one solution would be to hide up in the house itself till the Germans left and then to get out. Again it was just possible that the Second Army would continue their advance through the Division's bridgehead, and then the area would be liberated.

I could not see any way to escape that gave a better than fifty-fifty chance of success so I looked everywhere for a hiding place that would hold me for two or three days. The only possible place seemed to be a wall cupboard in one of the ground floor rooms, which had a flush fitting concealed door. The whole door was covered with the same sort of wallpaper as that of the rest of the room, and was difficult to see except on close examination. The cupboard was about four feet across, twelve inches deep, and about seven feet high. Its interior was divided horizontally by adjustable shelves, but by removing the shelves I was able to stand inside in tolerable comfort. Fastening the door was a problem. The cupboard was fitted with the normal type of mortice lock let into the thickness of the door, with a keyhole on the outside complete with key. By unscrewing the lock, and turning it back to front, the keyhole came on the inside of the door and I was able to lock myself in. A piece of wallpaper, torn from another part of the room and pasted over the outside keyhole, helped to conceal the cupboard's presence.

The next job was to lay in a stock of water and food. All I had was my waterbottle, and I found an old two-pound jam jar that I also filled up. A one-pound tin of lard and half a small loaf of bread completed all the provisioning I could do. Some of the officers very kindly offered to give me their waterbottles, but I refused. They would need them for their own escape, which, I reminded them, they must try to make or be a prisoner for the rest of the war.

Little did I think that I would be confined to my cramped little cupboard for thirteen days and nights before getting out. I thought that the limit of my endurance would be reached after three or four days, because I did not start off in the best condition for an endurance test. The Germans came round on the evening of the 2nd to take all names, and in order to avoid a record being taken I started standing in my cupboard. Pole squatting is I believe a time-honoured sport in the U.S.A. I cannot recommend cupboard standing to anybody who wants to try out something new. I stood first on one leg then on the other; then I leaned on one shoulder and then on the other. There was no room to sit down because the cupboard was too shallow. I managed to sleep all right although occasionally my knees would give way and would drop forward against the door making a hammer-like noise. Every bone in my body ached, and I felt quite light-headed from lack of food, water and rest.

The day after I locked myself in the cupboard the Germans turned the room into an interrogation centre. Every officer and man going through that cage was first interrogated in the room where my cupboard was. It was certainly an interesting experience, which I believe has never before been rivalled, though I scarcely appreciated its uniqueness at the time.

The questioning went on for several days, four or five I think, and by night the room was used as sleeping quarters for the German guard. I had no chances to get out at all, but as I had lasted so far, I resolved to try to remain a little longer. My luck must come to my rescue. It had always done so up till now.

Little by little I eked out my rations of water and bread. Four mouthfuls of water every four or five hours and just a bite or two of bread. The water was the chief shortage, and after nine or ten days I could not eat any more bread because my mouth was so dry.

It was now October 5th, 1944, and the thirteenth day of my voluntary confinement. My water was nearly at an end, and the cramp in my muscles hurt acutely most of the time. Patience and caution were now finished and I told myself that I would have to make an attempt to escape that evening or fail in the effort.

The room outside my cupboard was still full of Germans but provided no new prisoners came in that evening there would be a good chance of the whole guard leaving the room empty for half an hour or so at sunset. On the previous evening they had all cleared out of the room and hung over the garden wall adjoining the main road outside my window, to watch the passers-by in the twilight. I suppose it is a world-wide habit to come out of the houses on a warm evening for a breather before going back inside for the night. The only thing that might spoil it would be new prisoners; but there had not been any last night, so with any luck I would get away to-night.

I slowly shifted my weight from one leg to the other, and leaned alternately on my right shoulder and then my left. By now, shifting my position had become almost automatic, and no longer required any thought or even consciousness. My mouth was dry as a bone, but I had already had both my dawn and mid-day mouthfuls. My evening one was not due for another two hours yet. To-night I would take three mouthfuls of water. What bliss this promised to be!

It was due to get dark about 7.30 p.m. or 8 p.m., and I hoped the room would clear by about 7 p.m. I would then have to hide up in the bushes near the house for an hour, till it was really dark, before it would be possible to move round to the back of the house and get away.

The minutes slowly crept by while I waited anxiously, my ears taut for the sound of the Germans leaving the room. Occasionally one of them would go in or out, but I could hear snores from two or three having an after-lunch nap. At about 6 o'clock I pulled on my boots and smock and gathered all my equipment. Dressing in that cupboard was a work of art, and to avoid making a noise it was three-quarters of an hour before I was ready. While I was dressing I heard two Germans stumble out of the room, but I was fairly certain that there were one or two more. Sure enough, by their grunts and the bumping of boots on the floor, I heard two more get up and go out talking about a *fräulein*.

The time had come. Cautiously I unlocked my door. There might be the odd squarehead making up arrears of sleep. I opened the door an inch and had a quick look round. Damnation take it, there, not six feet away, was a solitary German soldier sleeping with his hands crossed over his tummy and his mouth wide open. As I had to walk across the floor and open the big french windows, which were both noisy operations, I decided to give him another half hour.

A few troops came clattering into the building with a couple of girls, all talking at the tops of their voices. I heard them go upstairs and enter the room directly over my head, and they soon had quite a merry party going with songs and a gramophone, and an occasional girlish giggle or scream. I was in luck. They were probably not expecting any prisoners to-night, and if the noise increased as the wine flowed I should have no worries about covering up squeaks as I opened a window.

The noise upstairs woke up my sleeping soldier after about twenty minutes, and he got up and walked out. This was my chance and, taking a couple of mouthfuls of water, I gently pushed the door open again. This time the room was empty. I could see the guards lining the garden fence on the main road and not ten yards away. My plan was to get the window open and then wait for a lorry or tank to go by before slipping out and into the shrubs growing almost under the sill. Germans would be most unlikely to look back towards the house when anything interesting was passing.

I was in luck and no sooner had I opened the windows when a large truck went clattering by. This was my cue, and I was quickly out and had dropped into the shrubbery. My luck held good on the 13th day in that Dutch cupboard.

I quickly crawled into the bushes where it was thickest at the corner of the house, and concealed myself as best I could with dead leaves. From where I was I could see eight or ten of the guard idly leaning against the garden fence a few yards away and could hear them chatting unconcernedly about the war in general and their sweethearts at home.

CHAPTER FIFTEEN

Dutch Courage

IT GRADUALLY grew dark and one by one the Germans left the fence and went back inside the house. Forty-five minutes later it was black enough to start moving, and stealthily I crept to the back and climbed over the fence into an adjoining garden. The bottom part of the garden was all vegetables and I quickly pulled some beetroots up, wiped off most of the mud on the seat of my trousers, and chewed them eagerly. The juicy sweetness of the beetroot tasted wonderful, but I don't suppose it did my stomach much good. From the garden I climbed through another fence into an orchard and was soon feasting on some excellent apples. I would not have bothered about the beetroot if I had known about the orchard, and rapidly I munched my way through half a dozen apples. I could feel renewed strength and vitality seeping back into my veins and I stretched my arms and legs with the joy of freedom and relief from that terrible cupboard. My legs were incredibly weak but I was now full of hope and my brain was again functioning more or less normally.

My plan was now to contact a friendly Dutch family, who might give me some civilian clothes. Once I had these, I should not find it too difficult to move about and find a way back to our lines. I decided I might as well try the houses nearby. If the Germans did suspect that the cupboard had housed an escaper, which I thought most unlikely, then they would never guess that he was hiding within a few hundred yards of his late prison. Also the more I moved around with a thirteen-day beard on my chin, the more likely I was to be discovered.

Stuffing a few apples into my pockets, I moved down to the bottom of the orchard where it joined on to some gardens at the back of a row of houses. The fence was a high one and made of close-mesh wire, but I soon found a hole underneath and wormed my way through. The houses were the usual brick-built semi-detached suburban types, and I could see no reason against tapping on the door of the first one I came to, telling them who I was, and asking for shelter.

I tiptoed past a coal shed and knocked gently on a door of a house with its bottom windows still lit up but screened with black-out curtains. Eventually I heard a voice asking who was there in Dutch. In halting German I stammered out:

" I am a British parachutist. Please give me food and shelter."

" Go away quickly," he replied in equally bad German, " my house is full. We have no food. Very dangerous to have you here."

The whole conversation was conducted through the closed door and in the end he did not wait for me to answer and I heard him stamping off to another room. I walked away feeling rather depressed.

Disconsolately I walked back a few paces and decided to rest in a small coal shed to collect my thoughts before my next move. I would cross the road and try a house on the opposite side. I would go round to the back where perhaps I might find a more friendly family than the one which I had tried first.

I came out of the shed, and after passing between two houses, crouched in the shadow of a wall while a German army truck swept by full of troops. As soon as it had rounded the bend, I walked quickly across the road and between two more houses on the opposite side. Once more I tapped on a door but to no avail. The time was now about 11 p.m. and all were in bed.

I tried three more houses and still got no reply. But I noticed saucers left lying outside the back doors of all three houses; they were full of scraps off plates and presumably left for cats. I was so hungry that I went from door to door wolfing the scraps which really tasted excellent. Eventually I had had quite a reasonable meal, and I decided that the best plan was to hide in one of the sheds at the back of the houses and wait there till morning. I chose the one which had the biggest plate of scraps—they surely must be charitable people—and soon nestled down in an old potting shed full of seed trays and broken furniture. I slept well and woke at dawn to watch for any sign of the inhabitants so that I could make myself known to them as early as possible. Gradually I heard the house wake up; the alarm clock go off, sleepy yawns come from a window, and finally a man looked out at the morning sky. Half an hour went by and the back door was opened so that I could look straight into the kitchen where a girl of about twenty was cooking on a stove and a man swept out the kitchen and then cleaned his shoes. Eventually he shaved, put on his jacket and came towards my hiding place, presumably to get some firewood.

As he came in through the door I said, " Good morning " in German, and, to give him his due, he did not appear to be in the least taken aback. Speaking German in whispers I told him my story and asked him if he could help. He understood me quite easily and replied that he would do his best but that there were a lot of children nearby who might stumble on me whilst playing and give me away. He said he could not hide me in his house, but he would try to find a place where I could go that night. He would also see about some food. I thanked him with a terrific handshake and with a wink he turned towards the house and beckoned his wife to come over to the shed.

At first she would not do so; but after a bit she came over, looking rather cross, and walked into the shed. She suddenly saw me and let out a scream, clutching her husband for protection and looking thoroughly frightened. I do not suppose I was a very edifying sight, with my ginger beard, camouflage airborne smock, and torn, dirty battledress trousers. However her fears were soon put at rest and she went back to the house with her husband to prepare a meal, although still with a rather scared look in her eyes.

In the meantime I had a look round my hut to find a possible hiding place in case any children came near, or the Germans made a search. There were some horizontal wooden beams under the roof, and at one end a few planks had been placed across them to hold up some bales of straw. At first sight this looked the best hiding place, but its big disadvantage was that it was also easily the most obvious. Anybody coming into that hut would immediately be attracted by the pile of straw up in the roof. I therefore decided to hide under a pile of loosely-stacked seed boxes and apple trays that littered the floor. By arranging these in the manner of a tunnel I crawled in underneath and pulled some old sacks on top of me. Even if somebody had peered down through the clutter of trays, he would only have seen a pile of sacks at the bottom.

Hiding, always hiding! What a monotonous and horrible business! But I could not afford to walk about in daylight, unwashed, unshaven and dressed as I was. Before I had had time to make myself really comfortable the good lady of the house brought out an enormous plate of boiled potatoes over which she had poured a savoury gravy. It smelt like a banquet fit for kings. I had soon wolfed this down and then swallowed about a pint of ersatz coffee, which made me feel as if I had not slept for weeks.

I woke up to the clink and thud of heavy military boots tramping in the yard outside and the sound of German voices. From the snatches of conversation I gathered that they were accusing the Dutch family of sheltering a British officer. In halting German he flatly denied the accusations, but I could imagine him being brushed aside and I could hear the Germans walking upstairs and banging open doors and cupboards. I was scared stiff and pulled the sacks even closer, hoping against hope that they would leave out my shed. Obviously the news of my presence had leaked out and the German security police were already on my trail. What a horrible thought.

I then heard them come banging downstairs, out into the yard and straight towards my hut. I could hear someone's heavy breathing as he paused just inside the doorway to allow his eyes to get used to the gloom, and also the expostulations of my good Dutch host in the background. As I had thought, the first place he looked at was the straw up in the rafters. Muttering oaths, the German climbed up and pulled away at the straw bales which came crashing down to the floor. As soon as he had satisfied himself that there was nobody there, he did not bother to look anywhere else and left the shed, after which I could hear them leaving the courtyard to go somewhere else. Once again my luck was in, and I was round another tight corner.

About four o'clock the Dutchman came back, and with a voice shaking with agitation, told me I would have to leave straight away. I replied that I would wait till dark, and in the meantime would he find somebody who would be prepared to take me in. The poor man was obviously in a complete dither and nearly incapable of any speech which was not really surprising. I asked him if he knew why the Germans had come, and he said he thought that it must have been the children who had given me away.

Evening came and he returned with an aluminium canteen full of sandwiches and a waterbottle full of milk. He was obviously longing for my departure but felt a bit guilty at turning me away, and so gave me all the food he could spare. When it was quite dark he led me outside and told me to follow the railway line for about a mile, when I should find open country on my left with a big white farm whose owners, he thought, would shelter me for a short time. Thanking him profusely for his kindness, I was soon on my way, walking down the cinder path alongside the railway track. It was pitch dark which was a help, and my host had told me that the line was free from German patrols.

I soon recognised the farmhouse and found the back door, upon which I gave an urgent Victory V tap. The door opened a crack and in a whisper I told the farmer who I was. He replied that German patrols were all round his house, and he could not help me, after which to my amazement he slammed the door in my face.

I walked away, and half a mile farther on I tried another house only to get the same treatment. By 10.30 p.m. I had walked two or three miles and tried two more houses with no success. I was very tired and disheartened and started wondering what on earth I should do if I was unable to find shelter by daybreak.

I heard a church clock strike eleven and decided to look for the vicarage and ask the parson to help me. The church was across some fields surrounded by trees, and after I had walked there I found a building joining on to it which would presumably be the vicarage. A light shone under the door, and I tapped gently for an entry which was only given me after five minutes anxious waiting outside.

A young priest dressed in a long black cassock was standing holding a lantern in one hand, while a group of about a dozen men, women and children were crowding round behind him interested to see who was knocking so gently after curfew hours. I quickly told him my story, and he said that although he could not let me stay in the house he thought he would be able to help me. Apparently I was in a Roman Catholic school that had been partly requisitioned to house some German troops serving an A.A. gun in some trees nearby. The remainder of the house was full of evacuees from Arnhem, and therefore it was a most unsuitable choice as a hiding place. My luck was in again. If I had tapped at the wrong door it would have been opened by a German and not the parson.

I was the centre of attraction, surrounded by about a dozen evacuees of all ages, with a couple of young priests hovering in the background. A large cup of milk was brought and was very welcome. Then followed a long discussion about where I should go, and eventually they decided to send for the school's private policeman who lived a few hundred yards away.

At last a real old character walked in. He looked more like

a gamekeeper than a policeman and was dressed in a black corduroy jacket and breeches with black leather leggings and boots. His hat was a green " pork-pie " and his face was thin and lined, but he had a twinkle of amusement in his eyes. Although he could not speak a word of English, he was obviously enjoying himself immensely. This was his chance to do something for Holland, and get fame as a patriot. I imagine his life must have been rather dull until now, and secretly he must have longed to take a more active part in the war, although his family would no doubt have kept him from doing anything rash.

He led me out through the school doorway and down an avenue of trees to his cottage at the end of the road. The time was about midnight, and his wife was waiting up for his return. A genial, fat old soul, she produced some bread and jam and I further sated my almost inexhaustible appetite. It must have been a strange scene. A shaded lamp stood on a shelf on one side of the room, in the middle of which was a heavy wooden table with a scrubbed top. Shining copper cooking pots hung over the stove while round the walls there were all sorts of bric-a-brac on shelves and brackets.

After washing down the bread with some strange beverage which was called tea, and made from dried apple and blackberry leaves, the old man suggested that I should shave and take off all my uniform. He would get me some clothes in the morning and it would be safe if he hid all evidence of his " Tommy " as he called me. After shaving with his old cut-throat razor, we climbed upstairs to the attic, one end of which had been converted into a bedroom. I was soon fast asleep between cool white sheets—what fantastic luxury!

The sun was streaming into the room and outside my window I could see an apple tree laden down with enormous red apples. My watch told me it was twelve o'clock, so I had slept continuously for about twelve hours. I lay back luxuriously in my bed and wondered what would happen next. I did not feel inclined to do anything except take it easy and recover some of my lost strength. Until now I had not realised quite how weak

I was. Nervous energy and excitement had been my fuel, but now natural processes had caught up and all I wanted to do was to lie back and breathe in the beautiful fresh free air and thank God that I was not a prisoner of war.

Suddenly the familiar whine of a shell passing overhead, followed by an explosion in a field or two away, brought me to my senses. I remembered that war was only a few miles away, and thought that I had better do something about getting back across the lines. I climbed out of bed and literally tottered across to the window. A mirror over the washstand gave me a shock. A more cadaverous, thin, lined face I have yet to see, and I could hardly believe that I was looking at myself. Outside, beyond some beautiful green fields across which I had trudged the night before, lay Velp and the outskirts of Arnhem. The shell I had heard pass had landed in amongst some cows, and I could see a farmer hurrying out to see what damage had been done. Milk was so short, in this dairyland of all Europe, that only small children had a ration. The Germans had taken ninety per cent of the dairy herds away to Germany, so the loss of one cow was felt by the whole small community.

There was a gentle knock on the door and in came the old man with a trayful of wonderful-looking macaroni, mashed potatoes and apple pie, in quantities normally sufficient to feed ten men. It all went down to his surprise, while he talked in a hushed whisper of everything he had done that morning. He said he had to keep quiet because he was not telling his children about me because he thought they would be bound to give the show away. It was wise.

I asked him in my mixture of English, German and French, whether he could get me some clothes and a bicycle. He thought he could to-morrow, but to-day I must stay where I was. I could do little else, as all I had on were my underclothes, so for the rest of the day I rested.

Next day I felt hot and feverish, with my chest wheezing like a steam engine. I had clearly got bronchitis which no doubt was partly the result of getting so run down during the previous fortnight. For four days I felt very ill and could not eat at all. The poor old couple looked very worried, and I think the man was beginning to wonder if he had a chronic invalid on his hands. Eventually on the fifth day the fever left me and I began to feel better, but my legs seemed weaker than ever. I decided that I must get in touch with the Resistance movement and ask for some help to get back across the Rhine. Kind as the old people were, I did not feel I was getting anywhere while I stayed with them, and I would achieve much more if I could get in with some more active members of the Resistance.

On the afternoon of the sixth day he came in to say that he had arranged for me to go somewhere where it was better organised for people like myself, and where there would not be so much chance of discovery. His one idea was to hide me. My one idea was to get away and back to England. My bronchitis had, however, enforced idleness upon me and so I was really most grateful for all the old couple had done for me.

I quickly dressed and went downstairs in the fading light, to meet another man who had a spare bicycle. I was to follow him at about a hundred yards distance to a new address. I took leave of the old pair, and thanked them from the bottom of my heart for all the kindness they had shown me. I will never forget them.

As we bicycled slowly along the streets, it felt quite queer to be once more on the road. I was dressed in an old dingy black pair of trousers and a blue shirt, which gave me local atmosphere. My only worry was that the Germans had an awkward habit of suddenly setting up a check-point, to round up able-bodied men for work on field defences which in this case they were building along the line of the Ijssel River. However we avoided all check-points although we saw a lot of Germans walking or marching about. In due course we arrived at the door of a suburban semi-detached villa in the side streets of Velp. Inside I was met by my new host and hostess, Mr. and Mrs. Huisman, and their two children aged eight and five. What an incredible family! They were already sheltering two refugees. One, a Dutchman who had escaped from a concentration camp and who had to lie low, and the other a Polish-German Jew whose race made him a marked man.

My host was the local schoolmaster from the primary school, and a more jovial, God-fearing, and brave man I have never met. His wife was equally wonderful, and in a tiny two-bedroomed villa squeezed seven people, cooked for them, using many gifts of food from friends, and even managed to keep the house looking extremely clean. Potatoes were the big filler-up at meals. We refugees used to peel them and wash up. Huge soup plates full of mashed potatoes with a little meat gravy were helped down by bread smeared with a scraping of butter and sugar sprinkled on top. Before and after every meal the schoolmaster said grace, while we dutifully stood with bowed heads behind each chair, our potatoes already doled out in front of us. The graces were impromptu and lasted about ten minutes. In the evenings the Bible was always read for ten minutes after the meal, and on Sundays a hymn was sung to the schoolmaster's accompaniment on a harmonium organ he had in his living-room. Most of the Dutch families I met followed similar routines, and were usually members of the Dutch Reform Church which I believe to be strictly Calvinistic in its preachings and outlook.

A hideout had been dug under the floor of the front room and was entered through a hatch formed from the floor boards which would be difficult to notice except during a very thorough inspection. At first we all slept in it, but I found it so dank and stuffy that I slept on the floor of the living-room just above.

Pete was my real contact with the world. I believe he was a proper member of the Resistance, although it was a question which was never asked in Holland at that time. He had light red hair and an open smiling face. He gave me the impression that he was prepared to take any risk in the service of his country and no job would be too much trouble for him. He came in on the evening of the first day, with my new host on one arm, and on the other a big basket-load of eggs, butter and potatoes for the household. He told me that a Major Hibbert was over near Ede, about ten miles away, and they were able to use a telephone that communicated direct to Nijmegen, fifteen miles inside the British lines. The line was a private one which had been installed by the local electric power company. The Germans apparently did not know of its existence and never discovered it. It was used by our Intelligence Services until the end of the war, and was an ideal way of getting information through quickly.

The plan being formed to get us to the British lines was divided into three parts. First, as many British troops as possible who were hiding up or living in the woods would be located and contacted. Then it would be necessary to concentrate them at the river at the right time and without the Germans discovering. Lastly there were the boats to get us across, together with any diversionary activities which might be laid on from the British side to distract the Germans' attention.

In the meantime everybody was to lie low and not excite too much attention, as it would take at least fourteen days to organise the whole affair. The magnitude of the problem can be understood when it is realised that more than a hundred and twenty British troops were scattered over as many square miles all round Arnhem, and all living more or less in secret. The majority had evaded capture and had been living for the previous ten days or so either off the land or thanks to the hospitality of our good Dutch friends. It would be the Resistance's task to make arrangements to gather us all together on a specified date and time a fortnight later.

CHAPTER SIXTEEN

Rhine Crossing

WE HAD a wonderful party the night before we left. Some friends came in with bottles of Arak gin, and a local baroness sent round a bottle of champagne for the " poor British officer who is so thin." All the Dutch became exceedingly merry, and by the light of flickering candles they were soon singing patriotic songs in quick succession at the tops of their voices. Thoughts of war and Germans were pressed into the background. Here, at least, was a little piece of patriotic Holland trying to forget its worries and anxieties.

By dawn next morning we were all dressed and ready to start on the final lap of our return home. A Red Cross lorry, used for evacuating civilians from Arnhem, would call for us and take us to the woods near Ede, where the major concentration was taking place. A wheezing old lorry, painted white with red crosses on the sides, drew up at the house, and already had six civilians seated in it. Who they were I do not know, and they exhibited no surprise when we climbed in and lay on the floor under some sacks—just in case a German check-point should ask for our passes.

The lorry was driven by charcoal gas and bumped and swayed through the streets of Arnhem and down the main road to Ede. From my place, on the floor, I could see the sky and trees overhanging the road and the second floors of houses as they went by. I began to feel an elation that I had not had for weeks. At last we were on the move again! I had a feeling of overwhelming gratitude to the good Dutch people for sheltering us and now getting us away. For their part, they were glad to have the opportunity of taking an active part in the war to help their country. But I was nevertheless exceedingly grateful for all they had done for us.

We were now on the road between Arnhem and Ede, and the forest was nearly continuous on either side except for an occasional white-fronted house set back in the trees. The lorry suddenly stopped and the passenger who had been sitting next to the driver jumped out and signalled us to follow suit. Nobody else was in sight and we had soon walked down a footpath leading into the forest, with the noise of the old Red Cross lorry getting fainter as it continued on its way to Ede.

After twenty minutes walk we came to a small clearing with a tiny hut in the middle. To my astonishment it was surrounded by about thirty British soldiers who were busying themselves in small groups all round. Some were sorting equipment, others cooking up some hot water, while nearly all were exchanging tales of their wanderings. Inside the hut, which was built as a shooting lodge, were crowded another twenty men or so, and a high old stench of unwashed bodies wafted out of the door as we looked in.

My only trouble was my shoes. My boots had been too obviously British and I had left them with my policeman friend in Velp. The shoes I had on were horribly uncomfortable and sharply-pointed with thin businessman's soles. Pat Glover, the quartermaster, soon fixed me up with a pair of boots he had scrounged off a dead British soldier. Pat had foreseen our requirements and had been collecting boots and smocks from British dead for the last few days.

The hut was one of two collection areas, the other being much nearer to our river crossing. Our area was about ten miles from the river, but the other was only about three miles from it. The plan was to concentrate everybody at the nearer one and we could move there by lorry at nightfall and then the whole party would be guided down to the crossing point.

By four o'clock everybody was sorted out into small groups

and the whole area had been scavenged for incriminating evidence. The Dutch were to provide the lorries, and we were to be hidden in the undergrowth fifty yards from the edge of the main road by ten minutes to six.

Slowly the minutes dragged by to zero hour and the start of our last lap. Our only immediate worry was the possibility of an inquisitive German patrol finding us, but unless they had information of our whereabouts, this was most unlikely. The only thing that worried me was the enormous size of our party. However quiet each one might try to be, a hundred and twenty men moving through woods at night would sound like an army.

I was half asleep when a low whistle woke me, and we were on our way to the roadside. At six sharp, three old covered lorries rattled down the road, and drew up opposite us with a squeal of brakes. The fifty of us piled in quickly and lay on the floor, while the Dutch drivers covered us with empty sacks, so that we looked like lorries full of potatoes. If a German check-point should stop us, which would be most unlikely, we would try and bluff it. If that failed we would have to jump out and overpower the post.

We were soon bumping on our way and after twenty minutes or so passed through Ede, which was being used as an H.Q. for the Division defending the sector of the river where we were to cross. It was now nearly dusk, and two German check-points waved us through without stopping us. We were obviously the rations convoy going up to the regiments on the river.

After another twenty minutes or so of most uncomfortable travelling, the lorries drew up at the side of the road and we all quickly jumped out. It was now nearly dark, and we filed off down a footpath. For ten minutes we stumbled over tree trunks and brambles till we came to an open area where we met the rest. The whole party was now a hundred and twenty strong.

Everybody was cheerful although we all knew that the most difficult part of the operation was still ahead. We would wait till the moon rose at 9 p.m. before we started, and that would give us four hours to cover the three miles to the crossing point which we were due to reach at 1 a.m.

We had about an hour and a half to wait, and, knowing that I would need all my energies later on, I quickly curled up in some leaves for a sleep. All the more experienced amongst us did likewise, although the younger ones were obviously so overcome with excitement that sleep was the last thing they wanted. At 9 p.m. the moon rose and we were on our way through the forest. Where possible we would go in pairs to reduce the length of the column, but sometimes the footpath was so narrow that we had to go in single file. All we asked each man to do was to keep in sight of the one in front, and to be as quiet as possible. The Dutch were providing guides for the first two miles or so, and they were invaluable as this was the densest part of the forest.

By 11 p.m. we had reached the edge of the forest, and about a mile of open fields now lay between us and the edge of the river. We wrung the hands of our brave Dutch guides and thanked them from the bottom of our hearts. One of them insisted on coming along with us and eventually he joined the Dutch forces then helping to liberate Holland. We had to pass between two German positions spaced about half a mile apart, each containing a Nebelwerfer mortar battery and some infantry. The mortars had been firing fitfully all night, and as we came closer the ear-splitting, tearing noise of these heavy mortars seemed to cut into the still night air and remind us that caution was still vital for success.

A four-foot deep drainage ditch ran along our route. We were able to use it as cover and bending ourselves double we half-crawled and half-walked down its length. After an hour we had covered about half a mile and were about level with the German position. Half a mile farther on we could see the line of the river, and just at that moment a burst of Bofors tracer came over and showed us that we were heading exactly right. It was midnight, and one hour was left to us to get to the crossing point.

More careful crawling using the best cover we could find, either from hedges or drainage ditches, brought us to a road, where we could see the Germans had dug slit trenches in the bank. After a quarter of an hour in which we all crawled up as close as possible, there seemed to be no Germans in the position, so we quickly ran across the road and jumped down the bank on the far side. The river was now only two or three hundred yards away, and we followed the line of a main drainage ditch down to its bank.

Nothing stirred on the river save the gurgle of flowing water, and a subdued swish from a nearby weir. A few marsh birds occasionally let out their plaintive cries, and it was difficult to believe that the river was no-man's land between Germans and Allies.

We could now see the other side through a layer of swirling mist that clung to the surface of the river. No sign of life or movement could be seen anywhere. Some of the men began to talk quite loudly as we walked down the bank to our crossing point a few hundred yards farther down. Somebody hissed, and a moment later a burst of German automatic fire sounded only fifty yards away. We all went flat on our tummies with the ear-shattering noise still ringing in our ears. Were we to be cheated of success at this stage? Would we have to swim for it? A thousand doubts went through my head as I wormed forward to see what was going on. Luckily nobody was hit, and we could hear sounds of a small German patrol withdrawing hurriedly back across the fields. The Germans must have been even more frightened than we were.

We reached the chosen point and gave a pre-arranged light signal. Five, ten, fifteen minutes went by and nothing happened, except for the occasional weird, tearing, screech of a German heavy mortar passing overhead. Our imagination conjured up a hundred and one things that might have gone wrong, but at last the rhythmical splashing of paddles could be heard, and a moment or two later three or four assault boats nosed upstream towards us out of the mist. The swift current in the centre of the river had carried them off course as they came across.

The boats were manned by sappers from 43rd Infantry Division, and three trips were needed to get us all back. This was my fourth Rhine crossing in six weeks. I had flown over it, I had swum it, I had been driven over it as a prisoner, and now I was carried across it in a boat. I preferred the last method, although I did not regret the first.

As soon as the boats grounded on the far side we leapt out, and guided by a white tape walked half a mile to a small farmhouse, where tea and buns had been provided. Everybody was now laughing and talking about what they would do when we arrived back in England, and in a carefree way we piled aboard some waiting transport that was hardly big enough for our large party.

At 3 a.m. on October 23rd we arrived at the Corps Casualty Clearing Station established in a school near Nijmegen and there we spent the rest of the night. Next day we were thoroughly questioned and I was able to pinpoint the German Divisional H.Q. in Arnhem for the benefit of some future air attack and also pass on the names of all those good Dutchmen who had helped me in the previous two and a half weeks.

After another night in the C.C.C.S. we were driven twenty miles to an airfield where six American C47s waited to fly us back to England.

At 2 p.m. we landed at the same Lincolnshire airfield from which I had taken off some six weeks previously. Near the control tower I could see a few cars waiting and I spotted one from my unit.

" Sergeant-major sent me, sir."

" Did you know I was coming?"

" Well, not exactly, sir. We heard that a party had got back from across the Rhine and the sergeant-major said you was a dead snip to be with it. I think he has had a bet, you see, sir."